THE INVENTION OF INTERNATIONAL ORDER

T0327309

Forceval, *Le Congrès*, 1815. Engraving, 18.6 × 27.5 cm. Bibliothèque nationale de France, Département des Estampes et de la photographie.

The Invention of International Order

REMAKING EUROPE AFTER NAPOLEON

Glenda Sluga

PRINCETON UNIVERSITY PRESS
PRINCETON & OXFORD

Copyright © 2021 by Princeton University Press

Princeton University Press is committed to the protection of copyright and the intellectual property our authors entrust to us. Copyright promotes the progress and integrity of knowledge. Thank you for supporting free speech and the global exchange of ideas by purchasing an authorized edition of this book. If you wish to reproduce or distribute any part of it in any form, please obtain permission.

Requests for permission to reproduce material from this work
should be sent to permissions@press.princeton.edu

Published by Princeton University Press
41 William Street, Princeton, New Jersey 08540
99 Banbury Road, Oxford OX2 6JX

press.princeton.edu

All Rights Reserved
First paperback printing, 2025
Paper ISBN 978-0-691-26461-5
Cloth ISBN 978-0-691-20821-3
ISBN (e-book) 978-0-691-22679-8
LCCN: 2021939077

British Library Cataloging-in-Publication Data is available

Editorial: Priya Nelson, Thalia Leaf and Barbara Shi
Production Editorial: Jenny Wolkowicki
Jacket/Cover design: Layla Mac Rory
Production: Danielle Amatucci
Publicity: Alyssa Sanford and Carmen Jimenez

Jacket/Cover art: *Le Congrès*, 1815. Catalogue of Political and Personal Satires in the Department of Prints and Drawings in the British Museum. © The Trustees of the British Museum

This book has been composed in Miller

For Vida Cetin (1934–2020)

When we study history, it seems to me that we acquire the conviction that all major events lead towards the same goal of a world civilization. We see that, in every century, new peoples have been introduced to the benefits of social order and that war, despite all its disasters, has often extended the empire of enlightenment.

—GERMAINE DE STAËL, *DE LA LITTÉRATURE*

[The Vienna generation had learned] from bitter experience that war was revolution . . . [and] that something else even more fundamental to the existence of ordered society as they knew it was vulnerable and could be overthrown: the existence of any international order at all, the very possibility of their states coexisting as independent members of a European family of nations.

—PAUL W. SCHROEDER, *THE TRANSFORMATION OF EUROPEAN POLITICS*

FIGURE 1. Thomas Rowlandson, *R. Ackermann's Transparency on the Victory of Waterloo*, 1 June 1815. Hand-colored etching, 22 × 33.8 cm. The Elisha Whittelsey Collection, The Elisha Whittelsey Fund, 1959, Metropolitan Museum of Art, NY.

CONTENTS

PREFACE

A HISTORIAN looking back at the early twenty-first century will find a world rife with predictions of the end of the international order. The nostalgia that tends to accompany these gloomy predictions looks to the end of World War II in 1945, when the United States and the U.S. dollar were globally ascendant. But the existing international order is the sum of much more than mid-twentieth-century alliances. At stake are at least *two centuries* of multilateral principles, practices, and expectations. The intention of this book is to return to the early nineteenth century as the origin of the conception of international order that shaped modern international politics.

In 1814, after decades of continental conflict, an alliance of European empires defeated French military expansionism and established the so-called "Concert of Europe." At this definitive moment, the empires of Russia, Prussia, Britain, and Austria agreed to elevate cooperation between states in unprecedented ways. Their efforts annexed multilateralism to moral purpose, not least the idea of a permanent or durable peace; they deployed diplomacy, conferencing, and cross-border commerce, even free trade, as methods to secure that peace. As importantly, the diplomacy-focused contours of this international "politics," from its committees to its salon-based sociability, drew the attention of a wider public whose opinions had begun to matter and who embraced the possibilities of the politics between states with enthusiasm. In the decades that followed, the combinations of new methods and new expectations became part of the history of the invention and reinvention of the parameters of international relations, with simultaneous invocations of humanity, on the one hand, and delineations of exclusive, consistently European, and hierarchical political authority, on the other. With the advantage of hindsight, this longer history helps us understand the extent of "international" thinking and "ordering" at stake in our own faltering international order: What counts as international politics? How might politics be organized? Who should or can participate, and to what end?

Over the last two centuries, since the end of the Napoleonic wars, fundamental changes have touched all dimensions of human existence. We have moved from horses to steam, to flying machines and virtual reality; from a Europe divided between a few empires and dynastic families to a system of nation-states; from salons and dueling to nuclear brinkmanship and war fought through artificial intelligence. Yet the fundamental elements of international order that still matter have deep practical and ideological roots in peacemaking policies and practices, as well as the politics that the promise of peace excited in early nineteenth-century Europe. When we consider the unprecedented existential threats the world faces now—systemic collapse of societies under pressures of war, disease, and social and economic injustice, a planetary-level ecological crisis—some might argue that historical lessons have their limits. But even a two-hundred-year-long history still matters, for getting our bearings and navigating the future, for its confirmation that peacemaking can be the mother of invention.

ACKNOWLEDGMENTS

IN THE SUMMER OF 2013, I participated in a documentary about women at the 1814 Congress of Vienna, the infamous gathering that signaled the end of the Napoleonic wars and the beginning of a new international era of European politics. The documentary was the idea of a wonderfully enthusiastic filmmaker intent on giving legitimacy to women as political actors in that history. Her film team followed me to a remote villa in the Umbrian countryside where, in suitably *ancien* surrounds, I shared my stories of Germaine de Staël, Anna Eynard-Lullin, Rahel Varnhagen, and others. Not least, I remember they had forgotten the filter that would ensure my face was not a mess of aging shadows; we filmed anyway. A year later, the writer contacted me about the launch at the Austrian Foreign Ministry and Chancellery on Vienna's Ballhausplatz, in the same rooms that had been the site of epoch-shifting political negotiations two hundred years earlier. If I felt some trepidation about the visual effects of the absent filter, it was soon overtaken by the news that production had been placed in the hands of a company less interested in the subtleties of gender politics. Indeed, the title of the documentary shown at the 2014 launch—*Diplomatic Affairs of the Mistresses of the Vienna Congress*—left little room for nuance, mimicking instead a long-standing view of 1814 peacemakers preoccupied with dancing and sex.

The idea for this book began to take on its own rhythms long before the making of the documentary or the contemplation of bicentennial commemorations for the Congress of Vienna. One of my earliest ambitions was to shift the lens on women away from the bodice-ripping that kept the history of the Congress of Vienna in print through the twentieth century, when almost everything else about it was forgotten. At least, that's one version of why I began this book. Motivations rarely come in singular form. Perhaps both Germaine de Staël and my interest in the UN directed me to the importance of this moment in the early nineteenth century. Around the same time, a few other scholars caught the same idea in the wind. Brian Vick, Beatrice de Graaf, and Mark Jarrett have all been able to imbue this historical moment with a new vitality. Our coinciding interests suggest a zeitgeist in which this history still matters, whether as a story of the complexity of foreign relations (Jarrett), the politics of influence (Vick), a new European security culture (Graaf), the valence of permanent peace, or even the invention of an international order. Reading their papers and publications and benefiting from their collegiality gave me the confidence to think of this period as important for our own time. It also confirmed that the history of the Congress of Vienna is about more than what Shane White—my friend, colleague, and writing role model—playfully coined for me as the "sexual congress."

Was I spineless not to use that title in selling my idea to the Australian Research Council (ARC)? They need to be thanked for investing so generously in my project when I named it "The International History of Nationalism and Cosmopolitanism, 1814–1822"—a framing that gives away another genealogy for this book. ARC funding allowed me to visit numerous European and North American archives and to order endless ILL. ARC funding gave me the chance to give talks at key bicentennial events including at the Austrian Academy of Sciences, Ingolstadt, at Columbia University (thank you, Victoria de Grazia), the World History Congress at Jinan (thanks to Laurence Badel and Matthias Middell), and Harvard University (thank you, David Armitage). Other seminars provided me with critical feedback at the Harvard Ginzburg Centre (Alison Johnson and Maya Jasanoff), Global History seminar (Odd Arne Westad); New York University's Remarque Centre (Stefanos Geroulanos), the Royal Academy of the Netherlands (Beatrice de Graaf), the University of Edinburgh (Penny Fielding), and University College London (Philippa Hetherington), among others. I also benefited from the time I spent researching, writing, and presenting the ideas for this book as a visiting fellow at All Souls, Oxford, the Fondation Maison des Sciences de l'Homme, Paris, the University of Vienna, and the Centre for History and Economics at Harvard. I wasn't always away from Australia. Most of this book was written in Sydney, while I was a full-time member of the History

Department at the University of Sydney, when that department led the university in research and teaching, and academic morale was high, and when the ARC led the world in sponsoring research ambition across the Humanities and Social Sciences—solidarity to the intellectual and administrative communities at both institutions.

Institutions count; so do people. In January 2020, I arrived in Florence and at the European University Institute, where the collegiality was so immediate it carried me through the last stages of my revisions: thanks to Giorgio Riello, Ann Thomson, Pieter Judson, Laura Lee Downs, Lucy Riall, Federico Romero, Corinna Unger, Laura Borgese, and Neha Jain. I am particularly grateful to Regina Grafe and Brigid Laffan for accommodating my participation from a distance while the pandemic raged; I zoomed all night and revised my manuscript by day. Through the turmoil, Peter Becker in Vienna has been an indulgent friend, advisor, and colleague, even when I was too faint-hearted to breach Covid borders; in Cambridge, Chris Clark pointed out errors and made me feel I might have something to say. In Sydney, Barbara Caine, Moira Gatens, Danielle Celermajer, Julia Kindt, Tess Lea, Helen Groth, Jennifer Milam, and Clare Monagle tolerated early chapters and my obsession with historical details, and always gave me the best writing advice, even if I have not always lived up to it. I am indebted to Madeleine Herren, Mark Jarrett, and Beatrice de Graaf for enduring the trial of reading the manuscript at crucial intervals and always offering astute and encouraging comments. Philippa Hetherington tutored me in Russian history, and Chris Reus-Smit and Sabine Selchow each helpfully brought their IR perspectives into the mix of influence and example. Thanks to Erik de Lange at Utrecht University for sharing his indispensable PhD, Jamie Martin, Bob Nye, and Garritt Van Dyk for commenting on the *AHR* article drafts that made their way into this study, and to Melanie Aspey at the Rothschild Archive for always being so helpful. The research for this book could not have been completed without the assistance of Roderic Campbell, who brought his extraordinary depth of knowledge and profound enthusiasm to bear. I am so grateful to him and for the years of his life this project stole—and to the other researchers who picked up the pieces for me at various times, not least Dr. Katja Heath and, for her German translating, Dr. Sabina Zulovic. At Princeton, my thanks to Eric Crahan for taking this book on and to Priya Nelson for stepping in and making it better, and Jenn Backer for her copyediting.

What started because of women got finished because of women: Anna-Sophia, Barbara, Moira, and Sabine, *thank you.*

THE INVENTION OF INTERNATIONAL ORDER

INTRODUCTION

THE 1814 CONGRESS of Vienna had not even begun when the idea of writing its history took hold. The initiator was the famously calculating French minister, the Prince de Talleyrand. The man cast in the role was Jean-Baptiste Gaétan Raxis de Flassan, the historian for the Ministry of Foreign Affairs and author of studies on diplomacy and slavery. Flassan became one of an impressive retinue of delegates, invitees, and observers who rode into Vienna from across the European continent in the autumn of 1814. The history he wrote would be published much later, in 1829, by which time Flassan self-consciously eschewed any mention of the sociability that was integral to the congress. Absent were the salons, goings-on in boudoirs, and the sentiment that, through the twentieth century, came to dominate accounts of peacemaking and the remaking of Europe after Napoleon. Instead, Flassan favored an official history of reasoning men who represented the dominating imperial powers and who united Europe through law and the idea of mutual protection.[1]

The story Flassan told of the Congress of Vienna offered only a hint of the intertwined social, economic, and political dimensions of the new international order that began to be invented in the spring of 1812, when Napoleon Bonaparte led an imperial army of conquest into Russian territory. The French attack ignited resistance and spurred the Russian tsar to forge a European coalition against Bonaparte's expansionism. It was not the first anti-French coalition of European powers, but it was the last. After more than two decades of wars on the European continent, the conflict between

Russia and France might have tallied as just another skirmish. Instead, Sweden, Prussia, Britain, and Austria joined Russia and claimed victory over France and its allies, and over the future. Although the word "international" was still rarely used, these imperial governments imagined the politics between states and their own authority in that politics on an international scale. In the course of their wartime and peace negotiations, men and women from across the European continent and the English Channel elevated new ideas, practices, and institutions of multilateral negotiation. They invented a new culture of international diplomacy that expanded the possibilities of politics between states, from resolving territorial and fiscal disputes to advocacy for liberal principles, rights, and humanitarianism.

The diversity of views of what international politics might be only underlines the extent of political engagement. Naturally cautious, even cynical, European statesmen as well as emperors marveled at their own inventiveness and each took some personal credit. From 1814 to 1822, over eight years of postwar conferencing and five public congresses, and through a repertoire of ambassadorial conferences, Tsar Alexander felt he had helped generate "some new European conception" on the model of a "federative European system."[2] British foreign secretary Viscount Castlereagh enthused over their discovery of "the Science of European Government . . . and almost the simplicity of a Single State."[3] At the heart of that "science" was the simple idea of cooperation through organized, bureaucratized forms of diplomatic consultation and negotiation between neighbors—or talking. Then there was their discursive focus. For Castlereagh, among the period's innovations was a moral commitment to Europe's future "security" or *sûreté* and *indépendance*, grounded in the prospects for peace, although he was less enamored of having to promote the international abolition of the slave trade under public pressure.[4] We know from the Austrian foreign minister Klemens von Metternich's private letters that he preened himself in the mirror of the new Europe they were making. Reflecting on these events later, Metternich celebrated what he believed was a general tendency "of nations to draw closer together and to set up a kind of corporate body resting on the same basis as the great human society which grew up at the heart of Christianity."[5]

Later histories were not always attuned to Metternich's or Castlereagh's perspectives on peacemaking, although scholars have agreed that this period marked a threshold. In the 1990s, Paul W. Schroeder saw in the introduction of new peacemaking methods of consensus and law and, as importantly, the idea of loyalty to something beyond one's state a "decisive turning point."[6] He depicted Tsar Alexander, Castlereagh, and Metternich as statesmen who, on the basis of their experience of the revolutionary wars, and their own coalition military campaigns against Bonaparte, intuited the importance of supporting "the existence of any international order at all, the very possibility of their states coexisting as independent members of a European family of nations." Schroeder even claimed that this transformation of "the governing rules, norms, and practices of international politics" was *more* consequential than the ideological earthquake of the 1789 French Revolution. Other historical accounts have been more restrained but still emphasize the weight given to "transnational affinities" and the idea of humanitarian intervention.[7]

Over the last two centuries historical versions of these same events have acknowledged the roles of key statesmen but concluded their efforts were "reactionary and shortsighted, contrary to the emerging liberal 'spirit of the age.'"[8] From this perspective, the Coalition fought Napoleon in order to force Europe back to its pre-revolutionary *ancien*, even cosmopolitan, past, to keep at bay a modern national future. Similarly, when historians have incorporated social evidence of men and women mingling, dancing, and forming intimate relationships in the new diplomatic settings of postwar peacemaking, they have accentuated the aristocratic and dissolute tenor of the transformations taking place. The mixing of private and public is taken as the antithesis of a modern, professional culture of politics. Unless, that is, the presence of a diversity of actors is analyzed in relation to the history of structural shifts underway in gender, class, and race relations, in which case, private relations and sociability become part of a history of the complexity of politics rather than of political failure. From this perspective—and we find it in the most recent cultural histories of the congress—older framings of this period as stories of political progress from the old to the new, ancien to the modern, or even cosmopolitan to the national appear reductively ahistorical, regardless of whether they are intended to serve an ideal or cynical view of peacemaking at the end of the Napoleonic wars.[9]

In tidying up the past, the impetus to anachronistic order and the temptation to smooth out wrinkles are certainly seductive. This international history studies the transformation in European politics at the end of the Napoleonic wars as a moment that breathes life into new ways of doing politics between states, when women as well as men, bourgeois as well as aristocratic, non-state as well as state "actors" engaged new political possibilities in unprecedented ways, to diverse ends. It also takes note of a contradictory, contiguous, contingent development: at this same moment of possibilities, the parameters of politics, whether within or between states, were being closely defined or "ordered" to determine what counted as politics and who could be political. In conjunction with developments taking place in national settings, women were determined to be beyond the pale of legitimate political agency; non-Europeans and non-Christians were eventually marginalized in political settings of peacemaking that were simultaneously European and international. When we include their conventionally discounted histories, the narrative of the invention of international order encompasses not only the ideas, practices, and institutions that remained influential but also long forgotten expectations of what international politics could become.

Almost a half century after the French invasion of Russia in 1812, Tolstoy's magisterial fictional account *War and Peace* was deeply immersed in the social history of its setting—a familiarity that inspired his opening gambit: a Russian noblewoman welcomes guests to her soirée in St. Petersburg with an intentionally provocative comment on the rapaciousness of Napoleon Bonaparte's foreign policy. She delivers her opinion in the universal French of elite society: "Well Prince, Genoa and Lucca are now nothing more than estates taken over by the Buonaparte family."[10] As early readers of *War and Peace* well knew, the fictional Anna Pavlovna Scherer, a St. Petersburg aristocrat, offered her warning nearly a decade before a Russian-led European coalition finally defeated Napoleon. Tolstoy was not only setting up the inevitability of the confrontation to come but launching a narrative that closely interweaves private relationships and public events through the prism of the salon and women's involvement. Indeed, in a reflective section at the end of the novel, Tolstoy singles out the role in the defeat of France of an exceptional woman, the *grand dame* (as he calls her) Madame de Staël.[11] Tolstoy's acknowledgment of Staël's influence rehearses Bonaparte's own naming of Staël as his grand nemesis and her popular reputation during the Napoleonic wars as one of three great powers of Europe alongside the empires Britain and Russia.

Some scholars of peacemaking have followed Tolstoy's historical instinct and remembered women as political actors, although they have been split in their assessments. For historians who dismiss peacemaking at the end of the Napoleonic wars as a restoration, women are to blame.[12] Less common is the more inquisitive view laid out in the 1960s by the Austrian writer Hilde Spiel, who noted that neither before the Congress of Vienna nor after, not at the peace deliberations of Versailles in 1919 or San Francisco in 1945, had "a group of statesmen and politicians, assembled solely and exclusively to deal with matters of commonweal interest, labored so extensively and decisively under the influence of women."[13] Recently, Brian Vick has convincingly argued for seeing women-led salons that took place alongside the formal conferencing of men as sites of "influence politics."[14]

At a time when the varnish of the international idea was still fresh, a large canvas of "non-state actors" imagined the possibilities of the politics between states as eagerly as politics within states. This repertoire of actors—beyond the small group of statesmen, monarchs, and foreign ministers who tend to dominate the view of this past—included, most flamboyantly, individual aristocratic and bourgeois women who, like Germaine de Staël, used their networks, wealth, reputations, and talent, as well as their social status as *salonnières* (hosts of gatherings in their homes) and *ambassadrices* (wives of diplomats). Certainly, Staël was exceptional in this setting, an intellectual who set a broad liberal political agenda for a cosmopolitan Europe built on the foundations of its national diversity. Still other women, such as Prussian Christian convert Rahel

Varnhagen, her compatriot Baroness Caroline von Humboldt, and the Swiss bourgeois Anna Eynard-Lullin, each marked out rival visions of the political future, even if to less effect, whether on the strength of their reputations as *salonnières* or as wives of better-known diplomatic delegates. From the origins of the "Concert of Europe" in 1814 to the outbreak of the Crimean War in 1853—a date often associated with the Concert's failure—the ideas and activities of the Baltic *ambassadrices* Barbara Juliane von Krüdener and Dorothea Lieven exemplified a further paradox: while gender norms increasingly defined the illegitimacy of women as political actors, individual women continued to pursue political involvement on an international scale.

Adding individual women to the history of the invention of an international order, even an exceptional woman such as Staël, reinforces the importance of taking women seriously as political actors in general. This case for integrating women is backed by the fact that the female-led salon was recognized as the origin of the conversational practices that defined the diplomat's art—and Staël's salon was regarded as its highest form. Indeed, through the nineteenth century, the decline of the *salonnière*'s importance in the diplomatic sphere was caught up in the rise of a new professional, procedural, and bureaucratic approach to diplomacy, based on the sociability of men. As the political focus moved to the model of formal conferencing in both national and international contexts, women's ambitions for being "political" shifted only to be accommodated elsewhere, mostly in the modes of philanthropy (or humanitarianism) and patriotism.

A second cohort of "non-state actors"—the banker and capitalist families empowered by their wealth and connections—was omnipresent in the informal sociability of postwar congressing. In the context of peacemaking, lines of influence connecting bankers and statesmen, economics and politics, do not always lead directly to outcomes, such as who got which territory. However, the political causes that benefited most from that influence included Jewish rights and the defense of Christians in the Ottoman Empire—causes that through the nineteenth century became associated with the philanthropy of the Europe-centered modern international order. The bourgeois ambitions of some bankers and capitalists, and their family members, were as implicated in the ordering that reinforced the gendered separation of public and private spheres.

Since the eighteenth century, the promise of modernity has offered an expansive horizon of political expectations but delivered a voice only for some. Adding non-state actors to the history of peacemaking redefines our understanding of the politics between states in the early nineteenth century. In some histories, the peacemaking decisions taken by statesmen tally as conservative because they seem to thwart the progress of national causes. By contrast, seeing this period through the eyes of both state and non-state actors reveals that women were vocal advocates for the political significance of national patriotism in this period, for a range of unpredictable reasons, not always self-identification with the nation. This evidence points us toward a history of national and international, even imperial, political structures and cultures, as mutually reinforcing ideas. As we will see, a genealogy of international order takes us across a sea of competing connected discourses and concepts; it exposes categories of historical analysis often understood as opposite as more often apposite, of nesting local, national, European, cosmopolitan, imperial, humanitarian, and universal accounts of the interconnected past, present, and future.

In the early nineteenth century, women and men navigated a complex and confusing field of ambiguous political ideas and possibilities for political action. They self-consciously encountered the novelties that defined that field, including ways of identifying themselves. There were no absolute borders separating liberals from conservatives or secular from religious practices in their perceptions of the importance of politics between states. A new experience of empathy enlivened rationales for peacemaking rather than war, for engaging philanthropic-cum-humanitarian causes. Contemporaries noted the "scriptomania" that had taken hold and drove men to keep memoirs and diaries of the events they participated in and observed. Women were often regarded as emotionally disinclined to this form of subjectivity, but they too picked up pens and recorded their thoughts, often in letters to their families and friends. When Austrian archduke John contemplated the Vienna congress as a "mistake," it was because it had generated too much introspection: "We have learned to know ourselves and our innermost thoughts, and thereby confidence sinks low; whereas our weaknesses are only too glaring." We might conjecture it was precisely the facility with which the boundaries between private and public could be breached that bothered him.[15] For the historically inclined, however, these same personal documents are the tools that allow us to pick up the threads of a lost past, to weave the connected stories of women and men, the private and the public, into the history of the invention of an international order, to identify the elusive and often interwoven liberal and conservative strands of the politics at stake. Individual stories return us to another paradox intrinsic to this history: the women and economic actors who helped create political norms became invisible in the histories that tracked the rise of modern formalized diplomacy and international politics—because historians shared the new modern premise that international politics was the terrain of properly masculine political actors, whether diplomats, foreign ministers, presidents, kings, or emperors.

The history of international order has long been the territory of international relations scholars, usually focused on the organization of political authority. Historians have the advantage of being able to add close-up views, to account for change and inconsistency, success and failure, as well as the broader structural shifts that set our bearings. A voluminous corpus of historical work on the first half of the nineteenth century, for example, has provided the outlines of the gender, class, and civilizational ordering that occurred in the context of state-based national and imperial politics, and, as I argue, inevitably shaped the politics between those states.[16] Taking a broader lens, Reinhart Koselleck's work on time situates the end of the Napoleonic wars in the middle of a bridging century or *Sattelzeit*, between the ancien and modern worlds that began around 1750 and lasted a hundred years.[17] On this chronology, the political ambitions heaped upon the invention of international order from 1812 are further evidence of a new capacity to imagine the future perched on an aspirational horizon of advancing and receding time.

The history of how an international order was invented at the end of the Napoleonic wars is as much about (in Schroeder's terms) "the transformation of European politics." My focus is on how "Europe," and a handful of European imperial powers, assumed authority for the world, who got to "do politics" and to "be political," what was understood as a legitimate terrain of politics, and how that changed. In this book, the end of the Napoleonic wars is the origin of the modern international order, of transformations that occurred in the midst of (and inevitably contributing to) structural shifts in society, economics, and politics—whether changing methods of diplomacy wrapped in gender relations, moral and universal, sometimes liberal, principles, or the objective of permanent peace itself.

In all these contexts, change occurred as processes of ordering that differentiated civilizations. It is not inconsequential that, by the mid-nineteenth century, Russia had gone from leading the European coalition and even espousing a liberal political agenda for the international order to assuming the status of a pariah state, or that the Ottoman Empire had lost the privileges of its European status in the ancien system of diplomatic relations. From 1856, after the Crimean War, the Ottoman Empire was legally and economically excluded from equal status in the burgeoning system of international precepts and institutions—thanks to its victor European allies in the war against Russia.

I have chosen to tell the history of these transformations in European politics as part of the invention of international order "after Napoleon" in chapters that alternate between analyses of themes and individuals, in the context of points of historical controversy. The incorporation of individual lives and relationships is meant to help elaborate the "themes" as well as more general structural developments in the history of diplomacy, including multilateralism, liberalism, capitalism, religion, humanitarianism, war, and peace. For example, the chapters trace *how* a new diplomacy conceived as masculine in its formal bureaucratized procedures usurped the informal politics of the salon and women's political agency. At the same time, the invention of international order harbored shifting gendered assumptions about appropriate forms of political subjectivity enmeshed in equally gendered conceptions of emotions and rationality in modern politics. These processes were gradual and uneven and they invaded private lives and relationships. The encroachment of capitalism on the politics of states and between them fits here too, involving the agency of female and male non-state actors with distinctive class interests that had moral as well as commercial dimensions. We learn how economic developments prompted lively debate in the public sphere about rights, security, and the threat of economic inequality. In this same way, I track the importance of religion and the specific impact of Christianity on the secular practices of European diplomacy and on the oscillating status of Russia and the Ottoman Empire in this erstwhile European "society of states."

As the chapters move between individual and structural analyses, they detail the shifts and paradoxes that emerged from the juxtaposition of an expanding scope of politics and the relative disempowerment of women and non-Christians, class and civilizational "others." In historicizing these processes, connections, and paradoxes, I have employed the present tense when I want to understand the reactions and strategies of women and men who invested themselves in the new possibilities of the world around them. How did they begin to imagine an international politics? How were their experiences and lessons passed on to succeeding generations? What have we since remembered, and what have we forgotten?

The modern world takes for granted the idea of an international order, but even the possibility of international politics had to be invented. By asking, "What kind of ordering was embedded in the invention of the politics that could take place between states two hundred years ago?" we stand to learn more about the practices and assumptions that still temper the international order today, for better and for worse. Ultimately, my attention to invention reveals how international politics came to bear the imprint of the political culture of the modern liberal state, with its bourgeois gender and class norms, and its concurrently inclusive and exclusive universal, imperial and European, national and international foundations. Before we can arrive at this point, let me start at the beginning: What was the politics between states when European empires took up arms against French hegemony and the power of Napoleon Bonaparte? How did an international order begin to be invented, and whom can we credit or blame?

CHAPTER ONE

Diplomacy

By Diplomacy we mean the course followed by states towards other states, and the rules that govern their external policy.

—ADAM JERZY CZARTORYSKI, *ESSAI SUR LA DIPLOMATIE*, 1827

IN 1812, THE creation of a Europe-wide military coalition against French hegemony relied on diplomacy. This was nothing new. Over the previous decade, a combination of military and diplomatic methods had served the famously short Corsican Napoleon Bonaparte well, aiding his consolidation of French hegemony across Europe's numerous sovereign states. The European governments that joined the coalition were each in some way entangled in this French-ruled web of relations, or order, not least its so-called Continental System. Designed with the intent of blocking British access to European markets and materials, from 1806 the French government enforced economic policies in territory directly under their military control or subject to their indirect influence. Bonaparte's minister for interior gloated that England was left helpless, watching on as "her merchandise is repulsed from the whole of Europe, and her vessels laden with useless wealth wandering around the wide seas, where they claim to rule as sole masters, seeking in vain from the Sound to the Hellespont for a port to open and receive them."[1]

The tensions between the French and the other continental imperial powers were as complicated by the history of bilateral relationships and treaty arrangements. The Russian tsar Alexander, who instigated the coalition against France, had once contemplated the diplomatic strategy of marrying his sister Grand-Duchess Ekaterina Pavlovna to Napoleon. In 1807, Alexander signed an agreement with Bonaparte allowing Russia to occupy Finland in exchange for support for the Continental System. Russia's gain was Sweden's loss, but the Swedish court too had its own history of courting Napoleon and fighting Russia, before eventually joining Russia in the coalition against France. By a curious twist of fate, the Swedish "Prince Royal" was in fact a French man, Jean-Baptiste Bernadotte, formerly Napoleon's Army Marshal and married to Desirée Clary, Bonaparte's own ex-fiancée.[2] Having established himself in Sweden as a rival of sorts to Napoleon, Bernadotte began to distance himself from French policy aims. In 1812, he committed Sweden to joining Russia in the formation of the "Sixth Coalition."

Since 1792, over a period of twenty years, there were five attempts to create multilateral European coalitions against French political and economic expansionism. Each failure, and the retribution that followed, became a reason for not taking up arms next time. In the circumstances, not only was the Sixth Coalition's success not inevitable, its timing and its makeup were constantly in contention. The Sixth Coalition's eventual success can be attributed to both existing forms of diplomacy and their adaptation. It is a history that begins when Bonaparte fatefully decides to lead a pan-European army of conscripted soldiers eastward against Russia, dramatically raising the stakes of French continental dominance—this is the historical event famously narrated in Tolstoy's *War and Peace*. As the fate of Europe hangs in the balance of French ambition and Russian reaction, Tsar Alexander decides to seek out allies. He sets in train a military campaign that will eventually lead to the transformation of European politics and a new international order. For the coalition, diplomacy's delicate task is the coordination of cooperation between themselves. This multilateral purposing has a relatively recent history, rooted in the eighteenth-century European Enlightenment cultivation of democracy as "the peaceful and continuous management of relations between states," bringing states ever closer together.[3] Even so, the diplomatic practices that might foster such coordination vary significantly from the norms that mark the modern era of international politics, still to come.

FIGURE 2. *An Ambassador's Audience with the Grand Vizier in his Yali on the Bosporus* (Ambassador Cornelis Calkoen, 12 August 1727), eighteenth century. Oil on canvas, 92.5×129.5 cm. Rijksmuseum, Amsterdam.

The European continent dominated by Napoleon's France was a mix of the old and the new, as we might expect. When it came to political forms, republics existed alongside constitutional monarchies; tiny principalities were lodged between large absolutist empires. Concepts as foundational to the modern political era as the nation and state were in their mutually dependent relative infancy—as was the idea of politics, regardless of whether politics done within or across sovereign borders. As a result, many of the characteristics of diplomatic arrangements and diplomatic actors are unfamiliar to the modern eye. Not least, the ancien template of diplomacy acknowledged the agency of some women, particularly *salonnières* and *ambassadrices*. It also oriented the world of diplomacy in distinctive ways.

The modernization of diplomacy is the story of who could legitimately engage in diplomacy and this new idea of politics in the sense of not only men and women but also Europeans and non-Europeans. Since trade, colonial, and consular relations connected Europe's courts and governments and populations with the world, the institutional and practical changes in the ways in which politics between states was conceived and conducted resonated beyond the continent's physical borders. By the war's end, the decisions taken among a small cohort of European men, representing an even smaller set of imperial courts, presumed to establish the *rules* and imperatives of a modern diplomacy and political engagement for Europe and the world engaged by Europeans. The limits, extent, and significance of the transformation of European politics—including how this transformation adds up to the invention of an "international order"—make more sense if we have a map of the existing landscape of diplomacy.

A European Diplomacy?

An early modern historian or international scholar might insist that the most important innovation in the invention of an international order occurred when the 1648 Treaty of Westphalia laid the foundation of the European international system. At that time, at the end of decades of wars of religion that cost eight million lives, a handful of European monarchs met in the Westphalian towns of Osnabrück and Münster and agreed to the terms of a peace that would mutually recognize territorial sovereignty. This was the moment that conjured the concept of "Westphalian sovereignty." In the modern era "Westphalia" has become the byword for the idea of the bounded sovereign state and the regulation of its legitimacy. Less noticed is that this same period saw innovations introduced in diplomatic practices. For the first time, diplomats sent to foreign courts actually took up residence in those foreign countries. The word "plenipotentiary" was newly introduced to describe diplomats who exercised full authority on behalf of monarchs and governments.[4] That said, in these European settings, diplomacy was still accorded a more literal meaning, as the study of documents or diplomas. It was only at the turn of the eighteenth century that diplomacy began to be conceived more broadly as the work of facilitating commerce and trade across borders or negotiating for peace before, during, and after wars. This emphasis on negotiation of the politics between states was given substantial form in diplomatic manuals and handbooks such as François de Callières's *De la manière de négocier avec les souverains* (1716).[5]

Was there a *European* diplomacy? Even in closely connected Enlightenment Europe, diplomatic practices and expectations varied as widely as did the political forms of European sovereignties.[6] At the turn of the nineteenth century, men still resolved their personal disputes by dueling, ambassadors in Europe were neither professionally trained nor paid, and the official protocols of diplomatic reception and legitimation were limited—even more incentive for the publication of unofficial handbooks! Since plenipotentiaries were expected to bring a title and a private income to the position, they tended to belong to the ranks of the aristocracy.[7] Once ensconced in an embassy post, a plenipotentiary might linger for up to thirty years, often with very little oversight from the governments he represented. Diplomacy focused on European courts and the politics of courtly life, to the extent that diplomatic postings were commonly identified with a royal court rather than a country: for example, the "Court of St. James's" was the relevant site of diplomacy, not England, nor Britain. Similarly, national identity was a weak political concept in comparison with the political force of dynastic relationships. Characteristically, in the eighteenth century, not every government presumed that its diplomats or even foreign ministers were subjects or citizens, or even that they spoke its local language.

The overall picture of early nineteenth-century diplomacy exhibits the predominantly ancien characteristics of a "cosmopolitan brotherhood."[8] Cosmopolitan in this context describes the ancien world of aristocratic rule and dynastic networks, a transnational elite. Russian diplomats and foreign ministers were cosmopolitan aristocrats in the sense that they were not Russians, men born into diplomacy rather than Russian-ness. In the early nineteenth century, the tsar's foreign ministers included Polish prince Adam Czartoryski, Corsican Catholic Count Carlo Andrea Pozzo di Borgo, and Corfu-born Greek Orthodox Ioannes Kapodistrias.[9] Count Charles de Nesselrode was born at sea near Lisbon, Portugal, to a Baltic German Protestant family. His diplomatic career in service to the tsar followed in the footsteps of his father, a count of the Holy Roman Empire who had been Russian ambassador to Portugal and then Prussia. Father and son were multilingual and Protestant without hindrance to their careers representing a Christian Orthodox empire. Nesselrode began as a diplomat for Russia, became Russian state secretary in 1814, and then foreign minister in 1816; he reappeared as Russian chancellor as late as the 1840s, at a crucial period in a new phase of European relations.

Of all Tsar Alexander's key foreign policy advisors, only Count Andrej Razumovsky was Russian by birth. Razumovsky could not write in Russian, was married to a German woman, and converted from the Russian Orthodox Church to Catholicism. In a period when many Russian-born aristocrats were equally limited in their capacity to speak, read, or write Russian, French would do. Tolstoy's *War and Peace* captures how the "officers and officials who were fighting with the French speak French with their wives and daughters, Russian to their subordinates, and mix the languages when talking to their peers."[10] Even the Russian tsar fit this cosmopolitan model to some extent. This absolutist monarch's mother and his wife were German princesses from the Holy Roman Empire; although Alexander was head of the Russian Orthodox Church, his tutor was a Protestant Swiss, French-speaking republican, Fréderic La Harpe. Like some of his forebears, Alexander was a Francophile and admirer of the Enlightenment. In this respect, too, Alexander mirrored the education of diplomats in this period. Reliant on French as a universal language, their correspondence is evidence that they read more popular authors in a variety of languages, including French Germaine de Staël, British Walter Scott, and German Goethe.[11]

Tsar Alexander was also exceptional in that during the campaign, he regularly assumed a prominent role in diplomatic negotiations, whether they took place in military encampments or the private residences of modest European towns. Not all diplomats were at ease with this "tsar-diplomat," not least for the embarrassment caused at finding themselves negotiating with an emperor rather than with his plenipotentiaries.[12] The tsar's equivalent in this respect was Bonaparte himself, who, despite having able statesmen such as the prince Charles-Périgord Talleyrand at the ministerial helm, kept a tight rein on foreign policy. Prussia's Frederick

William III had at one time tried to make diplomatic negotiation his own domain, but in 1807, when Bonaparte humiliated Prussia in the negotiations at Tilsit, it was decided diplomatic work should be left to the actual Prussian foreign minister. At this crucial period, Prussia appointed Count Karl August von Hardenberg, born in Hanover, a British-linked, German-speaking, Holy Roman Empire principality-cum-electorate.

During the Napoleonic wars, Hanover aristocrats could be found in the more bureaucratized British diplomatic service, men such as Baron Ernst zu Munster, a subject of the bishopric of Osnabrück, a territory incorporated into Hanover in 1803 by the French. Conversely, a British military figure such as Admiral Sidney Smith, who was sent on British diplomatic missions to Constantinople, might also act as plenipotentiary for Sweden and the Ottomans. The British case is of particular interest in this history because contemporaries recognized its institutions as characteristically coherent and modern. The British Foreign Office was established in 1782 and headed by a "Secretary of State for Foreign Affairs, a member of the Prince Regent's Government." In the critical year of 1812, this position was given to forty-three-year-old Viscount Castlereagh, whose career trajectory followed a familiar European model, albeit as a British subject. Born into the (Anglo-Irish) aristocracy, Castlereagh's maternal grandfather was British ambassador to France, his father-in-law, ambassador to Russia. Castlereagh's breeding ensured his political career, if not its diplomatic stamp. He began in Irish politics and ministries, then assumed positions in the English parliament and appointments such as secretary of state for war and the colonies. He arrived via this route to the post of secretary of state, where he remained until his suicide in 1822.

As the British secretary of state—or foreign secretary—Castlereagh made clear that the authority of all diplomats within his purview was carefully circumscribed by the institutions of governance. This was a theme that the prime minister drilled home to him: the secretary of state presided over a system that gave him "a discretion on all subjects on which you might have occasion to negociate [*sic*], which it is wholly unused to entrust to any Ambassador or ordinary Minister."[13] The merit of the system lay in its insistence on the use of "accustomed official channels" for any communication with foreign powers. Britain's reputation for being able to centralize control of policy was coveted by countries such as Russia, where relatively weak chains of command made irregularities in policy and reporting more common. However, Britain was not exempt from awkward cases of "double diplomacy," when rogue British diplomats exploited their distance from London to assert their own views.[14]

The diversity of the Austrian diplomatic corps, like its military staff, reflected the reach of the Habsburg empire. It included men from its imperial domains at either end of the European continent and in between, including the remnants of its dominion over the Holy Roman Empire that hugged the river Rhine and towns that spotted the territory of the Austrian Netherlands. The two most important Habsburg foreign ministers at the turn of the nineteenth century, Count Klemens von Metternich and Count Johann Philipp von Stadion, were born in Koblenz and Mainz, respectively. These were cities situated on the Rhine and, at different times, part of the Rhenish league, the Holy Roman Empire, and France (today these cities are part of a German state invented in 1871). The shifting ground of the Habsburg empire's cultural and territorial profile was repeated in Metternich's own upbringing. The Catholic Klemens was educated by a Protestant tutor in French, the *lingua franca* of diplomacy, and eventually he was regarded as speaking French better than Austrian German.

Of all the foreign ministers to feature in the history of peacemaking after the Napoleonic wars, none has accrued as cynical a reputation as Metternich. He was forty years old when history cast him the opportunity to change the course of Europe's progress.[15] How he came to be in that role was a predictable consequence of diplomatic conventions and family networks. His father was the Habsburg court's ambassador to the Holy Roman imperial cities of Trier, Cologne, and Mainz; his wife, Eleonore von Kaunitz, was the granddaughter of Prince Kaunitz, a famous Austrian diplomat and state chancellor. Kaunitz's social status gave Metternich entrée to every drawing room in Europe.[16] To the extent that Metternich encountered obstacles, they were largely the fault of his father's fiscal irresponsibility and accumulated debt. The son adapted by multitasking. Over the course of his diplomatic career, Metternich added to his inheritance and his wife's dowry by overseeing wineries, forests, and, eventually, iron and steel works at his estates.[17] But he was to his toes invested in his political role, including the modernization of Austrian diplomacy, whether by the introduction of new technologies for copying documents or by borrowing the "fixed framework" of the British model with its consolidation of the minister's authority over diplomats, noting "well, this is what I need!"[18]

The workings of the Prussian foreign ministry reflect the varying significance of class identification in early nineteenth-century European diplomacy. Neither the Prussian Chancellor Hardenberg, son of a Hanoverian military colonel, nor Prussian-born Baron Wilhelm von Humboldt, the son of a bourgeois French Huguenot father and German Scottish mother, inherited diplomatic networks; both rose through the institutions of their respective civil services. In the manner of the time, Humboldt's parents made the decision to have Wilhelm educated by private tutors recruited from among the leading figures of the Prussian Enlightenment. The young Wilhelm was able to take advantage of the relatively developed Prussian bureaucracy and its meritocratic exam system. Baron von Humboldt also drew a livelihood from the family's Berlin estate, Tegel, and the dowry of his wife, Caroline von Dacheröden. Through his various careers in Prussian ministries, he was able to develop the philosophical and scientific interests that earned him a reputation as a philosopher-cum-political figure, particularly in studies of language and education. When Humboldt arrived in Vienna as ambassador to the Habsburg court in 1812, however, war had broken out between Russia and France, and he was launched into the political maelstrom of Europe-wide coalition-building.

In the age of the "republic of letters," cross-hatched across expanding commercial and industrial opportunities, diplomatic Europe was connected by thick networks of intellectuals, aristocrats, and political and economic actors. Shared languages, particularly the European *Bindemittel* of French, helped circulate ideas, while the flow of money created opportunities for rapprochement, as well as borrowing and exchange across sovereign borders. The circumstances of coalition-building and the coalition campaign threw diplomats, ministers, and their entourages into a proximity that made them take notice of their differences. Some British delegates openly envied the Prussian practice of diplomatic uniforms reflecting rank. They wrote to their superiors wondering if they might not adopt a similar code of dress, expecting it would both build a sense of national cohort and help explain their status to other countries. Prussians and others admired the hierarchical bureaucratic order of "English" diplomacy, which in principle subordinated the actions and views of diplomats to their ministries and keenly regulated this structure. Most European foreign ministries determined the strategic utility of not only French, or even European languages, but also linguistic expertise in non-European languages. The Austrian Chancellery relied on French as the language of translation; nevertheless it worked in Latin (to address the Holy Roman Empire), German (the Federal Diet of Frankfurt), Italian (for Lombardy and Venice), and Turkish, Arabic and Persian for maintaining relations with crucial trading partners. The Austrians, like the French, boasted training academies for consular and diplomatic staff that taught 'Oriental' languages, sometimes recruiting trainees as young as eight years old.[19] During the Napoleonic wars Russia, too, embraced the idea of establishing an Academy of Asian Studies in St. Petersburg.[20]

Where expertise in a specific language was lacking, foreign ministries conventionally hired foreigners, in some cases women, to translate or even negotiate. For over two centuries, the British government used members of the Italian Pisani family to assist with consular issues across the Mediterranean.[21] The Russian and Ottoman foreign ministries were as well-practiced in the employment of Phanariots as middlemen or "dragomans." Drawn from a class of wealthy Orthodox Christian Greek families who lived in the quarter of Constantinople known as Phanar, for over two centuries they served as interpreters in discussions with ambassadors and wrote memoranda about their conversations. In the Russian court, Phanariot dragomans utilized their networks to channel news and goods across the vast distances of that empire. In the Ottoman case, dragomans were rewarded with clothing, coaches, and luxurious housing, and even promotion to the position of "second-in-charge" in the ministry of foreign affairs. This gave them significant economic power in the interstices of the empire's relatively weakly defined governmental structures.[22]

Given what would happen in the nineteenth century, the surprising feature of European diplomacy in this period was the status of the Ottoman Empire. In the dense diplomatic and commercial connections with European powers, the Ottomans regularly featured as part of a European tableau of labile geopolitical boundaries. In the early 1810s, contemporaries would not have been surprised by the decision of Austria and France to send to London the Persian ambassador Mirza-Abdul-Hassan-Khan to act on their behalf. In European diplomatic circles, Khan carried the reputation of a distinguished gentleman known for speaking Persian, Arabic, Indian, Turkish, English, and Russian, as well as French.[23] Indeed, from the late eighteenth century, Ottoman sovereigns and advisors respected French legal codes and fiscal regulations as useful tools of state-building and also adopted the French language as a means of exercising soft power on the European continent.[24] However, after 1812, as the coalition of imperial powers fighting Bonaparte began to organize under the rubric of Europe and humanity, that all began to change. The transition was gradual and uneven. Metternich would continue to insist for some time that in any peacemaking context the Ottomans should and would take their place alongside other European empires as Europe's seventh great power. The story of that empire's marginalization in the developing manner of politics between states is in part a modern story, not unlike nor unconnected to the exclusion of women as legitimate political actors on that same international scale.

Salonnières *and* Ambassadrices

By the time the tsar began to reach out to Sweden and Europe's other empires through diplomatic networks to form a coalition against France, official diplomats of all ranks comprised a relatively diverse aristocratic cosmopolitan brotherhood. When we add the metamorphosing bureaucratic structures that are part of the pre-1812 history of European foreign ministries, opportunities were slowly opening up in public life for men from non-aristocratic backgrounds. For women, however, developments in the theater of diplomacy were traveling in the opposite direction. In the existing system, women could not always be ignored and were often

FIGURE 3. Philibert-Louis Debucourt, *Meeting with Madame de Staël,* late eighteenth century. Gouache on tinted paper. Bibliothèque Nationale de France, Département des Estampes et de la photographie.

relied upon. The royal courts that remained the symbolic centers of diplomacy were domains where women often assumed formal roles—as queens, princesses, and duchesses. Even where they did not lead those courts, the monarch's wife, sisters, daughters, mistresses, and other noblewomen could exert influence over foreign policy through their networks, not least their dynastic connections to the courts of other sovereigns.[25] For this same reason, diplomacy by means of marriage was common practice. In 1810, Metternich managed to orchestrate the union of the eldest daughter of Austrian emperor Francis II, nineteen-year-old Marie-Louise, and forty-one-year-old Napoleon Bonaparte. Metternich's maneuver cemented an alliance between the two countries *and* prevented an alliance between France and Russia, should Bonaparte have married Tsar Alexander's sister Ekaterina Pavlovna instead.

Some women became well-known too in their roles as the wives of diplomats, or *ambassadrices* "who learned their trade alongside inexperienced husbands."[26] Many were simultaneously inclined to act as *salonnières,* utilizing their conversational skills and influence to open up channels of diplomatic negotiation. Once the famous French intellectual Germaine de Staël married the Swedish ambassador to France Baron Eric Magnus Staël-Holstein, she was able to exploit the diplomatic status of her Paris home to safely hold her salons and influence politics in revolutionary France. The salon was literally a space that constituted the foyer of a woman's home, "where affairs of state," as much as ideas and culture, could be discussed and where a woman could preside.[27] Staël's salon had the reputation of the highest form of the salon for these same reasons, and it is no coincidence that her home at Coppet, on Lake Geneva, was considered a "château-school of diplomacy."[28]

In its semipublic-semiprivate form, the salon constituted a labile space, enabling women who were otherwise not invited to take public roles, let alone official government positions, to participate, lead, and excel in conversations that could sway opinions and smooth out disagreements. Where the traditional salon ruled, it was the domain of women who by virtue of their wealth or connections—whether aristocratic or bourgeois-born, Christian or Jewish—might make their views heard, or at least their presence felt. Across Europe's urban centers, salons competed for influence with the spaces of royal courts. Authors of guides on diplomatic method regarded the formal dinners, receptions, and festivals of court sociability as less conducive to the kinds of conversational skills fundamental to diplomacy. For this same reason, those guides credited salons (and their *salonnières*) with cultivating "the more serious understanding of political negotiation" through their "understanding of conversation."[29]

While the history of the salon tends to be written about in the context of the French Enlightenment, the practice was widespread and endured into the nineteenth century, with some adaptation for local idiosyncrasies. Vienna's salons were as old as those of Paris and Berlin, even if the French ridiculed them as mediocre and *ennuyeux* because they were not political enough. Visitors to the quintessentially bourgeois German-speaking Swiss town of Basel remarked on its salons as sites of great ease and luxury, usually filled with about fifty people, the women elegant, and the servants in aprons bearing tea and refreshments.[30] In the Russian salons of St. Petersburg and Moscow meals were a feature of the archetypal salon, as well as the *salonnière* who asserted her authority gently.[31] Germaine de Staël, like the tsar, assessed the English salon as overly focused on food; it lacked the grace and good manners requisite to a French-style salon in which people were brought into conversation. Predictably perhaps, Staël regarded her own Paris salon as the model of negotiation, with its "spirit of enterprise," the "mixture of the two parties" "bringing together at dinner the most intelligent men of each side." In her view, the role of the salon was to call "men distinguished by their nature to eminent places in society."[32] The salon, she added, gave exceptional women, such as herself, the role of *legislateurs*, moderating hostility, teaching civility, and inspiring heroism.

Staël's self-regard was not unearned. Even before she brought her salon to the challenge of negotiating a Europe-wide coalition against Bonaparte, she was renowned throughout the European "republic of letters" as a *salonnière.* The enduring French foreign minister Charles-Maurice de Talleyrand-Périgord would never have gained his appointment in 1797 without her help. In the final years of the Napoleonic wars, Staël was at times referred to as the "ambassadrice triomphale" because she used her skills as a *salonnière* to fortify the moral and political resolve of statesmen, and even the Russian tsar.[33] Her archenemy the duc de Rovigo, Napoleon's police minister, acknowledged the impact of Staël's interventions.[34] Napoleon too hissed that "her salon was fatal"; she gathered in it "all the partisans, republicans, and royalists. She put them in each other's presence; she united them all against me. She attacked me from all sides."[35] Staël is an inevitable point of reference for the themes folded into this political moment: the changing nature of diplomacy, the prominence of an exceptional woman, the increasing marginalization of all women, the introduction of overtly gendered political ideas and practices on a European scale imagined as both universal and international. Coincidentally, in combination with her own actions and her salon, Staël's ideas of liberty and independence were integral to the making of war and peace, and a new international politics.

Germaine de Staël's life is an unavoidable axis for this history of diplomacy, in which the past is represented by a cosmopolitan brotherhood and the uncomfortable accommodation of the agency of women, and the future by the rise of national diplomats and a masculine bureaucratic diplomacy. Staël's own capacity to act depended on the legal and social ambiguities of ancien era social practices, in regard not only to the salon but also to the class mobility available to the wealthy. Her title as baroness and her status as *ambassadrice* were the consequence of an arranged marriage to the hapless Baron Staël-Holstein. More generally, her privileged personal situation was in large part due to her Swiss father, Jacques Necker, who was Louis XVI's celebrated minister of finances, a position that placed the family in the corridors of the French Royal Court, where Staël's mother, Suzanne Necker, became famous for her own salon. There the young Germaine imbibed the Enlightenment at the feet of its greatest spokespersons. By the time she had grown up, thanks to her father, Staël was an extremely rich woman with a flair for financial management and connections in the royal court and aristocratic circles. Conversely, she was a spokesperson for the bourgeois liberal politics that anticipated nineteenth-century developments, whether in the domain of individual rights or rule by law. These same developments and ideals modernized foreign ministries and encouraged the homosociality of diplomatic circles, explicitly discouraging the public participation of women in the politics between states.

The transformation in conventions around women's public and explicitly political roles was of course noticeable before the Coalition defeated Bonaparte. According to Staël, Bonaparte's enervation of "the public spirit" made the French salon less likely a place in which elite conversation subjected political issues to rigorous intellectual scrutiny.[36] By the 1810s, the French foreign ministry introduced a newfangled form of salon run by foreign ministers. In this state-sanctioned version of drawing room receptions or dinners hosting visiting dignitaries and diplomats, a woman's role was supplementary: an *ambassadrice* was the *maitresse de maison* who did "the honors of the house"; she cultivated "respect for the emperor by enforcing civility and silencing *frondeurs*" as a support for her husband.[37] This more restricted supplementary conception of women's roles was not comprehensive, but it accorded with modernizing trends elsewhere. In the British diplomatic service, wives were increasingly expected to assist their husbands, but not to act independently on their own initiatives as *ambassadrices*.[38] The more professionalized the cultures of diplomacy and politics became, the more the intervention of both sovereign and non-sovereign women in questions of foreign policy came to be viewed as illegitimate, and salons, like the women in charge of them, disappeared from our view of the international past, even when they continued to exist. It also became less likely that foreign ministries would recruit men with dancing skills in order that they might winkle out of women "the secrets of their husbands."[39]

It is no coincidence that through the nineteenth and twentieth centuries, historians of diplomacy will not record diplomatic lotharios, let alone Staël's part, or the impact on women, in the critical episode of coalition formation, diplomatic negotiations, and Bonaparte's defeat. This is despite the fact that Germaine de Staël in particular became so crucial to the building of the victorious coalition against France and the transformation of postwar European politics. Instead, historians will rehearse as a matter of fact that the salon, like women's presence at all, was the antithesis of modern diplomacy. They will conclude, like the famous twentieth-century British diplomat Harold Nicolson, that diplomacy is absolutely "not the art of conversation," it is "the art of negotiating agreements in precise and ratifiable form . . . far better left to the professional diplomat."[40] But in 1812, that's not what happened, at all.

CHAPTER TWO

War and Peace

The four great powers, England, Austria, Russia, and Prussia, who formed a coalition in 1813 to repel the aggressions of Bonaparte, had never before acted in union, and no Continental state was able to resist such a mass of force.

—GERMAINE DE STAËL, *CONSIDERATIONS ON THE PRINCIPAL EVENTS OF THE FRENCH REVOLUTION*

Bonaparte had so persecuted her that people said that in Europe one had to count three Great Powers: England, Russia, and Madame de Staël.

—MADAME DE CHASTENAY

Creating a Coalition

At the Europe-changing moment of 1812, Germaine de Staël is living in enforced exile in Coppet, a chateau on Lac Leman, in the small republic of Geneva, under French occupation. This is not the first time the French government has imposed conditions inhibiting her movement at a distance from Paris. For Bonaparte, the last straw is the news of Staël's manuscript *On Germany*, a thinly disguised critique and call to arms against him.[1] The Russian diplomat Nesselrode reports Napoleon is furious with Staël, and she is no longer allowed to venture beyond Geneva's borders.[2] Her family, her letters, every aspect of life that is important to her are subject to state control by the French-appointed Genevan police. When friends from Paris visit, they too are punished. As painful,

FIGURE 4. Vladimir Borovikovsky, *Portrait of Germaine de Stael*, 1812. Oil on canvas, 88.7×68.0 cm. Tretyakov gallery, Wikipedia user Shakko.

Staël's political ignominy is inflicted on the marriage prospects of her daughter and the careers of her two sons.[3] As the French state intensifies its effort to suppress *la Baronne* (one of Staël's soubriquets) she fears for her life and decides to flee.

On 23 May, at 2:39 p.m., bundling up only a few possessions, Staël leaves Coppet under the ruse of a regular afternoon carriage ride. Having told her staff they will be back for dinner, Staël and her companions—her daughter Albertine, her eldest son, Auguste, and secret husband John Rocca—begin a furtive voyage across Europe heading for Stockholm, the home of Swedish ambassador Baron Staël-Holstein, her first (now dead) husband.[4] In a Europe where ports and paths and passports are still difficult to negotiate for an open enemy of Napoleon, Staël's only preparation is to entrust the handwritten pages of *On Germany* to Auguste, the child of a liaison with Count Narbonne, son of King Louis XV. This remaining copy will escape the clutches of Napoleon's spies and police to eventually appear in English, in 1813, thanks to an enthusiastic London publisher.[5] The book is an immediate success. Reviews announce the arrival of a guide for a "future age" to "the state of Germany in the highest degree of its philosophical and poetical activity, at the moment before the pride of genius was humbled by foreign conquest."[6] Meanwhile, Staël's escape inadvertently leads her into the crucible of Bonaparte's Russian campaign.

In those urgent and dangerous circumstances, Staël puts her words, networks, and letters, her celebrity, and her informal diplomacy at the service of the creation of a coalition and its shaping principles. She is certainly not a lone crusader. As *ambassadrice* and *salonnière*, she operates in an embryonic international milieu, standing for a politics of *conviction*. In contrast to the *calcul* of diplomats and politicians, Staël situates herself at the symbolic heart of the transnational revolution in politics with its origins in ideas and her own insistence on "the liberties of Europe." Common parlance singles her out as one of three powers crucial in the campaign against France and the remaking of Europe, alongside Britain and Russia.[7] This is a fact less surprising to contemporaries than to later scholars of this period. Looking back, historians will define politics—national and international—as the actions of men, on the assumption that women are either irrelevant, interlopers, or a distraction.

Neither statesman nor soldier, of all the enemies that Bonaparte's reign and the Continental System incite, "Madame de Staël" is known as the most resolute and persistent opponent, his nemesis. At five feet and one thumb tall, she is only slightly shorter than the famously petite self-styled French emperor. Staël is invariably remembered for her own (gendered) shortcomings. On some views she is "heavy," with breasts and shoulders considered too big, "a cook's face, negress lips, and long protruding teeth."[8] Reports of her standard appearance are as distinctive. She sports short sleeves, the famous turban-like *cachemire* hugging her head, and she seems to be constantly twirling a small piece of rolled paper. Sometimes the paper is a twig; always its purpose is the same, a kind of baton keeping time with rhythms of her rapid, seductive speaking. Her eyes, men say, could make you forget what are identified as her physical faults. She can "produce at will a sort of electricity that causes sparks to fly, and that relieves some people of the burden of their excess vivacity and awakens others from a state of painful apathy."[9] Eric Bollmann, a Hanover-born American citizen who will impose himself on the Congress of Vienna, praises her "frank, open, unconstrained manner, and . . . air of honesty and truth not easily resisted."[10]

Few of Staël's contemporaries resist the opportunity to comment on *la Baronne*'s exceptional "genius"—even as conventions dictate that women such as Staël should be tolerated as the authors of less intellectually serious genres, such as novels.[11] They notice she sleeps only a very few hours and never rests; her conversation is "a series of treatises, or a piled-up mass of whim and wit." Staël writes constantly "while her hair is being curled, when at her breakfast, at an average a third of every day." Some of that writing, celebrated across the continent and Atlantic, gives subtle voice to her opposition to Bonaparte—from the novels *Delphine* (1802) and *Corinne, or, Italy* (1807), to her original study of a national culture, *On Germany* (1813). As importantly, Bonaparte's consolidation of power also provokes Staël's insistence on *liberal* principles and institutions—which, after 1812, she thrusts into the widening gyre of the politics between states.[12] She is committed to preserving the principles that she believes sponsor peace and prosperity and prevent the use of violence and the abuse of power by government: "rule of law and civil equality, constitutional and representative government," freedom of the press, and freedom of religion.[13] Staël is an acknowledged exponent of the virtues of heterogeneity in the political domain, including the diversity of national cultures. In the thick of peacemaking, she will become an important advocate of the abolition of slavery.

The impact of Staël's writing is accentuated by her reputation as an exceptional woman and the extent of her political and intellectual networks.[14] Her marriage to Baron Staël-Holstein accrues her a noble title and bestows social status and, as importantly, diplomatic immunity. Through the heady days of the French Revolution, under her supervision, the Swedish embassy in Paris's rue du Bac becomes the hearth of a celebrated political salon. After 1792, when the French political situation deteriorates further, as the monarch and his family are subject to physical attacks, Staël's immunity and money help rescue from peril individuals in her circle, as well as those outside. The twenty-eight-year-old Staël writes she prefers "real dangers" to a safe life removed from the center of political events, "woman as I am."[15]

The dangers become real when the "Terror" phase of the revolution leads to the denunciation of Staël's salon and she flees to England, returning to Paris only after Robespierre's death in 1794. Under both the revolutionary government of the Directory and during Napoleon's early years, Staël's reconstituted Paris salon in the Faubourg St. Germain is a gathering point for liberal republicans and moderate royalists, "diplomats, ambassadors, artists and men of letters."[16] Her home is a place for the cultivation of discussion, generation of ideas, dissemination of views, and orchestration of political favors.

Staël has not always been Bonaparte's enemy. In his first years as a military leader and consul, as he begins to garner a reputation in French political life, she is his unrequited admirer. However, she soon comes to see Bonaparte as a tyrant wielding "absolute power," to the extent (as she will write) "no person could any longer follow his own will, either in the most important circumstances or in the most trifling."[17] The truth of her analysis is proven when, in 1803, Bonaparte condemns Staël as "a perpetual motion machine, who stirs up the salons," and orders her to keep a distance of forty leagues from Paris. Staël refuses to call Bonaparte by his first name, Napoleon, as if he is more than mortal! She quips that under Bonaparte a whole social order is being organized to prevent an ambitious woman from rising to the reputation of that of a man.[18]

During her ten years of exile from Paris, Staël's most permanent address is her father's chateau at Coppet, near Geneva. She makes this home to the Coppet circle of liberal thinkers, most famously (alongside Staël herself) Benjamin Constant, August

Wilhelm Schlegel, and Simonde de Sismondi. At an enforced distance from Paris, Staël continues to speak out against Bonaparte's domestic despotism and the creeping hegemony of France over Europe. In particular, Staël's framing of the illiberal characteristics of Bonaparte's "system" defines the liberal bases of her opposition: rule of law, a rich pluralist public sphere. Her condemnations put ideological flesh on the bones of an instinctive rebellion: French society is governed by the emperor's whim rather than law; freedom of the press and the liberty of the individual are not guaranteed. As worryingly, Bonaparte's unyielding hegemonic expansionism poses a threat to "liberty and independence in Europe." While Bonaparte leads France, she warns "there will always be another war, another conquest."[19]

In the spring of 1812, the forty-five-year-old Staël takes flight from Coppet and Bonaparte. She is in the winter of her life span, barely recovered from the secret birth of a handicapped son. Within a year, her escape has landed her in England to an enthusiastic welcome. In between, she endures an arduous and constantly rerouted journey to her intended point of arrival, Sweden. When she takes a decision to travel through Russia, the curve of history shifts.

Staël arrives in St. Petersburg just as Tsar Alexander takes tentative steps toward the formation of an anti-Bonaparte coalition. He is preparing to travel to Abø (now Turku) on the southwest coast of Finland, newly part of the Russian empire, to meet the Swedish prince regent Bernadotte and discuss a military pact. Alexander hears of Staël's arrival and quickly seeks her out. He is aware that she has a history of collaboration with Bernadotte in earlier attempts to undermine Bonaparte. Staël grabs the opportunity to mobilize support for the tsar and Bernadotte as the leaders of a new coalition against the French emperor.

In her few weeks in St. Petersburg, Staël exercises a concerted informal diplomacy. She moves between the Russian court and the drawing rooms of established aristocratic Russian families. The wife of Nesselrode writes her husband that she saw Staël at the noble Orloffs, where Princess Dolgorouki presides.[20] Staël holds a

FIGURE 5. Domenico Bossi, *Portrait of Alexander I (1777–1825), Emperor of Russia*, 1805–1815. Ivory, metal, glass, 7.4×4.5 cm. Rijksmuseum.

regular salon at the Hôtel de l'Europe, which draws Russian military and diplomatic figures. This includes Koutouzoff, the general-to-be of the Coalition armies; General Souchtelen, the Russian ambassador to Sweden; and his son, the tsar's aide-de-camp fresh from a diplomatic mission to London with lots of news to dispense. At any time of day, her home hosts fifteen to twenty people, Russians, English, American, and Prussian diplomats and military men, even French plenipotentiaries.[21] This is not simply hosting for the sake of sociability; Staël uses her gatherings to strategize her views and to celebrate the tsar and England as the epitome of a liberal political culture that is Europe's future.

One cooler summer evening toward the end of her short stay, the German patriot Baron vom Stein sits transfixed by Staël's stirring recitation from the unpublished *On Germany*. "Energy of [masculine] action," Staël reads, "only develops in those free and powerful countries where patriotic sentiments are in the soul like blood in the veins."[22] Taking on Bonaparte requires an energetic and "knightly" military masculinity motivated by an enthusiasm for the defense of liberty. Stein is an imperial knight of the Duchy of Nassau and former Prussian civil servant turned advisor to the tsar on the preparation of a "German" insurrection against Napoleon.[23] Hearing Staël, he leaps on her espousal of militarism not for its own sake but for a future German polity. By virtue of its difference, Germany stands for the liberty and individuality at threat from Bonaparte's disregard for difference, political or cultural. Stein copies out and sends to his wife passages on the necessary *enthousiasme* of young German men to defend their right not to be subjugated by a foreign power.[24] He writes his wife he was moved to tears, captivated by the ugly woman with brilliant eyes.

Not everyone is as easily impressed, particularly given that Staël is a woman. The American ambassador to the Russian court, John Quincy Adams, barely registers Staël's arrival in August, for good reason: his child has just died. When he finally sees Staël, he suspects (like other men before him) more show than substance: "something a little too broad and direct in the substance of the panegyrics which she pronounced to allow them the claim of refinement. . . . expressed with so much variety and vivacity that the hearer had not time to examine the thread of their texture."[25]

Given that America is at war with Britain, and British troops have set fire to the capitol of the young American republic, we might anticipate Adams's lack of sympathy for Staël's view of Britain "as the most astonishing nation of ancient or modern times, the only preserver of social order, the exclusive defenders of the liberties of mankind." Still, when Staël requests a conversation with Adams before leaving for Stockholm, he acquiesces. Over a two- to three-hour discussion, he reports, she has "much to say about Social Order Much about Universal Monarchy much about the preservation of Religion in which she gave me to understand she did not herself believe and much about the Ambition and Tyranny of Buonaparte, upon which she soon discovered there was no difference of Sentiment between us."[26]

Staël is now devoted to promoting Tsar Alexander and Bernadotte as the men who can inspire and harden the resolve of vacillating political and military figures, who can defeat the French emperor, who can lead a new postwar European liberal order.[27] In her somewhat paradoxical view, Tsar Alexander is well-intentioned in his admiration for liberal principles, and Bernadotte has been busy dispensing liberal laws as Swedish ruler. Staël has in mind that the French Bernadotte might head a new liberal post-Napoleonic France.[28] She is not alone in her admiration. English diplomats and visitors also see Bernadotte's potential, noting his aquiline nose, "of most extraordinary projection," his eyes, full of penetration, and "a countenance darker than that of any Spaniard and Hair so black that the Portrait Painters can find no Tint to give its proper hue. It forms a vast bushy circumference round his head. . . . he is now absolutely adored."[29] Staël supports her claims of Bernadotte's suitability with a conventional Enlightenment geographical determinism: by virtue of being born in the south of France, he draws together northern traditions of liberty and southern energy. These qualities, she offers, will enable him to foster *enthousiasme* for opposing the Grand Armée and reconciling "the dispersed interests of Europe's governments and broader public"; as the French adopted son of King Gustav, too, he exemplifies the melding of republicanism and royalty.[30]

With the benefit of historical hindsight, we know that within a year the full force of a much larger coalition leads to the defeat of Bonaparte, assisted by Bernadotte's military prowess. Yet Bernadotte soon disappears from the main theater of international history, along with Sweden, while the tsar's reputation as a liberator, and even Russia's leadership, is gradually undone by his own allies.

FIGURE 6. François-Josèph Kinson, portrait of Jean-Baptiste-Jules Bernadotte, nineteenth century. Engraving, 29.8 × 22.7 cm. Biblioteka Narodowa, Warsaw.

Recovering these lost versions and ambitions for peace is as much a part of the history of the invention of international order. They remind us of the changing political foundations of the Coalition and the importance of the liberal thinking of Germaine de Staël in the various stages of wartime diplomacy as all eyes turn to the idea of a future peace.

Methods of Negotiation

On 24 September 1812, a week after Russian forces set Moscow alight and force French troops into a long and perilous retreat, Staël arrives safely in Stockholm equipped with only slight Swedish but a deep knowledge of local political life. In the years leading up to the French Revolution, *ambassadrice* Staël has been privy to her husband's Swedish diplomatic networks. She has assumed responsibility for writing dispatches on French politics on her husband's behalf to Gustave III, who prefers her analyses.[31] Now, Staël is able to bring her influence to bear directly and persistently on Bernadotte, while maintaining her extensive correspondence with the distant tsar. In Stockholm, she continues to exploit her friendships, networks, correspondence, and salon as spaces in which she can insist on the political principles she characterizes as *liberalisme*. From Staël's perspective, her salon is intrinsically a diplomatic forum. Although the salon form is undergoing substantial changes—even in France, where Bonaparte hopes to render the salon a masculine space in the interests of government policy—according to Madame de Remusat, Staël's salon continues to encourage people "to think who have never thought before, or who had forgotten how to think."[32]

From late 1812 until mid-1813, Staël cultivates her Stockholm salon in a four-room apartment on the Arsenalgatan, near the Swedish royal palace. There she mixes readings from *On Germany* with dancing. "Madame de Staël's conversational dances"[33] become, in the words of the Prussian envoy von Tarrach, "a central meeting point for the large-scale plot against Napoleon."[34] The Swedish foreign minister Lars von Engestrom describes the salon as a *café politique*, "where the chatter is about everything, and the doctrine preached is subversive of all order."[35] No diplomat can risk refusing Staël's invitations.[36] The French chargé d'affaires, Monsieur de Cabre—whose own star sinks as Staël's rises—reports back to Paris that her effect is "bomb-like." Staël is always at Bernadotte's side, "he tells her everything, and she sometimes advises him."[37]

What does Staël achieve? Certainly she is able to orchestrate Cabre's expulsion from Sweden. She successfully appeals to the British envoy to Stockholm, the young Sir Edward Thornton, for monetary aid for Sweden. When British foreign minister Castlereagh temporarily changes his view of Bernadotte, he is influenced by the reports of Thornton, who is influenced by Staël (although he never mentions her in his official reports). Staël's suggestion that Victor Moreau, the exiled former French general, take command of troops against the French emperor is less successful.[38] Most of all, she goads Bernadotte on. She advises him to respond to Bonaparte's threats on behalf of *la cause de l'humanité*, to keep firm with the Austrian and Prussian ambassadors so that the emperors of Austria and Prussia too will be forced into the Coalition.[39] In January 1813, when Bernadotte plans a meeting with von Tarrach to discuss the emerging alliance, it takes place at Staël's residence.[40] She takes credit for sending to France the news of the Abø agreement, the most important event of the century (up to that moment), even though the French ignore it. She promotes the idea of granting the country Norway to Sweden for reasons of security (not expansion), in exchange for Swedish involvement in the campaign, even though it goes against her liberal principles. Sweden is also granted the Caribbean territory of Guadeloupe in this agreement. John Quincy Adams jokingly represents this geopolitical policy—"it is not enough to expand, it is even better to surround oneself"—as "well suited to the conception of a lady-politician."[41] The duc de Rovigo—who, as Bonaparte's minister of police, pursued Staël and copies of her *On Germany* manuscript above and beyond the call of duty—records for posterity that it was Staël who finally convinces Bernadotte to trust Alexander.[42] Separately, Karl Gustav von Brinkman, the former secretary at the Swedish legation in Paris during the Baron Staël-Holstein's tenure, depicts her as the "conscience" of an outraged Europe and the single person who exerts the most influence on both the tsar and Bernadotte. Without Staël, the forging of bonds between the Coalition partners may have been less successful, the motivations of the tsar and Bernadotte themselves less primed.

We should not imagine that all of Staël's diplomacy relies on proximity. Stockholm is hardly at the epicenter of a wider European society. So Staël, an avid member of the self-consciously *European* "republic of letters," cultivates her extensive networks through correspondence, an indispensable means of opinion-making in the circumstances. Her courier heads west on Tuesdays and Fridays, a schedule that occasionally forces sudden sign-offs in order to make the pouch.[43] In a climate of widespread government surveillance, bankers are particularly useful points of *post-restante*: Merian in Basel, Desport in Geneva, Torlonia in Rome, or Messrs. Ferd. Fortis and C. in Milan. She makes good use of her banking connections for information too. Since no letter can be expected to evade interception, Staël cajoles and flatters Jacques Augustin Galiffe, the Genevan-born secretary to the Russian Court Banker in St. Petersburg, into passing on her letters to third parties.[44] Galiffe, in turn, writes twice a week, serving as an auxiliary source of information and lobbyist. While diplomats and other political representations in Stockholm meet at her salon, send off missives, and receive their own instructions, Staël uses Galiffe to send news from Sweden to Russia, and to keep both Russia and Sweden to their Abø promises. Employing her telegraphic style, she presses Bernadotte's requests for more troops and informs Galiffe of reasons for delays in Bernadotte's military campaign. The prince will probably head off in the spring, she promises Galiffe, expecting the news to be passed on to the tsar.[45]

Staël's correspondence also conveys her frustrations, not least the difficulty of getting Austria and Prussia into the Coalition. She makes her complaints known to correspondents around the continent, from the well-networked Prince de Ligne in Vienna to the Duchess of Saxe-Weimar, one of the tsar's sisters. While passing through Stockholm, Dorothea Lieven, the enterprising wife of the newly appointed Russian ambassador to England, is brought into her fold, temporarily.[46] Once Lieven is in London, Staël writes to her on the importance of promoting Bernadotte's suitability as the future king of France. On 16 February 1813, Lieven replies through the Russian diplomatic office referring to "our operations."[47] Staël pursues her English political interlocutors directly—whether Prime Minister Liverpool, Foreign Secretary Castlereagh, or Lord Grey, the former foreign secretary and Whig. Reaching out to Americans she knows, she resumes her epistolary acquaintance with Thomas Jefferson, having met him in the 1780s, when he was minister to France. Her aim now is to dissuade America from its ongoing war with England, so that they might join in defeating Bonaparte, as “free peoples” belonging to the same family. If the Americans destroy English naval power, Staël warns, they will find a new enemy in Bonaparte because he is against all liberties. Jefferson is dismissive. He advises her that Americans believe England to be the enemy of the liberty of the oceans and free commerce.

Through all this informal diplomacy, Staël remains focused on Bernadotte, stoking his resolve through letters after he has embarked with his troops. She reports her exchanges with either the British prime minister or the foreign minister, as she seeks backing for the universal applicability of a *constitution anglaise*.[48] She clarifies for Bernadotte the political discussion in England, or implies that the prospect of the French throne could turn to his favor, if only he would grab the mettle: “The deliverance of Europe depends on *You*”; “Drive on until the liberty of France granted and directed by You!”[49] She also persists in asking that Bernadotte give her orders and put her to work for him.[50] In his more sarcastic moments, Bernadotte is liable to proclaim that Staël is qualifying herself for appointment to the Swedish council of state. He writes to her privately in more obsequious fashion: “If I were Charles VII I would be tempted to make you play the role of Joan of Arc. . . . Give me your plume as an ally and I will have thousands more men to throw into the balance.”[51]

Visitors to Staël’s home in Stockholm have the chance to see the power of that plume on full display. Most mornings Staël receives in bed, ink-stained and animated. Strewn around her are the pages of her endless correspondence and manuscript drafts.[52] Her outpourings include the final version of *Reflections on Suicide*, newly prefaced with its call to Bernadotte to maintain his motivation. Early drafts of a memoir, later published as *Ten Years of Exile*, attack Napoleon, praise Russia, and enjoin the tsar to the defense of liberty. A new project (posthumously published), *Considerations on the Principal Events of the French Revolution*, offers an eyewitness account of the progress and significance of the French Revolution, with addenda that include the war and the peacemaking that follows. The tract *On the Continental System* first appears in Hamburg in 1813, attributed to an anonymous author. Although its authorship is disputed, *On the Continental System* bursts with Staël’s ideas and language. John Quincy Adams considers the biting attack hers, since it advocates her views "against the continental system," for "the doctrine that free ships make free goods," and in favor of Bernadotte's "chivalresque virtues."[53] It describes Bonaparte as the "archfiend of Europe," famously accuses him of being "not a man, but a system," and deftly describes the manner in which Bonaparte's foreign policy has cowed the sovereigns of Europe and set them against each other. Its message is a call for a European war of independence.[54]

Staël gets her wish. By February 1813, the political and military mood on the continent has shifted in favor of a broad coalition. Prussia agrees to join. In March, the British government agrees to provide Bernadotte with a million-pound subsidy to cover the cost of 30,000 soldiers in the cause, and naval support "to help compel the Danes to surrender Norway [to Sweden], and the island of Guadeloupe as a possible additional or consolation prize."[55] By May, all bonds between Sweden and France have been broken. One year after Staël left her home in Coppet, Bernadotte finally disembarks his Swedish forces on the continent. He is accompanied by Staël's confidant and family tutor August Wilhelm Schlegel as secretary and her youngest, wayward son Albert as aide-de-camp. Bernadotte carries a proclamation written by Staël to spread among the French soldiers, urging them to change sides.[56]

By the spring of 1813, the momentum toward a European coalition is growing, although the level of commitment and ultimate objectives are still not clear: Is this a campaign to remove Bonaparte or to force France back to its pre-expansion boundaries? The other major European empire, Habsburg Austria, remains outside the Coalition camp. Staël decides it is time to move on and plans her departure for England, where, she explains to Bernadotte, she will add her voice to those proclaiming his *beau caractère* and potential as the future head of a post-Bonaparte French government.[57] Stockholm, she complains to Lieven, "has the air of yesterday's town" and awaits "a great battle from one moment to the next never has humankind played so important a game . . . all your nation is electrified and the asiatics [*sic*] will save Europe."[58] In the balance of who played in that "game," we can weigh the diplomatic reports advising that Staël has the tsar's ear, and the tsar seeks her views on Napoleon's counteroffers and asks her to press Russia's case with Bernadotte. In turn, she makes Bernadotte's participation in the war against Bonaparte all but an obligation he owes her.[59]

The historical commentary on this period of coalition formation and Staël's distinctive role is thin, but it exists, mainly in the history of Sweden and biographies of Staël herself. One historian (who is otherwise loath to give her much credit) claims that "Bernadotte, guided and aided by Madame de Staël, August Schlegel, and Benjamin Constant, gives us the only example outside of France in this period of the deliberate use of propaganda for demoralizing the enemy."[60] Swedish historians have been more generous in their conclusion: all diplomatic activity was focused on Staël's Stockholm residence; she used her base to run an informal secret agency alongside the formal operations of the local embassies.[61] For our purposes, the evidence of Staël's salon, letters, networking, and writing brings into clear, instructive view the diverse methods of diplomacy, negotiating the politics between states on the cusp of a new era. This is a history that extends beyond an exceptional woman's feelings or her ideas in the European summer of 1812. It is integral to the changing conceptions of politics more generally, whether the expanding ambitions of individual women in wartime and in anticipation of peace or the structural shifts that will position the workings of the feminine salon as the antithesis of the operations of the masculine state.

CHAPTER THREE

Politics

AT A CRUCIAL MOMENT in the invention of international order, individual European women engaged the shifting political cultures of empires and nations. Cases of individual agency, such as the extraordinary role played by Germaine de Staël, occurred in the context of shifting social norms. In some cases, women negotiated loosely defined, relatively familiar social norms regarding appropriate public roles. In others, they found themselves confronting more calculated gendered demarcations of public and private spheres. This was particularly the case after 1804, when Bonaparte's introduction of a French Civil Code made familial male-female relations central to the authority and development of the power of the modern state and applied new national conditions of citizenship to men and women differently. The foreign woman who married a French man became French, just as all children born of a French father, even in a foreign country, were French. However, marriage to a French woman did not guarantee the man French citizenship, and a woman born of a French father lost her citizenship when she married a foreign man. Her children, too, assumed the nationality of her husband. In giving clearer legal definition to the patriarchal rights of men over women, and the limits of women's economic as well as political power, the Civil Code redefined the political future in gendered terms. As France expanded its military and political presence, so did the influence of these legalized conventions. Historian Isabel Hull usefully recounts how in Prussia the French Civil Code was layered over existing "gendered sexual assumptions of traditional society." Detached from their social context, developed and reified, those assumptions came to legally define "the essence of males and females in civil society."[1]

In the early nineteenth century, women's social, economic, and political disadvantages relative to men were certainly not new experiences. Nor were they experienced uniformly across European polities or between women of different class or religious identification. But in Britain, as in France or Prussia, military crisis and continuous political upheaval placed new pressure on the legitimacy of women's political participation and deprived them "of both formal and informal political rights."[2] As the Coalition and French forces fought over the future of Europe, women's publicity and any active political engagement provoked European governments to more clearly define women's difference through their special roles in the private sphere.

Not all the transformation was toward a singular definition of who could be political and how. The earlier events of the French Revolution, including disappointment with the gender-specific interpretations of the Declaration of the Rights of Man, had provoked calls for the "rights of women," most famously Olympe de Gouges in 1791 and Mary Wollstonecraft in 1792. Gouges linked the private concerns of women to their public (national) status; Wollstonecraft emphasized women's rationality as the basis of their right to be considered human. The sex difference debate was significant enough to draw the public commentary of men too. Wilhelm von Humboldt, Prussian ambassador to the Habsburg court from 1812 and a crucial negotiator in the formation of a coalition against Bonaparte and its broader mission, authored a treatise on the difference between the sexes in this same period arguing the natural gender order exhibited a functional complementarity: masculinity was the embodiment of reason, productivity, and "a striving which is keenly productive"; femininity inclined to fantasy and to "conserve through bonding."[3] Men looked forward, women were stationary, at best. Humboldt's claims caught the eye of Germaine de Staël, who exchanged public views with him on the implications of these differences and the idea that women inherently held progress back. In the context of opposition to Bonaparte, Staël elaborated her view on the importance of the differences between the sexes. Both her novel *Corinne, or, Italy* (1807) and *On Germany* (1813) maintained that Britain's relative political stability was due in part to the complementary roles taken by men and women, that is, men were appropriately public, women private. Although the instinctively political Staël warned against women exerting "influence in the public sphere for personal advantage," she also acknowledged that they behaved in such ways under the conditions of arbitrary and repressive government. In "free countries," she advised, "the true character of a woman and the true character of a man can be known and admired," because institutions objectively and transparently protected the interests of all.[4] In other words, both men and women behaved in non-transparent ways when they lacked the institutions that represented them.

Across Europe, the political implications of the sex difference debate percolated through diplomatic events and practices. As Europe's various polities rubbed up against each other, gender behavior became a useful measure of the differences between the ambiguities of the old cosmopolitan world, in which unbridled women might insist on a voice, and modern state-based regimens where the public roles of men and private roles of women complemented each other. Antagonists of women's publicity contemptuously described salons run by aristocratic and *haute bourgeois* women as blurring the boundaries between public and private—as if that blurring was itself politically dysfunctional.[5] When spies and police compiled reports for foreign ministers and monarchs on the words and activities of the representatives of other states, they too often focused on gender-appropriate behavior. Germaine de Staël was a favorite target of such observations. For the Corsican-born Russian diplomat Pozzo di Borgo, Staël was a "monstrous hybrid," speaking and writing "like a man" even though she comported herself "like a woman."[6] Austrian foreign minister Metternich attacked her as *la femme-homme* who "kills me."[7] It is little wonder that Staël responded by both privately reminding individuals of her diplomatic efforts and presence at key historical events and publicly disavowing any political agency. During her campaign against Bonaparte, Staël's signature directive was "burn my letters"—a form of self-censorship that protected her from surveillance and her children from the burden of social disrepute.[8]

The virulence of attacks on women who transgressed gender norms reveals as much as it represses about women's presence in the international past. The simplest assertions about the gendered behavior of men and women suggest the complex reality of individual experiences and their structural conditions. During the peacemaking process that followed the Coalition's victory against France, one witness commented on the memoir-writing rampant among participants as "Scriptomania." The witness also claimed that this was a practice only engaged in by men.[9] Even though the author was as likely a woman, they confidently asserted that women did not keep memoirs because their "violence of thought" precluded them from hiding their feelings or sentiments and, thus, left them nothing to confide to paper. Of course, the truth is women kept diaries, even if they did not always presume to publish them as men might. (Even Staël knew that if she wanted to write about politics, she had to turn to literary genres or work collaboratively with men who faced no such difficulties.) As importantly for us, women confided their thoughts in their letters. Like their diligently and daily scribbled notebooks, these remain accessible to us when they were stored in family archival collections. Sometimes they were even left in state archives because police tasked with tracking plots against governments or information on the politics of foreign powers thought it worth intercepting such letters. Their contents run against many of our conventional expectations about the past. They help color our view of the question that so regularly pursues the inclusion of women in political history: "What influence could a woman actually exercise, given the ideas, practices, and even laws that worked to marginalize women's voices?" Read closely, evidence of their writing jogs other questions too, not least, "What did individual women say and want?" Answering *this* question leads us to the peculiar importance of patriotism and philanthropy in the history of the invention of an international order, as well as the gender ordering it involved. It also helps us track the conceptions of the distinctive international politics that women and men could do as political cultures congealed around new ideals of separate spheres.

Feminine Politics

Women born in Europe between 1763 and 1771, and who lived through the Napoleonic wars—even those who lacked a formal education—were liable to remark on the limits to their life choices.[10] As the cultural, legal, and political profile of women's difference sharpened, some persisted in wanting the same experiences as men (including joining the military) or to be even better than men at what they did. When sixteen-year-old Theodor von Humboldt volunteered with the Prussian army to fight against Bonaparte, his mother, the Prussian *ambassadrice* Baroness Caroline von Humboldt, wished she were a man and could join him.[11] Female monarchs, whom we might imagine as having more scope to realize their ambitions, could be as frustrated. In the crucial first years of the Coalition campaign, 1812 and 1813, Austrian empress Maria Ludovica, third wife of Emperor Francis, announced her despair at the distance her neutral husband was keeping from the battlefields. She wrote to her son Archduke Johann lamenting, "Ah, would I were a man, to serve the State."[12]

Letters between the Russian grand-duchess Ekaterina and her brother Tsar Alexander during this period overflow with her ambitions for political agency. Ekaterina discussed politics, military dispositions, and the Russian economy.[13] She saw to the creation of a reserve army of 1,000 men to be sent off to join the Coalition forces.[14] When she wanted to do more for the Coalition campaign, Alexander directed her to help win over Austrian emperor Francis and other smaller sovereignties, providing her with a budget of 1,700 ducats to spend on necessities such as bribes.[15] By exercising conventional forms of female diplomatic influence, or "soft-power" diplomacy, the grand-duchess was able to bring the Kingdom of Württemberg over to the Coalition cause in November 1813—despite the kingdom's long history of capitalizing on an alliance with France.[16] Ekaterina also acquiesced to directing some of her energy to a newer form of female political agency. On the tsar's request, she agreed to join the Ladies' Philanthropic Society, established by her sister-in-law, Empress Elizabeth Alexeievna (née Louise of Baden).[17]

Once the coalition against France began its campaign, and the inevitable battles wounded and killed hundreds of thousands of

FIGURE 7. Louis de Saint-Aubin, *Elisabeth Alexeevna Imperatrice de toutes les Russies*, 1813. Engraving, 29 × 22.5 cm. Biblioteka Narodowa.

European men, bourgeois and aristocratic European women took up patriotic versions of philanthropy, along the lines of the Russian Ladies' Philanthropic Society.[18] In Britain and Prussia, the phenomenon of patriotic philanthropy provided an even broader-based outlet for women's "energies and organizational capacities and a public role of a kind."[19] Historian Karen Hagemann argues that in Prussia, patriotic philanthropy meant that for the first time "even middle-class women—like the men of their class—became an important part of wartime society."[20] Among those women was Rahel Levin, who had fled French-occupied Berlin for Prague. The philanthropy Levin practiced was akin to what later in the nineteenth century would be named humanitarianism. She drew on her meager resources to care for the soldiers who were otherwise left to die on the streets of the Bohemian town. "I am in touch with our [Prussian] commissariat and our staff surgeon," Levin wrote to the man then courting her, the low-level (Christian) Prussian diplomat Karl Varnhagen:

> I have a great number of *charpie*, bandages, rags, socks, shirts; I am having meals cooked in several quarters of the city; I personally see some thirty, forty riflemen and soldiers a day; I discuss and check on everything, and make the *most* of the sum entrusted to me! . . . The correspondence. . . . The accounts, addresses, receipts, errands, consultations: in short, my undertaking is ramifying into a large enterprise.[21]

The logistics of Levin's efforts are impressive. As she recorded in her expense notebooks, she bought blankets, bandages, medicine, clothing, and food and managed 150 women throughout the city to cook and distribute meals and visit the wounded. With little money of her own, Levin turned to correspondence as a fund-raising tool. Before leaving Berlin, even as a Jewish woman she had accrued a reputation as a *salonnière*, and she now had those substantial salon-based networks to draw upon. These stretched to the men leading the political and military effort against France and to their families. Levin soon approached Caroline von Humboldt in Vienna—where Wilhelm von Humboldt was ambassador—asking if she would start a collection among "the ladies of society" for the overwhelming numbers of abandoned and neglected soldiers of all the allied armies.[22] Writing to her Christian compatriot, Levin reinforced her plea by describing her feelings whenever she encountered a soldier who would tell her "I'm a Prussian." At that moment, she explained, "I could die. Alas! You don't know the feeling . . . I beg you, do send something!" Despite the Humboldt family's financial difficulties, the baroness donated more than a thousand gulden.[23] She also assured Levin that she completely understood her feelings, and

FIGURE 8. MR del, *Rahel Varnhagen von Ense* (1771–1833). Engraving, nineteenth century. Wikipedia Commons.

then upped the ante. The (light) injuries the Humboldts' son Theodore had sustained in battle inspired in her a patriotic epiphany of "beautiful, genuine/intrinsic and holy feelings," reconciling her to the necessity of sacrificing one's dearest.[24]

In the shifting early nineteenth-century terrain of politics, patriotism or "the love of the fatherland" was one of a number of socially acceptable forms of being political available to women. Patriotism's basis in "love" or personal feelings reflected a broader philosophy of thought that anchored political authenticity in emotions and made feeling the center of "civic identity."[25] Scottish philosopher David Hume evoked feelings as contagious passions that did not know "the boundaries of individuals."[26] For Jean-Jacques Rousseau, "the most heroic of all passions" were "capable of producing the greatest prodigies of virtue," namely tying people to a *patrie*. In one of

Staël's earliest essays on the "happiness of individuals and nations," she argued for a philosophical understanding of the passions—the desire for glory, or greed, vanity, love, the inclination to friendship, filial, paternal, or conjugal tenderness, and religion. That understanding, she believed, could be the basis of a "political science," a discipline which, of course, had not yet been invented.[27]

For women so often identified with their emotional life over their intellectual capacity—or even in relation to the "violence of their thought"—patriotism became a means of engaging politics as an emotional right.[28] For a Jewish woman such as Levin, philanthropy—literally the love of humans, or humanity—was a means of proving her patriotism toward a Prussia that, thanks in part to Wilhelm von Humboldt, had recently granted citizenship to Jews.[29] Levin uniquely conceptualized her philanthropic attention to the suffering of all the soldiers on the battlefields as a patriotic act and identified her patriotism with Prussia's defense of civil rights and peace. Writing to the poet Heinrich Heine, she described herself as a Prussian who abhorred wars and saw in any obsessively cultural "German" patriotism (such as that of Caroline von Humboldt) simply "a coincidence; and the puffed-up vanity of attaching prominence to this circumstance will end with this folly bursting asunder."[30] For pacifist reasons she conjured a *European* philanthropy: "I have *such* a plan in my heart," Levin wrote in her diary in 1813, "to call upon all European women to refuse ever to go along with war; and jointly to help all sufferers; then, at least we could be *tranquil* on *one* side; we women, I mean. Wouldn't something like that *work*?"[31] Even when we consider the question of influence, Levin's thinking matters. It expands our understanding of what women thought the politics between states should be, as well as how a woman might attempt to act politically—through philanthropy and through her writing. Levin's words also carried weight. Contemporaries such as Friedrich Gentz, Metternich's secretary, thought her an exceptional woman, even a genius. Although Levin published her philosophical writings anonymously, her salon and networks garnered her a reputation for the clarity of her thought.

It should already be apparent that in the early nineteenth century, in the midst of a Coalition military campaign against France, privileged or exceptional women could exercise unofficial, or soft, diplomacy through salons, letters, and networks, even publications. Alternatively, women found that philanthropy evoked as an emotional patriotism, or on behalf of humanity, was a respectable method of being political in the emerging forum of a shared European politics. They took up the paths of patriotism and philanthropy well aware that their participation in politics was subject to controversy. As a Jewish bourgeoise, Levin knew she could not control how her activities were interpreted. Any authority or influence she earned through her brilliance was ultimately delimited by the triple burden of being a woman, a Jew, and relatively poor—as she herself acknowledged. While she was in Prague, she was more than aware that Gentz feared that their friendship would be discovered by the aristocratic Duchess of Sagan—this was his "greatest *terreur*," she would recall: "He always thought he had to plump me underground, bury me alive, out of sheer desperate need to deny he knew me, just on account of the Duchess of Sagan."[32] After her marriage to the Christian diplomat Karl Varnhagen, and her conversion to Christianity, she bemoaned the social restrictions placed on her now as an *ambassadrice*: "Ah, only that I were an official person! Only that I were a duchess!"[33] Twenty years later, writing to Gentz, her lament had transformed to a more general sarcasm: "I should tell you about politics? . . . a mere woman!"[34]

As Levin noted, not all versions of an appropriate patriotism were alike. Baroness Caroline von Humboldt—whom Levin knew well and, as we have seen, certainly considered a friend—espoused war and spoke for an increasingly anti-Semitic version of Prussian patriotism as German patriotism. In this aspect, Baroness von Humboldt's views were contrary to those of her husband, Wilhelm, whom she tried to influence as he articulated the Coalition's political purpose. Both Levin's and Caroline von Humboldt's versions of patriotism share some qualities with Staël's contributions to the importance of patriotism in this period. Like Levin, Staël extolled the virtues of a cosmopolitan or heterogeneous framing of a "new Europe of nationalities," in contrast to Bonaparte's hegemonic political inclinations.[35] However, in the midst of her angst about the fate of France and Europe under Bonaparte's illiberal rule, Staël put to work an idea of patriotism more akin to Caroline von Humboldt's, as an instrumental emotion that could inspire enthusiasm for the greater political good. "Energy of [masculine] action," Staël ventured in her discourse on Germany, "only develops in those free and powerful countries where patriotic sentiments are in the soul like blood in the veins" and was crucial to resisting Bonaparte.[36] In countries where men were reduced to servitude, whether by governments or even overambitious women, the opposite was true. Staël brought this model to bear on the importance of being able to imagine the existence of "Germany," in the absence of that state. In her hands, this national idea was important to the extent that it could inspire an energetic and "knightly" military masculinity and motivate "German" men across the continent to defend their liberty. This was the national thinking that captured Baron vom Stein's imagination in St. Petersburg. The manuscript that Staël read to audiences across Europe from 1812 stipulated a direct correspondence between men assuming the superiority due them and their capacity (in contrast to women) to exercise the military virtues inspired by love of "patrie."

Masculine Politics

A history of international politics that features women is an invitation to write about the cultural ordering of politics more broadly. Masculinity and the interiority of men were as much at stake in the organization of political authority. In the context of war, and rapidly changing military and political landscape, legitimate domains of action for women were closely tied to historically specific norms of masculinity. Historian of German nationalism George Mosse maintained that the wars in Europe against the French Revolution and Bonaparte "were waged on behalf of patriotism and morality, both of which determined the direction of the new national self-consciousness."[37] In German-speaking regions hostile to the revolutionary aims of the French forces, the French were represented as essentially "loose living" in comparison with the German morality and masculinity on military display. We have some evidence that this conception of the masculinity of German military patriotism was readily internalized. When Ernst Moritz Arndt, the "prophet of German nationalism," returned victoriously from a French-Coalition battle at Leipzig (known as the Battle of Nations) in 1813, he wrote of having engaged in "a bloody quarrel fought out among men." Mosse argues that Arndt's evocation of a masculine national cause had its corollary in the cultivation of a bourgeois respectability which, in the course of the nineteenth century, became definitive of a "German" national identity.

During the Coalition campaign, the Prussian government fostered "valorous manliness" as the calling card for a new generation of patriotically minded, combat-ready soldiers.[38] This same language appears in contemporary British diplomatic correspondence, rendering the adjectives "manly" and "manliness" common terms of approbation. Manliness in turn was associated with specific emotional qualities; as British secretary of state, Castlereagh earned a reputation among his European peers as conciliatory, "intelligent and calm."[39] Metternich admired Castlereagh as "cold" *and* "a man," the most gallant man he had ever met, carrying a calm head and a heart in the right place.[40] When Staël wanted to defend the tsar against accusations of effeminacy, she described him as unaffected, calm, penetrating, judicious, wise, and consistent in his commitment to "the progress of social order" and "those rights which human reason at present calls for in all directions." Tsar Alexander, she declared, was ruled by his opinions more than by his passions, interested not in conquest but in "representative government, religious toleration, the improvement of mankind by liberty and the Christian religion."[41]

Despite the importance of emotions to the depiction of patriotism as a political motivation, men were more often represented as agents of sense than sensibility. As the French Civil Code confirmed, men were the default stakeholders of modern rational political state-based life, its national and international dimensions. Men who lived up to their masculinity were rational and emotionally controlled, in contrast with "the violence of women's thought." Conversely, just as women could turn an emotional authenticity to some political advantage, in the same way, men's political authority could be undermined by questioning their masculinity, their inclinations to femininity, or even a penchant for taking women seriously. Metternich damned the tsar as a peculiar mixture of *masculine* virtues and *feminine* weaknesses. Such depictions of Alexander were common among his critics, particularly those from rival states, who often took the tsar's allegedly compromised masculinity as emblematic of his Russian-ness, or sourced his failure to live up to masculine norms to a preference for discussing politics with ladies.[42] Similarly, the theme of Metternich's propensity to the distractions of love was taken up by Gentz, who complained that "on more than one occasion a political discussion had been permitted to drift into talk about the relation of the latter to the woman known as the Duchess of Sagan." Yet the accusation stuck mostly when used against the tsar.[43] A normative sexuality also counted in these representations. In private exchanges with the ubiquitous Duchess of Sagan, Metternich swung between accusing Tsar Alexander of being about to kill him and eyeing him up as the object of more "depraved" inclinations.[44]

Culturally charged representations of the emotional and rational self, private relations and public affairs, give us a handle on the world in which diplomats, statesmen, and even monarchs who are part of this history of the invention of international order lived as men and humans, perhaps all too human. From the perspective of non-Russians, the tsar's Russian-ness made him particularly susceptible to accusations of deviance. By contrast, among anglophone commentators and historians, characterizations of Prussian-ness or English-ness were enough to award some immunity from moral or political prosecution. Historians have tended to characterize Castlereagh as a Briton bringing to bear a controlled rational, even unemotional, masculine demeanor.[45] This is despite the fact that Castlereagh took ether to quell his anxiety about public speaking, was lampooned within Britain for his feminized characteristics and "ostentatious uxoriousness," and was exposed to blackmail for alleged homosexual activities (in a Britain that punished sodomy with the death sentence), and then, on the eve of the final congress in Verona, he slit his own throat.[46] Wilhelm von Humboldt, who has survived history with his reputation as a high-minded philosopher intact, regarded himself as serious and above gossip, above Metternich's view of diplomacy as a social affair, above his own boss Prince Hardenberg's inclination to take gifts and money from petitioners. Nevertheless, Humboldt's sexual fetishes—pregnant maids on the military campaign trail and an account book for sexual expenses—made him a target for his contemporaries' lampooning.[47] Together with the Duchess of Sagan, Metternich spread rumors about Humboldt's love life and mischievously opened his private letters (forcing Humboldt and his wife, Caroline, to write in code).[48] Sagan, who was suspicious of Humboldt's liberalism, mocked the lisp that butchered the Prussian minister's pronunciation of the French *ch*—Humboldt, she laughed, spoke of "des *soses*" and exclaimed everything *sarmant*.[49] Indeed, Metternich's letters to Sagan display a world in which the relations between statesmen were as susceptible to emotion and sexuality: how Prince Hardenberg kissed him; Emperor Franz "jumped on him"; the king of Prussia smiled; or Tsar Alexander said he loved him, lasciviously.

The next chapter examines the correspondence between Metternich and the Duchess of Sagan as part of this history of shifting gender norms entangled and unraveled in the private relationships between men and women, and negotiated on a daily basis in the context of war and diplomacy. Even as older, more ambiguous aristocratic diplomatic practices endured, new opportunities for engaging the politics between states encouraged appropriate forms of publicly performed femininity among the bourgeoisie as well as aristocracy, in the name of patriotism, Europe, and humanity. In the midst of these opportunities, there was a familiar noisy disapproval of women's emotional, even sexual, political "intriguing" (unless it could be assigned a patriotic or philanthropic role) and the less often heard sounds of women answering back.

CHAPTER FOUR

Public and Private

The past, my friend, is not you! This past is the domain of history.

—COUNT KLEMENS VON METTERNICH TO DUCHESS WILHELMINE VON SAGAN, OFFENBURG, 13 DECEMBER 1813

Ratiborschitz . . . is connected to the history of the world and to my relationship with you . . . I see you . . . floating between the present and the future!

—COUNT KLEMENS VON METTERNICH TO DUCHESS WILHELMINE VON SAGAN, CHAUMONT, 1 MARCH 1814

IN THE FIRST DAYS of June 1813, at a critical moment in the international history of Europe's "durable cooperation," Austrian foreign minister Count Klemens von Metternich orders his carriage and sets out from Vienna. He is headed for Dresden, the capital of the Kingdom of Saxony and the location of his first diplomatic posting more than a decade earlier, now the site of Bonaparte's makeshift military headquarters. Metternich works out a convenient geography for the pending diplomatic negotiations that he hopes will encourage the coalition of Russia, Sweden, Prussia, and Britain on the one side, and France on the other, to agree to end the war. If he is successful Austria will not be forced to pick sides. He has singled out the castle of Ratiborschitz (Ratibořice), located in the Austrian Bohemian area of Nachod, as the site of the discussions between Coalition statesmen. Here they will determine whether to acquiesce to Napoleon's demands or fight on until the French emperor

FIGURE 9. Franz Xaver Stöber, *Portrait of Klemens Wenzel Lothar, Fürst von Metternich*, 1830. Engraving, 16.6 × 10.8 cm. Rijksmuseum.

is deposed, while Austria's government decides whether it will join the Coalition against France at all. Russian foreign minister Nesselrode recalls the Ratiborschitz conferencing as the stormiest he has witnessed, "but the importance of rallying Austria was so great" that he puts up with whatever conditions are necessary.[1]

Ratiborschitz sits in hilly terrain directly north along the route between Vienna and Dresden. It is equally distant to Reichenbach, the Silesian town hosting the Coalition's military, and to Gitschin, where Tsar Alexander has his base.[2] As Metternich's talented advisor Friedrich Gentz reports, this small area "of some twenty-five miles in length and scarcely as much in breath" now eclipses Paris,

St. Petersburg, Vienna, and Berlin in significance; compressed there are "the four great sovereigns of Europe with their ministers, cabinets, foreign embassies, a part of their courts, and five to six hundred thousand armed men."[3]

As significantly from Metternich's point of view, Ratiborschitz is the country home of the Duchess of Sagan, born Katharina Friederike Wilhelmine Benigna, Princess of Courland, and sometimes referred to as "Cleopatra of Courland." On 6 June, Metternich writes to Sagan about the heights to which he has raised her home and its private significance for him.[4] "You see," he presses, "that Europe begins to reunite itself around the small foyer of activity that you have seen created under your very eyes."[5] He imagines the "Europe" that the Coalition is building through their private relationship, or, as he puts it to Sagan: "My friend and Europe, Europe and my friend!"[6] Early one morning, as Austria decides to join the Coalition, and anticipating victory, Metternich exclaims: "My life . . . is tied to the history of the world, and my relationship with you."[7]

Between 1813 and 1815, Sagan and Metternich share a voluminous correspondence. Later Metternich will try to destroy and hide from historical view these same letters. In his hurry to prove that he moved in masculine public spaces undistracted by women, he will erase Sagan from the record of his public life to the extent of culling the relevant sections of Gentz's papers.[8] His retrospective accounts of the male mastery of politics in this period deliberately try to destroy the evidence of how his personal relations shaped the idea of politics between states.[9] When the letters are accidentally recovered in the 1960s, they expose a private history that fills the gaps in our knowledge of how a powerful man (Metternich) redefines his expanding sense of self according to the motifs of a European public life and the masculinity of diplomacy, how the public and private intersected in the slowly evolving agenda for a future peace.[10] The emphatic repetition of the word *politique* in the correspondence between Metternich and Sagan underlines the novelty of the situation: a Europe transformed under Metternich's influence; a present that is the sum of his own past actions and exclusion of women from politics; Sagan's fate, as Metternich describes, left "floating between the present and the future."

From the married Metternich's perspective, despite the risks of interception and exposure, there is much to gain from writing to Sagan, including her physical acquiescence. While the Duchess of Sagan has only a liminal place in the international history of this period—usually as one of the femmes fatales of the "dancing Congress"—her objectives in 1813 are political, not least to convince Metternich that Austria should join the coalition against France. The two aristocrats write in French, resorting to German occasionally and rather awkwardly. They entrust their letters to army or professional couriers such as the Verwalter Flyers, or the diplomatic bag of the British foreign minister Castlereagh.[11] Since the order in which the letters arrive is unpredictable, they number them. As with all correspondence of the time, the challenges and contexts of communication lie in the unreliability of messengers and the omnipresent threat of public exposure; consequently, the letters bear the marks of self-censorship.[12] Nevertheless, Metternich's overwhelming tendency is to frankness. Sagan calls his letters monologues, and the disparity between his self-reflective, even narcissistic, style and her preference for focusing on news is apparent to them both.

The correspondence that flies between Sagan and Metternich from the summer of 1813, as Coalition negotiators arrive at her Bohemian estate, records her first taste of diplomacy. Like Metternich, Sagan was born outside the Habsburg empire. However, she is the proprietor of Ratiborschitz within Habsburg terrain and regularly resident in Vienna, and describes herself as "above all things . . . a good Austrian."[13] Unlike Metternich, she is convinced Austria should fight against France. Metternich really does not want to go to war. The man history remembers as the conservative repressor of Europe's liberal movements believes that war is a bloody waste of men and resources. He is mindful that to go against France is to risk defeat and undermine the basis of Austria's security and autonomy, namely the dynastic marriage he has orchestrated between the Austrian princess Marie-Louise and Bonaparte. Over the months that the Coalition takes form, as Staël waits in Stockholm and then in London, Metternich stalls, preferring to position Austria as the neutral negotiator of peace between the European powers.

By comparison with Metternich, Sagan explains her enthusiasm for the Coalition campaign is based on her sympathies with

FIGURE 10. Gerard Francois, *Duchess Wilhelmine von Sagan*, 1815. Oil on canvas. Musée de l'Histoire de France, Château de Versailles © Alamy.

the ancien principles of her upbringing. The same duchess whose opinion Rahel Levin fears, detests "with all her soul" the democratic associations that feed the values of self-love, vanity, insolence, unsociability, and "the inability to achieve an eminent degree of civilization."[14] That antipathy is fueled by the disastrous effects of French expansionism on her territorial and financial interests.[15] Metternich responds both by making much of the fact that Ratiborschitz is the "centre of European diplomacy at the moment when this poor

Europe is the foyer of the world's troubles" and by demanding that Sagan forgo being political.[16] As Europe becomes the focus of the war and peace, Metternich advises her, "The past, my friend, is not you! This past is the domain of history."[17]

It is hard *not* to read Metternich's comment as part of a process that delimits the political roles of men and women in this transformative moment, "floating," as he charges "between the present and the future." While the process of coalition formation reinforces his view that men and women have distinctive roles in the society of states, the emphatic parsing of politics with Sagan keeps alive the urgent question: What can and should politics be for men and women in the context of the world-scale events into which they are being drawn? Their answers elevate philanthropy as the legitimate form of politics for women.

A Baltic Woman

Often portrayed as duplicitous and immoral, the Duchess of Sagan is a complex woman who assumes diverse social and political roles and measures opportunities against constraints. Born in 1781, Sagan is twenty-nine years old when she first gets to know Metternich in Berlin, where the thirty-three-year-old Austrian diplomat holds a posting. By then Sagan has been married and separated. She has given up an illegitimate child and taken other children into her care, all the while moving around Europe between her estate in Bohemia and a residence in Vienna. When, in 1812, Metternich returns to Vienna as foreign minister, Sagan is installed in the Habsburg capital at the Palm Palace on Schenkenstrasse under the old city ramparts, a short distance from Metternich's headquarters at the Chancellery on Minoritenplatz. Her neighbor and rival in politics as in love is the Russian princess Ekaterina Bagration. The latter is Metternich's *former* lover (during his first posting in Dresden) and mother of his illegitimate daughter Klementina. Bagration's salon is famous for attracting the regular company of the Russian diplomatic corps as well as local luminaries such as Prussian ambassador Wilhelm von Humboldt and his wife, Caroline. Sagan and Bagration are not friendly, although they both have ties by birth to the Russian court and share a visceral hatred of Bonaparte.[18]

As with Bagration, Sagan's loathing of the French is provoked by her aristocratic objections to political revolution and the personal effects of French expansionism. Originally from the Duchy of Courland in the Baltic region (now part of Latvia), the family lived as cosmopolitan German-speaking aristocracy at home on the fringes of the Russian empire, abiding by feudal law and engaging in English-style hunts.[19] Until the eighteenth century, the Courland title even came with colonial properties on the Gambia river in Africa (eventually usurped by the Dutch) and in Tobago in the West Indies, which Sagan's impoverished forebears sold to the English.[20] When, in 1795, the family are forced from Courland by Catherine II (who absorbed the principality and brought the rights to the title), they move south into central Europe, purchasing the Duchy of Sagan in Prussian Silesia and the Bohemian Ratiborschitz estate.[21] Upon her father's death in 1800, nineteen-year-old Wilhelmina benefits from relatively unregulated Russian and Habsburg laws that do not discriminate between the property rights of sons and daughters and that allow her to assume the title and responsibility of duchess.[22]

The grown-up Sagan is relatively typical of wealthy, independent noblewomen. She is fluent in numerous languages, well-read in the complex history and politics of central Europe, and consumed by current affairs. She does not publish on political themes, but she is on familiar terms with statesmen and well-practiced at gleaning information through her vast network of family and friends in many of Europe's courts.[23] While growing up, Sagan does not lack for examples of women exercising political and economic agency. Her mother, Countess Anne-Charlotte Dorothée de Medem, manages the Baltic estates and is a special Russian *ambassadrice* to Warsaw. As duchess, Sagan shows similar abilities. In 1809, when Bonaparte's forces lay siege to Sagan's territory in her absence, the duchess supports a group of Hussars in their fight against French occupation. When Bonaparte threatens to confiscate the Duchy of Sagan in retaliation, she conscripts and outfits five hundred men to defend the property.[24] Her motives are as ideological as they are selfish, as she acknowledges to Metternich: "My God, how I hate and abhor all liberal ideas."[25]

Sagan undoubtedly has a combination of personal and political motives in her epistolary relationship with Metternich. The foreign minister is a useful friend for news of the progress of the Coalition's armies, and by implication the well-being of Prince Alfred Windischgratz, a younger Austrian officer who eventually distinguishes himself at the Battle of Leipzig and in whom Sagan has long been interested. (Metternich is somewhat irked by the fact that she does not hide her feelings.) She discusses her mother's pension and a position for her brother-in-law—which Metternich flatly refuses, on the grounds that even he cannot do anything for someone so useless. Her mother, too, takes advantage of Metternich, writing to him to discuss economic questions and underline how the war is threatening the family's livelihood. Sagan tries to persuade Metternich to intervene on her behalf with Tsar Alexander, upon whom she depends for many favors, including access to her capital and guarantees for credit. She taunts Metternich with not loving her, and then praises him or asks for bribe money for a compatriot in need of a French spy to replace a cheaper less useful Polish spy.[26] From Sagan's perspective, then, Metternich brings influence and connections, even opportunities. Diplomacy in particular is a revelation.

As Metternich draws Sagan into the dizzying days of coalition-building, the latest political news passes through the central European outpost under her charge. Sagan awaits "the world" at Ratiborschitz while watched over by Gentz. She keeps a lookout for news of "projects"—as she writes to Metternich, "I assure You that You have every reason to be content with me and hope that You will love me always as a consequence."[27] It may be for that same reason she promises not to speak to Metternich of politics when he comes. Occasionally Metternich—using the polite formal form of address they maintain for the first few months—gives her leave to tell him of her own projects.[28] She lets him know that, on 13 June, the first group arrives: Russia's Nesselrode, Austria's Count Stadion, and Prussia's Hardenberg and Wilhelm von Humboldt. The talk is not about the war but rather all about Egypt and Greece, the Hindustani plateau, transmigration, peoples, science, poetry—Slavic, Finnish, Sanskrit, "etc. etc." Sagan the bibliophile and polyglot is in her element in the salon-like setting.[29]

Through the weeks as the diplomats at Ratiborschitz negotiate various treaties, and Metternich works his appeasement preferences on the Coalition partners, Sagan hosts the more difficult conversations among the core group.[30] The debate one late night on 18 June goes "round and round in sometimes furious argument" about the terms of a peace that Metternich might take to Bonaparte.[31] Since Metternich holds the reins of Austria's appeasement policy, Sagan knows that it is important to maintain pressure on him if Austria is to fall in on the Coalition's side. When Humboldt, as Prussian ambassador to the Habsburg court, provides the group with a memorandum that insists on fighting Bonaparte to the end, he acknowledges Sagan's support during "the most critical period of my public life."[32]

Politics "of the bandaging kind"

The treaty agreed to by the Coalition on 27 June 1813 and named for Reichenbach sees Metternich, not Sagan, win the first negotiating round: Austria will enter the war *only* if France does not accept a minimum program of four points within five days. The existing partners agree they will not act unilaterally with Bonaparte, and Britain backs their cooperation by promising 666,666 pounds sterling as a subsidy for 80,000 Prussian troops, and 1,333,334 pounds subsidy to Russia for 160,000 soldiers to keep France on its toes.[33] When the French delay their response, a still ebullient Metternich writes to Sagan that a peace conference will open in Prague on 5 July to see if France and the Coalition can end the war. Metternich assures her that Ratiborschitz will go down in history for its role. He cannot know then that the armistice, like the Prague congress, will be viewed as *his* error. Instead of leading to peace, it allows the French to lead the Coalition by the nose and gives Bonaparte time to regroup. When the drawn-out Prague meeting inevitably fails, the Coalition is left with no choice but to continue fighting. Then, on 19 August, Austria joins the Coalition. By October, events seem to have proven the wisdom of that choice, as the force of five major European powers—Russia, Sweden, Prussia, Britain, and Austria—defeat France at the bloody Battle of Leipzig. Remembered as the Battle of the Nations—or "the slaughtering of nations"—it costs the lives of more than 54,000 Coalition and 38,000 French soldiers.[34] Against Metternich's deepest instincts, Austria's soldiers are now among those of Prussia, Russia, Sweden, and the Hanseatic region, Mecklenburg, and northern

"German" territories risking their lives; more than 400,000 troops are shared out between Field Marshal Gebhard von Blücher, Prince Bernadotte, and Prince Karl von Schwarzenberg.

The diplomatic and military history of this period is crucial and woven into the fabrication of a European multilateral politics. It is also part of the history of the gender norms that circulate in the setting of war, in private as much as public relationships. There is no doubt that even as the Ratiborschitz meeting gives Sagan opportunities to be political, those opportunities are constantly circumscribed by Metternich himself. When she criticizes plans for a postwar German federation because of the possible impact on the status of her own sovereignty and ability to reap taxes, Metternich mollifies her, all the while confirming the extent of his power.[35] He sends her copies of his declarations and suggests she compare Napoleon's language and texts from earlier on with those from the end of 1813, in order to mark the fall of a colossus. He acknowledges that her deep understanding of contemporary affairs is better than that of his ministers and extraordinarily helpful to him.[36] In the midst of their exchanges, Metternich sends Sagan pastilles of Italian olive gum, which she uses to perfume a room, or a chest, and "6 livres de bon tabac de pape gros" for snuff. He also insists she obey him in matters *en politique*. He is to be left to reign over this world "so vast, so strongly encumbered with ruins, so strongly exposed to the influence of all the destructive elements—leave me to govern—with the robust arms that God gave me—this world."[37]

At the same time, the more Sagan dives into being political, the more Metternich draws a line: if she finds a political idea coming to mind, she is to give it to him.[38] When Holland is in revolt against the French, Sagan is among the first to know. However, Metternich advises her to not tell anyone in large part because there are rumors "that *we have* a political correspondence."[39] Metternich may want to avoid being publicly thought of as indiscreet, but when he repeatedly chides Sagan, "you cannot believe that I love you when you are political," a different kind of ideological work is in process: Metternich lets Sagan know his opinion; the duchess actively negotiates the gender register of being political.

Occasionally Sagan reassures Metternich that she speaks little of politics. At other times, she confesses she cannot help but engage in politics: "sometimes I lose patience when I hear too many stupid things said, and it could be that I am given the honour of being thought informed by you."[40] She reserves the right to strike an acerbic tone: "You don't like us other women being involved in politics, you don't like us having ideas. I promise you never to dream up any of them [ideas] and to be circumspect about politics." Or, more cuttingly: "Knowing what you think of political letters, today I wanted to make honourable amends for daring the other day to write in this genre by sending you things of an extreme futility—I find like you that this suits me infinitely better."[41]

These exchanges manifest the intersections between a changing diplomacy, Metternich's changing sense of self, and his relationship to a "Europe" that lies palpably on the expanding horizon of political expectations. In the period between the failed Prague peace conference of August 1813 and the victorious Battle of Leipzig and after, Metternich continues to pass on news to Sagan as a way of puffing himself up.[42] Occasionally he ruminates on the horrors of the war and how many men are killed: "The Swedish Prince Royal, Blucher and us have certainly killed more than 50 thousand men from 23rd to the 30th."[43] He uses such figures as justification for his continuing preference for appeasement. Mostly he reflects on the grand fortune of being the minister of a great power, precisely at that time. Kings, emperors, the pope, and sultans are all his regular company.[44] He comments on days spent working happily with the Russian Nesselrode and the British ambassador to the Austrian court Earl of Aberdeen and sharing out Europe as if it were a piece of cheese. When the Swiss delegations seek him out, he is the distributor of the "golden apple," even though the Swiss are hardly the inhabitants of Olympus and he can barely understand their German.[45] He enjoys dismissing the Swiss cantons and their claims, as if their provinciality is too little for his larger concerns: "What the devil do you want me to know about the canton of this or that other town, or that village [*bourg*], or that corporation?" Writing to Sagan, Metternich names meetings that might go on for eight hours, ending at 2:00 in the morning, "ces conférences *de l'Europe!*"[46]

Some nights Metternich is woken up to six times to meet the couriers who travel twenty *lieues* each day moving among the allied camps and their diplomats. At one point, he figures he has managed three hours of sleep a night for eight days.[47] At 11:00 p.m., 25 October 1813, Metternich is in his hotel room in Weimar, in the Grand Duchy of Saxe-Weimar-Eisenach, receiving English and Bavarian couriers and twenty-five persons who, he claims, each now believes that the destiny of the world is in his, Metternich's, hands.[48] A few weeks later, in Frankfurt—once a free imperial city in the Holy Roman Empire and reinvented as a grand duchy by Bonaparte—he works from 7:00 a.m. until 2:00 p.m. in his antechamber. He receives ministers from the Grand Duchy of Baden, the Duchy of Nassau, and the Electorate of Hesse, who have come to throw themselves at his knees in the hope of securing their sovereign independence in a postwar future.[49] At the stroke of midnight in the town of Basel, Metternich's antechamber is "as full as an egg," brimming with sixteen local deputies, the reigning burgermeisters of Basel and Vienna, a Franc-Comtoise deputation, the widow of an Austrian pensioned officer, the Comte de Wintzingerode (minister of the Kingdom of Württemberg), two Spanish and Dutch prisoners, and his Viennese banker, Leopold von Herz, among others.[50] In their midst, Metternich feels like a king amusing himself.

Then there are impromptu conferences between "the 4 grands cabinets"—Russia, Prussia, Britain, Austria—with no space for Sweden at the table. Metternich claims these attempts to decide the points of negotiation for the anticipated general peace have no precedent in the annals of the world. As the prospect of peace grows closer, there are three days when he is unable to find even five minutes for anything that does not involve the fate of several million men. He portrays himself as a kind of "pivot" for Europe, "walking giant like between heaven and earth through the future of Europe."[51] It is difficult not to interpret Metternich's self-aggrandizement as a matter of negotiating both the impact of the changing circumstances of the war on the domain of his own power and his political roles in relation to those of Sagan.

There are some forms of politics that Metternich does approve for women. In February 1814, as the Coalition has Napoleon cornered, Metternich writes, "I love the politics you do"—by which he means Sagan's supportive research into the peerage he might adopt, a task she has taken up to humor him.[52] He begrudgingly approves when Sagan turns her hand to philanthropy, what he thinks of as work for humanity. This is specifically the management of the problem of wounded Austrian soldiers arriving in Prague by the cartload. Sagan, resident in the Bohemian capital since the failed peace congress, writes repeatedly to Metternich of the situation. She appeals to him to produce a *Handbillett* that will give orders for managing those dying of misery in Prague's streets, "with no one taking responsibility for their bed or cover." When he fails to act, she uses her own money to set up a hospital with a hundred beds, which she then supervises. At the same time that Rahel Levin is raising funds and locating medical resources, Sagan is overseeing her own philanthropic work with the soldiers whose wounded and disabled bodies lie strewn across Prague. The expanses of the Italian Renaissance–style Wallenstein Palace, her residence, are made available as an open house for feeding these men.[53] Metternich replies to her repeated requests for government intervention: "I would not love you if you did not feel the interest of humanity so inseparable of those of empires so warmly, and I would love you a little less still if you were political."[54]

As the waves of soldiers continue to arrive and there is still no state action, Sagan keeps up the pressure. She beseeches Metternich, *par humanité*, to find ways of protecting the injured and the prisoners that the Russians are taking in the battles, not just the soldiers on the Coalition side, "to order the civilized peoples of the Don, Dniester, Black Sea, and Asian deserts to not maltreat the prisoners, at least while they pass through Austrian territory."[55] Metternich's reply, from Frankfurt, is to remind her that even though what makes *him* happy is "Politics!" he does not love her when she "does politics."[56] He does not love "political women," "as a state of being, or a *métier*." However, he does give her permission to do politics "of the bandaging kind."[57]

What might Metternich have done if he had been aware that by this time Sagan was writing streams of love letters to the English diplomat Frederick Lamb, Byron's brother-in-law, a man she had met in Prague during the failed peace conference? As it is, in early April 1814, with Bonaparte defeated, Metternich addresses her with a sarcasm that hints at his insecurity: "Are you happy now? You who are so difficult to please politically? Do you think we've done well? . . . Do you want something else?"[58] Sometimes he reminds her of what he has given her: "You, then, you and Europe have had the benefit of an immense wave of well-being spreading throughout humankind."[59]

The public and the private are not simply coincidental, or even complementary; they implicate each other. In the course of their correspondence, Metternich not only lets Sagan know she is *trop indépendante*, as peace looks more likely he reminds her that if he were a woman what he would love about a man was his "essence," which only he as a man could have, namely the (often painful) privilege of "a real and useful activity."[60] Alternatively, he acknowledges if she were a man, they could achieve great things together; she would know all his political thoughts; she would be ambassador to his minister. Alongside such hypothesizing, Metternich insists women were invented as a sweet reward for men and to be dependent on them.[61] Men were made to be energetic by character, women to be good, to rely on men, and to sustain them.[62] Sagan's retort is characteristically evasive: "Well then I am not a woman for nothing, as you give me leave to speak politics, this time I will not say the word . . . I do not want to deny my Sex, if I were a man I would not please you at all."[63]

There is something to Sagan's insight. On numerous sleepless nights Metternich fights off images of a pipe-smoking Sagan.[64] His subconscious is hardly reassured by Gentz, who advises his employer, "My main and fundamental opinion remains unshaken: W[ilhelmine] has too much intellect and too noble a disposition that she would in pursuit of happiness arising from a solid relationship with you cut back on everything else without exception. She mustn't however be left to her own devices for too long."[65] Gentz insists Sagan is "not yet properly disciplined"; she is too subject to "impetuous passions."[66] (The authority of judgment will come full circle when Metternich comments that Gentz "really should have been a woman as his delicate skin, his coquetry and his sensitive nerves all suggested.")[67] Sagan herself acknowledges that there is a lesson to be learned, "my *philosophy* which teaches me to submit to my destiny."[68] By comparison, Metternich's sense of personal destiny is liberating and politically expansive. In the midst of the maelstrom of diplomacy that is the last months of the Coalition campaign, as couriers bearing memoranda and missives crisscross the army camps and the castles where sovereigns and diplomats wait, Metternich saddles up and moves from military sites to negotiating tables across Europe. His letters create in him a sense that he is watching his life take shape "from the outside."[69] As Austria finally helps turn the tide of the war in the Coalition's favor, Metternich has his reward, the title of prince.

CHAPTER FIVE

Europe

You see that Europe begins to reunite itself around this small foyer of activity that you have seen created in front of your eyes. Let all the world cry out and acclaim it.

—KLEMENS VON METTERNICH TO THE DUCHESS OF SAGAN, PRAGUE, 12 JUNE 1813

It was asked of me, what was meant by the Continent of Europe.

—EDWARD THORNTON, SCHWERIN, 25 JULY 1813

BY THE END OF 1813, Coalition partners forged their cooperation by envisioning a postwar peace that scaled from *patrie* to Europe to *humanité*.[1] This language resounded in Germaine de Staël's publications and private interventions with the tsar and Bernadotte in diplomatic circles, in mutually reinforcing references *à la cause de l'humanité*, in the push and pull of the Duchess of Sagan's relationship with Metternich and the Europe he imagined at his feet, and in the philanthropic idealism of Rahel Levin's Europe and Caroline von Humboldt's Prussia. Looking back—and with his attention resting purely on the men in this story—the late nineteenth-century German historian Friedrich Meinecke condensed the spectrum of the available conceptions of community into two specific categories: *national autonomy* and *universal federation*. Meinecke maintained that at the end of the Napoleonic wars, national autonomy and universal federation impelled each other "like two engaged gears."[2] He admitted that the idea of nationality was "circumscribed

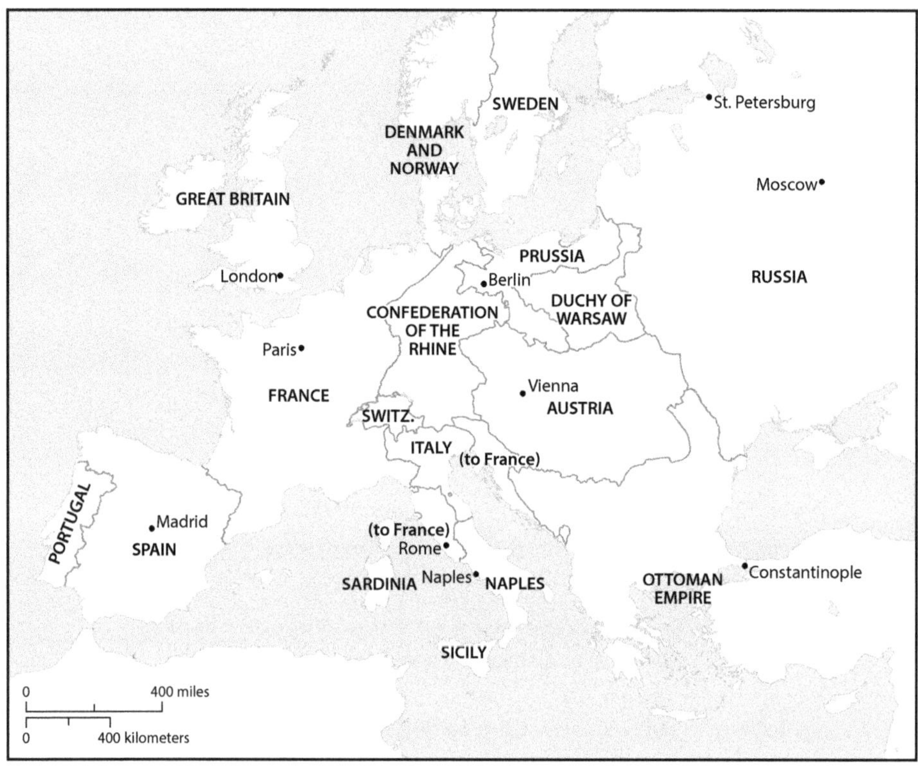

FIGURE 11. Map of Napoleon's empire, 1812.

by universalistic principles," and contemporaries viewed both the state and nation as "things that a man can create or search out to suit his ideas and needs."[3]

Undoubtedly, Meinecke's comparative view was colored by the tenor of the nationalism of his own era and a personal antagonism toward the universalizing and federative political ideas popular at the turn of the twentieth century.[4] A century earlier, explicitly *international* thinking was more closely identified with an Enlightenment-influenced palette of ideas about relations between states, including, notably, the *cosmopolitan* "principle of reciprocity" and a "society of states." Coalition statesmen and diplomats, and their supporters, mapped a future postwar landscape of what we would now call international relations by looking back to their recent past and referencing even older policy initiatives and rhetoric—some of which had been rehearsed by their archenemy Bonaparte. At stake were not only conceptualizations of the politics between states but also the ideological work that invocations of Europe, like humanity, could do, whether imagining the organization of political authority or its international scale, who was in and who was out.

A Society of States

In 1805, against the background of increasingly successful French expansionism across the European continent, and Bonaparte's accruing personal power, the young Polish nobleman Prince Adam Czartoryski drew up plans for a new coalition between Russia and Britain that would fight for a European order "founded upon the sacred rights of humanity," including national rights.[5] As the Russian tsar's minister of foreign affairs, Czartoryski argued that order would guarantee the cause he held uppermost: an independent Poland restored from the pieces of the former kingdom of Poland that had been distributed among Austria, Prussia, and Russia. Meanwhile, William Pitt, the leader of the British House of Commons, envisioned opposition to France in the form of a "confederacy" of Europeans. This would be constructed on the legal basis of "general agreement and guarantee for the mutual protection and security of different Powers and for re-establishing a general system of public law."[6] Pitt discussed with Russia redesigning Europe around the containment of French territory, on the one hand, and the creation of larger political units out of smaller sovereignties, on the other.

These federalizing and nation-building strategies were themselves hardly new. Only a few years earlier, in 1802, on the eve of the Treaty of Amiens that agreed a truce between Britain and France and brought an indeterminate end to a second (failed) coalition, Bonaparte himself had proposed a European confederation. As French First Consul, he pondered a Europe in which "all the powers" might reduce their standing armies, "and then, perhaps, as intelligence became universally diffused, one might be permitted to dream of the application to the great European family of an institution like the American Congress, or that of the Amphictyon, in Greece; and then what a perspective before us of greatness, of happiness, of prosperity—what a grand and magnificent spectacle!"[7] Bonaparte more than imagined federations, he federated whole regions of Europe. In 1808, the Confederation of the Rhine (or Rheinbund) consolidated the central European territory of the 1000-year-old Holy Roman Empire. What were formerly 300 sovereign polities of various forms were now combined into 39 agglomerations populated by 3 million people.[8] Bonaparte's invention of the Kingdom of Italy reduced the 10 political units in existence along the Italian peninsula to 3. The geopolitical creation of Illyria out of Austrian territory with present-day Ljubljana at its heart was likewise a strategic political agglomeration. Faced with the defeat of his ambition, and his life as an exile on the remote island of Saint Helena, Bonaparte would reminisce somewhat wistfully that he had simply wanted to concentrate "the same geographical peoples which revolutions and politics had broken down."[9] In each case, of course, these federations of a great European family of peoples were simultaneously the instruments of French security needs, firming up the Continental System.

The war against Bonaparte did not dampen appetites for applying either national or universal, political or economic ideas from that era to thinking about the postwar future. Instead, it renewed their discussion. The wartime plans under consideration by the Sixth Coalition committed to Bonaparte's defeat tinkered with similar imaginaries of the geopolitical reordering of postwar Europe. In a proposal reworked by the British foreign minister Castlereagh—previously Pitt's aide and secretary of state for war and the colonies—a "European confederacy" became the umbrella concept for "coordinating the several treaties which already existed between the allies into one binding document."[10] Few contemporaries (or historians since) would categorize Castlereagh as either a liberal or cosmopolitan thinker, or assume that his conception of a confederacy extended to an idea of Europe's political unification.[11] Rather, the British foreign secretary's emphasis on peace brought him into alignment with his political mentors and European statesmen wary of political extremes and extremism. Among them was the equally aristocratic Metternich, who supported the Coalition's "very bold enterprise" in the language of "making the constitution of Europe."[12] Given Metternich's influence, his heightened awareness of his role, and what we know of his conscious attempts at both private and public levels to identify with and mold Europe's political future, it is worth returning to the ideas he bought to bear and how he imagined the politics between states if we are to capture the intersecting liberal and conservative outlines of the idea of Europe and its significance.

Count (later Prince) Klemens von Metternich, a "Rhenish" gentleman who helped run the ancien Habsburg Austrian empire, and whom historians often paint as the archenemy of Europe's modern national future, was also a forward-looking creature of the late Enlightenment. The letters he wrote while foreign minister—whether to Sagan or his secretary Gentz, or even correspondents in Persia—reveal a man who kept up with scientific advances. He was a believer in vaccines and the virtues of a proto-psychology, the latter in evidence when he advised Sagan against the fallacies of mesmerism or analyzed his own dreams. He drew on discoveries in chemistry and pathology to understand and conceptualize the nature of government. Although his diplomatic career was all but determined by the fortune of his social circumstances and his father's legacy, Metternich brought to bear a deeper conception of how states, and the political relations between them, could and should work. Some of this conception was impressed upon him by his university teachers at Mainz, adherents of Immanuel Kant, whose famous 1784 essay *Idea for a Universal History from a Cosmopolitan Point of View* was published a few years before Metternich's arrival there as a student.[13] In this definitive Enlightenment text, Kant took the literal meaning of "cosmopolitanism" as belonging in or to the world and translated it into an argument for states coming to realize that their self-interest was best pursued through "the law-governed decisions of a united will," or an unstructured federation.[14] He emphasized this was not a romantic view of sociability but rather an unsocial sociability, a choice to choose the invention of a society of states out of self-interest.

In the late eighteenth century, Kantian cosmopolitanism was mirrored in an "inclusive and pluralistic understanding of the global legal order" that Metternich shared with otherwise unlike thinkers, and that ultimately did not prevail.[15] On Metternich's interpretation, in a society of states, "each state has outside its particular interests, the other interests which are communal to it, whether with all the other reunited states, or with more simply groups of States."[16] In his cosmopolitan imaginary, Europe was part of a wider world that extended at least to Persia and the Ottoman Empire, and that ought to be shaped by "the principle of solidarity" and "balance between States." The "law of nations" could be applied to encourage a "striking openness on the part of Europeans to the possibility of shared legal frameworks and mutual obligations between Christians and non-Christians, Europeans and non-Europeans."[17]

At the same time as Metternich conceived of the "society of States," as "this essential condition of the modern world," he took Christianity as the *model* for "the great human society/*la grande société humaine*." Its reciprocity principle, "do unto others as you would have them do unto you," was in many ways the ultimate rationale for an unsocial sociability.[18] As importantly, Metternich did *not* presume that the community for which this axiom was relevant was exclusively European or Christian—even if his vision premised only male political actors. For the Austrian foreign minister, the Ottoman "state" was a legitimate member of the society of states, not least because he fundamentally respected "existing international law, the sovereignty of the state, and its independence."[19] Metternich expected, wrongly as it turns out, that Ottoman delegates would participate in the making of peace once the war had come to an end.

The impact of ideas is rarely a matter of accident, relying as it does on texts and contexts. In the final year of the Coalition's campaign, Kant's cosmopolitan perspective suddenly became accessible to French- and English-language audiences thanks to Germaine de Staël's outlawed text *On Germany*. Not only was *On Germany* a new kind of study of the existence of a German culture, Staël's account of Kant emphasized his reconciliation of two human tendencies: "personal interest, and universal justice." Kant, Staël explained for her wartime reader, was the proponent of "a happy synthesis of realism and idealism, uniting the liberal principle of freedom of the individual with the needs of others."[20]

Staël's interpretation of Kant supported her own emphasis on "social order" (as John Quincy Adams recorded, she hit that note repeatedly) and her concern with the reconciliation of pluralism and order.[21] Her publications popularized an idea of Europe in which the undeniable "difference of one people to another" was social in origin, and relational, *and* national patriotisms were useful for fomenting opposition to French military expansionism.[22] Staël was as pragmatic in her conception of nations when she rendered them a "ressource normale" of diplomacy, a means of preventing wars by satisfying in advance the ambitions that threatened to clash with each other. Importantly, in her version of Kant's unsocial sociability, "nations must serve as guides for one another."[23] How did universal federation engage national autonomy? Reacting against Napoleon's illiberalism, Staël conceived of humanity's simultaneous progress toward "world civilization" and national diversity.[24] In *On Germany*, she mapped a new idea of the diversity of nations and their distinctive talents onto older Enlightenment configurations of European civilization as the sum of the fusion of northern and southern peoples. Each group could borrow from the other—whether at the level of nation, or north and south—while retaining the strengths of their own difference. Europe became the site of shared moral and political (liberal) values and institutions pushing humanity further along the path to social and political progress, liberty and political equality.[25]

Taken together with Metternich's cosmopolitan "society of states," Staël's reading of Kant, and her own idea of Germany, captures some of the spectrum of universal and national ideas, impelling each other "like two engaged gears." The letters of statesmen and diplomats indicate that they too moved between the worlds of philosophy and politics. As they made their way alongside the Coalition troops, through the German-speaking parts of central Europe, some took as their guide Staël's recently published English-language version of *On Germany*. If we are surprised that a woman's ideas mattered, we should be as attentive to Metternich as an unpredictable spokesperson for the more inclusive and pluralist roots of the cosmopolitan thinking behind the idea of Europe and its newfound multilateralism.

In the course of the campaign against Bonaparte, "universal federation" (Meinecke's term) was inflected through the Coalition's political program. In the spring of 1813, as Austria deliberated whether it would join the Coalition or try to remain neutral, Metternich preferred peace. As he wrote to his fellow Prussian ambassadors, his aim was to "create not a precarious state of affairs but a general arrangement which will put back the geographical and political relations of the powers on a just and lasting basis."[26] This included reimagining relations between European powers and polities, as well as the borders of Europe itself. In this context, Metternich responded to the imperative of Europe's reinvention by reference to framings that he had learned, including a Kantian "society of states."

In the early stages of imagining an international order, with Europe at its center, Metternich's cosmopolitan thinking made him an advocate for the equal standing of the Ottomans, and the eastern empires more generally, in respect of the "law of nations." He argued the Ottomans had reciprocal status "under the guarantee of the recognition of acquired rights, and of respect of legal faith."[27] This ardent defense of the Osman dynasty's equal sovereignty within the society of states and of Turkey as a sixth European power was also reinforced by a long history of Austrian-Ottoman economic engagement.[28] There were long-existing Habsburg trade policies and security plans that relied on good relations with the Ottomans. While each of the Coalition powers had a vested interest in trade with the Ottoman Empire, the Austrian foreign ministry educated its diplomats in the languages and particularities of Islamic societies through its long-established Imperial Oriental Academy. Historical evidence too shows that the geopolitical and civilizational idea of the Muslim world as the antithesis of a Western modernity only began to take a firm hold on the foreign policies of European powers *after* the Napoleonic wars. On some counts, that idea of the overwhelming difference of the Muslim Ottoman

Empire became especially relevant from the 1820s, in the context of the encroachment of the so-called "Greek question"—a question that initially concerned the status of Christian Orthodox Greeks in the predominantly Muslim empire. As these events unfolded, Metternich was exceptionally consistent in his geographical imagining of a society of states until sometime after the last of the postwar peacemaking congresses in 1822.

At the same time, across this period, the Sixth Coalition that conjoined to defeat an illiberal enemy was ultimately an amalgam of imperial powers. Consequently, ideas of international ordering that circulated after 1812, no matter how "cosmopolitan" or indebted to a formula of reciprocity or society of states, were also troubled by the questions of who was in and who was out. Even Kant's "cosmopolitan point of view" required that "the civilized states of our continent, especially the commercial states," change the way they treated "visiting foreign countries and peoples (which in their case is the same as *conquering* them)" and assumed that "the political constitution of our [European] continent . . . will probably legislate eventually for all the other continents."[29]

Cosmopolitan thinking did not preclude the privileging of Europe in the context of the existing relationships of European empires with the non-European world. Where the European continent began or ended (and the relevance of Europe's civilizational difference) mattered to the Ottoman Empire and to the parts of the world those powers had already colonized, often through violent dispossession of indigenous peoples. Kant's anticipation of an international legislative hierarchy reflected imperial relations and imagined cultural and civilizational borders. Russia as much as the Ottoman Empire was vulnerable to the non-European implications of this cosmopolitan "European" thinking.

Borders

From at least 1812 until 1814, Tsar Alexander's leadership of the Coalition coincided with his gradual designation as the hero of a *liberal* European peace. Anti-Bonapartists and anti-liberals who distrusted his leadership saw the feudal emperor as an advocate for a Europe of constitutions and rights. This same accruing reputation

FIGURE 12. John Pinkerton, *Turkey in Europe*, 1814. "A modern atlas, from the latest and best authorities, exhibiting the various divisions of the world, with its chief empires, kingdoms and states, in sixty maps, carefully reduced from the largest and most authentic sources." David Rumsey Map Collection.

of the tsar as the leader of the Coalition confirmed Metternich in his political view of Russia as a controversial (and rival) power on the border of Austria's northern territories and in the Ottoman Empire. Conversely, Staël's awareness that the tsar's authority was susceptible to cultural stereotypes drove her to portray a modernizing Russia in her autobiographical text, *Ten Years of Exile* (which she began to labor over while in Stockholm). Her intention was to bolster the tsar's status as a worthy leader of the anti-Bonaparte alliance. Although Staël herself addressed Russia's potential in terms of its "asiatic" difference, in *Ten Years of Exile* she portrayed the country's vibrant imaginative culture as only lacking the political element of a Third Estate to realize its potential. In her 1814 pamphlet on the importance of abolition of the slave trade, she enjoined Alexander to support the cause in postwar diplomatic negotiations on the grounds that "the emperor of Russia rules peoples of diverse degrees of civilization within the confines of Asia." In that role, she tasked him to mediate liberal principles across the Europe-Asia divide: "he tolerates all religions, he permits all customs, and the scepter, in his hands, is as equitable as law. Asia and Europe bless the name of Alexander. May that name resound as well on the savage shores of Africa! There is no country on earth unworthy of justice."[30]

Where did the Ottomans fit on this changing, if contested, map of Europe? They had their own view of whether they belonged in a European-derived "society of states," and on what terms. Through the decades of the Napoleonic wars, the Ottoman government routinely made the most of diplomatic relations by signing a series of bilateral treaties in order to fend off Russian threats or to use Russia as a defense against French opportunism. This fit a general pattern of hedging bets: the Ottoman Empire exploited good relations with Bonaparte when he portrayed himself as a friend of Islam; with Russia after the French invasion of Egypt; with Britain when Nelson defeated the French. Sometimes, the Ottoman military participated in joint naval operations in the Ionian seas with both Britain and Russia.

Even as the Russian court used Ottoman "dragomans" to assist their negotiations, and Austria instructed its diplomats in Turkic and Arabic languages, the Ottomans cultivated French as a means of communicating in the European world of consular and diplomatic activity. Ottoman sovereigns even sought to entrench the modernizing methods of their western neighbors—a habit that sometimes sparked suspicions too.[31] In September 1812, the British diplomat Sir Robert Wilson described the sultan as "a man of very extraordinary mind, and Energy," noting that his chiefs were "all convinced of the necessity of adapting the European Military systems."[32] The question of whether the Ottoman sultan or his ministers should be involved in the making of a postwar order was from their perspective a question of how that involvement might occur: on their terms or on those of the Coalition powers. On all accounts, the Sublime Porte was keeping a close watch.

Mapping the intellectual and ideological landscape of Europe, its horizon and limitations, its texts and contexts and varying perspectives, helps us connect the diplomatic events that took place during and after the Sixth Coalition war, with evolving cosmopolitan framings and conceptualization of politics between states, as well as the complex motivations of the individuals involved. In the last year of the Coalition war, invocations of *patrie*, Europe, and humanity were tied to forward-looking liberal constitutions, national states, and federal conglomerations, even as they jostled with the restoration of kings and kingdoms. These varied ambitions had unpredictable spokespersons and were often grafted onto each other in unique ways. Tsar Alexander's opinions of peace, historians tend to agree, were cultivated by the French Enlightenment and Genevan republicans. Like Metternich and Castlereagh, and despite their suspicions, he celebrated the European basis of their cooperation, to the extent of speaking of Europe as a federal project even when his ideas did not necessarily serve Russia's interests. In early 1814, the Prussian foreign minister, Hardenberg, was already thinking of Europe in statistical terms, arranged through the counting and balance of population. His secretary, Wilhelm von Humboldt, ambassador to the Habsburg court in Vienna—and brother of the exceptional naturalist Alexander—imagined "universal humanity" in relation to geophysical "natural" power blocs.[33] Humboldt presumed that German-speaking Austria and Prussia were a natural geophysical partnering at the center of Europe; Spain and Turkey or the Ottomans sat outside that natural ordering on either side of Europe; Britain, with its external reach beyond Europe, into the New World, constituted a separate geophysical system, as did Russia. Like all the statesmen and diplomats, and public, Humboldt also acknowledged that the idea of a German confederation was an inevitable item on the postwar agenda—because of the "facts on the ground" created by Bonaparte's Rhine Confederation and its convenience for recalibrating Europe's equilibrium. He supported the reestablishment of a German federation on the model of the existing French-invented confederation, upgraded with a federal army, court of justice, and guaranteed political liberties in the constituent states.

By the late nineteenth century, Friedrich Meinecke would depict Humboldt's view of Germany as unpatriotic, in thrall to "universal federation," "universal humanity," and a "world republic" with roots in "natural law and democracy."[34] At fault, according to Meinecke, was "the individualistic and cosmopolitan eighteenth century"—a critique that stuck.[35] And yet, usually classified a "liberal," Humboldt gave less thought than illiberal Metternich to a cosmopolitan "society of states" as the basis for the politics between states. The political distance between Metternich and Humboldt and Staël's innovative national cosmopolitanism, juxtaposed with Meinecke's depiction of the universal and national impelling each other like engaged gears, stretch the measure of political thought in the early 1800s and its distance from the century that would follow. This comparison suggests that looking back we can take neither the resonance nor the meaning of concepts for thinking about the politics between states for granted; they depended on texts and contexts, the voices of men and women. Just as there was no predictability to the borders of cosmopolitan and liberal ideas, change was not inclined to move in a single predictable direction, as if modernity sat perched, waiting, on a distant horizon.

CHAPTER SIX

Multilateralism

The establishment of international relations upon the basis of reciprocity, under the guarantee of respect for acquired rights, and the conscientious observance of [pledged] faith, constitutes, at the present day, the essence of politics, of which diplomacy is only the daily application.

—KLEMENS VON METTERNICH, *MÉMOIRES*, 1:31

Who would even attempt to find deep motives and impulses based on intellectual ideas in the notes of diplomats or in the préambules *of political agreements?*

—FRIEDRICH MEINECKE, *COSMOPOLITANISM AND THE NATIONAL STATE*, 1907

ONE OF THE MOST UNPREPOSSESSING symbolic moments in the history of European diplomacy takes place around a small card-playing table in the "dirty and dull" northern French town of Chaumont, on the river Marne. On 9 March 1814, at the Coalition's makeshift headquarters, the foreign ministers of Russia, Prussia, Britain, and Austria take a vow to pursue their alliance into the postwar period. This agreement between four empires, signed as a treaty, embeds the importance of politics between states in the fraternal bonds forged between them in battle. The meaning they give to their commitment rests on the promise of an enduring form of cooperation imagined as "ces conférences de l'Europe!" and that we now would identify as multilateralism. A term that literally means agreement between three or more countries, "multilateralism" does

FIGURE 13. Forceval, *Le Congrès*, 1815. Engraving, 18.6 × 27.5 cm. Bibliothèque Nationale de France, Département des Estampes et de la photographie.

not come into popular use until more than a century later. Yet for historians casting the net of meaning backward, the Chaumont moment lays the conceptual planks of multilateralism on which the modern international order is built. For Paul W. Schroeder, Chaumont exemplifies more than an agreement, it contributes a new ethos of "loyalty to something beyond the aims of one's own state."[1] Motivated by the "bitter experience" of war, the European statesmen gathered there learn, Schroeder conjectures, "something else even more fundamental to the existence of ordered society as they knew it was vulnerable and could be overthrown: the existence of any international order at all, the very possibility of their states coexisting as independent members of a European family of nations."[2] With the advantage of hindsight, the international, even cosmopolitan, aspects of this early nineteenth-century multilateralism are defined by what we know international thinking will become.

In the early nineteenth century, multilateralism begins modestly, with no possible premonition of the international future that lies ahead. There have been multilateral agreements of a kind too in the past. In 1748, at the end of the War of the Austrian Succession, the Peace of Aachen/Aix-la-Chapelle was signed by eight European powers.[3] Further, some of the language and concepts deployed in the Chaumont agreement were well-rehearsed over at least a century of earlier treaties, from calls for perpetual or permanent peace and equilibrium, the "rest and well-being of Europe," "a solid and durable peace on earth and over the seas," to "the happy future of Europe." Other phrases written into the 1814 document are already as generic, whether the reference to "[the] great work of the political reconstruction of Europe" or "the good harmony" of the allies.[4] However, at Chaumont, the familiar reprise of "rest and repose" is bolstered with specific imperatives "to concert together," on behalf of Europe. Among the Coalition allies, the term "concert" evokes a practice of negotiation, in deliberate contrast to Napoleon's rule by hegemony, and thereby becomes the source of the common identification of the "Concert of Europe."

There are no great paintings of the powers at Chaumont, nor rescued images that might establish its significance. What were the underlying emotions of these men, whose relations were the subject of other illustrations? Their extant correspondence from the frontlines in 1814, private and public, provides some answers, as Metternich gushes to Sagan that after Chaumont the world "is not and never will be what it has been formerly."[5] The experience at Chaumont convinces British foreign secretary Castlereagh that a template for a "European confederacy"—including Britain—has been set, on the model Pitt imagined less than a decade earlier.[6] For months, Castlereagh too is announcing his confidence in an already existing "European confederacy" with its origin in the "higher motives" of a moral bond resting "upon more solid principles than any of those that have preceded it, and the several Powers to be bound together for the first time by one paramount consideration of an imminent and common danger."[7] Now, after Chaumont, he wonders that it is "impossible not to perceive a great moral change coming in Europe, and that the principles of freedom are in full operation." In the past, questions of security were matters resolved by "a contest of sovereigns, in some instances perhaps, against the prevailing sentiment of their subjects." Now, European leaders are guided by "the feelings of the people of all ranks as well." We do not have to accept all of Castlereagh's claims to acknowledge the power of his enthusiasm. From Castlereagh's view, Chaumont is the next logical step in an evolving politics. From our perspective, it gives a quasi-legal form and adds pragmatic detail to the accentuated multilateralism of the early nineteenth century, anticipating its international dimensions.

In a period when, as English political philosopher Jeremy Bentham has already estimated, "security turns its eye exclusively to the future," some of those involved in Chaumont understand the principles of freedom with respect to legal codes and constitutions; others focus on growing state bureaucracies, not least its foreign ministries. The Coalition statesmen who identify with the cause of "Europe" and "peace" think and work in the context of circulating political possibilities: federation, a society of states, humanity, and, simultaneously, national state-building. They use Europe and an "equilibrium of justice" as metaphors for "collective sentiment," "onto which notions of peace, tranquillity and harmony were projected."[8] Although talk of "confederacy" and "the constitution of Europe" is not intended as a literal rendering of these ambitions, it evokes a mood of consensus that extends from military cooperation to moral imperative. Loftier ideals—oblique references to "principles of freedom"—are mixed in with practical motivations and methods. As allies they also agree to imagine Europe's collective security through the consolidation of four regions: the Netherlands, Italy, Switzerland, and a German confederation comprising the myriad polities of the former Holy Roman Empire.[9]

Historians have at times reduced the political thinking of this era to the "balance of power"—a well-rehearsed formula for balancing out the ratio of manpower, resources, and territory among Europe's empires, so that no one power has a strategic military advantage. Instead, as the Coalition moves forward from strength to military strength, its protagonists and supporters venture more ambitious plans for the postwar and achieving equilibrium. Maintaining the momentum of multilateral cooperation comes wrapped in new diplomatic principles that will significantly expand the ways in which politics between states is imagined.

Conférences

At its most basic, in early 1814, as the Coalition's war against Bonaparte and France continues, cooperation is built on the foundations of both bilateral and multilateral agreements, and on diplomatic conferencing meant to facilitate their relations. Some of these processes are established a few weeks before Chaumont, at a series of "very dull" meetings at Châtillon, a small, reputably prettier, provincial French town around 250 kilometers away, on the river Seine. Through February and March 1814, the *hôtel des conférences* for these meetings in Châtillon is the commandeered house of Marshal Marmont, one of Napoleon's most trusted military men. With Austrian grenadiers watchfully stationed outside, Coalition statesmen and lesser delegates gather around 1:00 p.m.: Austria's Count Stadion, Russia's Razumovsky, Britain's Aberdeen, Stewart, and Cathcart, Prussia's Humboldt, and French foreign minister Marquis de Caulaincourt. If there is unfinished business, they resume after 8:00 p.m. Their goal is to negotiate an end to the war. The negotiating methods devised at Châtillon are intended to finesse cooperation between the Coalition's state-based members. In hindsight, from the vantage point of more than a century of accumulated bureaucratic and diplomatic expertise, the detail of those methods can seem disarmingly banal. That they appear innovative to those involved is important to keep in mind.

Each Coalition member is expected to have access to full records of the meetings between them; meeting notes are laboriously written out in duplicate and collated for distribution.[10] At the beginning of each meeting, discussions are prefaced with the presentation of original documents—prepared copies of their agenda and protocols—for each other's perusal. This process also helps underscore the legitimacy of their authority. Only after the presentation of these documents can they declare their mission to make peace with France "in the name of Europe."[11] The allies deliberate all manner of methods that can help them avoid competitive friction, including the order of signatures on protocols and declarations. They decide that each Coalition plenipotentiary should sign on one side of the page in random order.[12] This way no one power can claim or demand precedence. Together, they agree to reject bilateralism: no one sovereign should make a separate arrangement with another sovereign in the alliance. They contend that inclusiveness—even to the extent of restoring a defeated France to good standing in the postwar "political system"—will establish the Coalition's commitment to the future "security/*sureté*" and *independence* of Europe.

Of course, for all the care the diplomats take, ultimately they will not keep all of their promises, and bilateralism will continue to be a part of the multilateral future. Châtillon fails more specifically to quell Bonaparte's ambitions. As he continues his deliberate stalling, the Coalition negotiators head to Chaumont. It is at this point that a smaller group of foreign ministers, the tsar among them, parley the politics and strength of their bond in the circumstances of war and after their victory.

The treaty signed by the Coalition members at Chaumont in early March 1814 continues the task of outlining the practical as well as ideal details of their European version of multilateralism. They determine that should any one of them face attack by the French, "the others shall employ their most strenuous efforts to prevent it, by friendly interposition." When more forthright action is required, they are to "come to the immediate assistance of the power attacked, each with a body of sixty thousand men."[13] The Coalition partners continue to back the promise of military aid with money, relying on the principle of "subsidy," a precedent already set in earlier bilateral agreements and the Treaty of Reichenbach.[14] Britain's obligation now is to all the Coalition. While more than 50,000 British troops are fighting the French in Spain, under the Duke of Wellington's command, Britain will also contribute subsidies to Coalition partners supporting 150,000 "men in the field," out of a total of 450,000 Coalition soldiers. The subsidy system will now take the form of an issue of £5 million in a paper currency to be used to pay for the military campaigns of Russia, Prussia, and Austria. These governments will cash the notes in after the war is over. As a further incentive, the British promise that the paper will accrue interest at the generous rate of 6 percent.[15]

Fiscal arrangements tie the Coalition allies to a shared currency and a financial stake in victory that will ultimately benefit bankers across the continent who are called upon to assist with the provision of credit and payments. For all the cost to the British government, the arrangements give it a serious footing on the continent, allowing it to pursue the disabling of Bonaparte's Continental System and restore its access to European markets. At the same time, Britain assumes a position of exceptionalism. A condition of its cooperation is the exclusion of all questions that affect its maritime policies, from its colonies to its war with America. The agreement bolsters Castlereagh's privately held conviction that he personally has gone from governing England to "governing the continent"—although we know another foreign minister, Metternich, thinks the same way about his own growing authority and power.[16]

The allies' Chaumont moment is bolstered by a new military governance structure, set up three months earlier. The Allied Central Administrative Authority led by the Prussian advisor to the tsar, Baron vom Stein, manages military logistics as well as the occupation in Saxony, Berg, Westphalia, and Frankfurt, and the sharing of spoils of war for the Coalition.[17] Vom Stein embodies the spirit of a Prussian enlightened bureaucracy, now brought to bear on the challenge of cementing relations between European powers and making sure the Coalition wins. His organizational acumen sets an important precedent for the postwar, when an Allied body will be tasked with overseeing the occupation of Paris and with conferencing key political questions.[18]

There are already strong clues about the Coalition's emerging postwar agenda and the spirit in which it will be tackled. In the wake of their Chaumont consensus, as the Coalition forces march, ride, and fight on their way through the French countryside, their sights set on Paris, they distribute pamphlets outlining the "principles of freedom" that are their shared motivation. They promise a future in which the "*reciprocal* independence" of "nations" will be respected, social institutions will be protected from daily upheavals, property will be secure, and commerce will be "free." Their propaganda links the old and new together, adapting the political palimpsest of the ancien world to transnational post-revolutionary expectations. The Coalition promises that "princes" endowed with the authority of divine will, or more simply dynastic inheritance, will fulfill their obligations to watch out for the well-being of their populations, without having to rely on prodding from "strangers."[19] They borrow from the potentially incendiary political language of the French philosopher Rousseau, tempered with the example of Bonaparte's own strategic rhetoric, to confirm that the whole of Europe has "one will" that is in turn the expression of "the people's needs." Like the French ambassador, the Marquis de Caulaincourt, we might be inclined to ask: When these men invoked the people's will, whom did they have in mind? Caulaincourt is convinced the allies are excluding France from "la société Européene."[20] As it turns out, however, France will quickly be restored to European society as a legitimate member, while the status of the Coalition leader Russia, like the Ottoman Empire, will remain precarious.

In 1814, multilateralism, much as the more expansive idea of loyalty to something beyond the aims of one's own state, has to be worked at; it cannot be taken for granted on the basis of a single agreement or experience. For all the homosocial or fraternal bonding of male protagonists, the divisions among them cut along the lines of entrenched Enlightenment cultural tropes of north-south and east-west differences. These are not simply geopolitical points of reference; they are constantly in play as points of geopolitical, even moral, orientation. In the midst of military and political tumult, at the moment of fraternal bonding between the men who represent Europe's major powers in their coalition against France, Metternich and Castlereagh bring these tropes to bear on depictions of Russia as a threat to the Europe they prefer to identify, respectively, with their own growing authority. Castlereagh's suspicion of Russian motivations relies on a theory of the "natural march of empires from north to south, from the regions of the frost, snow and famine, to the climates of warmth, verdure, and fertility."[21] The Russian tsar might imagine himself the spokesperson for a shared European multilateral future, yet from Castlereagh's perspective the movement of the tsar's armies west and south to warmer European climes looks to be in Russia's expansionary self-interest. Castlereagh's half brother Charles Stewart, British ambassador to Austria, is triggered by the image of Cossack Russian guards "from the Tartary region of Russia bordering China" crossing the river Rhine. Stewart will write in retrospect that "the whole system of European politics ought as its leading principle and feature to maintain as an axiom, the necessity of setting bounds to this [Russian] formidable and encroaching power."[22] Metternich's anxiety regarding Russia is as openly geopolitical. His perception of Russia as a clear and present threat to Austrian territory and commerce references a gendered moral geography of civilizational difference, including allegations of the tsar's inclination to female company and sexual deviance.

As the end of war seems in sight, it is not only the heads of state or their ministers who engage the possibilities of a new Europe and the imperative of peace. We have already seen how Germaine de Staël directly exerts her intellectual influence in the formation of a coalition. Some intellectuals use the tools of publication to appeal to the monarchs and statesmen with alternative framings of a post-war European society of states and the form of political culture they could foster. Among the more notable is the French thinker Claude-Henri de Saint-Simon, who, with his coauthor historian Augustin Thierry, produces a telling pamphlet, *De la réorganisation de la société européenne, ou De la nécessité et des moyens de rassembler les peuples de l'Europe en un seul corps politique, en conservant à chacun son indépendance nationale* (On the reorganization of European society, or on the necessity and the means of reassembling the peoples of Europe into a single political body, while conserving the national independence of each one).[23] This text takes as its unexpected premise the idea that peace in Europe cannot be built on a multilateralism of diplomatic practices and treaties alone. Saint-Simon and Thierry elaborate an argument for a more thorough scientific reorganization of Europe, for new ways of thinking about the relations between states and the political forms that might encourage peace and liberty.[24]

By this time, Saint-Simon is well-known for his entrepreneurial success as much as his social ideas. He has made his fortune as a capitalist, speculating on the anarchy of the French Revolution, buying and reselling the confiscated land and buildings of the Catholic Church. He has used that money to establish himself in the world of letters as a kind of visionary of the future, decades before he earns a reputation as a "utopian socialist," or proto-socialist thinker. In 1814, Saint-Simon and Thierry's argument relies on a more specific engagement with the importance of the "social": the habits of individuals and "peoples," even the *direction* of their sentiments and feelings, are socially determined. Saint-Simon and Thierry shift attention from feelings as foundational political emotions to the social contexts in which they are generated and reinforced. They explain that since the scale of social institutions and relations affects the scale of an individual's collective identification, the more comprehensive the society, the larger the social/political community with which an individual might be inclined to identify. On this same basis, the more connected the Coalition can make postwar Europe, the greater the possibility of generating "European patriotism."[25] Saint-Simon and Thierry acknowledge that such a process cannot happen on its own but believe that a "coactive force" can unite wills by providing the social context that can "concert movements, and render interests communal and engagements solid."[26]

Saint-Simon's intellectual debt to Staël runs through this emphasis on the "social" as *the* determinant of political life. Staël has made this point most emphatically in her *De la littérature considérée dans ses rapports avec les institutions sociales* (1800), which renders culture not simply the product of a writer's individuality but a sociological artefact, simultaneously shaped by and shaping a collective *esprit*.[27] The two certainly know each other well. Around the time of Staël's husband's death, the recently divorced Saint-Simon visited her to offer condolences, and a proposition: "Madame you are the most extraordinary woman in the world, just as I am the most extraordinary man; us two, we would without doubt have the most extraordinary child yet."[28] Staël refused him, but Saint-Simon is gracious enough to retain interest in her ideas.

In anticipation of an imminent peace, Staël too continues to promote her political vision, including the idea that France model its political institutions on those of Britain. Saint-Simon and Thierry build on this same idea but aim higher: they imagine a European parliament based on the model of the British parliament, seeded in the first instance in the creation of a combined Anglo-French parliament. Despite a quarter century of war between these countries, the authors insist that Britain and France now share a political form as constitutional monarchies standing for property rights, individual rights, and freedom of thought. As unrealistic as an Anglo-French parliament might appear now, their fancy illustrates just how wide the window of opportunity seems at the time. In *De la réorganisation de la société européenne*, a European parliament will oversee "enterprises of general utility," such as the freeing up of navigation along the Danube and Rhine, a European education program, and even a Europe-wide moral code. (The navigation of the Danube and the Rhine do in fact end up on the Coalition's peacemaking agenda, although for different reasons.)

There is much in Saint-Simon and Thierry's text, including the weight they give to the political authority of science and of a "second class" of entrepreneurs, that will echo in the peacemaking interventions of another future utopian socialist and well-known entrepreneur, Robert Owen.[29] In 1818, Owen's contribution will come in the more pessimistic form of a warning about the threat to Europe posed by increasingly endemic inequality. But in 1814, Saint-Simon and Thierry's proposal is distinctive because it anticipates a golden age in Europe, when Europeans will form a single society and consider the "general" interest more important than simply national concerns. Saint-Simon and Thierry let their imaginations run to the idea of a future European parliament that will undertake "external missions," populating the globe with the superior "European race," making everywhere else habitable on a European model.[30] This future liberal Europe will extend its influence through an international order of colonial dimensions.

Early nineteenth-century renditions of Europe produced by the multilateral mood of the Coalition's campaign inevitably veer to the non-European world, although they do not always intone a culturally aggressive European imperialism. The 1813 text of Staël's collaborator Benjamin Constant, *The Spirit of Conquest*, warns that an imperial approach to European unity will flatten local patriotisms and replace them with "fictitious passion for an abstract thing."[31] Constant's use of *imperial* tends to refer to the relations between the dominant powers, at the expense of the smaller or defeated European polities. In this scenario, he prefers to make commerce the guarantee of peace in a brave new European world. His argument returns to the promise of the "doux commerce" theme proposed by Kant in his *Universal History*: "It is the spirit of commerce that sooner or later takes hold of every nation, and it is incompatible with war."[32]

The other text that reverberates in debates about politics between states and its purpose in this period is authored by another

Staël collaborator, Simonde de Sismondi. His pamphlet against the slave trade, *De l'intérêt de la France à l'égard de la traite des nègres*, published in Geneva in 1814, is among the texts the British distribute in a liberated Paris to sway official and public opinion.[33] Its specific concern is the damage wrought by Bonaparte's economic policies, from the Continental System to the slave trade in French colonies. Sismondi admonishes the proposition popular among some French politicians that Saint Domingue (Haiti) should be recolonized and the slave trade restored. On his view, it makes no fiscal or moral sense; slavery perverts the ideals of free trade as much as freedom.[34] Instead, he contends that the more trade expands (and empires extend), the more competition, and the less slave trade–based agriculture, will run markets. Like Constant, and others of Staël's Coppet circle, Sismondi believes that the internal organization of nations and their political external relations are shaped as much by the new "spirit of commerce" as politics itself. Commerce is creating competition that will eventually force Europe to negotiate with countries such as India and America rather than fight them. In the same way, the spirit of commerce principle can be seen at work in the Barbary regions of the African Mediterranean, where, he maintains, piracy is being abandoned in favor of agricultural commodities and markets.

Running through the flurry of publications addressing the possibilities of politics in the postwar is a general view that the Coalition has Europe's fate in its hands. As importantly, few imagine that the organization of political institutions and political life within states and between them is simply a matter of negotiation and methods. It is as much about underlying ideas of peace and how a more permanent peace might be achieved. At their most imaginative level of inclusiveness, the stakes are an era of moral and economic equilibrium.

Are women of any consequence in the Chaumont moment of multilateralism? In Frankfurt only two months earlier, Coalition diplomats gathered to enjoy opera and dinner every night, and the emperor of Russia's delightful sisters, including Grand-Duchess Ekaterina, shone. The dinners often at Metternich's headquarters began at 3:00 p.m., so that, as Aberdeen wrote home, "the day is terribly shortened."[35] At Chaumont, by comparison, Castlereagh writes his wife waiting in Brussels that they work hard, and although he has met "all the great wigs," "I am not so great a hero as you suppose," and he never sees a single princess.[36] Lady Burghersh, the niece of the Duke of Wellington, is the one woman who travels with the diplomats on horseback in order to accompany her husband, and she leaves behind the correspondence of the hardships she endures on the military campaign trail.[37] However, Charles Stewart's letters imply that there are women in Châtillon, a "female society" intended to banish the "ennui" and to add to the "conviviality and harmony that reigns between the ministers." We can hear the tones of innuendo when he predicts that the women's presence "will be long recollected with sensations of pleasure by all the plenipotentiaries there engaged."[38]

The Allied Machine

Ten days after negotiating the Chaumont agreement, the allies march on Paris, on 1 April 1814. The future looks different when the armies of the Coalition finally arrive. The cries that can be heard are for the thirty-six-year-old Russian tsar: "Vive l'Empereur Alexandre—le liberateur—Le Paix!" All eyes are on him as Alexander enters the city, mounted on his gray charger Mars—gifted at the Châtillon talks by the Marquis de Caulaincourt. When Castlereagh and Metternich reach Paris ten days later, with the Prussian foreign minister, the deaf Prince Hardenberg in tow, they cannot contain their displeasure at the tsar's advantage. The advantage, however, may be as much Talleyrand's. The most senior of the French statesmen who take control of peacemaking, Talleyrand has been able to assume the role of formal representative of France as a defeated power and, as quickly, control of the political agenda. On the first day of liberation he convinces the tsar that Napoleon's former Champs-Élysée palace is mined and dangerous, and his own residence on the Rue St. Florentin is safer.[39] By bringing the tsar into close proximity, Talleyrand is able to maneuver an agreement on Napoleon's exile relatively close by, on the island of Elba, just off the coast of Tuscany, and retention of his title of emperor. From Castlereagh's perspective this should have been Britain's moment. It is hard not to imagine Castlereagh's rancor at the tsar's prominence, given the cost to Britain of the Coalition armies. He is of the camp who suspects that Napoleon's removal makes Russia the new threat to Britain's political and economic prominence on the continent. Regardless, Castlereagh's modus vivendi is conciliatory, "intelligent and calm."[40]

On 9 May, the Paris negotiations begin as an "informal conversation" between France and the ministers of the now four main Coalition powers: Britain, Russia, Prussia, and Austria. In a setting where the issues that have been researched and reported on are to be agreed through "conference" and "machinery," the naming of their first meeting as an informal conversation seems an anomaly, and is possibly a strategy for excluding Spain from their discussion. Around them the cogs of a multilateral bureaucracy begin to turn, on the model of organizational cooperation conceived en route to Paris. As Beatrice de Graaf notes, Vom Stein's Allied Administrative Authority is now the prototype of a new "collective security system" known as the "Paris Conference"—later it will be referred to as the "Allied Council" or Ministerial and Ambassadorial Conference; the presiding British celebrate it as "the Allied Machine." The work of the "Conference" is the organized occupation of France, the introduction of new practices of passport regulation, joint security service, military policy, and border control for the Coalition forces.[41] Among the Coalition administrators are Count Pozzo di Borgo, the Russian diplomat born in Corsica, Napoleon's own birthplace, and Robert Gordon, Aberdeen's brother.[42]

The business of occupation is entwined with the business of peacemaking, and Lord Aberdeen is not anxious for any speedy conclusion since "the manner in which the business is conducted" is as important as the issues themselves.[43] There are formal and informal *séances* or meetings, as well as commissions focused on researching and discussing territorial and financial questions. The *Commission des limites* is concerned with the fate of territory previously under French domination, and it proceeds on the assumption that the geographical borders of the new France were agreed at Chaumont.[44] The finance commission, also agreed at Chaumont, provides oversight of the payment of subsidies to the Coalition partners. For example, Austria accepts 104,155 pounds, which, the commission determines, will be paid through four Austrian banks:

Fries and Co., Steiner and Co., Geymuller, Arnstein and Eskeles. The commission's other tasks include the management of the financial implications of the transfer of territory beyond the "ancient limits" of France that have been set as the new French border. Now that this territory—in Belgium, the Rhine, and Alps—is no longer French, debts have to be settled, assets transferred, and the fate of "national domains" that have been purchased by private French individuals under the conditions of French occupation decided.

The outcomes of these commissions and discussions in Paris culminate in the Treaty of Paris, signed at the end of May 1814. The first of the postwar peacemaking treaties, it defines European security in terms of border adjustments already outlined at Chaumont: a reduced France will be surrounded by a territorially bolstered Netherlands ruled by the House of Orange to the north; a new confederation of independent states known as "Germany" and a free and independent Switzerland, east and south.[45] Despite the popularity of confederation, "Italy," a territorial entity created by Napoleon as a kingdom under his rule, is to be returned in its older sovereign pieces to the possession of Austria. In liberated Europe, dynasties will resume their thrones: Bourbon king Louis XVIII in France, Bourbon king Frederick VII in Spain, although both in territories reduced to their ancient limits.

The peacemakers accept that European interests beyond the continent are within the Coalition's remit. France will have back all its colonies in the Western Indies, Africa, and America, and all of its factories and establishments east of Cape of Good Hope—even though Britain captured these during the war. Britain keeps for itself the island of Tobago and Ile de St. Maurice and its dependencies, as well as French commercial territories on the Continent des Indes, where it promises not to build fortifications. Malta will also be Britain's, as well as the Septinsular Republic, territory in the Mediterranean that the Russian tsar's Corfu-born diplomat Ioannes Kapodistrias hoped would gain its independence.[46] France is required to prohibit the slave trade in its restored territories.

The liberal underpinnings of the Chaumont agreement are confirmed by the Paris treaty. Article 16 requires "The High Contracting Powers" to bury "in oblivion the dissensions which have agitated Europe" by guaranteeing the security of individual and property

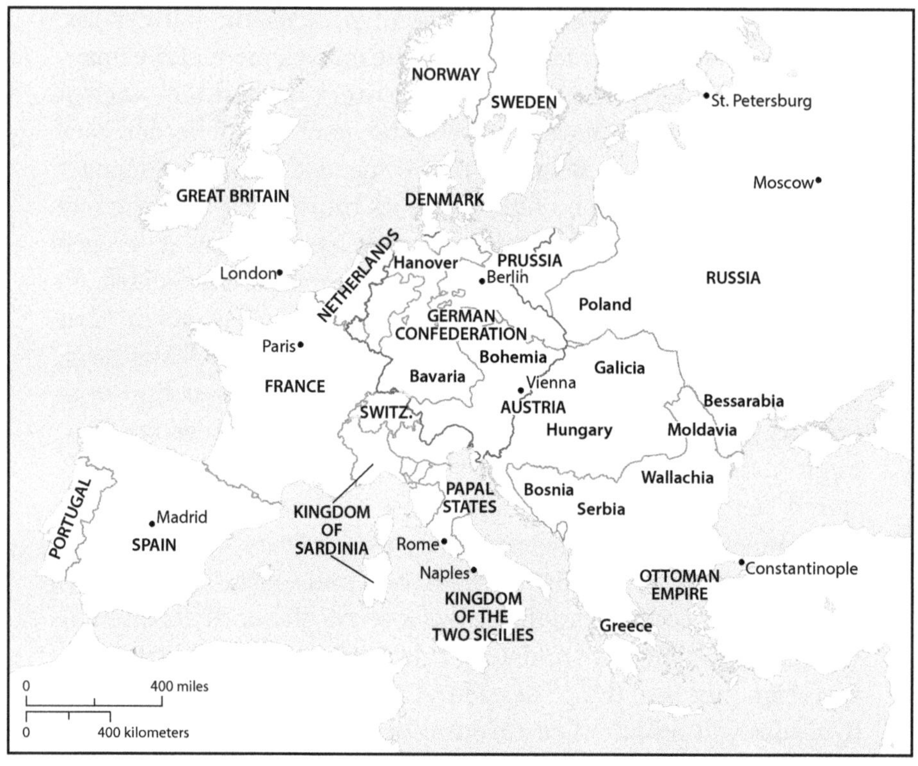

FIGURE 14. Map of Europe after the Congress of Vienna, 1815.

rights. In "countries restored and ceded by the present treaty," individuals cannot be "prosecuted, disturbed, or molested in his person or property, under any pretext whatsoever . . . for conduct of political opinions, etc."[47] All sums claimed from France during wars since 1792 are to be renounced, although the French are required to "liquidate and pay all debts owed outside borders due on contracts of formal engagements between individuals and authorities etc."[48] Security now is as much a question of securing private property as state sovereignty.

For all the treaty's practical detail deciding the imperial reach, territorial form, and commercial purposes of Europe, the peacemakers interpret its significance in philosophical terms. Castlereagh records that it is impossible not to perceive "a great moral change coming in Europe"; "the principles of freedom are in full operation."[49] Metternich is even ready to take full credit: "I've been telling myself for years—I will kill N[apoleon]—and I will make world peace . . . principles which guide us all including England."[50] However, if there is a historical lesson in the air, it is as much that any moral or political change comes at the cost of the exclusion of countries and whole groups of people. In Paris, these men take it upon themselves to speak in the name of Europe and humanity, in the midst of the many voices keen to be heard. Ultimately, the extent of liberal political ambitions associated with this historical moment is the product of that same conjunction.[51]

CHAPTER SEVEN

Liberties

IN THE EUROPEAN SPRING OF 1814, there are no simple or inevitable solutions to the questions of how to make peace and to "restore" order; too much of the world has been remade to simply turn back the clock. Even Britain has its imperial authority challenged by the breakaway colonies of the North American continent. In the preceding two decades, Bonaparte not only altered Europe's political boundaries, he created facts on the ground within France's extended empire that included new administrative units, legal codes, and forms of citizenship that premise national sovereignty. He granted rights to Jews, but took away from women their revolutionary gains. In planning for a post-Napoleonic order that ostensibly rejects Napoleon's legacy, what principles of political rights and exclusions are to decide the bases of political communities? These are among the questions that concern peacemakers in Paris, before and after they agree on the territorial and geopolitical terms of the peace. The path to agreement not only takes the route of official fora or treaties, it articulates through social contexts and a landscape of contested ideas.

As the prospect of peace takes form, Allied soldiers from the farthest reaches of the continent are camped at Château de Bondy, near Place Gambetta, and parading through the streets in "foreign costume and the most extraordinary dresses."[1] The boulevards are crammed with dandies, masked women, open recreational carriages, and cartage drivers, Cossacks are "riding in the streets, and innumerable groups of officers of the enemies," and "armies parade

FIGURE 15. Unknown artist, *Premier combat sous Paris en 1814*. Etching. Bibliotcka Narodowa.

in carriages on horseback and on foot."[2] The Cossack soldiers are particularly noticed as "mostly from the Don, men with whom nature has been lavish of her proportions and all selected from their height."[3] Coalition soldiers of all stripes fill the theaters and coffeehouses are overflowing, to the extent that some of these spaces feel as if they are in military possession. Cultural differences are also on display among Europe's civilians. Over two decades of cultural isolation, the English manner of dress has assumed a relative eccentricity. It is nearly a quarter of a century since the British foreign minister has last been in the city, as ambassador in the heady days of revolution, and now Castlereagh arrives, to some mirth, dressed like a prelate from 1780s, with horribly braided puffy sleeves and short fur jacket.[4]

In Paris, on the surface, the mood is light, and everyone is mixing and saluting each other cordially. Metternich writes home that it is as if there has been no war, despite the omnipresent military and the simmering political tensions. Locals proudly sport the royalist white "cocarde" in their caps, or cry "Vive le roi!" under the windows of Emperor Napoleon's palace.[5] Their voices are drowned by talk of constitutions, civil liberty, individual rights, property rights, free press, free trade, free thought, freedom of religion, and national rights.[6] The same police reports that cast the growth of journals and the variety of opinion as suspicious and potential threats to social order are evidence of a thriving public sphere.[7] However, even Tsar Alexander notices the Parisian papers' servility to the ruling Bourbon government.[8]

It is somewhat counterintuitive that the tsar of a quasi-feudal Russian empire that countenances indentured peasant labor has become the living symbol of Europe's liberties. Alexander is celebrated as the "le legislateur de l'Europe," much as Staël promotes him. She is not alone. Anticipating the peace, the elderly legal scholar Jeremy Bentham writes the tsar from London in January 1814, asking for a commission to devise a new body of penal and civil laws for Russia. Bentham brings to his offer a Europe-wide reputation as the theorist of utilitarianism.[9] The tsar has read Bentham's work in (Genevan) Étienne Dumont's French translation, and he was personally responsible for ordering the Russian translation of Bentham's *Treaties of Civil and Penal Law*, with its espousal of penal reform and a free press. The idea of universally relevant legal codes reflects the tsar's interest in the political forms that might bolster peace in Europe.[10] Bentham explains to the tsar that he would like to provide the legal basis for a more liberal Russian empire, creating laws that "are the same in all *places* and at all *times*; others which vary with the *place* and with the *time*."[11] He informs the tsar he is ready to provide a constitution for Poland too if the kingdom is likely to be restored as a political entity.

Neither Bentham's offers of a Polish constitution or a Russian legal code is taken up. Nevertheless, Bentham's invitation, like the tsar's philosophical curiosity, marks the entwined political and intellectual climate of the immediate postwar. Gentz will later gauge the breadth of ambition at this peacemaking moment by portraying the tsar as someone who sees "himself as the founder of a European federation and wanted to be regarded as its leader," who defends that project in every memoir and diplomatic note as "the glory of the age and the salvation of the world."[12] A few days after arriving in Paris, when Alexander announces the Coalition's victory in writing to Louis XVIII, brother of the guillotined Bourbon king Louis XVI, he adds a recommendation that this future king of France should acknowledge the existence of a French "national will" and the moderate and liberal institutions organic to France.[13] Louis, still in exile in London, is busy seeking support for his claims to the throne from Staël. Although a convinced republican, Staël is ready to accommodate a constitutional monarchy as a "temporary tool to politically stabilise continental Europe . . . a compromise."[14] This is despite the fact that she still backs Bernadotte and regards the obese Louis in his "rolling chair," "pulled from the front, and pushed from behind," as the living emblem of the worst self-indulgent aspects of pre-revolutionary France.[15] Staël's concerns seem validated when Louis XVIII assumes dynastic reign. Backed by the British government, his arrival indulges pomp and ceremony. He visits the tombs of his guillotined brother and sister-in-law, and then presents a charter that promises the French a constitutional monarchy and a parliament with a dual chamber. These are based not on the "national will" or "the people" but on the king's divine right. Contrary to the tsar and Staël's liberal preferences, Louis XVIII's charter also chooses distinctions of aristocratic blood over merit in the formation of the new government.

For historians, the tussle between the Bourbon king's view of his divine political authority and agitation for a more liberal constitutional monarchy is the stuff of French national history. However, with the Coalition ensconced in France, overseeing the postwar administration of that country and deliberating the conditions of a peace settlement, what happens there inevitably has implications for elsewhere. The peacemakers are quick to offer an opinion about France as the laboratory for a postwar Europe and on behalf of humanity, although they hardly agree on its direction. Metternich expresses his dismay directly to Louis XVIII: "Your Majesty believes he has established Monarchy; You are mistaken, it's revolution that has taken hold through your work!"[16] Talleyrand, who has endured as a statesman through various versions of revolutionary France, including Bonaparte's empire, judges Louis's charter a success because it restores the Bourbons to a throne "solidly established on the fundamental monarchical and constitutional truths which has to render it not solely unwavering, but even unattackable."[17] Nor is it only the opinions of foreign ministers that matter in occupied Paris. Principles of political liberty sit on the horizon of expectations of the engaged men and women invested in the political outcomes, whether the fate of the slave trade or constitutions, or the prospects for commerce. There are two dominant, intersecting trends in the evolution of these talks: the evolving methods of modern diplomacy, with their homage to the innovations of state bureaucracies and science; and the mingling of ancien and Enlightenment thought that elevates the relations between states, as well as the political form of states, as a subject of political debate and institution-building. In this environment too, the liberties of Europe imply the possibilities for debate and the legitimacy of public opinion.

Public Spheres

The history of postwar peacemaking begins as a social history of informal conversations, not only among a small clique of diplomats. In the crowded conference setting of Paris, large and small ideas circulate and are lobbied for and against at familiar sites of sociability, conventionally understood as "society." Even if women are not regarded as necessary during the military campaign, victory and the liberation of Paris allows them to repair to the French capital. Castlereagh now provides Lady Emily with the passport she wants so as to join him from Brussels. Once in Paris she is oblivious to her reputation as "colossal and ungainly, her manner uncivilized and unconcerned," and immediately sets to organizing nightly dinners, champagne parties, and "petits soupers" (or suppers).[18] Even though the English dominate the social cohort, the Viennese banker's wife Fanny von Arnstein has traveled from Vienna, as has Wilhelmina Sagan, who is reported to be "good looking, with a pale complexion, and simply dressed." She is visiting her family, who are residing at Talleyrand's—along with his wife, Madame Grand, "either English or Scotch by birth," brought up in India, and often counted as "mullato."[19] Talleyrand's attentions are focused on Sagan's younger sister Dorothea, the estranged wife of his nephew Edmond de Périgord. He has begun to teach Dorothea diplomacy, starting her off with a "family dinner" for Tsar Alexander. Dorothea—"dark, with magnificent eyes, highly rouged, and gayly dressed in a pink gown, and roses on her head"—does hostessing honors alongside her mother, Anna-Dorothea, who has known Talleyrand since she aided his betrayal of Bonaparte.[20]

The presence of the Courland women in social circles is not always welcome. Lady Castlereagh tells her niece Emma, "I am afraid we live in very bad company," and is brought to nearly faint at the sight of them in her home.[21] Metternich does not allow his wife to come to Paris, perhaps because he hopes to spend time with Sagan there. However, Sagan is now in a serious relationship with Aberdeen's secretary, Frederick Lamb, who has escorted her as far as Munich. Once in Paris, Sagan shops for jewelry, wine, vinegar, and china for Lamb, herself, and her children.[22] She resists Metternich's continued advances while reminding him of her "archmonarchist" views and encouraging him to work against the liberal fancies of her monarch Alexander.[23] Oblivious to his rival, Metternich is buying silks for Sagan, as well as furniture for his Vienna house.[24] He still thinks himself the pivot of the new Europe and is preoccupied with preparing a text that will herald the first step of the peace negotiations.[25]

Contemporaries give credit for the framing of the first Paris treaty to Talleyrand's successful social diplomacy at his residence at 2, Rue St. Florentin.[26] Over this same period, Castlereagh competes for influence by holding gentlemen-only dinners at his borrowed Ministry of Finance quarters, with "the conquerors and the conquered." He seats Prussian princes Henry and William and military household names such as Wellington, Schwartzenberg, and Blucher alongside diplomats and local political figures.[27] When Lady Emily has her suppers, women are invited and offered armchairs placed in regular spacings along a wall, while the men gather separately to talk. Castlereagh does not prefer "social duties" to his actual work, but his niece reports that he believes they require his involvement. Other men, "French, Austrians, Russians and English," think likewise, and on any one night might gather at Talleyrand's, Castlereagh's, and Hardenberg's, successively, for smaller dining and discussion opportunities, and with only the occasional female partner.[28]

As statesmen and diplomats shuttle between public and private spaces, there are differences between the forms of sociability in play: petits soupers and grand balls, concerts and sermons, dinners and card parties. Charles Stewart, Castlereagh's half brother and the British Commissary, takes over the grandest of French buildings, the Hotel de Montesquiou, to supplement the pomp and parades marking the return of the Bourbon monarchy with his own Grand Ball.[29] Emperor Alexander is said to shine, "(dressed for the first time in a *Red* uniform) waltzing with some of their Daughters in the adjoining room. In another corner, Prince Metternich, Lord Castlereagh and Czartoryski, with the whole corps diplomatique and politique of Europe revolving around them."[30] The polonaise is a favorite, although it is considered less a dance and more a slow promenade, led by the man holding the hand of the female and giving them time to discourse. This is a world in rehearsal for the Congress of Vienna, where waltzing will become the signature pastime.

Although French court life resumes, it cannot match the variety of diplomatic sociability, in part because the regular Paris social season is at its peak, oiling the gears of the peacemakers' political machinery. While the king and the duchesse d'Angoulême each hold "an evening Court for ladies—the King in the great apartment upstairs, and *Madame* the *rez de chaussée* of the Tuileries Palace"[31]—they compete with a multitude of social options offered by the aristocracy and an emboldened bourgeoisie. At the duchesse de Duras's salon, literature is the hot topic; at the Princess de Tremoille's, the politics of the ultra-right.[32] In the quarter around la Chaussée-d'Antin—home to bankers and early nineteenth-century French industrialists such as Delessert, Ternaux, and Laffitte—Mme. Daville, the liberal and bonapartist daughter of an Alsatian manufacturer, presides. The twenty-two-year-old red-haired James de Rothschild, who runs the Paris branch of the London-based Rothschild banking house, is "seen everywhere," at diplomatic dinners, in government offices, and at the Bourse (a new stock exchange building has been under construction since 1808), all the while making "great efforts to establish himself in society."[33] The Rothschilds have funded the theater of Louis XVIII's return so that it could be "magnificent," and in Paris, the banking firm has been given the task of cashing English subsidies "without depressing the rate of exchange."[34]

By mid-May, the salon of Germaine de Staël is again a potent site of diplomatic connection and negotiation, this time at a peacemaking conference.[35] Staël waits six weeks after the Coalition's victory before returning to Paris from London. She has been in exile for ten years, and, desperate as she is to return, at this crucial moment she is so appalled by the foreign troops occupying her beloved city that she vows not to set foot there until they all have left. When she finally buys a berth across the channel, the armies are still there, but she is compelled by the need to petition repayment of the French state's substantial debt owed her father, as well as money Benjamin Constant owes her. She urgently needs these funds for the dowry that will enable her daughter Albertine to marry Duke Victor de Broglie, a liberal French politician. Although Constant is Albertine's father, he refuses to acknowledge paternity or his debt. Instead, he is anxious that Staël's return will disrupt his writing. Constant's lack of self-awareness is conspicuous when Staël finally arrives and he charges her with being "curt even, thinking of herself, listening little to others, bent on nothing except through duty—even her daughter, and myself not at all."[36] Staël's other friends are more sympathetic; they immediately notice her physical decline. Her younger son has been killed in a duel while serving with Bernadotte, and she has become reliant on opiates to help her sleep. She is thin, "pale, her face bearing the mark of suffering, otherwise little changed, but matured and ennobled by all she had experienced."[37]

In the context of peace imperatives, Staël's political reputation precedes her. The Earl of Aberdeen, a compulsive reader of Staël's works, lets his London friends know that he proposes to see a good deal of her, "indeed, she will be very attractive compared with the stupid society of this place." Her presence, he acknowledges, "where there is so much room for criticism . . . appears to be generally feared."[38] She has made known her critical opinion of Louis XVIII's attempted revival of the doctrine of "divine right" and the effect on liberties in France of the ongoing presence of foreign troops.[39] Staël's political concerns are by now familiar: to ensure the liberties of Europe. So too are her methods: the salon, publicity, and networks.[40]

As soon as Staël lands on French soil, she reestablishes a salon at two locations: in an inexpensive apartment in her old stomping ground of the Faubourg St. Germain; *and* on the outskirts of

Paris near the Allied encampment, in a dilapidated chateau owned by her best friend, Juliette Recamier. She has forgiven Talleyrand, who has relied on Staël's sponsorship in the past, and who repaid her with betrayal.[41] The parameters of French thinking are represented by her old ally General Lafayette, the veteran of the American Revolution bearing "the optimism of 1789 with all its surviving illusions," and Staël's Coppet circle, including Constant and Sismondi, who stand for "the new constitutional school."[42] Among the regulars are Gentz and the architects of modern Prussia, both Humboldt brothers (Wilhelm and Alexander), and the Baron vom Stein. There are also the men from her English networks, the newly arrived Duke of Wellington, who is British ambassador to France and wields influence over the country's military occupation, as well as onlookers such as Staël's good friend the Scottish intellectual James Mackintosh.[43] News spreads that the tsar spends the last part of his stay in Paris in Mme. de Staël's salon in close relations with the future French Opposition.

If we are in any doubt about Staël's influence, according to the Genevan diplomat Pictet Rochemont, it is at her gatherings that the tsar promises to suppress serfdom in Russia.[44] The tsar is a fellow disappointed supporter of Bernadotte and even joins Staël's criticism of the anti-liberal practices of the returned Bourbon king. The salon, it is said, once again encourages people "to think who have never thought before, or who had forgotten how to think."[45] Even the reliably cynical American ambassador John Quincy Adams, now in Paris, remarks that it is "a kind of temple of Apollo," where one can meet the world.[46]

In the crucial last weeks of conferencing in Paris in May 1814, the evenings at Staël's salon conjure a familiar mechanics of negotiation and influence, in a new multilateral context of thinking about politics and the purpose and techniques of diplomacy—although it will be the last such celebrated salon in the context of the new model of peacemaking.[47] As in St. Petersburg, Stockholm, and London, Staël actively directs the conversation at her Paris salon to the ends of a liberal cosmopolitan-national Europe as she understands it: constitutional guarantees against abuses of political power and in defense of freedom of religion, press, and association; meritocratic rather than hereditary government; parliamentary institutions on the British model; and a thriving public sphere.[48] Desperate to have France spared retribution for Napoleon's sins, she uses the salon setting to remind the tsar of the connection between the French Enlightenment and Russia's Peter the Great; blame and punishment should be directed not at France but at Napoleon, a foreign Corsican. She finds ways of giving Genevans access to key statesmen to push their claims to territory on the French border; like other delegations representing the smaller powers and interest groups, the Genevan delegates find the salon the only means they have for penetrating the limited official circles of the new European diplomacy.

At Paris, Staël takes particular interest in the abolition of the slave trade and brings to bear not only her salon but also her pen. The formal initiative for introducing abolition to the conference agenda is Britain's—a circular dispatch from the Prince Regent directing Castlereagh to make eradication of "that inhuman traffic" and "the principle on which it exists" "an integral part" of the "public Law of Europe." In formal and informal conversation, Castlereagh is now compelled to argue that abolition offers the Coalition an opportunity to "severally jointly bind" "every nation of the European family" on a "firm and durable Basis." He wants to give France five years to abolish a "traffic repugnant to the principles of natural justice and of the enlightened age in which we live."[49] Attributing Britain's leadership on the slave trade question to its thriving public sphere, Staël is also aware that abolition does not have the same public purchase in France. The slave trade was outlawed in the early 1790s, during the French Revolution, but resumed by Napoleon. Staël decides to prime French and Coalition opinion by circulating (in English and French) a summary of the abolitionist argument.[50] Published against the background of the peace deliberations, "Call to the Sovereigns Convened in Paris to Grant the Abolition of the Slave Trade" appeals to a French audience and to the tsar's vanity. If Alexander supports abolition, she proclaims, it will cement his reputation as "an absolute sovereign [who] fought to found the wise principles of political liberty," and it will be remembered that at the Paris peace accord "the slave trade was abolished by all of Europe."[51]

For all Staël's efforts, abolition ends up among the Paris treaty's most glaring failures, although it will be taken up again at the

FIGURE 16. Georg Emanuel Opitz, *Le défilé militaire*. Watercolor, 37.1 × 47 cm. Anne S. K. Brown Military Collection, Brown University Library.

Congress of Vienna. In other issues, salon sociability, press campaigns, and petitions are more successful—particularly demands for a Norwegian constitution, Jewish rights, and compromise over the territorial demands of Geneva.[52] Effectively, the limits of liberalism reflect the limits of postwar politics. In France, new electoral laws legitimate the opinions of high society, or the privileged few. The result (and here historian Steven Kale is our guide) is that absent other forms of representation, preexisting institutions of elite sociability remain significant sites of political influence.[53] In the peacemaking setting, these same sites are the milieu of a mixed sociability, temporarily drawing in a broader public.

Unfinished Business

At 2:00 a.m. on 31 May 1814, the Treaty of Paris is signed, sealing the fate of France and acknowledging the unfinished business of peacemaking. The Duchess of Sagan witnesses the treaty's signing at Talleyrand's, where many are assembled for the great moment. She admits to Frederick Lamb, the absent British diplomat and object of her affections, that she is not particularly on top of the conditions agreed (such as Europe's new internal borders). However, she does know that there are key points that *have not* been decided. Will the Kingdom of Saxony disappear from the map of Europe? Will Poland be revived as Russian? Then there is the detail of a federal Germany and the status of abolition. (She is particularly critical of the idea of a German federation—*cette malheureux Allemagne*—since it will undermine the sovereignty of the smaller principalities of the former Holy Roman Empire.)[54] The lack of agreement leads to an *additional* article stating that the slave trade will be addressed in the future "with all the powers of Christianity."[55] Castlereagh confesses to his prime minister that he did not press abolition too much, in case it might give the French more leverage in other areas, particularly the allocation of colonial possessions.[56] Yet another *secret* article proposes the need for a second meeting, a congress that will build "a system of real and lasting equilibrium for Europe"; London is canvassed as a possible site, but Vienna is determined to be safer.[57] The treaty emphasizes "a system of real and permanent balance of power in Europe." Like the meetings between the plenipotentiaries that continue to bring diplomats together to manage the detail of their shared obligations, this conclusion mollifies both those who seek reassurance in a return to an older order and those who are newly invested in the Chaumont multilateral ethos exemplified by the "Allied Machine."

In June, the Allied Council takes a practical decision to create a more efficient method of goods transportation and to use the revenue of the Rhine navigation customs body established by Napoleon to fund the garrison occupying Paris.[58] Practical governance arrangements are supplemented with ongoing debate about the political form of this postwar Europe. Both themes seep into planning for the designated follow-up "Congress of Vienna." It is agreed that the plenipotentiaries of the seven European courts—Austria, Russia, France, Britain, Prussia, Spain, and Sweden—will meet as a committee to prepare "the affairs of Europe."[59] The Austrian government is advised that a circular should be sent by mid-August 1814 to Europe's courts alerting them of the protocols for the arrival of plenipotentiaries in Vienna.[60] Central to these preparations for more talks is the durability of the accord between the Coalition partners—a point underlined in the preamble to the Treaty of Paris. Coalition statesmen are acutely aware that the continuing close proximity of the occupying allied troops in Paris could leave their respective soldiers vulnerable should any disagreements between their governments suddenly overheat. Baron Munster from Hanover, speaking for Britain, reports his preference "to represent as strongly as possible the necessity of avoiding at present, almost at any price, a new war, which would embarrass everything, and which will be kindled less easily when all the military have returned to their homes."[61] The delicate situation reminds all the European powers that good relations, their commitment to each other and a higher ideal of cooperation, are not inevitable. The challenge implicit in the new model of diplomacy and the politics between states is precisely the maintenance of the momentum of cooperation in peacetime and avoidance of fracture and friction. One strategy they light upon is public symbolism and spectacle, elements that will feature in Vienna.

Within days of the signing of the Treaty of Paris, "the Emperor of Russia, the King of Prussia, his sons, and all the foreigners" arrive in London to celebrate the peace to much public interest.[62] The tsar is the hero of the crowds, "the deliverer of the world."[63] As if to underscore his liberal credentials, he visits Bentham in York Street, while an entourage of Cossacks on horseback waits outside.[64] If we are to believe London-based Russian *ambassadrice* Dorothea Lieven, the Austrian and British foreign ministers immediately establish "an identity of thought and feeling," agreeing on a cynical view of the tsar's motivations.[65] Perceptions of *unnegotiable* differences between Europe's polities abound in the thick of victory. Castlereagh and Metternich make good use of conventional tropes of Russians as asiatics, of terrifying Cossacks, and of the idea that the tsar is too much like a woman in his love of women.

At the end of the treaty negotiations as the center of politics moves from Paris to London, and from London to Vienna, women are vulnerable to charges of political illegitimacy as they are central to events. Privately Germaine de Staël chides the Genevan-born American secretary of treasury Albert Gallatin for not keeping her in the political loop when her interventions with the tsar on behalf of the United States have led to a separate conference in Ghent for resolving the war with Britain: "I perhaps merit some kindness for my efforts to help you. Lord Wellington claims that I never see him without lecturing to him about America."[66] She continues to censor her publicity out of concern for its effects on her daughter's marriage opportunities, beseeching her correspondents to not quote her "on anything" and to burn her letters after reading them.[67]

There is good reason for Staël's anxiety. Another Genevan acquaintance, Jean-Gabriel Eynard, records in his diaries a "grand diner diplomatique" at the outset of the follow-up congress in Vienna at Talleyrand's temporary residence in the palais Kaunitz, where "Mme de Staël was our first subject of conversation, and, as there is so much to say about her, our meeting was very animated."[68] There too the ancient but still enigmatic Prince de Ligne—whom Staël has often helped—ponders her ugliness, disdain of female company, and loss of celebrity.[69] Once, Staël could have taken comfort from the fact that her appearances at the Parisian theater inspire "cries of Viva Viva,"[70] or from Lady Melbourne's confidence to Lord Byron that British politicians regard her as having "such a *powerful* pen, that it was of great consequence to make her speak well of this country." Now, however, Lady Melbourne asserts "it is quite over with Madame de Staël," "nobody can bear her; she thinks only of courting Ministers but they will have nothing to say to her."[71]

Staël repeatedly vows off politics and consistently engages the diplomatic and political scene. Although she is forced to absent herself from the congress in Vienna for the sake of her husband's health, she maintains her network of correspondents, Alexander, Wellington, and Jefferson, among others. She develops vital lines of information from bases in Paris, Geneva, and the Italian peninsula. Staël remains the touchstone for a liberal political agenda, arguing for representative liberal constitutions and institutions as the future of Europe, along the imperfect lines of both American and English models. In the social context of congressing, news circulates through the last half of 1814, and into 1815, of Staël's ongoing "efforts to engender constitutional heat" and her controversial reputation as "the high-priestess of liberty and peace."[72] French spies denounce her salon in occupied Paris as a "center of opinion," of criticisms of the weakness of the French charter and political institutions, as well as of government attacks on religious and press freedom.[73] When Staël retreats to Geneva, she continues her petitioning, including meeting regularly with the local governor, who reports to Talleyrand at Vienna: "She is a real slut." Talleyrand writes to Staël advising her to cease her activities.[74]

Responding to news of the negotiations in train after Paris, Staël denounces "all those political reasonings on the balance of Europe, those old systems which serve as a pretext to new usurpations."[75] "Humankind," she writes to Bernadotte (now back in Sweden), "is very far from liberty at this moment. The miscarried revolution in France has caused those enlightened spirits everywhere to step back."[76] Staël's forgotten impact on the invention of international order at the end of the Napoleonic wars unpacks the paradoxes of this early nineteenth-century moment. She occupies a world that is simultaneously ancien, where ambiguous social spaces such as a congress might give more room to exceptional women, equipped by title or money to participate in political culture, and where a Concert of Europe begins to celebrate its innovations as the modern bureaucratized method of conferencing, with no women in sight.

CHAPTER EIGHT

Science

Qu'est-ce donc que le Congrès de Vienne?

—"BARON HUMBOLDT'S PROJECT FOR THE REGULATION OF THE CONGRESS," SEPTEMBER 1814

Till now however I have never heard of these high-flying sentiments among official people or Diplomates, and—I suppose it is one of the happy results of the Congress of Vienna. But I suppose these are not the news you want.

—LETTER TO FREDERICK LAMB, 28 FEBRUARY 1816

WHAT WAS THE Congress of Vienna? An organizational afterthought, it became the iconic symbol of international order—the version that emphasized the aristocratic conservative, cosmopolitan roots of postwar Europe. In September 1814, as the corteges of rulers (we need to remember some were women) and statesmen began to arrive in the Austrian capital, even participants still pondering what they might expect were convinced of the moment's historical significance. The congress, Castlereagh assured Talleyrand, was "a solemn date in the diplomatic history of Europe." Its form and manner of proceeding were to remain an example for the future, a "monument" to the existence of a European legal *public code.*[1] One observer, likely Dorothea Lieven, wrote that "one of the happy results" of the Congress of Vienna was that "among official people or Diplomates," "high-flying sentiments" had become the common expression.[2] The Prussian ambassador Wilhelm von Humboldt,

FIGURE 17. Franz Wolf (after Johann Nepomuk Hoechle), reception of the Allied monarchs in Vienna on the occasion of the Congress of Vienna, 1814. Lithograph, 1834. Austrian National Library © Alamy.

whose public profile already exceeded his official position, offered an extended memorandum on how it all should work. Europe, his document declared, had been indelibly altered by the French Revolution and by Napoleon's adventurism. Now, the plenipotentiaries of all Europe's princes and states were gathering in the spirit of the "general interest," and his own ambition was for nothing less than ensuring the continent's peace and happiness.[3]

In devising the Vienna congress, diplomats and their respective ministries devoted as much reflection to the detail of the ideas and practices that would be pursued. Some of these were easily adopted from the experience of Châtillon and agreement at Chaumont, or the stipulations of the 1814 Paris treaty. Lower-level British, Russian, Prussian, and Austrian staff had met in Paris and London through the European summer and into the autumn to tackle how best to arrange "Europe."[4] As they laid out, the Austrian Chancellery took responsibility for publishing a notice in the Vienna court gazette announcing the preparations underway to the interested public. An office at the Chancellery was given the task of allocating meeting spaces and guards and authenticating the credentials of persons claiming to represent a sovereign or state. It decided that embassy status would be given to the meeting spaces, placing them beyond the legal reach of the Habsburg government. Similarly, in theory at least, Habsburg police were required to be under the direction of the congress rather than subject to Austrian supervision, attentive to the interests of the whole.

When it came to *who* should have the power to speak or decide questions and *how* the congress should be organized to make it functional and effective, the unevenness of representation and authority impacted the Europeans and non-Europeans alike. Looking out from their new vantage point, individual monarchs, foreign ministers, and diplomats insisted that their decisions about how to do diplomacy and what it was for would apply to powers not given a formal voice at the congress. This list included the papacy, the United Provinces of the Pays Bas, the Swiss Confederation, and America, a country still at war with Britain.[5] The Ottoman Empire's place in these discussions was not as Europe's sixth power, as Metternich had presumed, but rather "the rank of a fourth class," equivalent to the smaller European sovereignties.[6] An offended Sultan Mahmud II (r. 1808–1839) sent his familiar "dragoman" proxy, Ioannis (Yanko) Mavrogheni, anyway. Some of the powers responded unilaterally to the sensitive situation with personal placations of this important trading partner—not least because the (substantial) commercial rights held by European traders operating in the Ottoman-ruled Black Sea were at risk. Castlereagh let the Porte know that he was talking to the Russians (through Nesselrode) about commercial navigation in the Black Sea and would be happy to ensure that the principle of free navigation being discussed at the congress would not be extended there. Reportedly, the tsar directed similar assurances to Mavrogheni's wife: "he was as disposed to guarantee the conservation of the Ottoman empire along with the other powers—even given the treatment of Serbia in Ottoman territory."[7] Castlereagh gave Mavrogheni his own assurance more directly: "the interests and 'intact conservation' of the Ottoman Empire were necessary to the 'established system' and general order." He explained that Britain, like Austria and France, would use the congress to confirm the integrity of the Sublime Porte and thus ensure the security and peace of Europe.[8] However, what the Ottomans wanted, a guarantee of their sovereignty in writing, they could not have.

A country's status in the overarching negotiation structure depended on its contribution to the war and the size of the territory. This meant many European queens and princes were not always able to obtain an audience if the four major victor powers—Britain, Russia, Prussia, and Austria—thought their territory or efforts insignificant. By contrast, France, the defeated power, was part of a "Committee of the Five Powers" at the heart of decision making. Occasionally, this committee shared power with Spain, Portugal, and the relatively invisible Sweden (represented by Count Carl Löwenhielm) as the "Committee of Eight" or the "Assembly of Eight Courts." Sweden noticed that despite its critical role in the campaign against Bonaparte, the arrangements gave France more of a voice. Further, the imbalance in the committee arrangements made it easier for the Five (often reduced to Four), who held forty-one meetings, to overwhelm the Eight, who met only nine times. From Castlereagh's perspective, the objective of this structure was a "coincidence of sentiment" between the French and the allies, "balancing" Russia's influence. Indeed, at his most blasé, the British foreign secretary admitted he would have preferred to present the other plenipotentiaries with a fait accompli. "The advantage of this latter mode of proceeding," he ruminated, "is that you treat the plenipotentiaries as a body with real and becoming respect. You keep the power by concert and management in your own hands, but without openly assuming authority to their exclusion."[9]

For all the circulating "high-flying sentiments" about the value of congressing, Castlereagh preferred a strategy of exclusion by stealth. The fact of "concert" could be used in practice to give each empire the power to pursue their unilateral interests. The trend was set at the informal opening attended only by the representatives of four "Puissances" (or powers): Castlereagh, Metternich, Nesselrode, and Prince Hardenberg assisted by Humboldt for Prussia. During the first week of the congress, these men held four conferences around desks and dinner tables in order to decide who would have the power to sit and deliberate and who could petition and negotiate. In a precedent followed through the modern era of scientific peacemaking, they gave carriage of business to themselves as the most powerful among the victors, claiming to represent the unified voice of Europe. The developments at Vienna added new structures and performative aspects to diplomacy and added to the structural governance shifts in the politics between states underway, not least enacting their measures on behalf of "humanity."[10] The focus in this chapter is on their bureaucratic methods and their agenda, since these became the stock characteristics of modern peacemaking into the twentieth century, with their mutually reinforcing attention to scientificity and universality.

Commissions

Among the novel decisions taken by the Committee of Four was the appointment of a suite of commissions to deal with the work agenda set for the congress by the Paris treaty, on the model of the smaller-scale commissions used in the Paris case. It can be no coincidence that the turn to commissions reflected the incorporation of modernizing bureaucratic templates being employed by imperial and national governments in their own ministries. Of course, in the context of the Vienna congress, the scope of these commissions and their operations were transnational, deployed to decide still unresolved territorial questions: the future of a German federation, as well as the fate of the Kingdom of Sardinia and republics of Genoa and Switzerland, Poland, Tuscany, and the Duchy of Bouillon.[11] Separate commissions debated the "Abolition of the Slave Trade" and the "Free Navigation of Rivers"; others tackled "Statistics," "Drafting of Agreements," and "Diplomatic Precedence."

In this transnational milieu, the peacemaking commissions reinforced the trust between diplomats crucial to the maintenance of peace between states by adopting the practices developed in their wartime negotiations: providing protocols of record to each of the participants across the various commissions; giving detailed instructions to chairs on how to effectively introduce their agenda so as to encourage consensus; apprising panels of the available background reading, such as memoranda, and providing those relevant materials.[12] The role of the designated commission on "Diplomatic Precedence" went further in the cause of preventing "the kinds of embarrassment" to the various Crowns and their courts that might exacerbate tensions.[13] After four meetings presided over by Humboldt and Lord William Cathcart (British ambassador to the Russian court, and military commander), the commission arrived at a new three-tiered classification system for diplomatic hierarchy: ambassadors, legates, or nonces; envoyés accredited by sovereigns; chargés d'affaires accredited by the relevant foreign ministry. Their rationalization of the order of precedence gave representative status to only the first classification—ambassadors, legates, or nonces—a practice that spread, and endured.[14]

There had never been anything like the Commission on Statistics. In the twentieth century, statistics were grist to the mill of scientific approaches to peacemaking. For diplomat-cum-historian Harold Nicolson, looking back from the end of World War I, the Congress of Vienna's statistics commission was "one of the most efficient and useful of all the bodies."[15] In 1919, statistics were deemed to offer an impartial method for resolving emotionally overheated conflicts over territory. In 1814, according to other historical comparisons, the resort to statistics "did not imply any passion for a scientific and disinterested peace settlement"; rather, "opinions and prejudice must have dominated."[16]

Certainly, statistics only began to insinuate a numerical science from around the 1820s. Prior to this, the commonly used German term *statistiks* indicated a written, synthetic account of a state rather than the political arithmetic that became a distinct governmental practice. Even so, by the early decades of the nineteenth century, the political and economic power vested in knowledge of population numbers as the basis for calculating potential tax bases or estimating military conscripts was already well understood by sovereigns, particularly in Sweden, France, Britain, and Prussia.

At the Congress of Vienna the commission's task was to provide statistical information on the population of territories liberated from French occupation, where a sovereign had not ceded power to France, and thus the territory could not be classified as "conquered." The statistics commission had no say in the fate of French agglomerations such as the Kingdom of Illyria, or the Grand Duchy of Frankfurt, or in the (Tuscan) city-state of Piombino that had been taken from the Queen of Etruria and given to Bonaparte's sister Elisa. Instead, its focus was on the Kingdom of Poland, wrought asunder by European powers in the late eighteenth century and pieced back together by Napoleon as a confederation. Poland was only belatedly added to the Congress of Vienna agenda on the insistence of the tsar, who was influenced by his former foreign minister, Prince Czartoryski. Following Czartoryski, the tsar argued that the Kingdom of Poland had to be returned to the Polish as "the most secure means of calming the anxiety with which they are reproached, and of reconciling interests."[17] But how was the extent of a new Poland's territory to be determined, given that the former kingdom had for two decades been divided between Russia, Austria, and Prussia?

The statistics commission was Metternich's initiative, but the practical job of digging out the necessary statistical information was given to the Prussian privy councillor and statistician Baron Hoffmann.[18] From Hoffmann's appointment to the controversies that surrounded his methods and conclusions (Should numbers rather than human desires decide borders? How *reliable* are statistics?), the Commission on Statistics is one more point of connection between the history of state administration and the prospect of international governance. The common use of the nickname Seelen-Hoffmann, "Souls-Hoffmann," hints at the combination of resignation and disquiet that met this man's methods of counting populations as *âmes* or *seelen*. French foreign minister Talleyrand protested that Hoffmann's obsession with numbers "made an inhabitant of Poland and a resident of the rich territories of Saxony and Rhine as of equal worth." Metternich grumbled that the committee might do "something more than a mere evaluation of numbers." His own suggestion that they make room for "the riches of the respective provinces and the quality of their inhabitants" tallied with the brief he had given the commission: to assess the "relative value of the territories conquered from Napoleon and his allies, from the aspect of population, as regards not only number but also kind and quality."[19]

These tensions shaped and interrupted the commission's work from its first meeting on Christmas Eve, 1814.[20] The major difficulty Hoffmann faced was the unreliability of numbers in a territory that had shifted its borders under successive governments. During their various periods of rule, Russian, Austrian, Prussian, and French governments had each imposed their own forms of counting and recording population numbers, as well as distinctive municipal boundaries. Out-of-date and unreliable local government sources and publications added to the challenge of tracking consistent records of population numbers. Consequently, Hoffmann decided the only way to manage these obstacles was to *smooth out* imprecise and uncertain published government figures. In the case of the Duchy of Warsaw, he began with an 1813 French Interior Ministry Directory, which took its numbers from an 1812 source that counted 3,800,362 souls. He added this figure to a more up-to-date survey that estimated 4,334,656 souls over a larger area. He then added the disparate totals and divided them by two, took the average, and applied its quotient. That quotient became the basis for counting the populations of the duchy's neighboring spaces, regardless of whether they were once part of Austria or Prussia.

Disagreement over Hoffmann's method and his results was perhaps inevitable when the numbers ended up benefiting one or another government's claims to territory. Regardless, the commission eventually accepted Hoffmann's figures for lack of alternatives and agreed to the contours of an independent Duchy of Warsaw situated at the core of a new Polish Kingdom. On these statistical grounds, only a few districts were returned to Austria and Prussia.[21] The territorial commission used the findings to decide other political details of the new Kingdom of Poland: its official language would be Polish, and public office was to be a prerogative for Poles, even as the kingdom was "irrevocably tied to the Russian empire." This new Poland was under the oversight of the tsar, who put Czartoryski in charge of introducing reforms, and a new constitution, but gave control of a Polish army and its military budget to his belligerent brother Grand-Duke Constantine.[22] The process awarded the franchise to 100,000 new Polish subjects on the basis of a tax census and literary and artistic merit. However, despite the Polish prince's insistence, neither peasant reforms nor Jewish rights were entertained. By the end of 1815, with Czartoryski's influence over Polish affairs almost nonexistent, the Polish kingdom was restored only "in principle." In practice, it was most fully defined as an economic entity that offered Europe's empires free navigation on "all Polish rivers within frontiers of 1772" and free circulation of goods within the same area.[23]

The foundation of the new Polish kingdom on the principles of free trade and the free navigation of rivers mirrored the work of another peacemaking commission. The Commission on the Free Navigation of Rivers traveled down the ideological tributary of international thinking that equated free trade with peace. In the wording of the 1814 Treaty of Paris, free navigation was to assist "communications between nations" to "render them less strangers to each other," "in the mode the most impartial, and the most favorable to the commerce of all nations." The language was Wilhelm von Humboldt's, a particularly enthusiastic proponent of the idea that the free navigation scheme should be applied to all navigable European rivers that bordered, separated, or traversed different states. He had in mind not only the Rhine—where the free navigation principle had already been put into practice by Bonaparte—but also the Danube and the Escaut/Scheldt, a 350-kilometer-long river that cut through northern France and the southwestern part of the Netherlands.[24]

In Vienna, the Commission on the Free Navigation of Rivers was once again a forum of a few men. There were precedents for its underlying principle in natural law theory and in Pitt's earlier plan for Europe.[25] There were working examples too, such as in the Austrian Netherlands, where the 1792 French "Scheldt decree" had established freedom of river navigation as a "natural right"; there was also the template set by Bonaparte, the 1804 Rhine Octroi Convention agreed between the French empire and the Holy Roman Empire. This had freed up commercial navigation on the Rhine river, stretching over more than a thousand kilometers from the Swiss alps to its outlet into the North Sea.[26] By reducing state tolls and abolishing shipping monopolies, navigation was made free where the river was navigable to the sea. The governance of compliance and management was as much a part of this innovation: a central commission oversaw communication between the riparian, or riverside, states, and a court of appeal was available to manage disputes and costs. A decade later, the retreat of French forces had placed this arrangement in jeopardy. Returning local sovereigns preferred to reclaim the right to exact tolls from passing ships and boats.[27] Humboldt saw the commission's work as an opportunity to reinvent institutions and structures that could circumvent the piecemeal division of the river's sovereignty and improve on the French experiment. The aim, he explained, should be to identify principles and practices that are "so general" that the free movement of commerce cannot in the future "be affected by local diverse circumstances, or by war."[28]

Over seven well-documented meetings held in February 1815, the commission traversed "free navigation" as a manifestation of the liberty of mobility and the antithesis of the medieval right of smaller sovereigns to impose taxes on itinerant *commerçants*. How could river bureaucracy and taxes be reduced? They suggested using general classifications for taxable objects so that detailed inspections did not slow commercial traffic. Humboldt conceived of a general levy to fund a central administration that could hire inspectors or diplomatic agents, negotiate complaints, and act in concert to reinforce the principles of free navigation, and possibly even a common river policing force.[29] On one plan, a voice and a vote on any Rhine administration would be proportional to river-bank sovereignty: Prussia would have a third of the vote, France one-sixth, Holland one-sixth, and the other "riparian" sovereigns one-third.

For Humboldt, the conceptual significance of "free navigation" was of equal importance. The Rhine was a communal resource and deserved to be overseen by a central administration that represented no single power but "un ensemble."[30] Not everyone agreed. Among the sovereigns of the smaller riparian polities Bavaria, Baden, Hesse Darmstadt, and Nassau, there was a clear preference for a co-administration that maintained their respective sovereignty, rather than co-ownership or administration "for the benefit of world commerce."[31] Backed by the French representative, the duc d'Alberg, and supported by the British, the conservative view won out; individual riparian states assumed responsibility for the maintenance of tow-paths and tolls. The commission's decision maintained the principle of diplomatic conferencing in its version of an intergovernmental river body, but it fell back on older models of communication between riparian states: no detached general administrative body, only a central committee comprising the representatives of the riparian sovereignties; decisions taken by majority vote; and, crucially, no decision binding on any state. Contrary to Humboldt's vision, there was no international court for Rhine navigation, the river administration's authority and tasks of the commission were decreased, and there was no basis for enforcing compliance. In the end the commission confirmed the principle of free commerce but only thinly upheld the "natural right" of navigation.

Slavery

The commission discussing "free navigation of rivers" contemplated opening up the flow of commerce to the alleged benefit of humanity. The commission dealing with abolition of the slave trade concentrated on ending the commerce in humans. Even though contemporaries identified the abolition cause with the British political system, its moral underpinnings incorporated a universalist basis for the new culture of an international politics. In 1807, under pressure of public opinion, the British government had outlawed its slave trade and stemmed the buying, selling, and transporting of slaves between its colonies in Africa, the West Indies, and America. As we have seen, in 1814, it was the British government that insisted on abolition as a point of negotiation at Paris, where failure to reach agreement had passed the problem on to the Vienna congress, and to the same man who had admitted his hesitation on this same principle.

As chair, Castlereagh ran the abolition commission according to the new practices of conferencing. He oversaw the translation of all relevant documents into French and then their distribution among the commission delegates. Among these documents were British parliamentary papers, abrogated texts of the abolition movement, reports on the effects of abolition of the trade on the livelihoods of planters who employed slaves, and survival of the colonies themselves. Castlereagh reported in October to his prime minister that before the congress discussions he also tried nonprocedural methods to get Talleyrand to agree to abolition of the slave trade in France. He assured Liverpool of his efforts to "prepare the minds" of the plenipotentiaries.[32]

The abolition commission eventually had its first meeting four months into the congress, relatively late, on 20 January 1815.[33] For the benefit of his fellow commissioners, Castlereagh described the slave trade as "a commerce incompatible with the Christian religious principles of universal morality and of humanity." He reasoned that "after the calamities of a war unparalleled for the Extent to which it was waged, and for the changes it has introduced in the different branches of the European Confederacy," the abolition of the slave trade would contribute to Europe's "repose" and "tranquility," placing it on a "firm and durable Basis."[34] His language evoked the self-consciously humanitarian inflection of the popular English abolitionist campaign, now directed at making ending the slave trade a universal imperative of peace. To counter suspicions that England was only concerned to make sure no one else profited from a trade it had already outlawed, he reassured his committee that abolition concerned "the natural principles of justice and of the Enlightenment," which shaped "the times in which we live." Even the recalcitrant (and well-informed) Talleyrand picked up the rhetorical cue, adding that "a similar declaration would be well received by the sane and *enlightened* public of all countries, and that it would bring honor to the Congress."[35] By the last meeting on 8 February, Metternich briefly put aside his opinion that the "British public" were determining laws for other nations, affirming that even for countries without slave-based colonies, such as Austria, there was nothing foreign "in regard to the importance of the good of humanity."[36]

Once the commission began its discussions, it became difficult to move beyond agreement that abolition of the slave trade constituted a natural and *enlightened* justice for the good of humanity. Castlereagh's proposal for the deployment of a maritime police north of the equator—where the geopolitical border of the abolition plan was drawn—was met with vehement resistance from Talleyrand as well as the Duke of Palmella and Marquis of Labrador, respectively, Portugal's and Spain's ambassadors. They loudly opposed the resort to sanctions against states that refused to end the slave trade. Talleyrand, Palmella, and Labrador each agreed to vote with the general sentiment in favor of abolition, on the condition that a clause would reserve to their governments "the freedom to determine the period when the abolition of the slave trade could pass into law in states without hurting the interests that required a great deal of management."[37]

Early in their second meeting, Castlereagh was happy enough to agree to this conditional clause as a pragmatic compromise, as a way of melding "the wish of humanity" with "the interests and rights of independent powers." The result was the "Declaration of the Powers, on the Abolition of the Slave Trade." It emphasized the civilized "sentiments" of the European powers but offered no details of when the slave trade would end. Further progress on abolition was deferred to a series of annual post-peace "ministerial conferences and permanent communications consecrated to this objective," to be held in London and Paris. The task of these meetings would be to report on the commerce in African "Negroes" and to capture any progress in the reduction or abolition of that trade.

Ultimately, the Vienna slave trade commission was not able to find agreement on its core issue. However, its discussions reinforced the broader principle of the need for contiguity between the rights of states and interests of humanity, as the normative responsibility of politics between states. In 1815, only Portugal claimed that the congress had no remit over the laws of states or moral questions. More generally, the participants in the Congress of Vienna could not have predicted the legacies of their words or actions; however, in 1815, they invoked a community of "civilized countries" on the premise of international-scale "sentiments." Historians agree that the commissions on diplomatic precedence, the principle of free navigation, and abolition of the slave trade constituted "the first multilateral codifications of international law."[38] In the early years of congressing, the abolition debate also led to bilateral anti–slave trade treaties, including between Britain and the Netherlands and the United States, and to the establishment by Britain and Spain of so-called mixed commissions to oversee compliance with new anti–slave trade conditions. By some accounts these commissions eventually liberated 85,000 slaves.[39] Paradoxically, hindsight also tells us that the "civilizing mission" norms established in the 1815 declaration on abolition became the core of justifications for imperialism through the nineteenth century. Seventy years later, the 1885 General Act of the Berlin Conference, attended by twelve European empires, the Ottoman Empire, and the United States, claimed abolition a principle of the law of nations and granted Europe's empires "the right to 'employ all means and their power' to quell the slave trade in the Congo area." Abolition became the curtain behind which European empires rationalized colonial oversight, "expressly making colonisation into an instrument of abolition, to the extent of masking genocide in the Congo."[40]

ACT, No. XV.—Declaration of the Powers, on the Abolition of the Slave Trade, of the 8th February 1815, Vienna

Having taken into consideration that the commerce, known by the name of "the Slave Trade," has been considered, by just and enlightened men of all ages, as repugnant to the principles of humanity and universal morality; that the particular circumstances from which this commerce has originated, and the difficulty of abruptly arresting its progress, may have concealed, to a certain extent, what was odious in its continuance, but that at length the public voice, in all civilized countries, calls aloud for its prompt suppression; that since the character and the details of this traffic have been better known, and the evils of every kind which attend it, completely developed, several European governments have virtually come to the resolution of putting a stop to it, and that successively all the Powers possessing colonies in different parts of the world have acknowledged, either by legislative Acts, or by Treaties, or other formal engagements, the duty and necessity of abolishing it;

In communicating this Declaration to the knowledge of Europe, and of all civilized countries, the said Plenipotentiaries hope to prevail on every other government, and particularly on those which, in abolishing the Slave Trade, have already manifested the same sentiments, to give them their support in a cause, the final triumph of which will be one of the noblest monuments of the age which embraced it, and which shall have brought it to a glorious termination.

For all the confidence the Congress of Vienna inspired, through the months of its proceedings the question "What was the congress?" did not go away. Amid the (now) modern-sounding commissions on the slave trade and on international waterways sat the commission concerned with the various claims to the Duchy of Bouillon, disputed between Bavaria and Baden on the grounds of shifting dynastic laws. The Grand-Duke of Baden, who was married to the tsar's sister, ruled Bouillon but had no male heirs, only three daughters who had married into the Beauharnais family. Absent other heirs, the duke declared the children of his late grandfather eligible to inherit Bouillon, even though they were born of a union between a prince and a commoner. Ultimately the Bouillon question too boiled down to a contest between old and new visions of governance, whether sovereignty should be determined by gendered laws of inheritance and dynasty or on behalf of the "nation" or people.[41]

Other older diplomatic practices also continued. Dynastic marriages, like bilateral arrangements between the European empires, were hardly abandoned in the middle of this changing, modernizing political landscape of methods and objectives. In the spring of 1814, the tsar had sent his sister Catherine to London on a mission to rupture the anticipated engagement of the English princess Charlotte—only child of George Prince of Wales and thus in line for the British throne—and William of Orange, the new sovereign of the expanded territories of Holland. The match was among Castlereagh's diplomatic priorities, as a means of consummating a British alliance with the Netherlands.[42] The tsar sought the same alliance and thought his other sister Anne would be a better match—indeed, his informal intervention led to the eventual union of Anne and William. The sovereigns and representatives of the European powers, floating between the past and present, hedging their bets on the future, pursued an amalgam of old and new methods side by side. Castlereagh and Humboldt might separately acknowledge that the Vienna congress was not a European *ensemble*, because it lacked any European political structure, but they also celebrated the congress as gathering "all Europe," allowing each representative the liberty to speak his mind and put his contrary opinion. For anyone paying attention, even as diplomacy and "High Politics" were what a specific group of European men laid claim to, the politics of "high-flying sentiments" was also something that women of more and less experience and influence engaged. In the circumstances, it was difficult to discern whether the Congress of Vienna stood for an old world or represented the rumblings of the new, and where progress lay.

CHAPTER NINE

Society

Here everything is spectacle, it is literally the theatre of the world.

—"N" TO MADAME DE STAËL FROM VIENNA, 27 NOVEMBER 1814

A tale so formless that it could not be told.

—GOETHE ON THE CONGRESS OF VIENNA

HISTORIANS HAVE OFTEN ANSWERED the question "What was the Congress of Vienna?" by turning to the titillating details of a dancing congress. One way of interpreting versions of the international past that flirt with its distractions—whether its waltzes or seductions—is that they capture the historical confusion surrounding the transformations in politics and diplomacy. The conviction that international history—as the domain of diplomacy and politics—is an exclusively masculine realm has given histories of the era after the Napoleonic wars a curious split personality. The memoirs of the relevant statesmen reinforce this trend, by insisting that the Congress of Vienna was indeed a *conference* of *men* who agreed in gentlemanly fashion on their principles of accord and that it was *not* a *congress* sounding with the swish of skirts, or involving women at all. The gender implications are evident too in visual records. The history of peacemaking as the promise of reasoned discussion among diplomats, sovereigns, and statesmen is a scenario best captured in Jean-Baptiste Isabey's official portrait of the Vienna congress. The scene gathers all the official male

FIGURE 18. Bernhard J. Dondorf, after Jean-Baptiste Isabey, *Delegates to the Congress of Vienna, 1814–1815*. Lithograph, 1833–1872, 34.5×41.1 cm. Rijksmuseum.

protagonists in the one room—even though, in fact, there was no such comprehensive gathering of all these men.

Then there is the dancing congress version, replete with salacious stories of romance, affairs, suicides, and the irrational emotions of some (usually) non-British men who succumb to women's wiles. This version penetrates the multiple memoirs and popular representations of peacemaking and paints a picture of ancien female-led intrigue, dragging down with it the modern-minded congressing statesmen. The dancing congress conjures the end of the Napoleonic wars as the restoration of pre-revolutionary political values, aristocratic indulgence, and dissipation.

When we look closer, drawing the private and public together, laying the archives of ministries over the correspondence and memoirs of contemporaries driven by their "scriptomania," a muddier picture emerges, blurring the lines between masculine methods of diplomacy and the feminine work of sociability. For those not given a formal role or allowed a voice in this new Europe—whether any of the smaller European powers, the marginalized Genevans or Ottoman Empire, women, or colonized subjects—other, older, methods of diplomacy remain available. Monarchs are petitioned, and, in salons,

FIGURE 19. Johann Nepomuk Hoechle, *Redoute paré during the Congress of Vienna on October 9, 1814*, c. 1815. Austrian National Library, Vienna © Alamy.

the voices and ambitions of statesmen mingle with those of female rulers, aristocrats, and the bourgeoisie of both sexes, Catholics with Protestants and Jews. This is how the chief of the Supreme Police and Censorship Court Office Baron Francois Hager understands congress politics, directing his agents to surveil "the high spheres, old and new, of society and diplomacy, in the actions and conversation of sovereigns, and their entourages, and their ministers."[1]

As in Paris in the spring of 1814, the weight given to "society" as a political domain helps us take the measure of peacemaking participation. Official logistics count five sovereigns, eleven princes, ninety plenipotentiary envoys, the retinues of the lesser powers, the "uninvited representatives," wives, clerks, secretaries, and servants, and arrive at six hundred as an approximate number. Then there are the foreign and local men and women with commerce on their minds, prostitutes, pimps, spies, and the simply curious who contribute to the ballooning of Vienna's population.[2] There is some overlap between those categories and all manner of lobbyists who flock to the presence of royalty and leading statesmen—from booksellers in search of copyright laws to the defenders of Jewish rights. The congress appears to one Swedish delegate "as a court of law before which all kinds of pretensions and claims, however superannuated, may be brought."[3]

The curious combination of the old and the new is on full display in the presence of British admiral Sir William Sidney Smith, a standard-bearer of ancien diplomacy—who is there as *Sweden's* "chargé d'affaires." Smith writes and distributes a pamphlet on the need to end piracy and organizes two philanthropic fundraising events.[4] On the eve of the congress's opening, in late October 1814, the fifty-year-old white-haired admiral, his short, stout, slightly deformed physique weighed down by military badges and chains, hosts a party to support "negro slaves," followed by a picnic on behalf of Christian slaves in Tunis.[5] The money is intended to set up hospitals and provide subsistence for captives, and possibly even a multilateral fleet that Smith will command to battle Barbary pirates. The aristocratic women who attend complain that by asking them for donations Smith has compromised the honor of the attending sovereigns.

Women representing all social classes are at the congress; they are not only dance partners but also philanthropists and femmes fatales. Returned to the bosom of her Austrian family, Napoleon's second wife, Archduchess Marie-Louise, is defending the claims of her son Charles Frances Napoleon to the French throne. She argues that her son is, at the least, entitled to the duchies of Parma, Placentia, and Guastalla, since a treaty agreed with Bonaparte before Castlereagh's arrival in Paris gave them to *her*.[6] The Spanish Bourbon former queen of the same region, Maria Luisa, also known as Maria Luigia, asserts her personal rights over this same Tuscan territory, once known as Etruria. Maria Luisa's petition is presented by the Genevan Jean-Gabriel Eynard, her banker and estate manager. She also decides to circulate an autobiographical pamphlet at the congress that relates how in 1808 the Spanish court ceded "Etruria" to France and shut her away in a monastery with her daughter. In the document, Maria Luisa declares her interest in governing "to advance the happiness of my subjects." She does her cause few favors by complaining of the hardship of having to eat off porcelain rather than gold and silver.[7] In the end, she is not successful, and the territory is divided between the two Habsburg contenders, Archduchess Marie-Louise and Archduke Ferdinand. Bourbon Maria Luisa's failed claim becomes one of the reasons given by Spain for refusing to sign the final Vienna treaty.

Women, aristocratic and bourgeois, monarchical and republican, are at the balls and soirées organized by Metternich, Castlereagh, and Baron Gagern, who represents both the German duchy of Nassau and King Willem of the Netherlands. They assist at the less conspicuous gatherings at the homes of the aspiring bourgeoisie, including the temporary homes of Hanseatic town delegates; they orchestrate their own events. Familiar *salonnières*, as diverse as Sagan and the Austrian novelist Karoline Pichler, resume conventional political-cum-diplomatic roles, although both women downplay their independence and public persona.[8] The neighboring apartments of Sagan and Princess Bagration, down the road from Metternich's Chancellery office, are filled with persons in search of connections and information.[9] Bagration's role is consistent with her status in earlier periods of Austrian political history—as "one of those diplomatic sybils whose mission was to gain friends abroad for Russia's political aims."[10] Her salon is well-known for influencing the "young and old" who "gathered around [her] skirts," and some of whom took up her anti-Napoleon message. In the past it gathered Austria's Count Stadion, Prince Lobkowitz, Prince de Ligne, and a "second class" of local Jewish bankers.[11] At the congress, Bagration's main visitors are the tsar and the Russian diplomatic corps—Nesselrode, Stackelberg, and Kapodistrias. She considers herself a loyal Russian but criticizes Alexander's "Jacobin" fascination with constitutions, even though she depends on his financial generosity.

Bagration's salon is monitored by the spies of governments with similar concerns. They watch the tsar's comings and goings in order to determine her influence on his foreign policy thinking. Austrian spies suspect Sagan because of her connections to the tsar and Talleyrand, both of whom circulate in her modest rooms at the Palm Palais. By documenting intercepted letters, Austrian and French police reports have left us a vital record of absent women, and the intensity of long-distance politics, whether in support of Jewish rights and anti-Semitism, national questions, and patriotism, or the maintenance of an ancien status quo. In the hybrid sociability of the congress and its capacity for politics, "soft" diplomacy is Janus-faced, the provenance of the old and the new, and women its practitioners.

National Questions

At the Congress of Vienna, "national" questions are future-oriented, yet they are advocated in accordance with the plan agreed by the European imperial powers in the 1814 Treaty of Paris to establish a commission on German federation, at a time when there is no Germany. The creation of a German polity of some form out of the vestiges of Bonaparte's Confederation of the Rhine is primarily a strategic security measure intended as a bulwark against French expansionism eastward. Regardless, the prospect cannot avoid generating cultural and political debate. It draws in the competing interests of Prussia and Austria, and the thorny political issue of the fate of Saxony, whose king sided with Napoleon until the last minute and is now being threatened with loss of his territory.[12] Prussia wants this territory as compensation for its war efforts and in exchange for giving up its Polish provinces to Russia. For Prussian patriots too, Saxony represents a depleted aristocratic order. In Paris, Baron vom Stein has argued for supporting German federation in the interests of inventing a Europe comprised of organic national units, "as a community that should be so formed, to oppose the threat of France."[13] From all these perspectives, as Meinecke puts it, "state and nation appear to be things that a man can create or search out to suit his ideas and needs."[14]

In the circumstances of creation, the form of this federated Germany raises even more questions: Should it be an independent state, a union, or an association? As a confederation will it give rights of sovereignty to each of its constituent parts or, at the level of individuals, to all its populations, Christian and Jew alike? What are the rights of approximately 12 million subjects in the 380 vulnerable polities in the middle of Europe that will comprise the heart of this new entity? Once upon a time, these mini-sovereigns of the Holy Roman Empire exercised "the highest executive, legislative and judicial authority within their domains," ceding only the right of war or alliance to their emperor, the Habsburg monarch.[15] In 1806, when Bonaparte imposed a confederation in this same territory, many were absorbed by larger states, reducing them to a "mediatized" status without their former privileges and independence, not even the right to levy taxes. Frederick Augustus I's Electorate of Saxony was among the exceptions; it became a kingdom with expanded territory.

The Grand-Duke of Baden (whose own territory is at stake) is made a member of the territorial commission dealing with Germany, with reference to "the principles of International Law."[16] Other central European sovereigns—princesses, duchesses, and countesses with territory up for grabs—who want a voice have to find other platforms. The grand-duchess of Saxe-Weimar Maria Pavlovna writes her brother Tsar Alexander on behalf of the duchy into which she has married.[17] The princess dowager von Fürstenberg—a Thurn und Taxis who married into the Fürstenberg dynasty, and whose domains were absorbed by the Duchy of Baden in 1806—is one of the most important spokespersons for the "mediatized" sovereigns.[18] She wants back the territory Napoleon forced her to relinquish to Baden and her "rights" of conscription over 82,000 subjects. She advocates a confederation based on an older idea of Germany as an ancient empire, represented by Austria. Germany, she argues, should be "a voluntary political and military defensive union of the lesser estates with the great powers; that is what the German patriot can wish, and what each lesser estate must wish."[19] Working on the assumption that royalty will empathize with royalty, she turns to the British Prince Regent. England, she strokes, is the upholder of principles of justice, and Bonaparte's Confederation of the Rhine has stolen the prerogatives and ancient Rights, the fortunes, and the Honor of its sovereigns. Nobles such as herself, Fürstenberg writes, are enlightened, they have a long history of desiring liberty and justice, including supporting the grand coalition of the liberators of Europe. Now they want constitutions that will guarantee these ancient rights, prerogatives, and property, as well as the happiness of their subjects.

The promise of a German confederation inspires the Prussian patriot Caroline von Humboldt to offer quite different opinions to husband Wilhelm, even though she is not in Vienna. We have already encountered the baroness's views on patriotism; her letters to Wilhelm only confirm her passionate support of Prussian strategic interests and the breadth of her thinking on a future Germany. From her perspective, "the spirit of German liberty and unity" can be credited with Bonaparte's defeat; it is "still powerful and guides the course of the world."[20] She celebrates Prussia as a beacon of Enlightenment and political progress, a military power wielding its "superior weapon's glory." On her map of Europe, France is the past, England represents the tyranny of the present. Prussia is the future.

The fact that Caroline von Humboldt is so determined to influence negotiations in Vienna, but is not there, is also indicative of the different ways in which the sociability of the congress is perceived. The Humboldts have lived in Vienna since 1812, when Wilhelm took up his position as Prussian ambassador to the Habsburg court and became embroiled in the Coalition campaign. With the congress on the horizon, Caroline anticipates financial expense and disruption, so she packs up the family and leaves.[21] Counter to the flow, and counter to her role as *ambassadrice*, she returns to Berlin, stopping briefly at Coppet to stay with the absent Staël. She writes Wilhelm, "I am still often regretful that I am not in Vienna in order to cheer you up now and again for a quarter of an hour at your work. For, without doubt, seeing so many persons must give one a distinctly disagreeable feeling." Berlin, by contrast, exudes "the clearest political atmosphere."[22]

It may have been to appease Caroline's sensitivities that Wilhelm, who addresses his wife as "Li," claims he avoids the congress balls and stays home to work.[23] Caroline was by nature disinclined to mix, finding Viennese society superficial and the official get-togethers at the royal court an irritant. Her absence is our gain, as the textured correspondence travels between Vienna and Berlin. While husband and wife are aware their letters are vulnerable to surveillance, this does not curb their frequency or apparent frankness.[24] Instead, Caroline puts her correspondence to use as a site of politics. She is an outspoken proponent of a Prussian-dominated German federation, and her husband knows it.[25] He writes to discuss the details of his "mission," "not because I know that it will please you, no matter how much this might be an impelling motive; but because you pass judgement so clearly, from such

FIGURE 20. Unknown artist, Karolina von Humboldt with a profile (1766–1829) in a hairstyle à la Grec, wife of Wilhelm, 1808. Miniature. National Museum in Warsaw.

deep understanding and such accurate insight into all the circumstances, that no man on earth would want to do without it."[26] Caroline obliges, egging him on to build a German confederation on the foundations of existing "national Germanness":

> *Deutschland, Deutsche und nationelle Deutschheit* is evidently still growing, and Austria will not keep pace with it. To hold back the spirit of the times no power is strong enough, and history is a good source of information on what the future conceals. But probably the gentlemen don't read history.[27]

The baroness makes the case for a Prussian Germany on the realist grounds of security (an "enlarged and consolidated" Prussia

FIGURE 21. Giovanni Vendramini (Eduard Ströhling), *Portrait of linguist Wilhelm von Humboldt*, 1814. Engraving, 30.1 × 22.9 cm. Rijksmuseum.

is the single guarantee against future French aggression) and of idealist political sentiment ("the desire for representative forms of government"). She details "public opinion" in the Prussian capital Berlin, which she often elides as "Germany." She insists the Prussian public want to subsume the defeated Kingdom of Saxony as much as she does. She argues that if Prussia does not get Saxony, *Prussians* will be resentful; if they get it, they will rule it with enlightenment.[28] How does she know? She claims to have taken a public poll of sorts that convinces her that Saxons really care more about their constitution than their king.[29] Humboldt targets the "petty tyrants" of the former Rhine confederation such as Fürstenberg who demand old powers and rights (a "foolish sovereignty") in the space where she believes a federated Germany should rule, with Prussia at its center. She warns that to give in to the mediatized regents is to deny the "rights of the people" to be German. If these rights are not recognized, she predicts there will be widespread unrest in the duchies of Württemberg and Baden: "The people are deeply embittered and severely oppressed, and the latest war has enabled the people to visualize their wants."[30]

When Caroline passes on her views to Wilhelm, she uses a German vocabulary that evokes national *sentiment* and *will*. She underlines the emotional depth of the German question by relaying the story of a friend's young daughter who divorced her husband "because the two could not agree on the question of the German and French temperaments."[31] Her emphasis on the importance of the sentiment-based rights of Europe's peoples—even if over the territory of other people—sits at odds with her husband's views and with the methods of the congress. As Caroline insists on the purpose of her Prussian patriotism, Wilhelm will reply that few of the sovereigns and their representatives "have any predilection for these purely patriotic objects, which in the opinion of the majority do not really belong to the domain of higher politics."[32] (Later, Metternich will claim that national sentiment was not in viable circulation at this time.) The statistics commission backs this analysis by counting "souls" as physical individuals and showing no interest in their sentiments. This is despite the Coalition's wartime support for "the people's will," the tsar's advice to Louis XVIII that "national will" should be represented, and aristocratic enthusiasm for the ideas of Rousseau. Notably, in her letters to the tsar, Grand-Duchess Ekaterina remarks that wherever she travels, "Our Country" is every third word, and the question of "how to create and organize Germany" is uppermost.[33]

Nations are not only the causes of men but also of women, not only of the bourgeoisie but also aristocrats. Individuals who can be identified with each of these categories equally apply the language of sentiment and will to the other national question taken up formally at the congress, the restoration of Poland. The status of Poland as a legitimate cause is partly due to the influence on the tsar of Prince Czartoryski, who seeks a constitutionalist state. But it is as inspired by the Lithuanian nobleman Tadeusz Kościuszko, who camps himself on the outskirts of Paris to be at hand for Poland's reinvention as a constitutional monarchy, with no serfdom.[34] For Princess Jablonowska (Teodora Walewska), wife of Russian diplomat Prince Jablonowski, Poland also appeals as a means of resuscitating the former kingdom's constitution. The princess writes from Paris to Staël's agent at Vienna, Simonde de Sismondi, asking him to intervene with a colonel close to the tsar, because "Europe's destiny" should be decided by the powers "according to the lessons of Rousseau."[35] By contrast, the Duchess of Sagan supports the revival of the majesty and prestige of a thousand-year-old Polish kingdom. Bagration, for her part, tries to talk the tsar out of granting Poland independence, preferring to support Russian predominance in the territory, even if it means that in exchange, Prussia might gain Saxony.[36] This is a position that also suits Caroline von Humboldt very well, since it might "give back" to Prussia Polish territory that is "the greater part of our former possessions."[37]

Soft Diplomacy

In congress, politics, public opinion, popular interests, constitutional ideals, and patriotic feelings are put forward as rationales for peacemaking decisions. At a time when it is becoming more appropriate for women to pursue philanthropy, the possibility of politics between states is a domain of interest and ambition for bourgeois and aristocratic women. In the circumstances, women practice forms of "influence politics" we can usefully conceptualize as "soft-power" diplomacy.

Even before the Congress of Vienna begins, Caroline Rothschild writes from her hometown of Frankfurt to her banker husband Salomon in London, cajoling him to ply his networks in the gathering diplomatic circles in the interest of Jewish rights:

> Can't you, my dearest Salomon, contribute to this through your acquaintances over there? This would be a heavenly good deed, which cannot be bought even with very much money. Perhaps a minister there would give you an introduction to Austria, Russia or whomsoever has a say in this matter. You may ask what has a woman to do with public affairs? Better she should write about soap and needles. However, I see what I am doing as necessary.[38]

The demands for Jewish rights at Vienna are not unprecedented; they have been put forward by Jewish communities through the many episodes of the Napoleonic wars. When Bonaparte's defeat

FIGURE 22 (A), (B). Unknown artist, *Miniature Portraits of Salomon von Rothschild (1774–1855) and his wife, Caroline, née Stern (1782–1854)*. © The Rothschild Archive. Reproduced with the permission of The Trustees of The Rothschild Archive.

leaves new political authorities in the position of choosing whether to affirm the rights introduced by the fleeing French occupiers, representatives of the Jewish populations from the "liberated" towns send delegations to Vienna to persuade the peacemakers. Frankfurt sends Jacob Baruch, G. G. Uffenheim, and J. J. Gumprecht; Hamburg, Bremen, and Lubeck send the Christian jurist Dr. Carl August Buchholz.[39] In this same context, bankers and their families from London and Vienna petition for the rights for Jews in the new German confederation.[40]

In October 1814, Rothschild men pick up the baton and prepare a petition on "the Question of Equal Rights for Jews in Frankfurt."[41] Rehearsing Caroline Rothschild's advice, Carl Rothschild, her brother-in-law, writes from Frankfurt to Nathan, the head of the House of Rothschild in London, asking whether an "'English Lord' then on his way to Vienna . . . could possibly help in the question of civil rights with regard to the Jews."[42] Nathan approaches the prime minister, Lord Liverpool, parleying the anxiety of "the Jews of Germany." He calls on Liverpool's "enlightened Mind" and power to influence the outcome through Castlereagh, "lest it be in contemplation to deprive them of the political privileges which they have for some latter years enjoyed in common with their fellow Subjects of other religious persuasions." Against the background of anti-Semitic uprisings in the Duchy of Frankfurt, the intended heart of the new Germany, they want to ensure that the Jewish population will not be subject to regulations restricting their "industry" in the "other German States," and the restoration of the Prussian example of "liberality and justice" "to their ancient possession under the powerful Confederacy." Liverpool acquiesces, sending Castlereagh instructions to take the Rothschilds and Jewish rights in the new German confederation seriously. He reminds Castlereagh that Mr. Rothschild is "a very useful friend. I do not know what we should have done without him last year."[43]

While the Rothschilds have stayed away from Vienna because of its anti-Semitic laws, other Viennese-based Jewish bankers take initiatives, often following their wives. Over the months of peace negotiations, fifty-six-year-old Fanny von Arnstein—the Berlin-born wife of Viennese (ennobled) Jewish banker Baron Nathan von Arnstein—holds spectacular evening gatherings in her Hohmarket residence, a space in which, contemporaries note, classes, religions, and interest groups mix Prussian-style. She and her sister Cecilia—married to Arnstein's business partner, the similarly ennobled Bernhard von Eskeles—are daughters of the Prussian royal banker Daniel Itzig. The Austrian police report on them as "high-ranking personages" who "scandalously" promote Prussian policies *and* Jewish rights.[44] The Prussian banker and privy councillor Friedrich August von Stagemann describes their Jewish Prussian patriotism as anomalous: "It is often said that the Jews have no fatherland. But Frau von Eskeles has a fit if anything is said against Prussia, and Frau von Arnstein showers abuse on people and is beside herself. She compromises one through her vehement patriotism, says [Wilhelm] Humboldt."[45] On 11 April 1815, the banker husbands of Fanny and Cecilia, who otherwise keep a low political profile, deliver a petition to the Austrian emperor requesting equality before the law for Jews in the German lands in rights of

FIGURE 23. Conrad Malte-Brun, *Germany in 1812*. Paris: Francois Buisson, 1812. © David Rumsey Map Collection.

purchase, trade, and possession, the same limited privileges Jews exercise in Austria.[46]

The soft-power diplomacy of the relatively young twenty-one-year-old respectable Genevan bourgeoise Anna Eynard-Lullin is officially put to the purpose of a Swiss republican patriotism. At Paris, and then Vienna, her husband, the wealthy financier Jean-Gabriel Eynard, is invited to assume official secretarial duties for Geneva because of Anna's family connections. Anna Eynard-Lullin is not only the daughter of a failed banker but a niece of the patrician Genevan ambassador Charles Pictet de Rochemont. Yet Eynard-Lullin does not expect to attend the Congress of Vienna. She did not accompany Jean-Gabriel to Paris in April 1814, and the republican Eynards imagine aristocratic Viennese society to have a corrupting influence. Her plans change, however, when compatriot and fellow financier Francois d'Ivernois decides to bring his wife,

Louise. Eynard agrees the presence of Anna too might improve the delegation's chances. Eynard-Lullin readies her bags to serve her *patrie* with a mix of trepidation and nervous delight.

The couple's respective detailed diaries tell us that when the Eynards set off for Vienna on 30 September 1814, they hold modest expectations. Jean-Gabriel packs only his uniform and Anna one or two *toilettes*. Either they plan to resist most social invitations or they presume there will be few.[47] Once they are installed, Eynard-Lullin marvels at her ability to attract monarchs and promote the cause of a united republican Switzerland.[48] She is as surprised as anyone that she is feted and flattered in a brilliant world where ordinarily she is not of interest—a young "small" republican in the midst of dancing monarchs. The attention disconcerts her husband, but it allows her to wield influence to Geneva's political advantage.[49] She uses the noun *société* to describe the company she keeps.

During the three months they attend the Congress of Vienna, the Eynards spend their time among the best *société* in Europe.[50] Some events require no invitation, just an entry fee. At the "public ball" in the Apollon, all who can afford to pay gather in rooms lush with gardens, grottos, rocks, and moss and where, despite a heavy investment in candles, it is almost too dark to see. Usually, on any one night the Eynards average four invitations to public events in private homes. The Sunday evening of 30 October 1814, they go first to Metternich's then to Talleyrand's, before attending the Württemberg minister's residence. They end finally at Castlereagh's. They compare Metternich's *soupers*—like his dinners and balls, *brillantes et beaucoup plus cérémonielles*—with Lady Castlereagh's simpler, friendly affairs, where there are often no sovereigns in sight. Familiarity grows among a relatively small network of Europe's educated elite, some of whom have emerged from wartime exile and who now come into social contact with self-identified republicans and bourgeoises. Catholics mix with Protestants and Jews, Orthodox Christians are there alongside Muslims and Freemasons.[51]

The bourgeois republican Eynards will be among those who find themselves building enduring congress friendships with the Castlereaghs. A few nights after a particularly busy Sunday, Eynard-Lullin is the only woman invited to a dinner at Talleyrand's. She

FIGURE 24. Firmin Massot, *Portrait of Madame Jean-Gabriel Eynard, née Anne Charlotte Adélaïde Lullin de Châteauvieux (1793–1868), called Anna Lullin,* around 1810. Oil on canvas, 30 × 44.8 cm. © Musées d'art et d'histoire, Geneva. Photograph: Bettina Jacot-Descombes.

takes every opportunity to talk with the British delegates, whether Castlereagh, Canning, or Stewart, about "our *patrie*" Geneva, its frontiers and difficult situation.[52] Even in the midst of the noise and flurry of a ball, soft diplomacy has a chance. Dancing the slow and stately polonaise with Lord Castlereagh, Eynard-Lullin mentions the beauties of Switzerland—its territorial claims on the

FIGURE 25. Antoine-Jean Gros, *Portrait de Jean-Gabriel Eynard (1775–1863)*, 1800 (date proposed by Michelle Bouvier, December 2012). Oil on canvas, 64.5 × 48.5 cm. © Musées d'art et d'histoire, Geneva. Photograph: Bettina Jacot-Descombes.

French border are under consideration by the statistics commission. When the Prussian king speaks with her privately and hopes that all the partying and pleasure do not distract from important affairs, Eynard-Lullin prompts that "our small republic of Geneva" is among those affairs. The king, according to her diary, takes note. In an environment in which convention dictates that women "learned to know only such as were enabled by their position and rank to take part in the polonaise," little bourgeois Eynard-Lullin finds herself in conversation with the tsar on the subject of "the Swiss" and their loyalty to the Coalition.[53]

Whether it is at their own home or others, whether the sociability is orchestrated or more relaxed, congressing *société* offers the means of exercising soft diplomacy. Just after the new year of 1815, Louise Ivernois miscarries and the responsibility of representing Geneva falls to the Eynards alone.[54] The couple oblige by hosting modest receptions, with the occasional *diner*. These hardly count as salons. More simply they involve a general conversation, and then tea with informal chatting and organized music or games. French, English, and Russian diplomats (the duc de Richelieu, Stratford Canning, Kapodistrias, Pozzo di Borgo) might form a circle around a table and make up a question to match a provided answer. The games are most successful with the strangers, while the French do not appreciate them at all.[55]

On some Swiss accounts, it is Eynard-Lullin who swings the English over to the Genevan side—in striking contrast to the failed efforts of Berne canton's representative Louis Zeerleeder, a banker without diplomatic experience or wife to assist him.[56] Is soft diplomacy enough to determine a political outcome? Certainly, despite the difficulty Genevans face gaining formal audiences with the Committee of Four, the Genevan situation after the Vienna congress is improved. Although not all Geneva's territorial claims are successful, the Swiss canton is given Versoix, parts of Pays de Gex, and further concessions in Savoy.[57]

The address of Jewish rights too is testament to the significance at Vienna of soft diplomacy—and its limits. Jewish rights are only accepted as a relevant issue for the political fate of Jews in German-speaking territories formerly occupied by the French, not elsewhere. The congress's failure to reach any substantial policy on this issue—like that of abolition—is also evidence of the mixed effect of "public opinion." The Humboldts, for example, are in fundamental disagreement. Wilhelm von Humboldt brings to the problem of Jewish rights the same rationale he brought to the Prussian emancipation measure of 1812: Jews should be assimilated through emancipation because their social oppression is the origin of "their undesirable qualities."[58] Caroline von Humboldt socializes with individual Jews, but she objects to their collective emancipation because she assumes their religious difference determines their cultural and, inevitably, political difference. Wilhelm turns the argument around by explaining that giving Jews rights would mean the couple would no longer have to socialize with them. Their overall objective is the same, as is clear from their shabby treatment of Rahel Levin, who was close to them in her Berlin *salonnière* days. Baron von Humboldt is repulsed by Levin's "mixed" marriage to the Christian Prussian diplomat Karl Varnhagen and the thought that it might earn Rahel normative status as "eine Gesandtenfrau und Exzellenz."[59] Caroline just simply cuts Levin off and consistently argues against Jewish rights as premature.

Other congress political questions that circulate in society are only slowly resolved, without easily delineated causal chains of influence. In 1815, the Saxony issue brings the German question to a climax. As Prussia's foreign minister Prince Hardenberg threatens war, and Austria enters a secret defensive alliance with France and England against Prussia and Russia, the commission exercises Solomon-like wisdom to divide Saxony into two unequal parts. Two-fifths of Saxony will become Prussian. The commission also finally agrees on a Germany confederation comprised of 39 states (instead of the former 360), excluding German-speaking Switzerland, Alsace, and eastern Prussia, with the Austrian emperor Frances I at its head, on the Holy Roman Empire model.[60] Its constitution divides up the voting power of each of the composite polities and leaves its future federal assembly to decide on the question of religious tolerance and Jewish rights, as well as other unresolved issues, such as the tax and property rights of the mediatized. Meanwhile, Poland gets a constitution drafted not by Jeremy Bentham but by Czartoryski and the tsar. It promises some of the liberal freedoms that have been in discussion since the campaign, including freedom of speech and religious tolerance. However, relative to an earlier Polish constitution, it is seen as revoking rights that Polish Jews and peasants have had in the past, since Polish sovereignty will be subject to Russian oversight.

The methods by which these decisions are arrived at are not transparent; balance of power, legitimacy, numbers, and nationality all play as rationalizations. When we ascertain that Wilhelm von

Humboldt *fails* to gain a liberal constitution for the German Confederation (Deutscher Bund) that would have guaranteed the rights of all citizens, including Jews, we need to also acknowledge that Caroline von Humboldt's vision of Prussian territory and nationhood wins out.

What lessons can we take away from these examples of society and sociability in the midst of an international order being erected on scientific principles of governance and diplomacy? Women have opinions, expressed through public and private channels, about the political questions at stake and the methods and progress of male-dominated politics. Witnesses of this historical moment such as Staël denounce the weakness and incompetency of the men in charge and their intriguing, blaming individual statesmen's cupidity for the evasion of the liberal principles that compelled the campaign against Bonaparte's authoritarianism in the first place. A noticeable world-weariness strains Staël's summation of the progress of the congressing as it seems from her distance, a "world spectacle made to inspire sadness, with the only consolation that discontent is being aroused."[61] Bagration dismisses the ineffective sovereigns "having fun" and criticizes their ministers who delay outcomes by squabbling.[62] Self-conscious of her privileged position as a witness, Sagan writes to Lamb not sparing the English in her wrath: "how did the stupid fools who govern the world manage things."[63] Some of the attacks are also more personal. Even though Sagan relies on the tsar's favor, she bemoans that "there is now nothing to be had from the Czar" because he is desperately in love with Gabriele Auersperg, "so that there is not one of his ministers who can lay hold of him for half an hour." She is as critical of Metternich, who, she claims, "grows a complete fool his love for me and Dorothea and god knows who besides makes him so stupid it is not to be borne—he goes on and he can't help it, but in doing very great things, he finds means to . . . and discontents everybody—there is no soul no heart in the man and . . . believe me he is little more than a wretched coxcomb . . . and a self-conceited fool—this sounds very severe but indeed it is true."[64] Eynard-Lullin records that the congress "had proven that Europe lacked men of merit, that its Kings and Ministers were very mediocre."[65] Reflecting on a dinner at the residence of a British diplomat in late December 1814, she records that although not in a position "to judge such great things," she watches "the cream of all that exists in Europe in terms of distinguished men assembled with the mission of dealing with the most essential affairs." These affairs are the fate of states and sovereign rights, but "every day, instead of taking a step forward, they take one back, . . . then when they are no longer able to walk, they take to dancing." Overall she fears "for humanity."[66]

These women's opinions, like their actual agency and soft diplomacy, leave few ripples in the ocean of public and private documents that shape historical narratives of the international past. The voices that are easier to hear are aristocratic, and they reflect the power of class and gender norms in determining political agency and diplomatic authority. Yet, from our long-distance perspective, we can see how the blurred edges of "society," as much as the relatively open sociability of the congress, increasingly give space to a rising bourgeoisie and the particular influence of a new financier class. As significantly, some of these men and women seek to personally benefit from the political operations involved in the politics between states, while some act in formal and informal capacities to influence outcomes on behalf of other political or economic interests. These interests are not always national; they are as often class-based, or religious, or even moral, according to new bourgeois conventions. There are congress thresholds Anna Eynard-Lullin will not cross for reasons of bourgeois morality, namely those of Bagration's and Sagan's respective salons. Even as balls, dinners, salons, and *soupers* punctuate the rhythms of the Eynards' daily routines, the couple take their leave when the Russian grand-duchess becomes too friendly. Anna and Jean-Gabriel fear the morally corrupting effect of such contacts on their worldview. In a similar vein, when correspondent "N" writes to Staël from the Congress of Vienna that he is witness to a "theatre of the world," he is not only intimating its diversity but also bemoaning its superficial and performative tendencies.[67]

CHAPTER TEN

Credit and Commerce

Credit . . . [is] the true modern discovery which binds a government to its people . . . [because] it obliges the executive power to treat public opinion with consideration.

—STAËL, *CONSIDERATIONS ON THE PRINCIPAL EVENTS OF THE FRENCH REVOLUTION*

The age of commerce has given man a new nature.

—BENJAMIN CONSTANT, 1820S

A DECADE BEFORE THE CONGRESS OF VIENNA, Friedrich Gentz remarks upon the economic "revolution" underway across Europe.[1] Within a few years, Benjamin Constant's *Spirit of Conquest* (1813) is one of numerous published essays connecting the world-scale expansion of commerce and trade with an anticipated European peace. Similarly, the French capitalist-cum-social utopian Henri de Saint-Simon's pamphlet on the need to reorganize Europe argues that the failed *philosophes* of the eighteenth century should cede political authority to the "second class" of the "commercial order" "so important for the power of a State."[2] He has in mind the same *banquiers*, *negocians*, and *fabricans* whose omnipresence Rahel Levin notes in the sociability of congress diplomacy.[3] As postwar Europe floats "between the present and the future," the age of commerce winds politics and economics tightly, and money matters in pressing questions of collective and individual security.

FIGURE 26. *Médaille Commémorative du congrès de Vienne*, featuring Coalition battles. Engraving, 1814. Bibliothèque Nationale de France.

The economic actors arriving in Vienna mark the arrival of a new era of politics. Although they make up a modest fraction of the hundreds of sovereigns and statesmen and servants, men and women who crowd the city, the impression they leave reflects the shifting postwar horizon of *moral* as well as economic expectations.[4] Mostly they are identified as the *banquiers* indispensable during the war as creditors, currency providers, and agents, and now, after the war, crucial for fulfilling peacetime obligations. As the Coalition's conferencing gathers pace, the bankers who dominate this scene are the London-based Rothschilds and Barings, and Napoleon's banker Gabriel-Julien Ouvrard. Having established their agile methods of wartime credit provision—whether for raising armies and military infrastructure or payment subsidies, or in their ability to secrete currencies across transnational borders—they now show interest in maintaining peacetime government business. In Paris in 1814, the Rothschilds' role is to cash English subsidies "without depressing the rate of exchange." The result is a saving for the English Treasury of "hundreds of thousands."[5] One or another of the Rothschild brothers attends all other congresses, from Aix-la-Chapelle to Verona. They might have been at Vienna too, were it not for Austria's anti-Semitic laws, which allow foreign Jews to visit for only short periods.[6] Instead, the Rothschilds turn for representation to two men: John Charles Herries, the British commissary-in-chief, with whom they work delivering British subsidies to allies; and the Elector of Hesse, a satisfied private Rothschild client. The Christian Barings also rely on a proxy for business purposes at Vienna, Eric Bollmann.

At times the term *capitalistes* is used by observers such as Rahel Levin, who notices the manufacturer's wife from the Saxon town of Chemnitz. This woman wears black velvet, her hair cropped and curled up with a comb across her forehead. She is seeking out the tsar and the "right, good ear" of the deaf Hardenberg to make "the case of the Hamburg and Berlin business people" and convince them that Chemnitz should become Prussian.[7] The Hanoverian expatriate Eric Bollmann, who eventually becomes Levin's close friend, is more in the category of *negocians*. He has traveled the long way from Philadelphia—via London—to Vienna to promote steamships for travel and quicksilver for the manufacture of coins.[8] Tubingen-based Johann Friedrich von Cotta, the most successful publisher in the German lands, is among the representatives of "booksellers of Germany" in Vienna to lobby against censorship and printing piracy and to argue for copyright and the lifting of free trade restrictions.[9] At a more modest level, the Eynards' compatriot Genevan Dr. Jean de Carro, known for his promotion of vaccination practices, is keen to sell to congress delegates his cures for *goitres* and other deformities.[10]

Among Europeans, the processes of industrialization that give rise to the "second class" are characteristically identified with the British Isles, but their geopolitical impact is more widespread. Awareness of a new age of commerce feeds continent-wide imaginaries of a modern age. In the summer after Bonaparte's initial defeat, when the tsar's sister the Grand-Duchess Ekaterina Pavlovna travels to London to prepare for the postwar victory celebrations, she goes out of her way to visit English factories. She is equally enthralled by the British systems of taxation and drainage as by its local religious sects, particularly the Quakers. Ekaterina juggles watching debates in Parliament with finding out about the manufacture of money, down to the detail of British minting machinery. Her goal is to investigate how these methods might be transplanted in still feudal Russian soil.[11]

These same developments amplify the political voice of the so-called "second class" or bourgeoisie whose claim to notice is their money and their cultural difference from the aristocracy.[12] Ambitious men with limited elite networks find their way into the poorly paid lower echelons of expanding foreign ministries. Alternatively, where there are limited relevant government structures, the financial and familial networks of a financier such as Jean-Gabriel Eynard lead to formal diplomatic roles, in his case for the Queen of Etruria, or as a "secretary" to the Genevan and Switzerland plenipotentiaries, simultaneously.[13] Then there are the wives and daughters in banking and financier families, such as Germaine de Staël, Anna Eynard-Lullin, and Rahel Levin, who find themselves with access to diplomatic circles.

When we follow the money, we are able to throw light into the less illuminated corners of the intersecting pasts of international politics and international finance, where the ambition and influence of Saint-Simon's "second class" grows, often unobserved, although rarely unremarked upon. There we find the imposing specter of accumulating war debt and conferencing costs and their impact on already stretched sovereign and individual purses. Not all economic actors or interests are equal in this history. As we will see, bankers are a specific subset of the commercial class who are indispensable as provisioners of credit to individuals as well as governments, while, at the same time, Jewish bankers (like independent women) become leitmotifs of the underside of international history. Following the money leads us to the history of both security and insecurity, to commerce as the antidote to war, and the threat of economic sabotage as "just another method of conducting war" in times of peace.[14]

The Second Class

At Vienna, the first person the Duke of Wellington visits upon his arrival at the Congress of Vienna is Leopold Edler von Herz, a Jewish Habsburg court banker. The previous year Herz is among the contractors responsible for distributing and winding up British subsidies to Austria in the aftermath of the Battle of Leipzig. At the congress, Herz, "a suave, easy-going person who was welcome at all aristocratic gambling tables," is Wellington's personal source of credit.[15] Gentz's diary tells of Herz's distinguished dinners attended by leading British and French delegates, as well as local guests such as Herz's uncle and partner Nathan von Arnstein, among the most socially prominent of the bankers in the Austrian capital.[16] That prominence is crowned by their ennoblement—Herz, Arnstein, and Arnstein's partner Eskeles are among the few Austrian Jews ennobled in the late eighteenth century by Francis II, in their case for "zealous services rendered."

Local Viennese bankers are able to exploit specific business advantages. Arnstein and Eskeles, like their relative Herz, provide credit and currency exchange for visiting delegates and facilitate transnational government transactions for the Habsburg court. Without the soft diplomacy of their wives, Fanny Arnstein and Cecilia Eskeles—the daughters of the Prussian banker to the royal court Daniel Itzig—they would not court as much influence or business as they do.[17] According to the memoirs of Countess Rzeweulska and others, Fanny Arnstein's salon, especially, holds its own against "any aristocratic prototype," as "the center of all the vanities of the world and some of its receptions were said to be even more splendid than the Emperor's."[18] In July 1814, in expectation of early congress arrivals, and despite the summer heat, the sisters return from their country homes to Vienna to begin networking.

Fanny's congress salon is well-known as a place where "persons of the highest rank and the greatest distinction, ladies and gentlemen, foreigners and natives, gather in her rooms."[19] Her home on Hoher Markt attracts the highest echelons of congress society, including individuals who might have avoided her in other circumstances.[20] The Jewish provenance of the Arnstein palais seems not to daunt the leader of the Catholic delegation, Cardinal Consalvi, who attends decked in red cap and red stockings. The extremely bourgeois Catholic Karoline Pichler, who has her own more understated salon, is a regular attendee at Cecilia Eskeles's gatherings.

Once the congress is in full swing, most days of the week the Arnstein salon hosts strangers, country people, ministers, and princes. Every Tuesday evening, there are popular entertainments: private concerts, chamber quartets, vocal duets, pianists. At her "tableaux vivants" famous wax figures are brought to life. Arnstein provides tea, lemonade, almond milk, ice cream, and light pastries; through the winter there are cherries, peaches, and apricots.[21] In a town where the restaurants are not to everyone's liking, and food is expensive, the Arnstein salon is a cornucopia. Then there is its reputation for attracting desirable women, whether Countess Engel, Rebecca Ephraim and her daughter, or Arnstein's niece Fraulein Saaling. General Ludwig Wolzogen enthuses that "there I had the best opportunity to improve my acquaintance with all the diplomats and distinguished friends who went in and out there," having in mind the men.[22] On one night at the Arnsteins', there are twenty-two men gathered around the table, "among them the Duke of Acerenza-Pignatelli, several Swedish barons, the Italian poet Carpani, Wanda, Werner, Stegmann, Jordan and others."[23] The connections that bring bankers into close connection with politics are often simply familial: Fanny and Cecilia's nephew, Jacob Salomon Bartholdy, is a member of the Prussian delegation accompanying Hardenberg. As importantly, the Arnstein salon famously enables otherwise difficult political meetings among an eclectic community of interested parties.

Not all economic actors at the congress fall back on providing salons, and they insinuate themselves in society to advance a range of interests. The less well-known hunchbacked Monsieur Foneron—resident in Vienna and previously a banker at Livorno, where he had amassed a large fortune—seeks to accumulate honor to himself by bankrolling "the most excellent dinners" in the company of illustrious peacemakers.[24] The Christian Johann Heinrich Geymüller, originally from Basel, has earned Habsburg imperial recognition for raising credit to help the state meet an indemnity imposed on Austria by Napoleon a few years earlier. (Geymüller will eventually help found the Austrian National Bank, serving as its vice-chairman for some years.) At the congress, Geymüller and his wife exploit the lively social program provided by others. They mix with aristocrats desperate to source credit for lavish parties and dinners, clothes, houses, carriages, and the gambling that regularly takes place in private homes.[25]

It is clear that economic and political interests mingle with soft diplomacy, in diverse social settings. The Arnsteins and Eskeleses use their status and the salon to support Prussian interests and Jewish rights. Money cannot buy everything, but the few who insist on not blurring politics and commerce confirm the extent to which the border between these domains is not always visible. Jewish bankers try to bribe Prussia's delegates, Prince Hardenberg and Humboldt, Austria's Metternich, and Friedrich Gentz, without much controversy. Simon von Lämel, an ennobled Prague-based banker who backs the Austrians in the war against Napoleon with his own money, but is refused the right to purchase a home in Vienna because he is a Jew, puts his wealth to work on behalf of Jewish rights elsewhere.[26] During the congress, Humboldt alone refuses Lämel's bribes on the grounds of "the most antique principles," which he describes to his wife, Caroline, as not taking "private advantage for things which are done for the good of the whole."[27] Gentz, Hardenberg, and Metternich are not troubled by the offers of payment, even though, like Humboldt, they support the Jewish cause anyway.

Once we attune our historical hearing to the discordant economic timbre of peacemaking in the early nineteenth century, it is easier to pick up the notes of its reputed get-rich-quick ethos as well as the spectrum of ambitions and anxieties. For all his self-confessed antique principles, Humboldt is as likely as any other diplomat to resort to collecting the diamonds from the snuffboxes gifted to diplomats as a means of paying his bills. Like Caroline he is only too well aware that thriving or failing requires some initiative. In the context of a new age of credit and commerce in which bankers, politicians, and diplomats alike make a meal of government treasuries in search of European stability or status, this is a lesson learned by a newly self-conscious bourgeois class and the aristocratic elite alike.

Economic Insecurity

Within a year of the end of the Sixth Coalition war, across Europe concatenations of government debt, recession, icy winters, volcano eruption, crop failures, typhus, and plague-fueled famine taint the years of postwar peace. Even the prospect of change feeds an atmosphere of threats, some more real than others. This is the environment in which economic insecurity leads to the scapegoating of independent women, Jews, and foreigners. In Britain, public criticism of spending turns to the cost of peace. Accountants are appalled at the amount of "crayfish" consumed, giving us some sense of the opulence of these affairs and the fiscal correctness that the English bring to the professionalization of soft-power sociability.[28] By the next congress at Aix-la-Chapelle, the British government will consider money-saving schemes such as hauling three large "portable rooms" across the channel to Prussia for the use of the official painter, Sir Thomas Lawrence. Eventually they realize that the cost of building rooms and transport will exceed the expense of rent. No one debates the need for an official painter, or the accompanying group of Royal Academicians, despite what the *Times* describes as "the dawning symptoms of an approaching system of economy."[29]

Back in 1814, the government most fiscally stretched by the Congress of Vienna is the hosting Habsburg court. Princess Bagration chides Metternich that it cost him less trouble to defeat Bonaparte than it is costing him to agree over the spoils.[30] Over nearly a year of talks, the court secretary organizes extravagant public balls and novelty events, a hundred-piano extravaganza, and a "Grand Carousel" featuring 24 chevaliers dressed in medieval garb saluting their *belles d'amour*. Twelve thousand revelers turn up for the first public ball; 20,000 soldiers attend a sit-down dinner on the Prater on the anniversary of the Battle of Leipzig. The imperial table is kept abundant at a cost of 15,000 guldens a day, let alone the 34 sledges for a *Schlittage* to Schonbrunn, or the 300 new carriages placed at the disposal of visiting royalty, all borne by the Austrian exchequer.[31] Observing a concert held in the Hofburg on 1 October 1814, the Danish *ambassadrice* Countess Bernstorff describes "this new, strange world" with its "dazzling procession" of Europe's courts and dancing.[32] The dancing theme is captured in the Prince de Ligne's immortalized pun: "Le Congrès ne marche pas, il danse" (the Congress does not walk/work, it dances).[33]

Unable to meet its bills, the Austrian government decides to print 500 million guldens' worth of promissory notes. There are precedents for the measure, as the public knows too well. When it is revealed that the promissory notes are backed only by a guarantee of *future* revenues, memories of the state's strategy three years earlier quickly flood back. In 1811, the decision to print paper money—known as "Zotells"—to pay off Austrian public debt ended in state bankruptcy, "cruel hardship," "widespread dislocation," and "one of the most disastrous experiences of their own or their fathers' lives."[34] In late 1814, reactions to this same manufacturing paper money measure are affected by postwar uncertainty, endless examples of excess, daily currency fluctuations, and the still vital memory of the earlier bankruptcy.[35] Johann Emanuel von Küster, the Prussian ambassador to the courts of the South German princes, notes that "all levels of the Viennese public" complain about both the stock exchange and paper money.[36] Prussian diplomat Karl von Varnhagen describes the prevalent mood to his Berlin-based (banker) brother-in-law as "images of collapsing conditions and violent awakening forces."[37]

The general fearful atmosphere makes Fanny Arnstein's salon even more popular as a site of reliable information. Guests seek out the opinion of Nathan von Arnstein on the state of the economy and the real sources of financial threat. On one account, the otherwise retiring banker explains to those assembled that the government's issue of paper money is evidence of the parlous state of the Austrian economy. Arnstein assures his guests that a "return to peaceful conditions that do away with the fear of war, a reduction in the armed forces, and a recall of the promissory notes will, without recourse to any other financial manipulations, greatly improve the monetary situation and bring back prosperity."[38] The banker emphasizes peace (rather than war) as a prerequisite for economic security. He also affirms the critical role of economic prosperity as the only guarantee of peace, linking commerce more tightly to the objectives of peacemaking.

Prosperity is hard to imagine for many of the congress cohorts. Caroline von Humboldt was determined to leave Vienna prior to the congress, anticipating the explosion in costs. The Countess Bentivoglio of Bologna, who is coincidentally in Vienna to obtain the emperor's intervention in a financial matter, decides to stay and is soon aghast at the cost of food, hiring a cook, renting a house, paying cleaners and a wood porter, and procuring a carriage.[39] The self-identified bourgeoisie feel the expense of congressing as a personal cost, whether skyrocketing house rents or living prices. Even the wealthy Eynards actively seek economies in lodging and food upon their arrival. Their temporary residence in Vienna—three rooms and a salon on Kuglerstrasse found for them by their compatriot Dr. Carro—symbolizes their modesty, on behalf of the Genevan government footing their bills. The rent for the meager space is 600 florins a month (a postal employee earns 400 florins per annum) and more expensive than Paris rates. Their budgeting factors in a carriage without driver, and dining out, which is as expensive as Paris but leaves them hungry. The Eynards joke that Switzerland will be expanded at the cost of its financial ruin.[40]

At Vienna, Rahel Levin is a relatively lowly *ambassadrice*, and her husband, Karl Varnhagen, who is tasked with dispensing "official information concerning the proceedings" to the interested public, barely makes a living.[41] Money is constantly short; she relies on receiving family funds, at her brothers' discretion, to pay for a wagon, for example. She requests—or as she more colorfully describes, "marching, shitting, plundering, raging again"—that they send her money quarterly instead of monthly. In the landscape of congressing, Levin engages the nitty-gritty of fiscal investment and speculation as a means of survival from her one-room "bourgeois" apartment. There, with her husband, she sleeps, writes, dresses, eats, receives people, and does business and what she terms "economics." She sends her banker brothers news of exchange rates and diplomatic decisions that impact those rates, all the while assessing their bearing on her limited Prussian income.[42]

Levin may not have much money, but she does have connections, thanks to her experience growing up in Berlin banking circles and her Europe-wide reputation as a Berlin *salonnière*. Her friends include Pauline Weisel, the daughter of the director of the Banque Royale de Prusse, and she knows bankers in Prague, Berlin, Hamburg, Frankfurt, Leipzig, and Paris, and the Arnsteins, Eskeleses, and Geymüllers in Vienna. At the congress she brings these networks and her intelligence to the everyday practices of currency exchange, speculation, and investment.[43] She tackles the geopolitical realities of the time in the context of the "profusion of kingdoms, principalities, municipalities and other political jurisdictions" of German lands that David Landes considers a "money-changer paradise." And she draws on her keen sense of the economic consequences of peacemaking decisions, including the possible expansion of Prussian territory into Saxony, the Rhine, and Westphalia.[44]

In the freezing cold of January 1815, Levin is writing about currency exchange and its impact on her limited Prussian income. Her efforts to discover the currency rates, let alone predict them, are crucial to the success of her ventures. She litters her letters with the rate predictions offered by different outlets, such as occasional published currency reports, although they are only one source for determining the business of financial gain. A relative, she claims, has told her the rate will improve. Over the following days, however, it gets worse. She is frustrated enough to complain, "I don't believe anyone anymore, because nobody knows anything now."[45] Within less than a week, however, the Austrian currency shoots up in value.[46] On 16 March, her brother Marcus Theodor replies to her from his end, "The exchange rate reached 5% and only today does it seem as if it will settle."[47] When Napoleon suddenly escapes from exile and returns to Paris, the congress finds itself in dramatic tumult; Levin mentions that the Austrian exchange rate opened high in the morning and closed nearly 10 percent lower, "where it is now." She punctuates her comments with the exclamation that plays on the German term for economics, "Das ist ein Wirtschaft!" (This is some mess!).[48]

Predicting rates of exchange is also about the advantage to be gained from insider information. Levin's sources include Berlin compatriots such as Fanny Arnstein but also Count Johann Philipp Stadion, the Austrian finance minister.[49] In January 1815, she writes her brother about Stadion's plan for an Austrian bank, passed on by "an acquaintance of ours, who you know":

> It is a secret and he has told only us. If the thing works, all of the *Papier* that are now falling will rise infinitely. Therefore there is work to be done; if it becomes known everyone will speculate. So I will attempt to receive the first news of the approval and then you can do something. But I cannot send a completely secure message because if I know the *Banquiers* know too.[50]

The source in this case is Eric Bollmann, a typical cosmopolitan product of the complex map of European sovereignties in this period and newfangled entrepreneur.

Born in Hanover, Bollmann has lived in London, Paris, Karlsruhe, Vienna, and New Orleans. He knows the Humboldts from his education at Göttingen University, the French delegation from his time in Paris and Talleyrand's exile in America. The Austrians know Bollmann from the era of revolution, when his attempts to help the French general Lafayette escape led to his imprisonment in Vienna. During the congress, Bollmann grows particularly close to the Varnhagens, with whom he shares plans to "conduct big business in America with quicksilver, which is piled up here and is otherwise only able to be found in Peru."[51] Levin explains to her brother, "If his project is adopted, silver coins will come here again."[52] While the occasional historian has noted Bollmann's commercial failures at the congress, Levin knows him to be working with Stadion on encouraging Austro-American trade in primary goods and shipbroking through the Habsburg ports of Venice, Fiume, and Trieste. He is also promoting the establishment of an Austrian bank, in the image of the Bank of England and the First Bank of the United States.

Bollmann's networks work to Levin's advantage. In February 1815, before Napoleon's escape provokes a further collapse in political and economic confidence, Levin writes to her brother Moritz about the effect of territorial decisions on the value of the Austrian currency. Rumors that the congress is considering a Kingdom of Poland at the expense of Austria's Galician northern border region trigger the mass dumping of Austrian paper money. This is the paper money, or *das Papier*, printed and put into circulation by the government as promissory notes on the expectation of future government revenue: "I don't know what the exchange rate is, either *das Papier* has risen a little more, or it has stayed the same," Levin reports, "the previous fall is apparently due to the opinion in Poland that they will cease to be Austrians, so they sold *die Papiere à tout prix*. It was the same in the provinces, as in Prague and other towns earlier, cheaper than here. Such positions and shocks will happen more frequently."[53] Levin is pointing out that Austrian currency rates are vulnerable to the Polish question at the congress and the empire's dependence on the printing of paper money. She knows that Stadion is pressing for Bollmann's idea of a national bank as a way of implementing *eine Papierkuhr* that would "cure" the fragile monetary system. Bollmann has a plan for taking the destabilizing *papier* out of circulation by using the depreciating paper money to pay for the new bank's capital.[54] Levin reliably passes on to Moritz this news as a financial opportunity. She warns him at the same time of the need for discretion: "if you say anything to anyone—and I will certainly find out about it—then I will never tell you about anything again!"[55]

The same conditions that generate unpredictable currency fluctuations and the government's dependence on paper money inspire individuals of both classes and genders to seek ways of privately benefiting from the peacemaking process, as well as its sociability. Over the period that Levin keeps a close watch on the Austrian currency, its value declines by up to a third over three and a half months—from "200 to 300 guldens at the opening of the Congress to 320 guldens for 100 guldens silver."[56] When the situation begins to improve a year later, in 1816, it is credited to Stadion's long-awaited financial reforms. Levin herself, however—a Jew who has converted to Christianity, and a woman with banker connections and insider knowledge—continues to exist on the precarious margins of economic and social respectability. Her story directs us to the more treacherous political implications of the climate of economic insecurity and financial precarity, as well as the distinctive positions of women and men, particularly women with no independent means. Levin understands finance as fundamentally connected to diplomacy and peacemaking—not uncoincidentally, her husband calls her a "fine statesman," "ambassadorial secretary," or "commissioner."[57] When we glimpse daily congress life through her correspondence, the significance of banking networks extends in different social directions—up and down the ladder of class and beyond the boundaries of gender or religion.

The general climate of fiscal anxiety coaxes suspicion of the same bankers who are in some contexts the sources of "special knowledge" and in others accused of being agents of opaque and unwanted political influence, especially if they are Jewish or foreign. Austrian secret police reports accuse Metternich of protecting "the Jew, banker Herz," "the most unscrupulous of brokers," because he is literally in the banker's debt.[58] Others allege the tsar is paying a certain St. Petersburg banker, Monsieur Schwarz, present at the congress with his wife (also reputed to be one of Tsar Alexander's many mistresses), to sabotage the Austrian economy. When Schwarz is overheard to say, "The rate of exchange will soon drop to one thousand," the conclusion is that he is conspiring a manipulation of the rate of exchange through speculation.[59] The Danish delegation at the congress tips off the Austrians because they believe that the previous year the Russians paid the Schwarzes to undermine the Danish economy.[60] The Danish king goes so far as to instruct his chamberlain, von Scholten, to cultivate Mme. Schwarz at the congress, "at whatever cost." It is reported that the irresistible combination of Scholten's "dashing figure" and expensive gifts he lavishes on his mark enables him "to pump [the banker's wife] about Alexander's conversation with her, the latter visiting her at least twice a week and possibly giving her secret missions."[61] These same secret police reports eventually acknowledge that there is no evidence that Russians commissioned Schwarz to influence the exchange rate. It is more likely that Talleyrand has started the rumor of a Russian conspiracy to draw Austria closer to France.[62]

Austrian secret police spies are also important intermediaries of stereotypes of independent women, not least *salonnières*, as threats to political security.[63] A favorite scapegoat is thirty-three-year-old Princess Bagration, suspected of influencing Austrian sovereigns and statesmen to Russian ends through "political and amorous intrigues."[64] Monitored by a government wary of Russia's leadership at the congress, Bagration's salon is closely watched for details of the comings and goings of the tsar and her possible influence on his foreign policy thinking—although spies are as likely to explain Alexander's nocturnal visits to Bagration as a consequence of his venereal disease, which, they claim, the princess is curing with special lotions or *cataplasmes* and *pansements*.[65] In general, like the Duchess of Sagan, Bagration is suspect because of her independence and complicated personal history with Metternich. It is assumed that both women debauch themselves for financial reasons.[66] Bagration's need for money, despite her fortune, is said to make her particularly vulnerable to the entreaties of foreign governments and a threat to Austria.[67] The lavish entertainment that has given her salon its reputation—as *le paradis de Mahomet*—has drained her resources to the extent that she is on the verge of insolvency and presumed to be for sale.[68] Bagration does indeed need money, and she seeks it from a wide range of the bankers present—as do all the official delegates and representatives. In her case, like that of Sagan, precarious finances accentuate readings of the sexual power of women over men.[69] The tables of suspicion can also be turned. Early in the formal proceedings of the congress, the ubiquitous informer known as Nota cannot resist adding in his reports: "This is not the first time that the intrigues of women have influenced the politics of States. That's men for you!"[70]

By the time the Congress of Vienna finishes up—eight months after it begins—managing Europe's security is more than the completion of "this general pacification," or creation of new institutions to replace those uprooted by the war, or even territorial agreements that encircle France with enlarged sovereign powers. When Bonaparte's escape from exile on the Tuscan island of Elba in late March 1815 leads to the (in)famous Hundred Days of rule over France, a second Coalition victory over France at Waterloo culminates in the 1815 (second) Treaty of Paris, more punitive than the unexpectedly magnanimous 1814 first treaty. The Coalition powers now focus on a financial punishment, burdening France with the bill for reparations and, to add to the indignity, the cost of occupation. Until the reparations are paid, the Coalition will not leave France. As we will see in chapter 13, bankers are crucial to the resolution of this debt and to peace in Europe. They invent the international sovereign debt market and generate a new era in international finance rooted in the diplomacy of the new international order. In these same circumstances of the growing significance of credit and commerce, the politics between states are increasingly oriented around new bourgeois norms of national, gender, and class, even religious, differentiation.

CHAPTER ELEVEN

Religion

The Three contracting Monarchs will remain united by the bonds of a true and indissoluble fraternity, and considering each other as fellow countrymen, they will, on all occasions and in all places, lend each other aid and assistance; and, regarding themselves towards their subjects and armies as fathers of families, they will lead them, in the same spirit of fraternity with which they are animated, to project Religion, Peace and Justice.

—THE HOLY ALLIANCE TREATY, 26 SEPTEMBER 1815

IN THE LONG HISTORY of the idea of an international order, the influence of religion has been more controversial than money. Nowhere are these notes of controversy more apparent than in accounts of the treaty of the Holy Alliance. Signed in Paris *after* the Congress of Vienna, on 26 September 1815—the date of the Christian feast of the Exaltation of the Cross—the Holy Alliance celebrated the shared Christianity of Europe's sovereigns, "united by the bonds of a true and indissoluble fraternity and considering each other as fellow countrymen." It stipulated "their conduct would be absolutely regulated by the principles of the Christian religion."[1] Was this emphasis on Christianity a diversion from the political cooperation established at Chaumont, as some charged?

For critics of the Holy Alliance since, the name insinuates a backward-looking emotional intervention, an interruption of progress toward the scientific idea of politics that sat on the future's horizon. From a forward-looking perspective, the Holy Alliance is

FIGURE 27. Holy Alliance *Beaker*, ca. 1815. German. Metropolitan Museum.

shorthand for proving the illiberal character of the project of peacemaking European statesmen had in mind. It also links the end of the Napoleonic wars to the enduring Christian bias of a European-made international order. As historians usually end up discovering, the past is a complex place.

To begin with, the Holy Alliance was not a political aberration. If religion did not always determine foreign policies in predictable ways, it riddled the connective tissue of politics within and external to states. The last European battle over religious sovereignty per se, between Russia and the Ottomans, ended in 1784. Thirty years later, abolition of the slave trade and Jewish rights were accepted as legitimate concerns for peacemaking on the grounds of specifically "Christian Charity," as well as "Justice" and "Peace."[2] In an era when the integration of church and state remained a critical foundation of sovereign legitimacy, monarchical *Divine* right was manifest in the framing of the 1814 French Charter and in the roles taken by monarchs as heads of state religions, whether the Church of England or the Russian Orthodox Church.

When Castlereagh and Metternich among others denounced the Holy Alliance as an eccentrically religious rather than political idea, they alerted Europeans to alternative ways of imagining the politics between states, and what it was for. At the same time, they saw no inconsistency in signing peace treaties that invoked the protection and legitimacy of a Christian god. Christianity was a defining characteristic of the ideal of European fraternity, evoking a "general romantic concept of a Europe that should be united by allegiance to a common Christian faith."[3] In 1814 and after, both mainstream and alternative religious sects left their marks on attitudes toward the peacemaking agenda: Quakers worked to impose the slave trade debate on the postwar order; Jewish families pursued religious rights whether by petitioning or bribes. These are useful examples of how the politics of religion did not simply manifest as the antithesis of secular or Enlightenment or even revolutionary values. The signatures of the state representatives of three different Christian faiths—Protestant, Catholic, and Orthodox—that legitimated the Holy Alliance treaty referenced a "Whole Plan of Universal Peace" and echoed earlier Christian-inflected plans for world peace, even Metternich's secular thinking on the "society of states."

The detail of how religion was woven into the practices of a European-cum-international politics in this period helps us tease out the relevance of the Holy Alliance idea, but it also raises questions.[4] Is religion just "there," or does its controversial status reflect the transformations of politics taking place? Is the Holy Alliance evidence of attempts by imperial powers to control the civilizational borders of a Europe-centered international order on Christian grounds? Did religion matter to the constitution of a *European* international politics?

The Politics of the Holy Alliance

At the end of the Napoleonic wars, the significance of religion was on prominent display in everyday devotional practices and incorporated into the performance of peacemaking and the sociability of European society—despite the fractures among the Coalition powers' Christian communities. Not long after the Coalition forces arrived as conquerors in Paris in April 1814, the Russian tsar celebrated Mass for Easter Sunday on Place de la Concorde with his troops.[5] At Vienna, there were regular church services for various Christian denominations, a Greek Orthodox wedding, and a Catholic funeral for the Prince de Ligne.

For non-state actors, religion offered a method of opposition to the European political status quo. In Vienna, the state-regulated religious services that punctuated diplomacy and sociability competed with the impromptu fire-and-brimstone performances of the Prussian preacher-mystic Zacharias Werner, a man in his mid-fifties whose rhetoric attracted immense crowds. Through the weeks and months of congressing, Werner rebuked the immorality of the goings-on and spoke to the uneasy feelings of onlookers, many of whom were deeply invested in state religions.[6] Roxandra Stourdza—the empress of Russia's lady-in-waiting and sister to the tsar's advisor Alexander Stourdza—went to hear Werner out of curiosity and left converted. While she could not remember exactly what he said, Werner's speech was "vulgar" and "bizarre," but its effect was sweet and profound. He made her weep. So strong was her feeling that she felt in the presence of a divine love.[7]

Werner's personal popularity was indicative of interest in religious sects in Europe, from Britain to Russia. Some sects had emerged in the second half of the eighteenth century among Protestant and Orthodox Christian communities. The methodism of Joanna Southcott in England echoed in the Masonic societies of northern and western Europe; the Talmudism of Jewish communities spread through the Baltic; Lutheran, Orthodox, Moravian, and pietist cults were prominent in Switzerland, Prussia, Holland, Denmark, and Sweden. The confabulations of Lavateriens, Illuministes, and Swedenborgians melded with the supernatural promises of science-based experimentation.[8] Greek Orthodox Roxandra

Stourdza was excited by the pseudoscience of animal magnetism as much as Werner's version of pietism. Often regarded as subversive by sovereign governments, the political contours of these religious groupings were sometimes blurry. The Duchess of Sagan turned to mesmerists to cure her migraines, much to the mirth of the cynical Metternich. Mesmerists were also believed by some to be behind the Holy Alliance text itself.

By 1815, when it came to the influence of religion on politics, there was, as Germaine de Staël noted, something in the air.[9] At one of the banker Herz's dinners at the Congress of Vienna, Wellington, Castlereagh, Metternich, and Talleyrand sat alongside devout Enlightenment thinkers such as Dorothea Mendelssohn (a Catholic convert and the ex-wife of a Prussian banker) and her new husband, Friedrich von Schlegel (the brother of Staël's children's tutor August). Mendelssohn and Schlegel were there to help draft the Austrian version of a German constitution. That version, presented to the commission on German questions in March 1815, specified the "benefit of religious liberty," so that "the Israelites also . . . shall receive complete civil rights."[10] Watching the congress from a distance, the German Danish writer Frederike Brun—the estranged wife of the financier Johan Christian Constantin Brun—promoted Christianity as the antidote to blind nationalism and partisanship. Brun ran a salon in Copenhagen and Rome and regularly corresponded with Caroline von Humboldt and Staël in regard to peacemaking. She held the view that Protestantism was the religion of liberty and that Christ was against "exclusionary pride of country" and in favor of "openminded consciousness of the citizen of the world."[11]

Staël, a Protestant living in a predominantly Catholic country, was inclined to think of the Holy Alliance treaty as the tsar's attempt to defend religious tolerance. From her perspective, the tsar's text was in keeping with the political sympathies of the man she had believed in since 1812 as a liberal leader. The Holy Alliance, she argued, was a consequence of Alexander's embrace of "intimate religion," reuniting "what is good in Catholicism and Protestantism and which completely separates religion from the political influence of the priests."[12] It connected the desire for the "noble perfection of humankind" and "representative government!"[13] She explained her view in September 1815: "I have no need to tell you that liberty and religion stand in my thoughts—enlightened religion, liberty with justice: it is the end, it is the way."[14]

The urgency of Staël's praise for Alexander and his Holy Alliance idea was prompted by postwar episodes of religious intolerance. Staël was painfully aware that Protestants were being murdered in riots in the French *midi* and that the government, overseen by a Coalition administration, had failed to respond. Similarly, while in newly liberated parts of the former Holy Roman Empire Jews were subject to intensified attacks and discrimination, official resolution of their rights remained in abeyance. The fire of religious dissension was on display in the diplomatic corps itself, in the narrowed versions of Christian Europeanism of Joseph Le Maistre, a Piedmont-Sardinian ambassador and so-called father of conservatism, and Francois-René Chateaubriand, who sold a view of Christianity as "the most poetic, the most human, the most favourable towards liberty" of all the religions that had existed and the foundation of an enduring superior anti-revolutionary culture.[15] For the Russian advisor Alexander Stourdza, the Holy Alliance would sustain the Orthodox Eastern Church led by the Russian tsar.[16] Stourdza shared with his sister Roxandra and her friend Madame de Krüdener an "idealist vision of politics, grounded in the values of Christian fraternity."[17] Only a few months after the Holy Alliance declaration, Alexander Stourdza was the orchestrator of growing religious intolerance in Russia that led to the expulsion of Jesuits.

In 1815, the treaty of the Holy Alliance was perceived as either a threat to a conservative Christianity and state-based Christian institutions or contiguous with Coalition ambitions for a European peace based on fraternity and religious tolerance. The tsar's original version of the Holy Alliance treaty echoed many of the Chaumont- and Vienna-linked precepts of living "as brothers, not in enmity and malice, but in peace and love."[18] Anecdotal reports of Alexander talking of "little else during the journey from Frankfurt to Paris, in July 1815, than Castlereagh's own idea for a public declaration drafted 'by all the signatories to the effect that the general settlement will be upheld'" suggest that the echoes were deliberate. As the Coalition reassembled in Paris in order to conference the fate of France after their second defeat of Bonaparte at

Waterloo, Alexander told Castlereagh the fundamental idea of this declaration "had never passed from his mind."[19] The British prime minister was told the same by Castlereagh, who described the tsar's attribution of inspiration for the Holy Alliance treaty as "a Project of Declaration, with which I proposed the Congress [of Vienna] should Close, and which the Sovereigns there solemnly to pledge themselves in the face of the World to preserve to their People the Peace they had conquered and to treat as a Common Enemy whatever Power should violate it."[20]

It is perhaps most realistic to see in the tsar's version of the Holy Alliance a confirmation of multiple objectives: an attempt to consolidate the "indissoluble bonds" of Chaumont; a kind of soother to the rancorous disagreements at the Congress of Vienna. His effort was not completely in vain. All the Coalition powers except Britain signed the treaty. To the extent that the Catholic pope refused to sign it was because the Holy Alliance was too ecumenical in its Christian outlook, and *he* did not want to be associated with "heretics."[21] Two republics, Switzerland and America, were less cynical. Switzerland signed on, and although the American government eventually declined, it was "without any great show of horror," and the local press "was at first inclined to applaud its religious tone."[22]

In the circumstances, if the tsar was guilty of any miscalculation, it was his misreading of the extent of the Coalition allies' discomfort with his own authority. For those already suspicious of the tsar as a cultural, political, and religious outsider—including as the head of the Russian Orthodox Church and a feudal empire—the proposed Holy Alliance was one more example of his presumptions. Enemies depicted the Holy Alliance text as a rude intervention in the new politics, a manifestation of the tsar's overly emotional feminized self, attested to by his susceptibility to women and emotion. Castlereagh famously preferred to judge the tsar's "Whole Plan of Universal Peace" as "sublime mysticism and nonsense" and the tsar himself of "not Completely sound mind."[23] Austrian emperor Franz and Prussian king Friedrich Wilhelm balked at the representation of their unity, as if the subjects of the three powers would "see each other as fellow-countrymen" and their armies as "part of one army."[24]

The alliance powers made sure to modify the text, although without challenging its Christian undertones. They substituted the tsar's reference to "a single people designated a Christian nation" with "a single Christian people." Instead of representing their Christian affinity with Russia as "three sectors of this one people," they proposed "three branches of a single family."[25] Metternich dismissed the treaty as a "useless scheme," "nothing more than a philanthropic aspiration clothed in a religious garb, which supplied no material for a treaty between the monarchs, and which contained many phrases that might even have given occasion to religious misconstructions."[26] Yet he too bothered to edit the text, first, for the liberal implications of its rhetorical extension of fraternity to the *populations* of the signatory sovereigns, and second, for its implicit positioning of the non-Christian world. He began by deleting the tsar's reference to "the true principles" on which political relations between European powers should be based to ensure "the tranquility and prosperity of peoples."[27] The final version tempered the assertion that only "the precepts of this holy faith" could guide "the will of the monarchs directly and govern all their actions," as well as the directive requiring the "form of mutual relations" between the powers to be "*based on* the supreme truths inspired by the eternal law of the Divine Savior."[28] This became the more nuanced imperative—"*subject to* the supreme truths inspired by the eternal law of the Divine Savior."

The circulated final version of the Holy Alliance treaty still troubled contemporaries, many of whom could not agree on what the text meant, stood for, or intended. The French publicist Abbé Dominique de Pradt bemoaned its replacement of a European concert ascendant on "the principle of diplomacy by conference" with "the apocalypse of diplomacy."[29] Pradt vented his concerns that the secular state-based foundations of the new politics were being undermined. The Holy Alliance not only muddied the waters of political intentions and objectives at the time; it has since acted as a kind of cultural Rorschach test that everyone reads differently and that reflects the spectrum of interests and expectations invested in the new European international order. Its place in this international history underscores the difficulty of establishing the terms for the politics between states, among communities and individuals with so many positions on how the future should look and the extent to which the past could be shaken off.

Intolerance

At the dawn of a new era of international politics, as commercial and trading interests continued to determine membership and authority in an evolving international order, Metternich's fear was in part that the Holy Alliance privileged Christian relationships at the expense of treaty relations between European and Ottoman polities. These relations profited Europeans operating in the farther shores of the Ottoman-ruled Mediterranean, offering them reduced duty rates and fees in comparison with the costs of trade imposed on other countries as well as on local Muslim subjects. While the standing of Europeans was not constant across time or different imperial policies, ostensibly Christian commercial companies and traders had accrued substantial privileges from treaties with the Muslim empire. Over centuries, these agreements had allowed British, French, Genoese, and Spanish traders to establish themselves in foreign concessions in the ports of eastern Algeria and northwestern Tunisia. European companies could bank on "reserved markets" in these European "enclaves" and military forts.[30] Indeed, in 1792 Austria felt comfortable enough with its commercial relationship with the Ottomans that it renewed an agreement that would protect Austrian shipping in the Mediterranean from piracy by putting the Austrian flag "under the commandment of the Sultan, which meant that if a ship would be taken, the Sultan would arrange for reclamations from his North African vassals."[31] The benefit was mutual in more ways than one; Ottoman Regencies based in Algiers, Tunis, and Tripoli gained regular income and access to arms and shipbuilding materials.

At the end of the Napoleonic wars, this longer history of commercial arrangements in law bolstered the status of the Ottoman Empire as important to the future of European security, and even to the equilibrium between the European powers. If, for example, Russia was to fulfill a long-held ambition to expand south into the profitable trading arena of the Black Sea at the expense of the Ottoman Empire, then other European powers could be at a commercial disadvantage. Against this background, it is not surprising to see how, in the early days of postwar diplomacy, the attitudes of some statesmen to religious questions were decided by an almost reflex economic conditioning.

Existing treaties between European powers and the Ottomans also kept blurred economic and political sovereignty in tension with religious imperatives. The 1784 Treaty of Küçük Kaynarca had given Russia the right to protect Orthodox Christians on its southern border in the unstable Ottoman region of Bessarabia. This was where families such as the Stourdzas came from, benefiting from their status as "the most privileged Christian denomination."[32] The region's diaspora or expatriate population—including the Stourdzas—sought commercial and government career opportunities in the court of the tsar. In 1812, just prior to the French invasion of Russia, the Ottoman Empire had been forced by a Russian military campaign to cede sections of lower Danube land, but Orthodox Christians from the rest of the region and other parts of the Ottoman Empire continued to seek the protection of the Russian emperor.

The legacies of Christian Europe's relationship with the Muslim Ottoman Empire were made apparent at the Congress of Vienna by the arrival of a Serbian Orthodox priest named Matija Nenadovic. The priest had traveled over more than four and a half days from Belgrade to Vienna to alert the gathered diplomats that "Turks" were plundering, enslaving, impaling, and hanging Serbs in Ottoman lands. Nenadovic sought some forms of diplomatic intervention from "all the Christian rulers and allies." He hoped they could "reconcile the Serbian people with the Sultan" and encourage the sultan to act toward Serbs "as towards his subjects and not as if they were victims."[33] The peace negotiators' unenthusiastic response is indicative of the European powers' commercial concerns. Some diplomats stalled by advising Nenadovic to add more Russian words to his petition if he wanted to capture the tsar's interest or, alternatively, to produce a German version for (the German-speaking) Russian plenipotentiary Count Nesselrode. Eventually, after Nenadovic added Latin and English translations, a few Russian diplomats agreed to send a memorandum of Serb complaints on the status of Christians in the Ottoman Empire to the congress at large.[34] The response was still lukewarm; any sympathy for the Serbian community was overridden by support for the existing "terms of close friendship with the Ottoman Porte."[35] Metternich accused the Belgrade pro-Serbian authorities for mistreating locally resident Habsburg subjects, listing illegal arrests, fines, beatings, and killings.

At Vienna, the political demands of Orthodox Greek Ottoman subjects competed with the prioritizing of commercial relations with the Ottoman Empire. Bilateral commercial relations were not enough to grant the Ottomans equal status at the congress, but the potential threat that challenging Ottoman sovereignty posed to the multilateral relations of the Europeans themselves held sway. Eventually, it took less than a decade for the "Greek question" to break up the Coalition and recast the tenor of the Concert of Europe. However, in 1814, Europe's empires met Greek complaints with skepticism. This stance required them to ignore a growing European vogue for philhellenism based on fascination with the ancient world as the origin of European civilization. Germaine de Staël had talked of going to Greece to write, and the English poet Byron was among the most high-profile of philhellenes; Byron's cousin, Châtillon alumnus and British ambassador to the Habsburg court Lord Aberdeen, had helped Elgin remove the Parthenon marbles and founded the London Athenian society. Significantly, Aberdeen's philhellenism was not driven by any idealization of modern Greeks, whom he described to Castlereagh as "a bastard and a mongrel breed, derived from many sources, Romans, Sclavonians, Gauls and Catalans, and others: they have little connection with the ancient Greeks in blood, and still less in mind, being in fact as contemptible for their vices as for their lofty pretensions." He insisted that Greeks did not share "our views of preserving the tranquility of Europe . . . our love of peace, in the blessing of which they have no share whatever." The saving grace of Ottoman Greeks was their Christian character, which rendered them, according to Lord Aberdeen, "capable of improvement" and deserving of the empathy of "every man of common humanity" with "the feelings of the Greeks themselves" and "a struggle to which nothing in the civilized world can present the least analogy."[36]

Although the "Greek question" was not taken up at the Congress of Vienna officially, its future diplomatic influence was seeded there. Anna Eynard-Lullin recalled a dinner at the British diplomat Stratford Canning's where she listened to an English colonel "who had lived in Greece for five years forming four indigenous regiments." The colonel related his ambition to "train these men who wore *des tuniques, des cuirasses et des casques* to defend their liberty from Turkish attack; these Greeks had the bearing of their ancient ancestors and believed in the supremacy of their nation." That is where the conversation ended, however, since "the etiquette of Society required a polite shift of conversation."[37] Eynard-Lullin did not mention she had access to other sources of information when it came to the Greek cause.

Eventually, it was the philhellenism of her husband, Jean-Gabriel Eynard, that would change the fate of the Greeks. Monsieur Eynard discovered "Greece" through his friend Kapodistrias, the Russian diplomat of Corfu origin who would go on to become the first Greek president. They had met in Geneva while Kapodistrias was Coalition emissary sent to resolve the question of Swiss federation. At the Congress of Vienna, Eynard visited the residence of Kapodistrias's close friends the Stourdzas. There, together with Ignatius, the former bishop of the Bessarabian territory of Moldavia and Wallachia, they established a local branch of the Philomousos Eteria of Vienna (Vienna Society of the Friends of the Muses) on the model of an Athens-based organization that furnished assistance "to the poor young Hellenes thirsty for education."[38] Their intention was to fund Greek students who studied abroad and the protection of Greek antiquities. Roxandra Stourdza wrote in her memoirs that Kapodistrias had told her of "a sweeping plan that he would soon announce to me, and in which he asked me to take a leading part. . . . I answered him not with my lips, but with my eyes. My voice was choked with emotion." Roxandra's role, as Elisavet Papalexopoulou writes, was to oversee the finances of the secret society and prise donations from the tsar and his wife, and Metternich, using a diplomacy of sorts to get Greeks recognized in the "ranks of civilisation."[39]

These efforts to support Greeks were not yet focused on the creation of a Greek nation-state. Kapodistrias himself was more interested in his native island Corfu becoming part of a Septinsular Republic on an existing French template. Instead, much to his chagrin, at Vienna, Corfu and the Ionian islands of which it was a

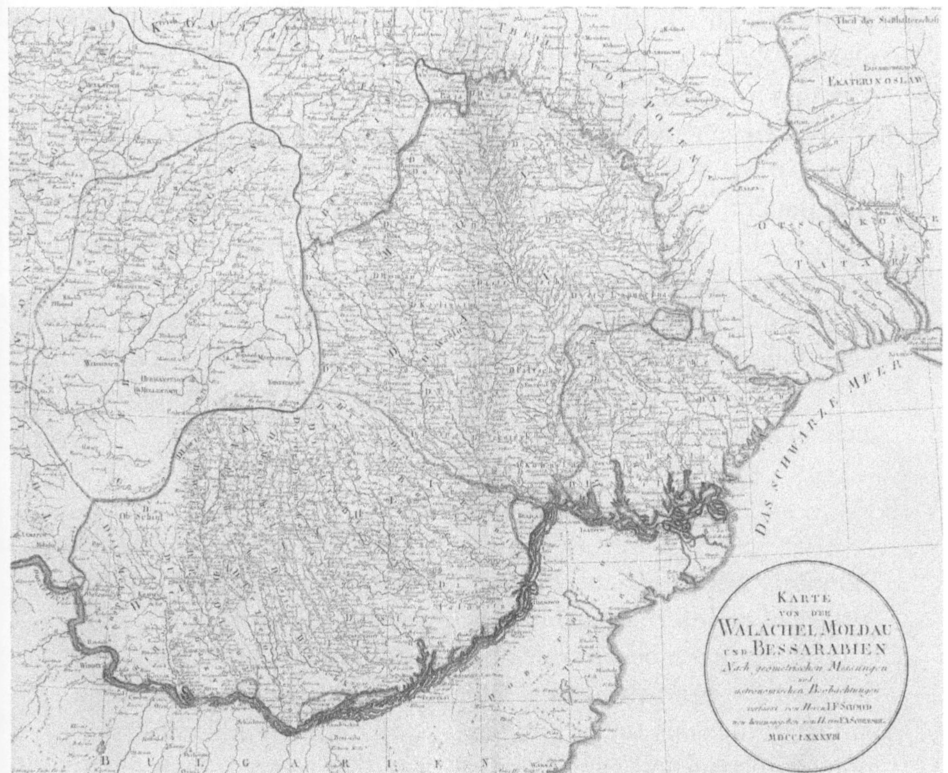

FIGURE 28. Black Sea region. Anton Schraembl, *Map of Wallachia, Moldova and Bessarabia* (Vienna: Joseph Philipp Schalbacher, 1800). © David Rumsey Map Collection.

part were given over to Britain under the loose legal conditions of "protectorate." Kapodistrias harbored equally adventurous plans to federate the Bessarabian principalities that counted Greek and Serbian Orthodox populations across Russian and Ottoman borders. His idea was that they should remain under Turkish suzerainty and have their autonomy guaranteed by the European powers. Again, his plans gained no traction. At the end of 1815, the Austrian secret police was accusing Russia of promoting Serbian and Greek dissension in order to undermine the Ottoman Empire (contra to both the tsar's and Metternich's policy priorities). By this time too, the Protestant Jean-Gabriel Eynard's friendship with Kapodistrias and his visits to the Stourdzas' had inspired him to personally support the religious rights of Orthodox Greeks as an intertwined religious, moral, and political European imperative.

In 1814, Greek allegations of religious discrimination at Ottoman hands did not translate into a multilateral policy question. The rejection by Europe's statesmen of the Holy Alliance treaty fits here as part of a general rejection of the politics of Christianity—at least where it had potential commercial implications or might unbalance the Concert, or bolster the tsar's authority. While the outcome temporarily suited the Ottoman government, the sultanate also understood that in this new self-consciously Christian Europe its sovereignty remained vulnerable. The point was proven when the Coalition powers turned their attention to the problems of piracy and white slavery and pondered the defense of Christians for commercial as well as religious reasons.

Religious principles and imperatives sit like a carbuncle on the surface of an international history conventionally told as the story of progress to a modern "rules-based" politics and diplomacy. Evidence of the pervasiveness of Christianity in postwar politics and culture returns us to the significance of the Holy Alliance's religious emphasis and what the history of that treaty reveals about the political culture being shaped at the end of the Napoleonic wars. We have seen that, in Europe, Christianity was a normative condition of political legitimacy. Indeed, within a few weeks of the signing of the Holy Alliance, a second more successful treaty was drafted that also evoked religion as the basis of the confraternity of the Coalition partners. The "Quadruple Alliance" treaty was a British initiative released simultaneously with the terms of the second Treaty of Paris, on 20 November 1815. It was signed by Great Britain and Austria, Russia, and Prussia (as a series of bilateral agreements), "in the name of the most holy and undivided Trinity." It diverged from the Holy Alliance only by adding a new more political emphasis on both "Royal Authority" and "the Constitutional Charter."[40]

Like the Holy Alliance, the Quadruple Alliance called yet again for conferences to be held periodically in the spirit of Chaumont, "to facilitate and to secure the execution of the present Treaty," "common interests," "measures . . . the most salutary for the repose and prosperity of The Nations, and for the maintenance of the Peace of Europe."[41] It repeated the convention that "the Repose of Europe" was "*essentially interwoven*" with the existing "order of things." In effect, it was a more ideologically conservative document than the tsar's version. Repose was "the object of the wishes of mankind" and required resistance of the "Revolutionary Principles" that had given scope to Bonaparte and convulsed France. Alongside "concert among themselves," military measures now overruled spiritual adhesion as a means of ensuring solidarity. The Quadruple Alliance invested in the ongoing occupation of France by allied troops and the restatement of the Chaumont principles of military and financial support should France attack any one of them, estimating "Sixty Thousand Men, in addition to the forces left in France," and more if necessary. The Coalition empires reserved to themselves "the right to prescribe, by common consent, such Conditions of Peace as shall hold out to Europe a sufficient Guarantee against the recurrence of a similar calamity."

The rejection of the Holy Alliance and its replacement with the Quadruple Alliance effectively marked the marginalization of the tsar, even though he was consistently the most vocal and determined supporter of the Chaumont-based principle of fraternity and purpose. Alexander persisted through this period of "Concert," until the mid-1820s, in putting the ideals of a European order before the traditional interests of Russian foreign policy. This included rejecting the opportunity that repeatedly presented of using religion as an excuse for commercial expansion into long-desired Ottoman territory. While Alexander Stourdza questioned the ability of large conferences to settle problems, the tsar continued to believe in them.[42]

Staël went so far as to attribute the tsar's motivations in proposing the Holy Alliance to his "liberal ideals": "I wish, with all my heart," she wrote, "for all that can raise up this man, who appears to me to be a miracle of Providence, to save liberty which is threatened from all quarters."[43] The Quadruple Alliance gave authority over the definition of liberty to the four powers, not just the tsar. The tsar might have taken comfort in the Quadruple Alliance agreement's reassertion of the importance of Christianity in support of "the Happiness of the World" and a commitment "to renew their meetings at fixed periods." Those "European Councils" included meetings of ministers, or more lowly diplomats, "for the purpose of consulting upon their common interests."[44] Those same conditions marked the tsar's point of vulnerability, namely his reputation for listening to women outside of such formal structures and practices. In this case, the woman whose feelings mattered was Madame de Krüdener, as the other members of the Quadruple Alliance charged.

CHAPTER TWELVE

Christianity

Madame de Krüdener has passed through here. I saw her once and did not care to repeat my visit. She said publicly that it was she who made the Holy Alliance, that the Emperor is the elect of God, and that the Turks will overwhelm Europe.

—ROXANDRA STOURDZA TO KAPODISTRIAS, 1817

Madame de Krüdener, que j'ai beaucoup connue, était à Paris. Elle avait passé du roman au mysticisme; elle exercait un grand empire sur l'esprit de l'Empereur Alexandre.

—CHATEAUBRIAND, *MÉMOIRES D'OUTRE-TOMBE*

MADAME DE KRÜDENER—ALSO KNOWN as Baroness or Frau von Krüdener—is one of the few women who retains her place in mainstream narratives of international politics. When she is remembered by historians, she survives as a narrative device, an emblem of the Eastern origins of irrationalism, where the East extends from Russia to the Ottoman Empire.[1] In 1815 and after, attacks on her as "an old Fanatick" contribute to a common conceit that renders Russia and religious women threats to a secular, professional ideal of political culture and to the statesmen's fraternity. Persistent criticism of the tsar's propensity to talk with and listen to women is lumped in with his interest in "Frau von Krüdener," a "teacher of mystical theology," who is, in turn, indicative of his "deeply religious" turn from championing liberalism to spiritual redemption. Through the latter half of 1815, Metternich rehearses

FIGURE 29. Friedrich Wilhelm Meyer the Elder, *Portrait of Barbara Juliane von Krüdener (1764–1824)*. Private collection © Alamy.

the rumors that Gentz helps circulate and that Castlereagh confirms: it is Krüdener who turns the tsar toward her "aventure mystique" and "this loud-sounding nothing" that is the treaty of the Holy Alliance.[2]

Born a Lutheran in the Baltic regions of the Russian empire, Krüdener is drawn to pietism, and more specifically *illuminisme*, a mysticism of the highest order. This chapter parses the details of Krüdener's life, her roles in the months leading up to the drafting of the Holy Alliance, and the historically specific religious sensibility and political motivations of the tsar himself. Does "Madame de Krüdener" determine the course of European history and the international past, or does she count as a historical red herring? Does it matter that Krüdener is convinced of her powers to channel communication with God, or that she is eager to persuade others that her destiny is to convert humankind? Should we be as convinced of those powers? Does she render asunder what a group of men has forged together? The history of Krüdener and the tsar returns us to the controversies that surround women's agency in the invention of international order, in the context of the structural shifts in gender, class, cultural, and religious norms that knit the politics between states into its modern versions.

A Man's Feelings

On 9 June 1815, Madame de/Baroness von Krüdener and her entourage—a teenage daughter Juliette, future son-in-law Monsieur de Berckheim, and the Genevan pastor Henri-Louis Empaytaz—find themselves in the small town of Heilbronn, on the Neckar river, in the Kingdom of Württemberg. This is the heart of the Romantic Black Forest region, now filled with the noise and dirt of 10,000 Coalition troops riding and marching to Waterloo, 500 kilometers away. They are headed there to fight a Napoleon-led French army once more, after Bonaparte's brief usurpation of Louis XVIII's throne.

Even as the head of the Russian Orthodox Church, Alexander is religiously curious. He gives favor to the spiritualist Russian Biblical Society, founded in 1812 on the principle of Christian ecumenicalism. His correspondence with Grand-Duchess Ekaterina Pavlovna in 1813 indicates that they are together responsible for having the texts of Swiss pietist Johann Georg Muller translated into Russian.[3] In the siblings' travels between the Paris and Vienna conferences, Alexander and Ekaterina seek out Quakers in London, Moravians in Holland, and a Carmelite convent in Prague. The head of the Russian Orthodox Church thinks of all of these people as members of his wider religious circle. Many of these religious groups represent movements for political reform—or as

Alexander's biographers acknowledge, religion "was no mere fig leaf for reaction, nor was it a doctrine of quietists' escapism; instead it frequently served as a guide to reformist activism."[4] We can also say that, at this stage, Alexander seems unconcerned by the political overtones of his religious ecumenicalism.

By the time Krüdener arrives in Heilbronn in 1815, the enthusiastic tsar, his foreign minister Ioannes Kapodistrias, advisor Baron vom Stein, and former tutor Fréderic La Harpe are already encamped in the Rauch'sche Palais in the nearby town of Heidelberg.[5] Krüdener has made the journey on the tsar's invitation. The meeting so overwhelms the tsar that he reports the encounter in emotional detail to the devout Roxandra Stourdza, lady-in-waiting to his wife, Empress Elizabeth, who first introduces him to Krüdener's prophecies. Several months earlier, Krüdener predicted that 1815 will be awful, that Napoleon will escape, wreak vengeance, and the "Bourbon lilies" will fall, *and* that the tsar "will accomplish great things, and guilty France will be chastised"—all of which seem to have passed![6]

When the tsar meets Krüdener, the first part of her prophecy has already come true. As he records for Stourdza's benefit, he is filled with anticipation about his own role in its fulfillment:

> I breathed freely at last, and my first resource was to take a book I always carry with me, but my mind, overcast by dark clouds, did not readily imbibe the meaning of what I read. My ideas were confused and my heart oppressed. I let the book fall, thinking "What a consolation to me at such a moment the talk of a pious friend would have been." The thought made me remember you I recalled also what you said to me about Mme. Krüdener, and my having expressed to you the desire to make her acquaintance. Where can she be now, and how can I ever meet her? Scarcely had I uttered this notion when I heard a knocking at my door. It was Prince Volkonsky, who, with an air of the greatest impatience, told me that he was disturbing me much against his will at that unearthly hour, but it was to appease a woman who was firmly bent on seeing me. At the same time he gave me Mme. Krüdener's name. You can imagine my surprise. I thought I was dreaming. "Mme. Krüdener! Mme. Krüdener" cried I! Such a prompt answer to my thought could not be mere chance. I saw her on the spot, and, as

> if she had read my soul, she plied me with some brave and consoling words which appeased the trouble I had been a victim to for so long.[7]

The diary kept by Krüdener's daughter Juliette corroborates the tsar's starstruck tone.[8] Secondhand accounts sympathetic to Krüdener have her holding forth for three hours and the tsar sitting "for the most part in rapt attention, the tears streaming down his cheeks."[9] Krüdener's group moves closer to the tsar's Heidelberg camp and "for several weeks they continued their devotional meetings." Alexander comes "usually late at night and staying sometimes until two o'clock in the morning." Stein, Kapodistrias, and La Harpe witness these meetings and claim politics is never discussed. Instead, the tsar fills himself "with the divine life."[10]

A week later British and Prussian-led forces defeat the escaped Bonaparte and his army at the Battle of Waterloo. As the allies reassemble in Paris to discuss the terms of a new peace agreement with France, Krüdener is there at the tsar's request, bearing a Russian passport organized especially. The two continue to write to each other, rehearsing the theme of the tsar's "special election" as the leader of the transformation of Europe. Krüdener sees her role as giving "religious consolation to the heads of the coalition." Whether the heads want that consolation is another matter. From the perspective of the other Coalition sovereigns and their ministers, the tsar has overstayed his welcome as the "saviour of Europe."[11] By the time the tsar announces the treaty of the Holy Alliance in the midst of negotiations for the second Paris treaty between the Coalition and France, Krüdener is viewed as a malevolent figure, poisoning the future of diplomacy with fake religious witness and elevation of the tsar.

A Woman's Politics

To many observers, Krüdener's place in this history of religion and politics could not have been predicted. The Catholic French writer and diplomat Comte de Chateaubriand knows her as *both* "Madame de Krüdener *worldly*, and . . . devout," and in each guise he finds her icy.[12] In the nineteenth century, her intriguing life draws the attention of biographers who declare the subtlety and rapidity "with which she rose from evil to good, from the merest worldliness to the highest religious aspirations, and to some of the most noble of religious virtues, self-denial and charity, are such as to (almost) baffle analysis."[13] There are two Madame de Krüdeners: the young ambitious worldly *ambassadrice* and the pious "Livonian Sybil."

Krüdener's presentation as two different people is hardly relieved by the inconsistent double details about her life. She is born in either the 1760s or the 1770s, her age at marriage is either fourteen or eighteen. Even her name and maiden name come in at least two forms, Barbara Julianne von Wietinghoff and Vietinghof. Her Baltic birthplace, Riga, has historically changed identities: at the time part of Livonia, now Estonia. The family are Lutheran, although the father is also, in the fashion of the time, a Teutonic knight who goes into commerce and becomes a Freemason.[14] In all these ways, Krüdener is typical of the lived cosmopolitanism of the period, its relatively mobile and unbounded forms of identification and attachment, at least among the upper classes.

With all the advantages available to a daughter of wealthy and influential landowners, Krüdener has no formal education but indulges French literature and fashion.[15] She is a baroness by virtue of marrying a significantly older (Leipzig-born) Russian diplomat, Baron von Krüdener. Marriage makes her yet another *ambassadrice* with access to diplomatic networks (her son Paul will become a diplomat). Despite the vast geographical and ideological distances separating the women in this international history, the connections between them occur at almost every turn, and not always through diplomatic networks. Krüdener's wedding takes place in what was still the Duchy of Courland in possession of Sagan's father. Baron von Krüdener is Russian minister to Courland and negotiator of the territory's return to the Russian Crown—which leads to the Courland family's move to central Europe and purchase of the Duchy of Sagan. As a young *ambassadrice*, Baroness von Krüdener entertains Tsar Paul and meets the seven-year-old Tsar Alexander. When her husband is posted to Venice, she joins diplomatic circles that include Emma Hamilton, an English *ambassadrice* who rises from prostitution to marry the British ambassador resident in Naples.[16]

In the magical, dangerous year of 1789, the still young Baroness von Krüdener rebels, shucking off her conventional life. She sets out for Paris leaving behind her husband, a daughter, and a son. In the French capital, she ventures into the salon circuit and begins to write, openly competing with Germaine de Staël to the extent of seeking out the men who are the object of her rival's affections. When Staël goes to Coppet, Krüdener follows her. Installed in Geneva, Krüdener has a mesmerist work on her nerves using bleedings and a diet of Epsom salts and asses' milk. She begins composing a novel, *Valerie*, her female version of Goethe's *Werther*, and her stab at literary fame. She hopes in this way to garner for herself some of Staël's celebrity.[17] When Staël leaves Coppet to return to Paris in late 1801, Krüdener is soon on her trail.[18] Staël seems not to mind the emulation and introduces Krüdener to Benjamin Constant and the Catholic conservative Vicomte de Chateaubriand. The latter becomes Krüdener's close associate in the crucial years of congressing; both, in their own way, become spokespersons for connecting religion and foreign policy, although Chateaubriand stands for a conservative state-sanctioned Catholic Christianity, and Krüdener for the authority of individualist Christian epiphany.

Before her religious transformation, Krüdener lives her life in stark contrast to the spiritual role she assumes in the Holy Alliance.[19] Most notably, there is the "hucksterism" surrounding her publication in 1804 of *Valerie*, which she markets with the sale of turbans and feathers.[20] Benjamin Constant's review is dismissive: if you take Chateaubriand and a couple of other writers, slice up their works, and reassemble the pages in a sequential order, that is *Valerie*. Regardless, the novel becomes famous as a barely disguised reflection of Krüdener's own worldly life, including her affairs. The heroine Valerie, like Krüdener, has an illegitimate child, and her husband refuses to give her a divorce. Then suddenly, not long after the notoriety of *Valerie*, and in the wake of her real husband's death, Krüdener rebels again, this time against her impious past. She now commences a journey to religious "enlightenment."[21] Like other Lutherans, she is attracted to pietism, a mix of Catholicism and Protestantism, devoted to the Virgin Mary and veneration of the Cross. Among her influences are a peasant prophet named Adam Müller and an occult pietist Johann Heinrich Jung-Stilling.

In the spa town of Karlsruhe favored by Europe's monarchs, she lives in the abode of Jung-Stilling's family, trying out their Swedenborgian tendencies, meeting miracle workers and somnambulists.[22] The idyll does not last long, however, as the government perceives the populist practices of these various mystics and pietists to be fomenting revolution and forces the community to leave. In a period when poor harvests and rising food prices provoke social unrest, the small kingdom can barely tolerate an alternative church fomenting the grievances of its agricultural class.[23]

While the Coalition fights Bonaparte in these same regions, Krüdener consolidates her reputation as a mystic, a prophetess with popular Europe-wide appeal and roots in the cause of the common man. She is no longer the femme fatale of *Valerie*. She is thin-looking with a "blotched complexion, eyes red from weeping, hair severely parted in the middle, plain black silk dress, harsh manner."[24] Ernst Moritz Arndt observes her in Karlsruhe as still bearing great evidence of beauty but "suffused with the magical radiance of a yearning and penitent Magdalene." There is no cynicism to his remark. She does not convey "the impression of a hypocrite and an impostor," he confirms, "but rather of an enthusiast: she had the passionate and powerful charm of an inspired person."[25] For Tsar Alexander's secretary, Admiral Shishkov, his first impressions of "a very clear-sighted and gifted woman" quickly turn to criticism of her abandonment of "the sphere of reason for high-flying sophisms" and her display of "a confident exaltation and inspiration instead of meekness and piety."[26] Staël approves of this changed Krüdener as "a fore-runner of a new religious age which is coming for the human race."[27] Krüdener is no longer as captivated by Staël; she has remade herself as a leader chosen by Christ with the ability to predict events and, as she maintains, to cure the sick with her prayer.

In 1813, Krüdener's mystical version of pietism is connected with a combination of causes: support for peasant workers and the diplomacy of peacemaking. In particular, her anger at the French imprisonment of her son Paul turns her against Bonaparte. She returns to the Swiss canton of Basel to establish a band of young pietists with a Genevan minister known as Empaytaz. Together with the local peasants they agitate against the conditions of rural work. Inevitably, they find themselves once again expelled. In February 1814, as the Coalition contemplates a direct military assault on France, Krüdener is in Baden and meets for the first time Roxandra Stourdza, who becomes her link to the tsar.[28]

Like Staël, Krüdener regards the tsar as the savior of Europe—although she is less interested in him as a defender of liberalism than a symbol of "profound piety" who ascribes "credit to God for all his victories."[29] While the negotiations of the first Treaty of Paris are taking place in Paris, in May 1814, Krüdener is at Staël's salon bending ears in the interests of a spiritual peace. In Vienna a few months later, she works indirectly through Stourdza, who is able to make use of her role in the Russian empress's entourage and her brother Alexander in the tsar's diplomatic delegation. From her modest room on the fourth floor of the Austrian imperial palace, Roxandra writes to Jung-Stilling and Krüdener to discuss the tsar as the elect of God. If we can believe the rumors and police reports, the tsar willingly swallows the bait. Witnesses note that his "longest talks were with Miss Sturdza [*sic*], whose intelligent conversation, into which she skilfully mixed subtle flattery, seemed to keep his interest the most."[30] He regularly visits Stourdza's room in search of consolation, to discuss mystical questions, or to read Krüdener's letters for hours.[31]

What do religious souls want from peacemaking? At one level, they heap their ambitions on the moral temper of Europe. Like Roxandra Stourdza and other exceptional women of the time, Krüdener will claim "I never mix myself up in politics."[32] Yet she is political enough to not leave the outcome of the renewed battle against Bonaparte entirely in God's hands. She corresponds with Russian foreign policy advisors Alexander Stourdza, Baron vom Stein, and Kapodistrias and meets the emperor in Heilbronn. The climax of her religious ambition is still to come, as the Coalition renegotiates the Paris treaty. In September 1815, she is all for convincing the tsar to maintain Cossack troops in France to support Louis XVIII. She believes God has tasked her to tell the truth and to inspire a love of the truth in the tsar, and to humble the French to ask for forgiveness at the feet of the Cross that they have deserted by virtue of their secular political revolution.[33] Staël, who is aware that under Coalition administration the French government is undermining the constitution and curtailing religious and press freedoms, may have misread Krüdener's thinking. Physically removed from the center of diplomatic negotiations, Staël tries to use Krüdener's influence to defend France from being punished for Bonaparte's sins and to reinforce liberalism in post-Napoleonic Europe.[34]

As Europe's leaders once again meet in Paris to discuss a second peace with France, the talk is all about the sway of a mystic who holds religious gatherings, and not all of it is denigratory. The Coalition's victory at the Battle of Waterloo sets the scene for the embellishment of Krüdener's reputation as an oracle among a much wider circle of diplomatic and political elites. Krüdener arrives in the capital on 14 July 1815. She takes simply furnished rooms at 35 rue du Faubourg-Saint-Honoré, not far from Palais Élysée- Bourbon where the tsar is staying. In the Paris of salons (minus Staël's salon) she invites people to prayer.[35] Every evening at 7:00 p.m., her small drawing room hosts whoever can fit: the duc de Richelieu (Talleyrand's eventual replacement as French foreign minister), Chateaubriand, Constant, Stein, and the duchesse de Duras, among others. Constant—Staël's erstwhile collaborator in liberalism and father of her illegitimate daughter, Albertine—goes to Krüdener in search of solace after his failed attempts at kindling a romance with Juliette Recamier, Staël's famously beautiful best friend.[36] Constant tells Recamier that Krüdener "gave to the passing moment a certain quality of eternity."[37] Staël's future son-in-law, a committed liberal, Victor de Broglie, seeks religious sustenance too from Krüdener.

Some witnesses describe Krüdener's Paris evenings as akin to the "mysterious *soirées* of Cagliostro."[38] Empaytaz conducts the religious services, while Krüdener holds forth before smaller groups, expounding her doctrines, at times for hours. She has worked on her voice, transforming its tones from their natural harshness to a "melodious, flexible, gentle" flow.[39] It is inevitable that Krüdener's attention-seeking makes her susceptible to ridicule. Disbelievers allege that at one meeting she talks herself into a coma.[40] Another story has her accruing substantial debt as she travels spreading her religion; she is so engrossed in her mission that she loses track of her poor finances. When she remembers, she prays to God, who consoles her that it all will be fine.[41]

When Castlereagh famously reports to Whitehall on the influence of "an old Fanatick,"[42] the tsar has not yet lost faith in Krüdener. Like many of those in town for the conferencing, he visits her frequently, since he is able to come and go discreetly at will; the "Livonian Sybil" is given access to a regular Mass in his private chapel.[43] The relationship continues through the months of diplomatic deliberation. On the sunny Monday of 11 September 1815, Krüdener's place by the tsar's side is in ostentatious public view on the outskirts of Paris, on the Plain de la Vertus: they are observing the spectacle of Alexander's name day celebration, a theatrical review of Russian troops, to which has been added the attraction of "a special secret revelation."[44] One hundred fifty thousand men or more organize into seven squares, or as Krüdener describes, "seven altars," representing "the seven churches whom Jesus addresses in the first three chapters of the Apocalypse, promising 'grace . . . and peace from him which is, and which was, and which is to come, and from the seven spirits which are before his throne.'"[45] At Vertus, each altar is the site of a prayer service. The central (fourth) altar is reserved for the tsar's entire staff, his Russian generals, and Krüdener. Among the vast crowds are the tsar's Courland compatriots the Duchess of Sagan and her sister Dorothea. They follow the tsar and his accompanying officers, and the other sovereigns and princes, on horseback.[46] The hefty cost of the review, like the great French chef Carême's catering, is charged to the defeated French.[47]

After the fact of Krüdener's soft-power diplomacy, she becomes "the official interpreter of the symbolism of the celebration." Her pamphlet, *The Camp at Vertus*, plays on the idea of a "field of virtue." It is composed as the tsar deliberates the idea of a Holy Alliance treaty and is immediately translated into Russian by imperial order.[48] In this document Krüdener presents the tsar as "the man with a great destiny" "come out of the deserts of Asia" (she herself is sometimes fetishized as "asiatic" because of her Baltic origins).[49] In her account, the tsar celebrates the review as the most beautiful day of his life, his heart is full with love for his enemies, he prayed fervently for them all, and he wept at the feet of Christ for the health of France.[50]

If Krüdener's intention is to convince the tsar to keep her by his side, it works. Two weeks later, on 26 September 1815, when the text of the Holy Alliance is signed, Krüdener has the honor of a second review of Russian troops in celebration of the treaty.

Can we blame Krüdener after all for the Holy Alliance text? Is it Krüdener's idea in the beginning to bring together Europe's sovereigns in a declaration of Christian "sublime truths"? Does she even insist on her opinion? Given the tumultuous intersecting and competing strands of Christian thinking and organization, as well as the number of individuals who had a stake in these events, we would do well to heed the relative skepticism of Madame de Krüdener's biographers when it comes to the impact of her influence on diplomacy: her "association with the Treaty of Holy Alliance" was "incidental" rather than "determinative"; she "mirrored rather than directed the tendencies of an age."[51] Among those incidentals is the tsar's fascination with Krüdener's spiritualism. Then there is the draft of the treaty prepared with the assistance of Kapodistrias and Alexander Stourdza, which the tsar asks Krüdener and her companion Empaytaz to read carefully: "If there are any expressions in it of which you disapprove, inform me about this. I want the emperor of Austria and the king of Prussia to join me in this act of worship so that we, like the Magi of the East, recognize the higher power of God the Savior."[52] When the tsar negotiates some changes to the Holy Alliance text with Metternich, he invites Krüdener along, so as to convince Austria of the treaty's purpose—as an act of good faith they lay out four dinner settings, adding one for Christ.[53] Finally, there is the status the tsar bestows on Krüdener at the Paris conference, through his visits and the place she assumes at his name day celebrations.

We know that there is a longer, thicker history of ideas motivating the tsar, not least his admiration for Castlereagh's vision of a European confederacy. Then there are the various religious actors who may have influenced him. Mystics linked to Krüdener send a summary of their version of a federation anchored in Christian religion to the Russian, Austrian, and Prussian sovereigns. This pamphlet outlines the ideal state as "a community ruled by a universal, or Catholic, church," as a new Christian theocracy.[54] Alternatively, Beatrice de Graaf has noted the hold on the tsar and well-positioned French figures of the spiritualism of the Austrian physician-charlatan Franz Mesmer.[55]

Krüdener's distinctive place in the events of 1815 is symptomatic of a range of social disruptions, not least what one biographer describes as "the strong undercurrents of sentimentalism, pietism, and mysticism, and the growing forces of romanticism, which underlay the harsh actualities of diplomacy and war."[56] Her entanglement in the politics between states reflects the rise of alternative, non-state-based religions. When historians latch on to Krüdener as evidence of the abnormality of women and religion in the evolution of a Western, liberal, Enlightenment-inspired international order, not only do they ignore the importance of contingent social conditions, they are inclined to erase women's political ambitions. When we ignore Krüdener's political ambitions, we also let go of the rumble of class politics that disturbed the idea of order on a European and international scale.

In the wake of the Holy Alliance controversy, Krüdener will continue her attempts to curry favor with the tsar. She will write him a letter documenting her version of her political importance in 1815. Alexander ignores her; she is now considered a nuisance.[57] In Switzerland, as she calls "sinners to repentance, preaching, comforting, and relieving the crowds of famished poor, victims of the disastrous wars," her acts annoy local magistrates wary of her anarchic influence.[58] In Karlsruhe, where she returns in 1816 to hold a prayer meeting of (reputedly) a thousand people, the government of the Grand-Duchy of Baden quickly moves her on. Even though her son is the local plenipotentiary, and her son-in-law the minister, she has no power to stay.

We have already seen that there is more to the history of religion at this moment than the influence of an exceptional woman. The threat posed by religious sects to the status quo in an age in which the heads of church and government often overlapped is among the reasons that politicians such as Metternich placed pietists and secret societies in the same subversive category.[59] The illegitimacy of alternative Christianities brings Krüdener's influence to a halt in Russia, where religious nationalism begins to take hold. Our historical antenna should also be alert to the ways in which women's political engagement is consistently a point of controversy and misconception. Stirring a woman such as Krüdener back into this history helps us understand how contemporaries understood power and security as gendered dimensions of politics between states. When Tsar Alexander—the only monarch who participated directly in diplomatic negotiations—asks the Duchess of Sagan to be in Vienna when he arrives, she boasts to Frederick Lamb: "Aren't I a very important person?"[60] The Danish foreign minister, however, was apt to view this same tendency of confiding in "des dames" as a sign of the tsar's incompetency, and no less the shortcomings of his masculinity.[61]

In all these ways, Krüdener is no anomaly in this postwar history. The potency of accusations made against her and against the tsar because of his relationship with her is one more chapter in the consistent history of threat posed by women's alleged sexual power to a normative politics and the gender norms undergirding the political authority of men. We need only remember Metternich's sleepless nights fitfully fighting off images of a pipe-smoking Sagan.[62] Krüdener's historical fate adds the festering political significance of religion, and to some extent class, in accounts of the international past. It also underlines the historically specific political suspicions aroused by emotions—where they are not simply about national patriotism.

The final act in Krüdener's story occurs in 1821, when she tries to convince the tsar to take up arms on behalf of Christendom in the Ottoman-ruled Danubian territories and free Greeks from Ottoman oppression. He resists. Alexander depicts Krüdener's zeal in urging "him to embrace the cause of struggling Greece" as hypocritical.[63] But Krüdener has spent her final years consistently, "calling sinners to repentance, preaching, comforting, and relieving the crowds of famished poor, victims of the disastrous wars."[64] She spends her inheritance on the poor, leaving little for herself, or her daughter, and earns the ire of magistrates in the towns where she spreads her alleged anarchic influence. The end of her life occurs in the same place as the tsar's, only one year earlier, in the Crimea, where she has gone to found a colony of sorts.[65] On the eve of his death, Tsar Alexander has finally agreed to make the Greek question a point of Russian foreign policy, much as Krüdener wanted and in complete contradiction of the Holy Alliance emphasis on the bond between the Christian powers and a European peace enlightened by religion. By this time, the threat of inequality finds new voices, and there is another woman, also from the Baltic region, who takes the credit and the blame for imagining a Christian-centered international order, the Russian *ambassadrice* Countess Dorothea Lieven.

CHAPTER THIRTEEN

International Finance

Who hold the balance of the world? Who reign
O'er Congress, whether royalist or liberal?
Who rouse the shirtless patriots of Spain
(That make old Europe's journals squeak and gibber all)?
Who keep the world, both old and new, in pain—
Or pleasure—
Who make politics run glibber all?
The Shade of Buonaparte's noble daring?—
Jew Rothschild and his fellow Christian Baring.

—BYRON, *DON JUAN*, CANTO XII.5, LL. 1–8

IN SEPTEMBER 1818, A posse of bankers heads for the Congress of Aix-la-Chapelle. Looking on, a correspondent for the London *Times* notes bankers are now as critical to the making of peace as the military to war. Within weeks, the English poet Lord Byron begins to pen the caustic stanzas of *Don Juan*, an epic poem he finishes after the final congress, at Verona in 1822. Byron's verses bestow an indelible image of "Jew Rothschild, and his fellow Christian Baring" as bankers who between them seem to rule the world. The strains of these economic themes run through the relatively short period of Aix-la-Chapelle congressing, from October to November 1818. We have already seen how peacemakers associated peace objectives with "free trade" and "free navigation," except for the curtailing of commerce in humans. These trends link the political and economic

FIGURE 30. William Heath (English, 1795–1840), *A kiss at the Congress.* Hand-colored etching on ivory laid paper, 1818. The Art Institute of Chicago.

elements of the emerging international order: conferencing and peace ideals, humanitarian *and* capitalist practices. Economic actors, particularly bankers and entrepreneurs, and their families, are a normative part of a political landscape in which credit and commerce are the instruments of nation-building on an international scale.

This chapter focuses on international thinking at the intersection of politics and finance and the more radical implications of the methods of international finance invented under the auspices of peacemaking. When France is handed an unaffordable reparations bill, the banker-devised solution goes beyond printing paper money to selling state debt to a transnational European public. This new method of credit raising is quickly adopted by the European empires, as well as aspiring postcolonial states, for their own purposes, bringing markets and foreign policy even closer together. Complicating these connections are the diverse motivations of economic actors, as mercenary interests and public good—whether Jewish rights or worker rights—intersect in an increasingly international public sphere. The prospect of the Aix-la-Chapelle congress entices a British factory owner named Robert Owen to travel from Scotland because he imagines that this gathering of statesmen will listen to his views on the threat posed to the future peace of Europe by industrialization. The failure of his relatively unique intervention does not undo Owen's confidence in the power of petitioning. At this originary moment in the invention of an international order, economic change impacts political thinking, inspiring a *capitaliste* to act for social justice and diplomats to invest in capitalism.

Nation-Building

Aix-la-Chapelle is a spa town as famous for its prostitutes as its waters. It was once the capital of Charlemagne's medieval European empire. By 1818, it is located within Prussian borders, thanks to the Treaty of Paris, and known in German as Aachen. There is less of a congress feeling around this gathering in Aix-la-Chapelle than at Vienna. Sociability is relatively diminished and foreign ministries feel they need to at least feign fiscal restraint. Organizationally, the congress conferencing format reflects a familiar template. The *Times* reports from Aix that treaties and conventions need to be signed "with all due solemnity" before "the determination of the Allied Sovereigns" can be officially announced.[1] The first conference is held at Hardenberg's, where the ministers meet and produce their credentials to each other. Daily meetings begin at 10:00 a.m. and continue until 12:00 p.m., and assemble again in the evening, alternating at the residence of one of the ministers of the three Allied Powers. There they consult each other's views and expedite the business of their mission.

While delegates and participants arrive in Aix-la-Chapelle in significant numbers, critics of the cost and length of the Congress of Vienna are convinced that Aix was chosen precisely because of the town's retired nature and the relative "absence of all amusements," "depriving the Ministers of all motives for a protracted stay, and . . . allowing them time to execute their political duties, without interfering with their social engagements."[2] The Russian *ambassadrice* Dorothea Lieven will remember the simplicity and concord at Aix-la-Chapelle as the beginning of "une époque memorable."[3] The French send fashion merchants and caterers, musicians and jugglers arrive from the German territories, and dandies and boxers travel from England, while female aeronauts compete with their helium balloons.[4] However, although the Coalition troops are present, there are no military parades. The King of Prussia puts up with "wretched theatre" every night out of boredom, but his brother monarchs do not even bother. The previous mingling of monarchs and their coteries and the public now can appear awkward because they involve the local burghers. Anna Eynard-Lullin is delighted and flattered when Lord and Lady Castlereagh treat her and her husband like long-lost friends, shaking their hands with a friendly familiarity, yet she believes "our *bourgeois* balls can have few attractions for Monarchs or Ministers."[5] Jean-Gabriel Eynard feels the mixing of men and women as a palpable sign of political dissipation. He is privately critical of the presence of Madame Quay, a novelist, and Madame Gail at one of Metternich's dinners, in what he describes as the diplomatic setting of a "société des hommes."[6]

Of the five hundred monarchs, statesmen, diplomats, and others attending the Congress of Aix-la-Chapelle, participating formally or informally in its *société*, the bankers are hardly an overwhelming number, but they are powerful. Among them are the Rothschild brothers, David Parish, Alexander Baring, and Pierre César Labouchère from the Dutch Hope bank.[7] Their role is to make sure that the financial arrangements that will bring the allies' occupation of France to an end run smoothly. However, there has been a hitch in the requirements imposed by the second Treaty of Paris in 1815. The French are asked to pay reparations of 1.95 billion francs for costs that include the 150,000-strong allied occupation—140 million francs per annum for clothing, equipment, and salaries. The reparations bill translates to the equivalent of 18 percent of French national GDP—or roughly the proportion levied on Germany after World War I. Yet, full payment within five years is a condition of the evacuation of foreign troops. When it is apparent that the French will not be able to meet the deadline, the British endorse a public loan to be repaid by the scheduled congress at Aix-la-Chapelle.[8]

The French indemnity loan is a banker's idea. In 1817, Gabriel-Julien Ouvrard turns to his Europe-wide networks to devise a system of selling French debt in tranches to a European public on the promise of attractive annual interest (*rentes*).[9] That network includes London-based Barings and the Dutch Hope banking houses, which, during the war, helped France recoup Spanish subsidies (even though Britain was on the other side). Now Barings has agreed to provide the French with the credit they need. The bonds Barings issues are quickly oversubscribed and celebrated as an extraordinary success. The sale of two further larger loans follow *suite*—in each case, Barings, along with a few other bankers with smaller allocations of the debt, pockets more than 10 percent of the overall loan cost.[10] With French finances in Barings' hands, and French indemnity bonds in fashion, the Duke of Wellington declares Alexander Baring to have "to a certain degree the command of the money market of the world and feels his power."[11] The duc de Richelieu, Talleyrand's successor as French foreign minister, quips that there are now six great European powers: Britain, France, Russia, Austria, Prussia, and Barings.

The statesmen and speculators who figure in this history are evidence of the vogue for sovereign debt launched by the Barings' loan: from governments who opt to sell their debt to investors to generate capital, to the individuals who buy debt to make more capital. Metternich, Hardenberg, Nesselrode, and Pozzo di Borgo all invest.[12] As if aware of a possible conflict of interest, Charles Stewart, Castlereagh's half brother and British ambassador to Vienna, asks the Rothschilds to purchase bonds on his behalf, in "strict confidence."[13] (Stewart accumulates extraordinary wealth in the decades that follow.) Although the Rothschilds are excluded from the larger tranches of business, they can buy and sell small amounts on the side. They accept Stewart's charge on the grounds that "it is a good idea to be friendly towards him and thus find out all the news." News is useful because, as Rahel Levin's experience shows, foreign policy can decide exchange rates and make or break the fate of these same bonds.

Then suddenly, just at the moment when the final payment is to be made, on the eve of Aix-la-Chapelle, a credit squeeze disrupts the momentum. Barings is not able to muster the expected currency, and the price of the *rentes* underwriting the loan collapses. Investors—among whom we need to add the diplomats at

Aix-la-Chapelle—fear widespread losses. A loan crisis is averted because the alliance statesmen meet with the bankers in the "Free City of Frankfurt" (now the seat of the new German Federal Assembly), en route to Aix-la-Chapelle. They resolve to give Barings a breathing space of eighteen months. Some observers claim the reprieve has been won because of the statesmen's personal interest. Certainly, the payment delay means that the bankers and speculators can recoup the *rentes* on their investments later in a more propitious market.[14] The diplomats determine that, in the meanwhile, the allies can still recall their occupation troops as planned.

The solemnity surrounding the conferencing protocols and processes at Aix-la-Chapelle belie the deliberations at Frankfurt. Diplomacy remains as much what happens in informal discussions, before and during the main event. The diplomatic experience of negotiation and community, at all its sites, and the precedents set in this world of diplomatic exchange all count in the fashioning of an international order. Once the idea of a transnational sovereign debt market is introduced, it travels along diplomatic circuits and charges the national ambitions of Europe's imperial powers. The success of the indemnity loan—particularly the interest it pays out to investors—has heightened the appeal of "foreign" government-issued bonds.[15] When William von Humboldt is made ambassador to the Court of St. James's in London in 1817, he uses his position to convince the local Rothschild banking house to float a "£5 million loan" for Prussia, on the French indemnity loan model. The money will be used to service Prussia's floating debt at 20 percent per annum interest and to pay civil servants and its army.[16] The Prussian loan adds some innovations. The capital is again raised transnationally, in Britain rather than in Prussia, European investors can buy these bonds regardless of whether they live in London, Frankfurt, Berlin, Hamburg, or Amsterdam, and they can be paid out in British sterling rather than Prussian thaler, thus carrying less exchange risk for non-Prussian investors.[17] The success of this loan issue and its method now propels the Rothschilds into a new pan-European market in sovereign debt.[18] Between 1818 and 1822, the previously marginalized Rothschilds add to their portfolio loans of over £23 million to Britain, the Kingdom of Naples, Russia, and Austria, on the Prussian model. Along with their expanded role as creditors come honors from the otherwise famously anti-Semitic Habsburg court. The House of Rothschild is able to establish an office in Vienna, and it rapidly accrues the status of necessary partner of the Concert of Europe.

Against this background, the connections between diplomacy and finance also reach into the Concert's major foreign policy challenges. In 1824, the Genevan financier Jean-Gabriel Eynard draws on his personal diplomatic networks and experience of congressing to issue sovereign debt loans to specifically humanitarian ends. He has in mind the Greek question. Eynard's efforts to cultivate support for Greeks in the Ottoman Empire occur in the absence of Coalition resolve at any of the congresses from Vienna onward. He claims to have written thousands of letters to European Greek committees, kings, diplomats, economists, and politicians. Ultimately it is his credit-provision strategy that brings Greece to the attention of a significant group of "investors."[19] Eynard arranges for Greek bonds to be issued at the Paris bourse that allow subscribers to purchase units for 59 francs each, with two years of interest at 9.5 percent. This gives the margin, Eynard claims, "to philanthropists and speculators alike," since "everyone plays at lending to government because they believe they offer the best chances of gain."[20] "Everyone" again includes statesmen and diplomats, for example, Chateaubriand, the liberal politician Baron Auguste de Staël (son of Germaine de Staël), and bankers Benjamin Delessert and André & Cottier.[21] For some subscribers, the philanthropic, religious, political, or even classical imperatives of an ancient civilization restored are of less interest than the desire to speculate, or just to ensure their Christian charity does not remain anonymous.[22]

Similar strategies are afoot elsewhere, although it is not clear if Eynard's influence has been at work. In 1824, visiting Greek deputies seeking to break from the Ottoman Empire request financial assistance from a London-based philhellenic organization known as the Greek Committee. The committee's members, too, decide to issues sovereign debt bonds, to the value of £800,000. Given the philhellenic committee's expertise, with its experienced economists, not least the famous David Ricardo, and with the (notional) national property of Greece as guarantee, these bonds are quickly and heavily oversubscribed. However, at a 41 percent discount, and bleeding banker commissions, the Greeks are left with less than a third of the original loan amount for their political purposes. In January 1825, a second loan for £2 million is arranged through the Ricardo banking house (David Ricardo himself is dead by this time). Once costs and embezzled money are subtracted, £980,000 remains for the Greek cause.[23]

This period of international finance embeds a sovereign debt culture in the history of European diplomacy. The implications are fascinating as transnational credit-raising potentially binds investors to the fates of foreign nations as well as to capitalism.[24] At the least, the connections between transnational finance infrastructures and nation-building complicate our picture of philanthropy and politics in the sphere of international relations. They also confuse otherwise segregated historical narratives of national and humanitarian sentiments, and even what international politics is for.

Social Justice

The French indemnity loan episode is relatively well-known, at least in the truncated versions rehearsed in histories of the origins of international finance. By contrast, the links between the international history of finance and questions of social justice are all but forgotten. It is Robert Owen who links them, when he arrives at the Congress of Aix-la-Chapelle with a radical message. The reputation that precedes him is not that of the utopian socialist we might identify now, in hindsight, but rather as the manager and owner of New Lanark, a cotton mill town development located on the Clyde river near the Scottish city of Glasgow. New Lanark has put into practice Owen's ideals of communitarian industrial living. Russia's grand-duke Nicholas and grand-duchess Ekaterina have visited and expressed interest in transporting Owen's vision of beneficent industrialization to Russia. Even so, in 1818, Owen is not confident enough to approach the bankers and politicians without a letter of introduction from the London Rothschilds.

Owen's mission, first in Frankfurt and then at Aix-la-Chapelle, is to present two "memorials" he has had written and printed "on behalf of the working classes." In these memorials, he claims to have spent thirty years studying and practicing "political economy"—a relatively new area of scholarship focused on economics as a statecraft. He declares his desire to share this accumulated knowledge with "those who govern the civilized world and . . . the public," without prejudice against "any class, sect, party, or country."[25] Owen charges that throughout Europe industrialization is exacerbating economic inequality: "the overwhelming effects of new scientific power"—the steam engine and the factory system—are undermining the exchangeable value of manual labor as the source of individual wealth. He offers as evidence the industrialization underway in Britain and the forecasting made possible by the new science of statistics. On these bases, Owen predicts a future in which everyone's needs are able to be satisfied, but only if the existing system of the distribution of the wealth produced is not maintained. Based on the available trends, he predicts that only one person out of every thousand will benefit from industrialization. The challenge is not "how a sufficiency of wealth for all may be produced" but "how the excess of riches . . . may be generally distributed throughout society advantageously for all ranks without prematurely disturbing the existing institutions in any country."[26] Owen interprets this inequality as a dangerous threat to future peace. If not managed, he warns, this new situation will result in violence, "in which a greater change in human affairs will be forced on the world than the world has yet witnessed."[27]

Distributing his texts in multiple languages, Owen invites the congress participants, regardless of their origin, to create a commission that will come to New Lanark to study his program for worker education. What Owen offers the statesmen is a "new plan for the regeneration of the world" that will address "the grand question" of economic inequality. For all the vehemence of the mission, his antidote is emotional and psychological rather than overtly political: a concerted effort by the European powers to address inequality through education that will teach people "to esteem, to love, and to aid each other." Drawing on the social determinism of Saint-Simon and Staël, Owen maintains that since *men* are products of their environment, governments can use education to encourage a more communitarian European consciousness and ward off future revolution that way. His assumption is that the new practice of recurring diplomatic reunions also opens up the opportunity "to establish a permanent system of peace, conservation and charity in its true sense throughout Christendom and effectually to supersede the system of war and of almost every evil arising from uncharitable notions among men, produced solely by the circumstances of birth."[28]

At Aix-la-Chapelle, Owen delivers his plan as diplomats maneuver their meetings and outcomes. Whenever he is given the chance he speaks at length in English (with a translator at hand) about his projects to improve the whole world. The London *Times* is "at least extremely curious" to reproduce in full the "memorials" addressed on behalf of the working classes "to the Governments of Europe and America"—even though America is not represented at the congress.[29] The newspaper reports that Owen submits all his developments to Congress "and requests a commission to examine his schemes, and to report to their next meeting."[30] Owen tells the sovereigns and ministers "it is owing to the merest accident they were not cannibals and heathens. . . . the reformer starts up into a prophet, and warns the nations of their danger, if they do not immediately call in his assistance to secure them from the accumulating evils of 'misdirected scientific power.'"[31] Anna Lullin-Eynard, who knows Owen through her uncle, thinks him a strange mix of happiness in his preoccupation with goodness, and unhappiness "when he saw how many people were uninterested in adopting his precepts."[32] Indeed, despite his reputation and the public interest his presence generates, there is no evidence that any statesman or diplomat at Aix-la-Chapelle takes Owen seriously.

When we put Owen's thinking back into a bigger picture of changing ideas of politics at this time, his Christian approach to tackling economic inequality on an international scale is hard to ignore. But so is his understanding of the economic origins of the threat of "disequilibrium." Ultimately, Owen's efforts expand our view of the range of political ambitions and expectations associated with this new simultaneously European and international order. His failure underscores the limitations of that same "order."

At the end of the Napoleonic wars, capitalists, entrepreneurs, industrialists, and bankers involve themselves in the Concert of Europe as creditors and opportunists, and as petitioners for social and economic justice. Their status as economic actors does not always translate into the political realm, and religion is often as important. The fact that the Barings are Christian is said to favor them for the indemnity commission; nevertheless, through this period Coalition statesmen and bankers alike advocate "en faveur des juifs."[33] In Frankfurt, while the impact of the credit squeeze on the indemnity loan is being addressed before the more public meetings of Aix-la-Chapelle, the Rothschilds work with Lämel, Eskeles, and the Christian banker Simon Moritz Bethmann to drum up support for the rights of Jews in their hometown.[34] Solomon Rothschild hands Gentz 800 ducats, telling him he should consider it money won by speculating in British funds. Gentz, who is again congress secretary, "the whole of the next day" to "a memorandum stating the case for the Jews of Frankfurt."[35]

At the Congress of Aix-la-Chapelle, the issue of Jewish rights may not be on the official agenda, but it remains a concern. Metternich and Hardenberg, who continue to accept payment from bankers in exchange for supporting Jewish rights, write to the local governments to remind them that the postwar European order supports "general civil rights" for Jews. They detail the Jewish soldiers who earned those rights by fighting alongside Christians in the war against Napoleon, the Jewish women who "mingled with the Christians in sacrifices of every kind," and the "Jewish houses" wielding influence over "the system of credit and commerce of the various German states, which cannot escape the notice of the Congress."[36] At the end of Aix-la-Chapelle, Castlereagh and Metternich together confirm that the status of Jews "must claim the attention equally of the statesman and the humanitarian."[37]

These political efforts on behalf of Jewish rights have become all the more urgent because of escalating religious intolerance and ongoing economic insecurity, including anti-Semitic riots in Frankfurt and other newly confederated German towns. Not uncoincidentally, the expansion of Rothschild business in Frankfurt, London, Paris, and now Vienna belies the persistent discrimination against Jews. Austria, for example, awards the Rothschilds royal and state honors but refuses its Jewish population basic civil rights. Humboldt is happy to recommend the Rothschilds to the Prussian government as the best and most trustworthy bankers for this "foreign loan"; the Rothschilds also manage his brother Alexander's estate. Still, Humboldt does not hesitate to call the bankers "crude and uneducated."[38]

As the House of Rothschild grows in European repute as a provisioner of credit and capital for Europe's imperial governments, the brothers find themselves the focus of racialized anxieties. At first, Amschel Rothschild is convinced that the problem is *not* anti-Semitism, as he explains to his brother James in March 1817: "Anyone who plays a prominent role will attract jealousy and people will try everything against them."[39] Nevertheless, the Rothschilds turn to Gentz as a paid publicist in order to fend off the anti-Semitic attacks they regularly face, especially in the Frankfurt press.[40] Gentz takes the Rothschild money to defend their interests in public but in private speaks about them as "vulgar, ignorant Jews, outwardly presentable," operating on instinct and "the principles of naturalism, having no suspicion of a higher order of things."[41] In Frankfurt, the philanthropist banker Bethmann—who, in the mode of the time, has also acted as a diplomat for Russia at the Confederation of the Rhine—is the *only* Christian local who sees fit to invite Jewish bankers into his dining room. When, in 1818, the Banque de France's monetary policy creates the credit squeeze that derails the final loan repayment, the Rothschilds are widely blamed, without evidence. Their alleged motive is revenge for their marginalization in the indemnity loan bonanza.[42]

The more the Rothschilds, like other bankers, consolidate their government business, drawing on the political networks maneuvered at the congresses that follow Vienna—whether Aix-la-Chapelle, Laibach, Troppau, or Verona—the more anti-Semitic attacks they are forced to weather.[43] By the final congress, in Habsburg Verona in 1822, the Rothschilds are an established dominant presence; it is their couriers that Austrian and French diplomats rely upon, it is their money that pays all of Metternich's expenses, and it is their cash that keeps the sociability of the congress well-oiled. The brothers have taken to referring to themselves as bankers to the European "Holy Alliance," possibly enjoying the Christian overtones of that now conventional, if misleading, identification of the congress system.[44] One evening, when two Rothschild brothers find themselves seated next to Eynard, they are the

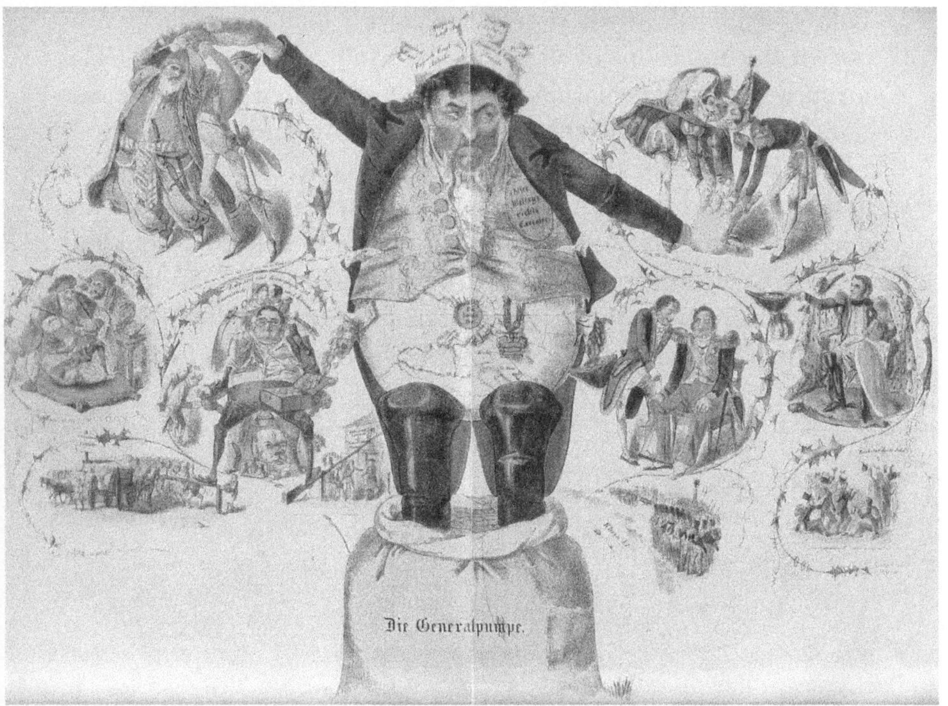

FIGURE 31. Eduard Fuchs, "Die Generalpumpe" (The general pump), (caricature on Rothschild), 1843. Lithograph, Germany (supplement to Eduard Fuchs and Hans Kraemer, "Die Karikatur" (The caricature). © Photograph by Christos Varsos, Wikimedia Commons.

subjects of the Genevan republican's barely disguised prejudice. Eynard records his impression of them as the ugly representatives of "la tribu d'Isai," the elder Amschel the worst of all, with his "air of an old merchant butcher."[45]

By this time, the treacherous tide of anti-Semitism has made its way into Byron's epic poem *Don Juan*, as he imagines the currents of a changing world, its political and economic complexities. Although a relatively meager *historical* document, in specific sections the poem's themes reflect contemporary developments in the internationalization of a new culture of credit and markets. Byron's tone is at times sarcastic, anti-Semitic, and ambivalent in regard to the role of credit in the realization of *national* ambitions. *Don Juan* speaks to the influence of Rothschild and Baring, and singles out the "truly liberal" ambitions of the (Catholic) French banker Jacques

Lafitte—who was involved in the indemnity loans and fiscally supported the ambitions of the utopian socialist Saint-Simon.[46] The invention of an international order has generated a new international political culture with indelible economic dimensions, as well as new critiques of these transformations and the entanglement of politics and capital. A crucial paradox of this period is that the opportunity to consolidate bonds between Europe's sovereigns and societies, whether in the name of Christianity or humanity, coincides with an inclination to fragment Europeans and their relations with the wider world, along class and religious as much as national and gender lines.

CHAPTER FOURTEEN

Humanity

"EUROPE" AND "HUMANITY" were among the most potent ideas shaping the scope and power, even internalization, of international "ordering." During the Sixth Coalition's campaign against France, and in the early stages of peacemaking, the call to humanity imbued the allegiances forged at Chaumont with both European and universal significance. Europe and humanity interlaced cause and effect; they were ideological wellsprings of the Coalition campaign against France, imperatives for a range of political causes, from politics "of the bandaging kind" and the slave trade, awarding rights to Jews, and even, in the rarer case, seeking economic justice for workers. Humanity helped expand the scope of a self-consciously European diplomacy and international imaginaries as an explanation and authorization of the stakes of cooperation—all while establishing the boundaries of that authority. Over eight years of conferencing, a Christian "humanity" became the significant reference point for collective—sometimes multilateral at other times simply bilateral—intervention in problems beyond the borders of the five main powers, Britain, Russia, Austria, Prussia, and France, as the representatives of Europe.

Coincidental with the opening out of multilateral international thinking was the European powers' careful segregation of bureaucratic oversight of their internal affairs and external relations. In particular, there was little overlap between expanding domains of diplomatic influence and international ambition, and their respective (trade-driven) imperial and colonial business. Foreign

FIGURE 32. John ("HB") Doyle, published by Thomas McLean, *The Greek Papers*. Lithograph, published 30 June 1830. 28.6×412 cm, 1900. Reference Collection, National Portrait Gallery, London.

ministries did act as hubs for extensive networks of consuls working on behalf of cross-border commerce and trade; however, "colonial affairs" were distinguished from "foreign affairs" and kept from the purview of this new "science of European government." Britain's colonies were administered through its War and Colonial Office, although its relatively new Foreign Office oversaw the more ambiguously governed protectorates. Russia, which did not institute a colonial office analogous to the British or French version, concentrated the administration of its colonial territories in a Ministry of Internal Affairs, not the Ministry of Foreign Affairs established by Tsar Alexander's 1802 ministerial reforms.[1] Of course, such neat divisions of oversight were belied by the addition and exchange of colonial territories at stake in peacemaking. Britain, for example, gained Trinidad, Demerara, Berbice, Essequio, Ceylon, Mauritius, and the South African Cape of Good Hope; Russia retained oversight of Poland and Finland.

In the European peacemaking context, the "internal affairs" of the dominant states rarely came under consideration as legitimate international concerns. It was assumed, for example, that Jewish rights might be relevant in territories formerly occupied by the French, but not in Austria or Britain. Staël was also quick to notice that the illiberal nature of British rule in Ireland and its war with the United States were somehow exempt from peace discussions. The exceptions to this rule of great power exemption were most forcefully applied in the condemnation of the slave trade (although not slavery itself) on the grounds of "humanity and universal morality." This language, according to legal historians, "introduced a powerful new norm into international law" and was intended as an indictment of the trading practices of each of the imperial powers.[2] Nevertheless, each empire still found good reason to continue its trade. Portugal finally agreed to end its slave trade north of equator (although it continued south of the equator); Spain would formally conclude its slave trade only after a hiatus of five years, in 1820. The 1814 Treaty of Paris agreement had given France until 1819 to end its citizens' involvement in the slave trade, yet the French slave trade resumed and peaked through the 1820s, persisting in previously liberated French West Indies islands Martinique and Guadeloupe until 1848. Ultimately, the commitment to humanity could not defeat the commitment of French political figures, for example, to colonization and the sugar plantation system.

The new congressing ethos played its part in encouraging a wider remit for European intervention. That ethos was reinforced by the introduction of regular lower-profile London- and Paris-based gatherings of plenipotentiaries at "ambassadorial conferences." A subset of the congress system originally devised by the Coalition as a means of multilateral oversight of territory they conquered as they campaigned through central Europe, they became, on Castlereagh's view, "a sort of permanent European Congress," an "upgrade of the Vienna Congress based on Vienna Commission," an "Allied Machine."[3] There were distinctive permutations of this idea, such as the "Committee of Diplomatic Conference," which was based at the British embassy and oversaw negotiations for the second Treaty of Paris agreed in late 1815. Then, for a number of decades, the ambassadorial conference model remained the modus operandi for discussion of contingent challenges to the European political status quo—whether the fate of Tuscan territory fought over by Spain and Austria, the Portuguese and Spanish conflict in liberated territories of South America, or the Danish-Swedish conflict over Norway.

This chapter probes the ways in which repertoires of Europe and Humanity came to frame and legitimate Coalition intervention in the problem of Barbary piracy and the status of Ottoman Greeks—both of which involved intervention in the internal affairs of the Ottoman Empire. These were the issues that shifted Coalition policies with respect to the Ottoman Empire and rendered that empire an important boundary marker of the new international order. As we have seen, most European imperial powers (including Britain) had long had diplomatic relations with the Ottoman Empire and its various autonomous regents. These relationships were established through the presence of consuls and treaties and, in many cases, gave European traders a privileged legal and concessional tax status. The history of the invention of an international order dominated by Europe is also the story of the forgetting of this earlier history of an Ottoman Empire with equal legal standing under an older "natural law," coincident with the reinvention of the empire's inequality in the new order.[4] Like so many dimensions of the remaking of Europe after Napoleon, and the transformation of European politics, the Ottoman Empire's changing status was knitted into place through a combination of cultural ideas, individual agency, and the invention of international political and economic practices, even under the sign of Humanity.[5]

Barbary Pirates

At the last of the formal peacemaking congresses, in Verona in 1822, "humanity" was a familiar incantation. Between Vienna and Verona, the European empires had added piracy to their list of "humanity" causes. The piracy on the formal agenda was a problem in the Mediterranean—along a coastline dominated by the North African ports of Algiers, Tunis, and Tripoli, under the authority of "Barbary Regencies," ambiguously autonomous regions of the Ottoman Empire, and it was often referred to as "corsairing." By the late eighteenth century, according to Erik de Lange, corsairing had become "a state-managed affair, with the Regencies possessing or holding shares in most of the vessels." If corsairing appeared as a kind of protection racket, it was not simply a Barbary practice. The Christian Maltese Order and the Tuscan Order of Saint Stephen conducted similar raiding of ships in the Mediterranean, including kidnapping sailors and travelers, Muslim and Christian, for ransom.[6] Corsairing was also a military strategy in wartime for the European powers when it suited them, including the French republic, and other operatives working under British protection.

Barbary piracy had a specific and complicated place in the larger scheme of Ottoman-European relations. Since the eighteenth century, despite being part of the larger Ottoman Empire, these Mediterranean Regencies had sent their ambassadors to Europe to negotiate bilateral treaties. In turn, Europeans recognized the Barbary Regencies as organized states with autonomous territorial sovereignty—or at least as another layer of sovereignty. The Europeans' motivations included the strategic utility of the Barbary coastline, with its importance for transatlantic trade networks and access to Maghreb agricultural produce such as grains and fruits. Individual European countries invested in these relations by installing consular offices and commercial houses and developing whole "foreign concessions" in a coastal terrain that today encompasses Algeria and Tunisia.

From the Barbary side, the advantages of signing bilateral treaties with various European powers included stipulating tributes and other sources of income, money, arms, and shipbuilding materials. In this way, trading treaties could be as lucrative as corsairing for the Regency powers keen to reduce their reliance on the removed Ottoman court and even reject its oversight.[7] During the revolutionary wars in Europe, the Regencies were able to profit from provisioning European supply chains, that is, until fighting disrupted established practices. Thus, in 1807, for example, the Compagnie Royale d'Afrique established by the French to manage exports from foreign Barbary coast concessions was taken over by the British, forcing Barbary sovereigns to resume corsairing to supplement their income. Given this fluctuating history, it should have come as no surprise to the European powers that in peacetime, and in straitened circumstances that included the failure of European governments to pay their agreed tribute, Barbary corsairs would once again ply their ships on European trade routes. For Tunis Bey (the regent of Tunisia), piracy was a means of not only recuperating unpaid tribute but also addressing what he believed was the unfair growing competition of Europeans in the region's merchant trade.[8]

In the context of peacemaking at Vienna, there was no shortage of complaints about the threats corsairing posed to European commerce and Humanity. The eccentric British admiral William Sidney Smith was among the most strident of voices urging action against corsairing as a cause for "humanity" equivalent to the slave trade because it involved Christians being held for ransom.[9] He proposed that the congress support raising a multinational fleet under his leadership to pursue the pirates. Smith's approach denied the Barbary Regencies' sovereignty, insisting instead that the Europeans had to resort to force and threat, rather than the diplomacy, treaties, or tributes that had long been the practice.

In 1814, the Committee of Four preferred to ignore the rather eccentric Smith. The British Foreign Office considered him too much of a rogue actor to be supported—it probably did not help that even though he was an admiral in their navy, he also represented Sweden at Vienna. By 1816, however, the European powers were openly debating Barbary piracy as an endemic problem, and Britain resorted to bilateral military action as the solution. British delegates spoke out in the London ambassadorial conference forum on behalf of "the great principles of justice, humanity, and the Law of Nations mutually between the States and People of Africa and Europe." Castlereagh signaled a growing interest in the seizure of Christian Europeans by Barbary pirates as worthy of the multilateral purpose of the European alliance because of its "natural connection" to the slave trade in Africans: "If we all draw heartily together," he argued, they could provide "a lasting service to mankind."[10] The relatively landlocked Austrian government was as vocal in their concern and condemnation, bending in their case to the agitation of lobbyists sent from the Habsburg port of Trieste, whose ships sailed those same insecure waters. In the course of two years, the congressing system collectively shifted policy on piracy as a legitimate cause for international intervention on behalf of the universal peacemaking principles that defined European authority in this postwar order, not only slavery but also the "concert" principle of "free navigation." European rationales for intervention in the Barbary question now stretched from invocations of "humanity" to the equation of peace and commerce.

Estimates that place the numbers of victims of piracy in this period in their thousands help us understand why the ambassadorial conferences on abolition of the African slave trade might have reconsidered "the question of Barbary, and Christian slavery." Historian Brian Vick has argued that even though any comparison between Barbary captivity for Europeans and race-based plantation slavery of Africans in the Atlantic world was absolutely incommensurate, the consequences of ransoming were "bad enough, with potential physical and sexual abuse, and five-year mortality rates near 20%."[11] As significant was the form of intervention the Europeans finally chose to manage the problem: not diplomacy but military power. In 1816, British and Dutch governments took a bilateral decision to bombard Algiers in order to force the local bey's hand.[12] Over the next decade, repeated military incursions of this kind would contribute to the infamous transformation of the Mediterranean into a "colonial sea."[13]

At Aix-la-Chapelle, in 1818, piracy was officially conjoined to abolition on the congress agenda on commercial grounds—"free navigation" rather than religion. Under the guidance of Wilhelm Humboldt, still ambassador to the Court of St. James's, the principle of free navigation was intended to ensure a "system of common security" and "the liberty of their subjects."[14] When Tsar Alexander agitated for a fleet of Christian nations to advance on Regencies that pursued captivity practices, his motive was not any more exclusivist than in the Holy Alliance treaty episode. The rejection of the tsar's plan, and of his idea of a joint fleet overseeing compliance with the abolition of the slave trade, said as much about the intertwined fates of the Russian and Ottoman empires in the shifting ground of European concert and authority. In the midst of all this the Ottoman Maghreb regions, once regarded as legitimate sovereignties, experienced "a gradual hollowing out of 'Barbary' statehood."[15]

Ottoman Greeks

The stories of individuals complicate our view of the past. They nuance, even muddle, the moving historical landscape of ideas, agency, institutions, and structures. They tell us who engaged and invested in international and national politics, how states assumed authority, and how their legitimacy was challenged or denied. In the decade after Staël escaped from the shore of Lake Geneva to begin her journey of international opposition against Bonaparte, the opportunities for soft diplomacy were focused on conferencing and congressing. Congresses in particular drew an elite keen for diversion but also political participation. This is as true for the congresses held in the small provincial Habsburg towns of Troppau (now Opava) in 1820 and Laibach (now Ljubljana) in 1821, where housing and facilities spoke to a diminished publicity and glamour.

At the 1822 Congress of Verona, there were no public balls and only a few salons. Over a relatively short two months of negotiation, Verona was written off as "a galloping congress—kings and ministers have come and gone like shadows."[16] As wife of the Russian ambassador to the Court of St. James's, Countess Dorothea Lieven bemoaned the lack of organization and general confusion. "Quelle leçon que ce Congrès!" she wrote surreptitiously to the Russian embassy in London.[17] There were relatively few women compared to Vienna, and in the small circle of *ambassadrices* marooned in the otherwise culturally attractive Italian-speaking Habsburg-ruled town, Lieven reigned supreme.

Among the big questions at Verona was whether to intervene in Spain on behalf of the ruling Bourbon monarchy that had been usurped by a constitution-bearing liberal government. James Rothschild, the Paris-based scion of the family, acted against his London-based brother's advice and provided "a Spanish loan payable to France." The French banker Ouvrard made a personal loan to the Spanish monarch in support of the Bourbon cause (Lafitte funded the constitutionalists).[18] The new French foreign minister,

Vicomte de Montmorency—formerly an ally of Staël's punished by Bonaparte for his proximity to her—asked Vicomte de Chateaubriand to promote the interests of the Bourbons in Spain. In his ambassadorial role, Chateaubriand introduced Ouvrard to Metternich "to hear what he has to say." He recorded that the deployment of Ouvrard may be "chimerical as far as regarded moral interests," but "the imaginative banker amused Prince Metternich: the idea of carrying on war by dint of money . . . and making France no party in the cause, was a scheme quite congenial."[19] Ultimately, the alliance members did not take a unified position, but they authorized French intervention in Spanish affairs on behalf of a dynastic relationship against liberalism.

The issue of intervention in the situation of Ottoman Greeks inspired less consensus among the Quintuple Alliance (France was now included). As with piracy, they had avoided this problem since the days of Vienna. Indeed, the appearance of the "Greek question" on the Verona congress agenda was forced upon the reluctant alliance in 1821, when the Greek renegade Alexander Ypsilanti led a successful revolt in the Ottoman-ruled Peloponnese region, creating new "facts on the ground." The crisis was compounded by Mahmud II Sultan's response to Ypsilanti's venture: rescinding the position of Greeks in key administrative positions and ordering the hanging of Greek patriarch Gregorius V at the gates of his Constantinople office on Easter Sunday of March 1821, despite the fact that Gregorius condemned the Greek revolt.[20] Supporters of the Greeks insisted that it was the religious responsibility of European powers, and particularly Orthodox Russia, to step up.

The Russian tsar was no more inclined to intervene on behalf of Greeks in the Ottoman Empire than was Metternich, who clung to his view of the principle of reciprocity and the equal legitimacy of Ottoman sovereignty. Alexander prioritized the "tranquility of Europe," and the alliance, rather than Russia's geopolitics.[21] He wanted to avoid any possible interpretation of Russia pursuing imperial ambition in preference to a commitment to Europe, even if it meant resisting the legally reinforced convention that deemed Russia the natural defender of the Orthodox Christian Greeks. This position required him to resist pressure from his own reactionary government and to ignore the effect of Ottoman anti-Greek policies on Russian trade in the Danubian principalities. Ironically, the tsar's prioritization of relations between the Europeans was accentuated when he agreed to French intervention in Spain in defense of Bourbon interests, but not intervention in Greece to defend Christians. Some congress visitors observed that the tsar had become unrecognizable in his political opinions to the extent of accusing him of becoming an interventionist in the interests of conservatism and against "les liberaux."[22]

By 1822, the defense of Greeks had taken on the swagger of a high-profile liberal and "humanity" cause thanks in large part to the influence of British, Swiss, and French public interest and the popularity of the latest capitalist fundraising schemes. Philhellene Lord Aberdeen's attempts to convince Castlereagh of intervention against the Ottoman Empire hit the humanitarian note of the growing public manifestations of empathy for the suffering endured by slaves. "A considerable change has taken place in the feelings of mankind on this subject," Aberdeen explained. "The attempt of any Government in Europe to support the Turkish power for the avowed purpose of diverting the claims of their unhappy Christian subjects would scarcely be tolerated."[23] In this public context, the Greek question marked a growing equivalence between Christian and humanitarian causes; nevertheless, the allies continued to keep the prospect of intervention at a cultivated distance.

Through the final years of formal public congressing and into the decades of ambassadorial conferencing, there were two individuals who contributed to the shift of European policy on the Greek question. One of them was Dorothea Lieven, the other, Jean-Gabriel Eynard. After Vienna, Eynard supported both taking steps to end corsairing because it was a humiliation against all Europe and acting on behalf of Christian Greeks (whether on the Greek peninsula or on the borders of the Russian empire), as *la cause de l'humanité*.[24] In particular, he cultivated his philhellenism in ways that were exemplary of the humanitarian sentiment Lord Aberdeen believed had a profound hold on early nineteenth-century politics. Although he died never having set foot on Greek territory, Eynard described assisting the Greeks as a great and noble project of "philanthropy" in the interest of "reality" and "the regeneration of *un peuple intéressant*."[25] At Verona, once more acting as a formal participant in congressing, Eynard noted the tsar's refusal to intervene on behalf of the Greeks and blamed the policy on the diminished influence of his friend and the tsar's former foreign minister Kapodistrias.[26] Like other bankers and financiers acting in the Spanish question, Eynard did not wait for the alliance government to decide on intervention in the Greek question. Instead, he took matters into his own hands, maximizing the diplomacy of philanthropy and humanity he had by then learned.

Neither Jean-Gabriel Eynard's pro bono work in the case of the Queen of Etruria nor his work on behalf of Geneva, whether at Paris or Vienna or Aix-la-Chapelle, prepares us for the intensity of his philhellenism, tutored in the international political networks of the peacemaking process. In his efforts to build and shore up Greek autonomy, he worked his diplomatic connections to financially back Greek independence from Ottoman rule and, eventually, Kapodistrias as first president of independent Greece. Eynard was a republican, Freemason, and Calvinist. His wife, Anna, by contrast, was devoted to doing God's Will. Late in life Jean-Gabriel would credit Anna with inspiring in him a (Calvinist) religiosity, and he came to insist on the need to defend the Greeks because they were Christians, regardless of the form of political autonomy that their defense might require.[27]

As the alliance statesmen procrastinated over intervention on the Greek side, Eynard entwined the financing of Greek independence with his diplomatic experience.[28] In 1821, before Verona, he visited the Paris bourse to convince "rich capitalists" to support Greek independence.[29] There the Rothschilds skirted around Eynard's propositions, wary of the risks of war in promoting the Greek cause. However, Eynard was able to get twenty-five politicians, philosophers, and leaders of French banking, including Jacques Lafitte, the liberal, former governor of the Bank of France, to help "procure for [the Greeks] all the resources that mechanical arts, sciences and French civilization could offer."[30] Together with the Paris-based bankers and capitalists, Eynard created a committee for the organization of a subscription in favor of Greek refugees under the auspices of the Society for Christian Morality, a French charity focused on abolition and social reform.[31] He also explored the possibilities of selling sovereign bonds to raise money for "the most holy rights of humanity and justice." At a diplomatic dinner in Paris organized by Pozzo di Borgo—the same dinner attended by the Rothschilds—the Genevan combined discussion of another lucrative French government bond sale with the possibility of raising funds for Greek sovereignty on the stock market.[32] He claimed that while orchestrating capital-raising methods he always kept "an eye on the politics of the European states" in order "to be certain not to commit a diplomatic error."[33] This meant maintaining contact with diplomats—Metternich when he was in Paris, or Canning in London—and tracking the movement of foreign policy in order to predict movement in the value of bonds. When the Paris press announced the founding of the Comité Grec de Paris, Eynard issued a round of Greek bonds to the value of 15 million francs through the French bourse.[34] While there was some obscurity around Eynard's connection to the rise of Greek committees in London and the sale of Greek bonds on the London Stock Exchange in 1824 (we know Eynard hosted London Greek committee members at his Swiss summer residence, Beaulieu), it is clear that his personal agency was critical to the spread of both tactics.[35]

In the long history of Greek independence, Eynard became known as the president's "principal agent for raising private loans in western Europe and even for extracting subsidies from friendly but cautious governments."[36] His project of a Greek financial institution was realized in the short-lived National Finance Bank with his own money, 750,000 French francs, as a guarantee for any French investment in Greece.[37] In 1831, after the assassination of Kapodistrias, Eynard continued to involve himself in the future of Greece, providing the funds (including his own) for the creation of a discounting office and supporting state Treasury bills. He was made an honorary director of the National Bank of Greece established in 1841 and a principal shareholder (along with the Rothschilds and others). Lord Palmerston, otherwise cagey in his support for Greece, conceded that Eynard had no equal in the cause of Greek independence "not only by the indefatigable exertion of your personal influence, but by advances of money larger than were probably ever before made by a private individual in the cause of a country not his own, and not acting as the Agent of a Government."[38]

How important was the ideal of humanity in the history of multilateral intervention? As Castlereagh's biographer notes, intervention was as often motivated by national interest as "humanitarian moralism."[39] Contemporaries were more than aware that the appeal of humanity was a consequence of changes in how humanity was understood, including changing emotional subjectivities. Aberdeen embraced the novelty of "the common impulse of humanity" understood as "an instinct, deeply and universally implanted in our nature," and justification for extending "protection to the persecuted and unfortunate." Even so, he accepted that "humanity" was not always enough to determine "interference." Instead, "interference" was "conduct which is intended to direct or influence the course of events, and to promote the accomplishment of some particular object."[40]

In 1822, "humanity" did not yet win the argument for European intervention in the Greek question, despite Eynard's and Aberdeen's efforts to convince the Concert statesmen. This moment highlights the still unpredictable and uneven progress of what we have come to think of as "the Eurocentric, globalizing and liberal nature of this nascent world order."[41] Ultimately, humanity, along with the qualifying noun "civilization," would do much of the work of situating both Russia and the Ottoman Empire outside the remit of the European society of states that assumed political authority of international affairs. The closer we look, the more entangled the histories of humanity and the institutionalized and internalized dimensions of the invention of an international order appear.

CHAPTER FIFTEEN

Realpolitik

Le roman est fini, nous entrons dans l'histoire.

—METTERNICH TO LIEVEN, DECEMBER 1825

What always seemed more important and serious to me . . . this grand drama of the Orient of which we haven't yet seen the first act. If we are to commence this piece of drama we need to assemble the actors! Don't you see?

—DOROTHEA LIEVEN TO LORD ABERDEEN, PARIS, 27 FEBRUARY 1840

IN 1825, while on a tour of the Russian Black Sea regions, Tsar Alexander mysteriously disappears and then is pronounced dead, likely the victim of an infectious virus. He is forty-eight years old. A wave of regret washes over Dorothea Lieven, now forty and wearing the tsar's gift of the title "princess." When she writes to Metternich in search of sympathy, his condolences are tempered. He takes the tsar's death as a sign that the era of "romance" is over and that they have entered the era of "history."[1] The idea that European relations moved from a brief window of romance in 1814 to a cynical view of foreign policy and politics has shadowed the history of multilateralism at the end of the Napoleonic wars ever since. Some historians argue that to the extent this new society of states' ideal manifests a romance, its death knell occurs not with the death of Tsar Alexander, who commits to it most consistently, but a quarter of a century later, in 1853, when the outbreak of the Crimean War pits Tsar Nicholas's Russia against a coalition of the French, British,

Austrian, and Ottoman empires. That same year sees the coinage of "Realpolitik," a term that pits realism against idealism. Alternatively, British historian Harold Temperley locates the origin of this break in the months just prior to the tsar's death: Dorothea Lieven convinces Alexander to prioritize Russia's foreign policy interests over those of the Quintuple Alliance, thereby launching "the end of the Neo-Holy Alliance and the congressional or international system of government," even "the beginning of the break-up of the Turkish empire."[2]

The aim of this chapter is not to argue that Lieven alone brings to an abrupt end the postwar "romantic" era of European multilateralism. Instead, closer examination of her reputation as a "diplomatic Sybil" combining "the arts of Society with those of policy" is a gauge of the uneven transformations in the conduct of diplomacy and politics between states through the first half of the nineteenth century. In that long history, Lieven is one more *ambassadrice*, maneuvering networks, correspondence, and salons, although in a rapidly altering social, economic, and political European landscape. Acting as an independent information collector and negotiator in multiple European metropoles—London, Paris, and St. Petersburg—Lieven seems the epitome of an early nineteenth-century multilateralist. The difference is that, without office, she is answerable to no one, even as political norms increasingly emphasize modern principles of national representation, merit, and transparency. She calls "civilised Europe" her *patrie*, and "all the diplomats of all its countries" are her compatriots. She is aware that her ambitions do not align with changing social conventions, but in 1825 she represents as "new and something to laugh at" the fact that "the most cautious and discreet of Ministers [had been] compelled to entrust the most confidential, most intimate and most bold political projects to a woman."[3]

The political drama that unfolds around Lieven as protagonist has more than one opening scene. She will mark the Congress of Verona, the final public congress of peacemaking connected to the romance of the Coalition's concert, as the moment of her introduction to diplomacy. It is after that congress that she assumes a prominent role in the Greek question. The dramatic denouement of her soft diplomacy occurs in 1853, with the outbreak of the Crimean

War. Her individual agency through this period, engaging available diplomatic ideas and practices—including private correspondence, but not publication—exposes a woman intent on maintaining an old role in the new politics between states. In 1856, as we will see, Lieven finds herself at the Congress of Paris, the setting for peacemaking after the Crimean War, where once again women, bankers, and *capitalistes* are among the assembled actors, but telegraphy and trains now connect policy, opinion, and communication across the continent.[4] The stakes, again, include hierarchies of culture, religion, and gender and the relative European status of Russia and the Ottoman Empire. Significantly, peacemaking after Napoleon has become a factor itself in the reinvention of international order.

The Diplomatic Sybil

Born von Benckendorff in the Russian vassal state of the Duchy of Courland, Dorothea takes her new name from her husband, the much older Russian ambassador Count Christopher Lieven. The marriage has been arranged by Tsar Alexander, in gratitude to Dorothea's mother, his governess.[5] From at least 1813, when Lieven arrives in London, where Count Lieven is installed as Russian ambassador to the Court of St. James's, she is involved in the politics that takes place between Europe's courts and governments. En route, she briefly conspires with Staël in Stockholm to support the Coalition, but then, counter to Staël, she supports the return of Louis XVIII to the French throne.

In British political circles, the young Dorothea becomes known for her charm, grace, and ease of conversation and the mastery of her letter writing.[6] The pronouncedly liberal Staël will consider her a political traitor, but the determinedly monarchist Lieven is likewise admired for her "extraordinary intelligence," "d'une finesse extreme," and her diplomatic reports too are received as superior to those of her ambassador husband.[7] At St. James's Court and Parliament, Lieven finds herself deep in what she insists on naming "politics." She moves in the circles of the Prince Regent and the Duke of Wellington and is especially close to Castlereagh.[8] Sympathetic biographers will describe her as "an *intrigante*, a type of female politician familiar in eighteenth century Europe."[9] For Metternich,

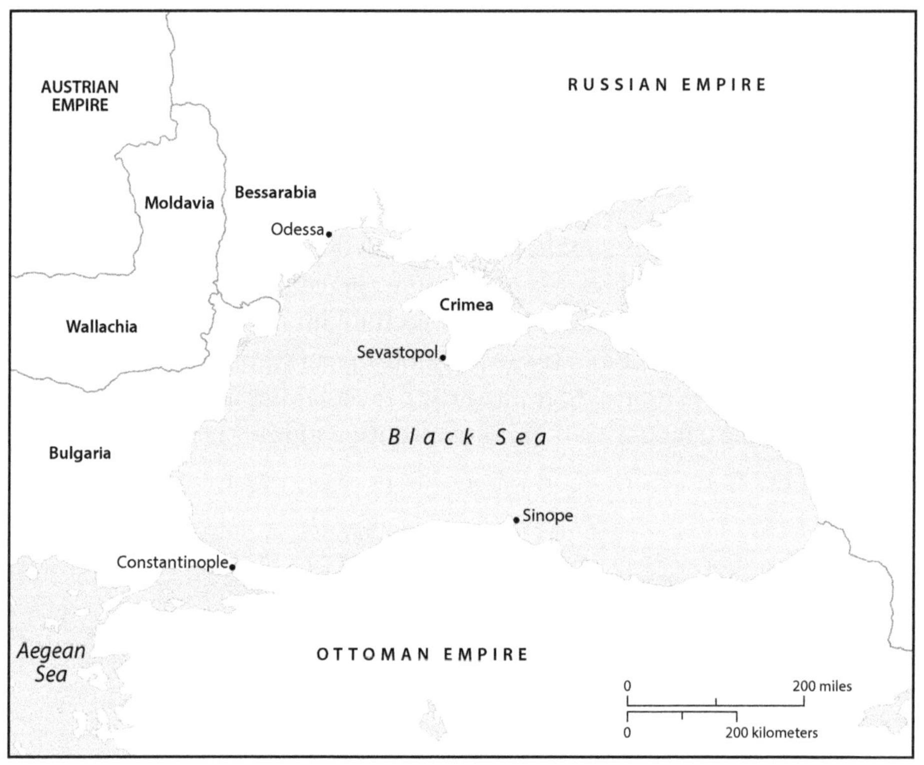

FIGURE 33. Sites of the Crimean War.

soured by his experience with the Duchess of Sagan, formerly of Courland, the Countess Lieven is another "northern Baltic" woman. He quips that these women overcompensate for the barbarism of their birthplace.[10]

The turning point in Lieven's diplomatic life occurs in 1818, when she meets Metternich at the Congress of Aix-la-Chapelle. The two strike up an intimate correspondence that lasts eight years, although they only ever meet three times in person.[11] Despite their pronouncements of affection, Metternich's self-love is not dependent on Lieven's admiration, in contrast with his earlier relationship with Sagan. He is less interested in using his correspondence to control or tutor her. We even find Metternich reflecting sympathetically on the significance of gender to Lieven's fate in life: "If you had been born as a man, you would have climbed to historic

FIGURE 34. Thomas Lawrence, Dorothea Lieven, 1812. Pencil, red and white chalk, 77 × 64 cm. State Hermitage Museum © Alamy.

heights. With a mind and courageousness one can achieve everything."[12] Whether we believe him or not, Metternich explains that his own "liberalisms and simultaneous despotism" have led him to fancy "that the best monarchical regime would be a female sovereign with plenty of intellect and tactfulness, which women possess to a much greater extent than men."[13] We know too that he is ready to take advantage of her political networks for his own ends.

At the Congress of Verona, Lieven participates in overt soft-power diplomacy. Sociability is still conducted through balls, opera, concerts, banquets, and soirées, but Metternich and the Russian minister Nesselrode ask her to open her home to the delegates.[14] Although Lieven's salon is not organized around any intellectual method, as Staël's once was, presiding monarchs, from Tsar Alexander to the kings of Sardinia, Naples, and Prussia, all collect there every evening until two in the morning. Notable women also attend, including Bonaparte's second wife, Archduchess Marie-Louise, and Castlereagh's sister-in-law, Lady Londonderry. Lieven trumpets that she is in daily contact with the most remarkable persons in Europe. She seizes the moment to facilitate discussion to the ends of British, Russian, and even Austrian policymaking. She secretly sends information on to Russia's London embassy and asks for information she sometimes shares with Metternich.[15] She brags that her knowledge of events and people, particularly her relationships with Metternich and Wellington—"these two constellations antipathetic to the [Russian] Emperor's ante-chamber"—are of more use than anything her husband or other Russian diplomats offer. Even so, many Russians distrust her because she has lived in England for ten years and because she sees Metternich every day. Nesselrode, Pozzo di Borgo, and Tattischeff, all of whom she regards as part of the tsar's "ante-chamber," attend her salon out of obligation rather than preference.[16]

It is around this time that, in the vacuum of congress action, Lieven begins her ardent interventions on behalf of Greek independence from the Ottoman Empire. She calls on the defense of Christian Europe and the interests of "humanity."[17] Although Lieven is Lutheran, she insists on Orthodox Russia's duty to protect the Ottoman Greeks; Greek nationalism is not a question of liberalism for this conservative woman but rather of Russian patriotism. Her position goes against Metternich, who still prefers non-intervention on the grounds of not disrupting relations with the Ottomans. He stands by his concept of a "society of states" and the right of the Ottoman Empire to defend its territorial sovereignty as the core of a European peace.[18] The more Metternich is determined to avoid war, the more Lieven's appetite for war grows.[19] Their rival views come to a head in 1825, when Metternich's wife, Eleanor, dies and he marries the twenty-one-year-old Antonia von Leykam. Despite Lieven's eight years of correspondence with Metternich, she is taken by surprise and feels betrayed. Her opposition to Metternich is now galvanized.[20] She questions "Metternich's talents and intelligence," reminding her correspondents that even Castlereagh, otherwise Metternich's ally, sometimes called him "a political harlequin."[21]

Neither Prince Metternich nor Princess Lieven has decisive control of the unraveling of European multilateralism entwined as it is in the progress of Greek national history. In 1825, the year of Metternich's remarriage, the continental credit bubble bursts, sending Europe's stock exchanges into turmoil and rendering worthless the Greek bonds sold by philhellenes. This same year Lieven finds herself on a mission in St. Petersburg, pressing Tsar Alexander to change foreign policy course. "I said to him," she writes, "'Put your foot down Sire, and you will make the whole world tremble,' for that was precisely what the emperor did not think that he could dare to do." According to Lieven, Alexander marvels at her transformation into "a stateswoman."[22]

There is evidence other than Lieven's memoirs that supports her version of events. The tsar screws up his courage and sends her back to London as his "living dispatch." She is to deliver the tsar's "living secret" to the English government, namely, the possibility of Russian intervention in the Greek question. Lieven must negotiate with Castlereagh's successor, George Canning, an open anti-interventionist critical of the "congressing" impetus, and with the Duke of Wellington as the British envoy determined to prevent British foreign policy from being decided by European consensus. Within months, Lieven obtains the agreement of Canning and Wellington to intervention on behalf of Greek renegades and at the expense of the Ottomans. Britain moves from refusing Russian requests for a conference on the Greek question to a bold alliance in defense of Greek independence. Temperley glosses this historical moment as Lieven's "first great diplomatic triumph" and "a turning point in the diplomacy of England and of Russia."[23]

What Lieven has started continues the following year, under the auspices of Alexander's successor, Tsar Nicholas. The Protocol of St. Petersburg is signed in April 1826 by men who connect the future of Greece with the 1814 past: Wellington, Nesselrode, and Dorothea Lieven's husband. Their agreement consolidates the revolution in Anglo-Russian relations and rationalizes their bilateral intervention in the Greek question as an act of invited mediation on "principles of religion, justice, and humanity."[24] They politely presume the Ottoman Empire's sovereignty cannot simply be usurped and that Greek autonomy, whether on the peninsula or in Ottoman/Russian borderlands, does not require a national state. Instead, autonomous Greek regions will pay tribute to the Ottomans and gain, in return, "complete liberty of conscience, entire freedom of commerce." By now, such conditions comfortably echo the liberal tenets of the 1814 order. But the protocol adds a novel condition: the territory in question will separate the "Individuals of the two Nations" by giving Greeks the right to "purchase the property of Turks, whether situated on the Continent of Greece, or in the Islands."[25]

A second agreement "for the pacification of Greece," "sentiments of humanity," and "the tranquillity of Europe" adds one more European signatory: France. The Ottoman parties have no say in the 1827 "Treaty of London," which claims to be dealing with "all the disorders of anarchy," not least the piracy that impedes "the Commerce of the States of Europe." The treaty tackles these problems by accentuating religious separation as the principle of Greek independence within the Ottoman Empire and by making Greeks "the possessor of all Turkish Property situated either upon the Continent, or in the Islands of Greece."[26] The three European powers warn that any rejection of these terms is to be met with the recognition of Greece de facto through the initiation of commercial relations and sending and receiving consular agents.

Instead of resolving tensions, the trilateral intervention provokes Ottoman military resistance; then, in response, a British squadron infamously bombs Ottoman ships anchored in the Bay of Navarino in the southwestern Peloponnese, as Russian and French ships stand by. Russia feels emboldened to declare war on the Ottoman Empire, which leads Britain and France to regret having assisted Russian expansionism. Against this background, a new Hellenic state is carved out of the Greek peninsula, and Kapodistrias becomes its president. When Kapodistrias is assassinated two years later, Britain, France, and Russia replace him with a seventeen-year-old Roman Catholic Bavarian prince. Backed by Rothschild loans, King Otto practices absolute rule in peninsular

Greece, while the Ottomans retain authority in areas south of Russia's border populated by Greek Orthodox subjects.

Through this decade of erratic British, Russian, and French relations, and the shifting organization of Europe-identified political authority, Lieven works the transnational webs of her influence on behalf of Orthodox Greeks in the Ottoman Empire. Her admirers celebrate her London salon as a distraction from politics, "the point of reunion for all errant diplomats who did not allow public affairs to interfere with that part of the evening which is legitimately due to digestion and society." But her critics accuse her of thinking "only of politics."[27] In 1834, allegations of political meddling lead to Lieven's banishment by Lord Palmerston—even though Palmerston is an old friend who in the past relied on Lieven's support for the position of foreign secretary.[28] Lieven is clearly traumatized by her forced return to Russia, but within a few years, she makes her home in Paris, from where she indefatigably pursues politics and her version of soft-power diplomacy.

In Paris, Lieven rents a section of the Rue St. Florentin residence of the recently deceased Talleyrand. It does not escape her that this was where Talleyrand as French foreign minister often hosted statesmen and diplomats. The building is owned by the Rothschilds, who have bought it from her good friend the Duchess of Dino (Sagan's sister), who inherited it from Talleyrand. Lieven is not modest about her ambitions. On the assumption that she will be left out of the grand historical narratives of diplomacy, she records for posterity her career as a diplomat. However, the widespread rumors of her relationship with François Guizot, a fellow widower and Protestant, rest on *his* fame. Through the decades of Guizot's relationship with Lieven, he is French ambassador to Britain, French foreign minister, and ultimately prime minister. As in London, where, together with the Duchess of Dino, Lieven maneuvered ministerial roles and proclaimed a female shadow cabinet, in Paris she is keen to develop her networks.[29] Like Guizot, she utilizes her connections with the Rothschilds to find out gossip and news that might help her anticipate policy directions—even against Guizot, who is an adherent of the "Doctrinaires" in the footsteps of Staël's moderate, pragmatic liberalism.[30]

According to historian Steven Kale, throughout this period, Lieven's influence "was the subject of the most elaborate suspicions

FIGURE 35. Daniel Pound, *George Hamilton-Gordon, 4th Earl of Aberdeen*, 1860. Steel engraving. Library of Congress.

and far-reaching exaggerations"; Guizot's "scandalous intimacy" with a Russian princess causes great resentment among French politicians and "a violent outcry" in the French diplomatic corps: whose diplomacy is Guizot practicing? No one in Paris can agree whether Lieven is "a mastermind or a puppet," whether she is trying to turn Guizot against Austria and toward Russia, or perhaps she wants to see her own brother "replace Nesselrode as Russian foreign minister"?[31] Lieven's salon is described as a "hive of intrigue," and her circle of *ambassadrices*—including the French duchesse Decazes, Hungarian Madame Apponyi, and Austrian

Maria-Theresa—is taken as proof that Russia possesses "a completely organized female diplomacy" run by a "concealed army of amphibious agents."[32] These "political Amazons with acute masculine minds and feminine language . . . gather information, obtain reports and give advice to the Czar's court." On some views, "she and her salon were controlled alternatively by the English and the Russians, with the two influences cancelling each other out."[33]

In the decade of difficult tensions in Anglo-Russian and Anglo-French relations, prior to the outbreak of the Crimean War, Lieven is in deep correspondence with the increasingly powerful Earl of Aberdeen, an enemy of Lord Palmerston. It turns out a solid investment on her part. Lieven broaches her epistolary relationship with Aberdeen while he is out of office, in retreat at his inherited Scottish estate. They write secretly. She tells him to put a "D" on the envelope intended for her, inside another envelope addressed by another hand to "Monsieur Paul de Tolstoy." He advises her to write to "John Newman Esquire" with "the letter D. upon the inclosure."[34] An alumnus of Chaumont, Aberdeen has in the past urged intervention on behalf of Greeks in the Ottoman Empire on the grounds of religious kinship and humanity. In 1841, Aberdeen is returned to Parliament as secretary for foreign affairs, and then, in 1852, he is prime minister just as Lieven seeks backing for Russian and Christian interests on behalf of Tsar Nicholas, who has for three decades pursued a policy of brinkmanship around the Greek question.

Lieven has the opportunity to see Aberdeen in London in 1848, in the midst of Europe's revolutionary tumult. She flees Paris, first by seeking refuge in the Austrian embassy and then traveling dressed as the wife of the English painter David Roberts, with gold and jewels hidden in her clothes. A lot has changed since she first arrived in London in 1813. She now travels by train; the same train carries Guizot via Belgium. Other things have not changed. The now redundant Metternich is also in exile in England and has taken a villa on Brighton Beach, where he occasionally runs into Lieven. Dorothea records caustically that he is talkative, repetitive, and "always infallible!" and his wife is fat and vulgar.[35]

Within a year Lieven is back in post-revolution Paris, and Palmerston complains that she is plotting against him in cahoots with Guizot. Lieven's correspondence with Aberdeen suggests that she is less interested in Palmerston than in priming Russia to go hard on the Greek question, negotiating Britain and France into submission. At the outset of 1853, as the ebullient Tsar Nicholas tests the waters of British opinion on a possible partition of the Ottoman Empire and sends a "man of war" to the straits of Constantinople to make demands of the Turkish government, Lieven and Aberdeen dance around the prospects for peace. She navigates her relationship with Aberdeen in order to have the British see events from an official Russian point of view. Aberdeen's intention is to make clear to Lieven that the British government answers to its public. Her letters commonly include reports intended to prove Britain's unilateral intervention in Ottoman policy against Russia in this period.[36]

During this time, Lieven is a conduit of communication between Paris and St. Petersburg for the French and Russians too.[37] When the Russian ambassador in France urges Tsar Nicholas to be moderate in his dealings with the French, Lieven revels in the opportunity to prompt this tsar to play tough in the defense of Orthodox minorities in the Ottoman Empire, which he obliges. In May 1853, Russia occupies the perennially contested Ottoman territories on its southern border; six months later British ships enter the Black Sea alongside the French navy and provoke the Crimean War. Lieven tries to help Russia defuse British reactions to its demands on Turkey, accusing Aberdeen of belligerence and opportunism; Aberdeen puts the British case that Tsar Nicholas has all the cards in his hands. She tries to reason with Aberdeen that Britain should not defend "Turkey" (as the Ottoman Empire is increasingly called) because that would mean protecting the priests of a foreign religion.[38] Aberdeen is as ready as Lieven to blame the Ottomans for their "fanatical spirit . . . encouraged by the hope of being able to rely on the assistance of England and France." Both correspondents testify that war is "a disgrace to the civilized world."[39]

As prime minister, it is Aberdeen's decision to go to war with France against Russia—*not* on the romantic argument of Christian or European kinship but on behalf of commercial interests in the Black Sea region.[40] Ironically, four decades after Chaumont, Aberdeen is attacked by his compatriots for being an appeaser, for preferring the values of the European "concert" over confidence in British interests and military capacity; his reputation barely survives. In turn, Lieven is accused by all sides of being an enemy agent, as well as a living symbol of the unchecked covert political influence of women. She flees Paris for London yet again, a Russian persona non grata.

The Crimean War is fought out over nearly two and a half bloody years, between Russia under Nicholas I, on one side, and a coalition led by Britain, Napoleon III's France, and Austria, with the Ottoman Empire, on the other. According to some historical arguments the war was "minor" because it involved the death of less than 100,000 combatants. However, it is as infamous for the terrible effect on civilians who, like the soldiers, succumb to disease as much as guns.[41] This aspect of the war is the context in which Florence Nightingale becomes the figure of modern nursing, transforming politics "of the bandaging kind" from an informal practice of patriotic women to the scientific mobilization of Christian humanitarianism. Within three years of the Crimean War's end, similar humanitarian sentiments will invent the Red Cross; hopes eventually hang on international laws making war more humane rather than entrenching peace.

The 1856 Congress of Paris

At the Congress of Paris, Europe's imperial powers attempt to pick up where the Congress of Vienna left off. For Emperor Napoleon III, the comparison between 1814 and 1856 is personal, rewriting the earlier history of defeat. The French monarch, who traces his roots to his uncle Bonaparte, is not interested in European solidarity. He revels in France's moral and military victory over Russia. He has invested substantially in a state-enhancing new diplomacy by building a sumptuous Ministry of Foreign Affairs at the Quai d'Orsay, now the congress stage. At the Congress of Paris, meetings are held in the salon of the ambassadors in the new ministry building, the men seated in alphabetical order around a table especially made and covered with green velvet cloth. The Ottoman Empire is represented at the Congress of Paris by its secular reformist foreign minister Mehmed Emin Ali Pasha. Britain sends its ambassador to France, Lord Cowley, a nephew of the Duke of Wellington. Over the efficient less than two months of the Paris congress that begins on 25 February 1856, twenty-four meetings are held at the Quai d'Orsay, with some commissions, and only five general sessions. The diplomats' work is rationalized with a familiar language of humanity, increasingly inflected through qualifying claims of civilization.[42] Their discussions and agreements are enhanced by the technology of the telegraph, which allows them to communicate in real time with their respective ministries and monarchs. The telegraph also allows an expanded European press to report for a global audience, and they are all conscious of the historical comparison with the 1814 "grande assemblée déliberante de l'Europe."[43] *Le Figaro* proclaims that, unlike Vienna, *this* congress works, dines, dances, and sleeps hardly at all.[44]

In 1856, as in 1814, a limited public navigates the diplomacy of peacemaking through its avenues of sociability and networking. Non-state actors even exert some influence on the international concerns of the congress agenda. Three members of the English Peace Society, founded in 1816 in London by the Quakers so admired by Tsar Alexander, attend in order to lobby the congress diplomats on the importance of arbitration as a method of preventing war.[45] The result is that the congress expresses a "wish" that mediation might be the first port of call when disagreement occurs among treaty partners; states in conflict should appeal to the "good offices of a friendly power before resort to force."[46]

The Congress of Paris continues the paradoxes of the transformations in diplomacy and international politics. The French ministry's offices are a testament to the substantial modernity of France's bureaucracy; even though its staff run to less than one hundred people, aristocrats and military figures are still the staple of French diplomacy, and there is still no meritocratic exam for entry. Ancien aristocratic forms of sociability mingle with modern legal and institutional forms of diplomatic practice and political convention. Paris has recently held the Universal Exposition, celebrating the industry of imperial empires and a new culture of international awareness. It is also the height of the Paris season and receptions are de rigeur on the basis that the "excellencies" are at a congress and not on a diet.

Diplomatic soirées at the Congress of Paris are organized by state delegates, including the emperor and empress, as part of diplomacy. Women continue to have an "unstable" political status in this ancien and modern social setting. Lieven, now seventy-one years old, has returned, along with other Russians who reappear on the social scene after an early absence at the beginning of the war. Although frail, she runs her salon as a focal point for Russian diplomats hoping to meet with French counterparts, to no less controversial effect than before. The capriciousness of women in questions of security occupies contemporaries, even the victorious Ottomans. The latter blame their diminished military capacity on a crippling state deficit and the extravagant "conspicuous consumption by palace women," "sisters, daughters and harem favourites of the Sultan." The women's behavior, in turn, is traced to "the influence of Europeans and Egyptian ladies," occasionally the sultan himself, whose "love for his wives [including a Christian woman] . . . was ruining the country."[47]

Ottoman historians have remarked that what mattered in the making of the 1856 peace were the interests of the ruling classes of France and Britain, not the Ottomans; "the great powers tried to find solutions with little reference to the Porte." While visual records of peacemaking diplomacy now include a Turkish figure wearing the characteristic fez, and legal documents refer to the Ottoman sultan as "His Majesty," a titular elevation, integration is more complicated.[48] Article 7 of the agreed Treaty of Paris "explicitly states that Istanbul could partake in the advantages of European Public Law." But before then, the European powers legalize their interference in the Ottoman state at a preemptive side conference held in January 1856 in Constantinople.

The Constantinople conference is one more nail in the coffin of the Ottoman Empire as an equal European treaty partner. Legal historian Mostafa Minawi helps us understand how this "break with the past" is "performed" and "enforced," in order to legally re-create Ottoman sovereignty "according to the moving targets of European notions of international law." According to Minawi, a parallel European legal system redraws the boundaries of Ottoman sovereignty on the international stage, "just as international law was incorporated into the toolkit of justifying the usurping of sovereignty through direct and indirect forms of colonialism."[49]

Some of the groundwork for this indirect colonialism is laid during the Crimean War, when European bankers oversee the integration of the Ottoman Empire into the European financial system through the provision of sovereign debt loans. Under the fiscal pressure of its war effort, the Ottoman government takes out three "tribute loans" backed by Egyptian tribute revenue and a "guaranteed loan" backed by British and French governments. The credit enablers are the Vienna House of Eskeles (now run by the son of Cecilia and Bernhard), which regularly acts as an intermediary between French and Austrian diplomats passing on correspondence, and the Paris and London Rothschild branches.[50] In 1853, the Ottoman grand vizier gives instructions to his London-based diplomat Namik Pasha to contract a loan for 500,000 *kese* "in favourable terms." (This is 2.5 million Ottoman pounds or around 2.27 million pounds sterling.)[51] This 1853 Rothschild loan is followed the next year by a second larger loan of 5 million pounds at 6 percent, with the "issue price of 85 percent," and a third in 1855. In one of the more perverse principles of investment, creditors calculating the risk of their investment find the prospect of peace less appealing than war. The Ottoman government will default on all of these loans by the 1870s.

At the secret Constantinople talks, British, French, and Austrian plenipotentiaries pursue the theme of economic sovereignty. They return to the Vienna "Free Navigation" agenda of "free ships, free goods," although with less emphasis on its importance for cultivating peaceful relations between neighboring states.[52] Navigation on the Danube, a river that connects European and Ottoman trade routes, is declared free and subject to the European Commission of the Danube, removing Russia from a position of control at the river's mouth. Similarly, the European empires declare the Black Sea "neutral" and the Turkish Straits closed to warships, taking away from Russia and the Ottoman Empire their right to position their navies there. Meanwhile, the new regulations also subject the Ottoman Empire's sovereign rights on the Black Sea to unilateral conditions favoring the European allies.

Religion is as much the focus of discussions that have equally debilitating implications for Russian and Ottoman sovereignty. Britain and France agree (among themselves) first to repeal the Treaty of Küçük Kaynarca, which for nearly a century has given Russia the duty of care of Greek Orthodox subjects of the Ottoman Empire, blaming the war on its "misinterpretation."[53] On the one hand, they make Russia cede southern Bessarabia to Turkey's province of Moldavia; on the other, they do not give the Ottomans the duty of care of their Christian subjects—they give it to themselves.[54] Negotiating under the banner of Europe, Britain and France (primarily) add a requirement that their Ottoman allies must allow conversion to Christianity within the empire, thereby opening the floodgates to Christian missionary activity in that predominantly Muslim realm.[55] They act as if the Ottoman Empire has not previously attempted its own reforms improving the Christians' status under Sultan Mahmud (1808–1839), as though Christian groups were not complicit in fomenting dissension by rejecting those reforms precisely in order to be able to call upon the protection of foreign powers.[56] Instead, now they reinvent the Ottoman state's unequal status through a regime of commercial and religious relations and so-called "capitulations" that bestow privileges on Christians and the European empires.[57]

Some of the steps taken in the Europeans' peace terms look to the international future. This includes the "timid attempt" to codify a law for the prevention of war, which, along with the Danube commission, will later claim a place in histories of a liberal international order. Their Declaration of Maritime Law is presented as adding to the "high-flying sentiments" embodied in the post-1814 engagement of the slave trade and freedom of navigation, and piracy, and as codifying "the first general agreement about naval war valid even beyond the jurisdiction of European international law," in the name of "the spirit of the century and the progress of civilization."[58] However, their practical focus is less romantic and more Realpolitik, namely preventing the seizure of either enemy goods under neutral flags or neutral goods under enemy flags and reducing the strategic use of blockades because of their impact on "free ships, free goods." Within a few years, this new legal infrastructure enables the French to exercise a *droit d'intervention* in Ottoman Lebanon and Syria on *humanitarian* grounds. The logic of the separation of religious communities will become a mainstay of the arsenal of peacemaking, culminating in the 1923 Treaty of Lausanne.[59]

Dorothea Lieven dies in 1857, the year after the Congress of Paris, her body discovered alone at her abode on Rue St. Florentin. Guizot almost immediately takes up with the Duchess of Sagan—not

Wilhelmina, who dies in 1839 in Vienna, but her younger sister Dorothea. What is Lieven's legacy? She has neither prevented a war nor ensured Russia's success in the Greek question. She can be said to represent the force of women's political ambitions and the appeal of diplomacy as a site of political agency. As an actor in the drama of Greece, her interventions reflected her interest in Russian foreign policy and the imperative of Christian collective security. Indeed, grasping the mix of Lieven's motivations significantly nuances the history of nineteenth-century national causes, the range of emotions and practices concealed in histories of state-building.[60] In this history, Lieven's and Eynard's national sentiments similarly connect humanitarianism, religious identification, patriotism for other people's independence, and even cupidity.

The period that follows the Congress of Paris marks the end of an era in other ways. Metternich, among the longest-living protagonists of the peacemaking period, also passes away. For thirty-five years he did his best to rewrite the international past by publishing his version of events as if private relationships and feelings mattered not at all. Instead he focused his memoirs on his mastery of the past, as if he always knew the direction the future would take him and Europe. He restated the tendency of nations "to draw closer together and to set up a kind of corporate body resting on the same basis as the great human society which grew up at the heart of Christianity."[61] By contrast, the changed landscape of European diplomacy marks at least in part the victory of Lieven's Realpolitik vision, especially in regard to her motivations for war and the diminution of the Ottoman Empire's international status to "European protectorate."[62] Religion has bled openly into humanitarianism as an imperative for war, and the romantic rationale of multilateralism has been all but displaced by "free trade," which in turn barely masks the commercial interests of a small group of empires. At the same time, the more detailed the legal conditions of international politics become, the less the scope for political ambiguity. The aspect of these developments in which Metternich might have taken most comfort, perhaps, was the definitive delegitimation of women as political actors and, not least, Lieven's reduction in this history to the status of *femme intrigante*.

CHAPTER SIXTEEN

History

A society of states exists when a group of states conscious of certain common interests and common values form a society in the sense that they conceive themselves to be bound by a common set of rules in their relations with one another, and share in the working of common institutions.

—HEDLEY BULL, *THE ANARCHICAL SOCIETY*

IF FIRSTHAND EXPERIENCE of the wartime Coalition shaped the multilateral and pacifist ambitions of Europe's statesmen and foreign ministers, as some historians claim, how did their historically specific ideas, approaches, and experiences come to influence future generations? Can we attribute the persistence or influence of their ambitions to memory? How would that work? Historians of memory argue that there are two distinct phases in the creation of the historical facts that link the past to the future: witnesses with firsthand knowledge of the events contribute to a "communicative memory"; when that generation dies, a cultural memory is mediated through public histories and memorializations.[1] Even if we disregard the problem of competing memories, or their different status, there is also the selection that occurs at all of these stages. What connects this past to future imaginaries of international order, or the possibilities of international politics at all?

Two hundred years ago, the "scriptomania" of peacemaking made memoirists and correspondents the narrators and archivists of the international order negotiated and written into place. Into these international narratives they poured their feelings, ideas, ideals, and sense of self, their experience of participating in the drama of peace. This is as true for Dorothea Lieven, striving for relevance and envying a diplomatic career, resorting to scraps of self-glorifying autobiography, as for Metternich, penning his letters to the Duchess of Sagan, his memoirs to posterity, and imagining himself striding like a giant through the landscape of Europe. Lieven self-consciously cultivated her place in the history of diplomacy for future audiences and worked on her memoirs to that end over decades—although her abbreviated notes never progressed to more than unpublished scraps. Who got to impress their view of the events in the "communicative" phase of memory was skewed toward gender as much as class or capability. Jean-Gabriel and Anna Eynard both kept diaries of the congresses they attended, but only his version was published.

The protagonists of 1814 were selective in the memories they recorded and wrote as history. Metternich and Lieven, who lived through a half century of the transformations of politics, and Germaine de Staël, who stirred her witness accounts into a general history of the period, reinvented earlier events. Staël was always exceptional, as a woman writing about politics, in disguise, and the author of the first historical overview of the French Revolution. Published posthumously in 1818, Staël's *Considérations sur la révolution française* criticized not only Bonaparte but also members of the Coalition fighting against him. She represented peacemaking at the end of the Napoleonic wars as a lost opportunity, chastising Castlereagh, Talleyrand, and the allied occupying government for abandoning moderate liberal principles such as rule of law, freedom of press, and freedom of religion in favor of personal enrichment. She also censored her personal contribution to events, giving substance to the caveat of her earliest biographer, close friend and cousin Albertine Necker de Saussure: "Only men have been given the right to portray themselves through their actions and to match their external lives to their thoughts."[2]

Although communicative memories of Staël's roles in the playing out of international events were fraying, her stroke-induced death in early 1817 gave rise to a chorus of nostalgia for the new spirit of congressing into which she breathed life. The French novelist Stendhal (no friend of Staël) recalled the popularity of her château on Lake Geneva in the summer of 1816, when, six hundred or so persons, "the most distinguished of Europe," "men [*sic*] of intellect, of wealth, of the greatest titles," gathered in "the most astonishing reunion," carrying themselves like a "parliament," "as if they were states general of European opinion."[3] Early on, Swedish historians comfortably credited Staël with creating "a platform" for the political principles that shaped the liberal view of the war against Bonaparte.[4] The French historian Duvergier de Hauranne inadvertently recorded rumors of a diplomatic stoush in Paris, in which English consuls Sir Charles Stuart and Stratford Canning (aide to Castlereagh at Vienna, and George Canning's cousin) attacked Staël's criticisms of the English and blamed her for "exciting national passions by her language."[5]

Eventually, the cultural memory of Staël's role in Bonaparte's downfall knit together censorious accounts of feminine "intriguing" by the "mistress of her age" and the occasional congenial assessment. Tolstoy acknowledged in passing Staël's importance in the downfall of Bonaparte; Lord Acton, the future editor of the *Cambridge Modern History*, admitted Staël's indirect intellectual contribution to historical progress, although only in writing to George Eliot. In this personal correspondence, he gave Staël credit for rendering liberalism a thing of *bon gout* (good taste), but in the *Cambridge Modern History*, the transformation of European politics is a tale of male diplomats, statesmen, or sovereigns.[6] Until as late as the end of the twentieth century, Staël's place in the histories that kept the memory of peacemaking alive—like her even less well-remembered female compatriots and competitors, Sagan, Levin, Eynard-Lullin, Krüdener, or Lieven—was hostage to the conventions of gendered separate spheres.[7] Subscribed to wholesale by generations of political and intellectual historians, these conventions contributed to the effacement of women in the international past. When women were too significant to ignore, it was as common to reinvent their actions and ideas as cases of individual eccentricity or social trespass rather than worthy of integration into our understanding of the history of politics—national or international.

Narratives of the international past, as much as national pasts, are the end products of who got to remember for a broader public, and what they forgot. It is never inevitable that any communicative or cultural memory retains the perspective of wartime and postwar multilateral possibilities. After the Congress of Verona, the new British foreign minister, George Canning, who lived through Britain's involvement in the campaign against France, defined himself *against* his predecessor Castlereagh's legacy, including his identification with the Coalition and Concert of Europe. With Castlereagh gone, and peacemaking over, Canning was jubilant at the prospect of the "one and indivisible alliance" splitting into its irreconcilable parts, "England, France and Muscovy," and things "getting back to a wholesome state for us all. Every nation for itself, and God for us all."[8] Over the next two hundred years, the romance of peacemaking at the end of the Napoleonic wars becomes a usable past, sometimes celebrated, as often trashed or purposely elided.[9] Sorting through the rubble of memory and history is one way of determining what bearing this past has on possibilities of politics between states, and how the past shapes the future.

Remembering

In 1826, the new Russian tsar Nicholas teamed with the new British foreign minister Canning to intervene in Ottoman affairs and abandon their commitment to the Concert of Europe—an idea to which neither had personally subscribed. That same year, Austrian emperor Francis I, who *was* part of that earlier history of the Concert of Europe, initiated a project in memory of multilateral European peacemaking. His Arco di Pace project refers to a triumphal arch that Napoleon had ordered built in the Italian city of Milan to record his conquest and that Francis now reinvented and completed as a monument to the Coalition. The arch is decorated with marble depictions of the Coalition's victory at the Battle of Leipzig and their conferencing at the Congress of Prague and the Congress of Vienna.[10]

The sites of cultural memory-making are not just to be found in memoirs or brick-and-mortar monuments. In 1814, Castlereagh imagined the form and manner of the Congress of Vienna as a "monument" to the existence of a European *public code* for future generations.[11] In 1828, the New York–based American Peace Society launches an essay prize on the subject of "A Congress of Nations

FIGURE 36. Giambattista Perabò, *The Congress of Vienna*. Bas-relief on the Arch of Peace, Milan, 1826–1838. Wikimedia Commons.

for the adjustment of international disputes and for the promotion of universal peace without resort to arms."[12] The prize, subscribed to by a burgeoning class of international lawyers, continues for decades, its winning entries published for a general readership. The decades of ambassadorial conferences in London and Paris also helped impose an institutional memory of the multilateral ambitions of the Coalition. As Beatrice de Graaf has outlined in her book *Fighting Terror*, these gatherings quietly offer an enduring space for negotiation of security issues, whether borders, colonies, or humanitarian questions.

Through the nineteenth century, a cultural memory of the "Congress of Vienna"—which has come to stand for the period of postwar peacemaking in toto—was purposely regenerated in the context of peacemaking as a template and point of differentiation. In 1856, at

FIGURE 37. Edouard Louis Dubufe, *The Congress of Paris, 1856* (*Le congrès de Paris, 25 février au 30 mars 1856*), published in *The history of the world; a survey of a man's record*, ed. H. F. Helmolt, vol. 8 (New York: Dodd, Mead, 1902).

the end of the Crimean War, when delegates gathered in the French capital to negotiate the terms of peace, the comparisons with the Vienna past were everywhere. The French government fashioned the Paris congress as a means of reclaiming the past—the memory of French defeat was now reinvented in the French victory, and the passage from Napoleon I to Napoleon III was told as an uninterrupted narrative.[13] The now generic methods of peacemaking diplomacy were repeated, and they were captured in the familiar visual representations of statesmen gathered around a table, on the template of Jean-Baptiste Isabey's framing of male sociability. However, this time the Ottoman ally was present, the sign of the fez foregrounded.

Other visual evidence records another familiar sociability, where men and women mingled, although at the separate conference at Constantinople. When we bring the iconography of these two sides of 1856 peacemaking together—the formal and informal, the public and secret—there is no one cultural memory of the forms and practices of an international order. Instead, the evidence exudes unsettledness, from the contradictions of the gender ordering that shaped the new international order to what Cemil Aydin describes as the "asymmetries and unevenness in globalized Christian-Muslim political imaginations."[14]

FIGURE 38. *The Sultan Abdülmecid I at The Fancy Dress Ball Given By The Viscountess Stratford de Redcliffe at the British Embassy at Pera*, from the *Illustrated London News*, 1856. © Alamy.

Diverse, even contradictory, perspectives on the shifting significance of the era of peacemaking were voiced almost from the outset, not least in the critical private narratives of women who found the responsible men barely up to the task. Disillusionment with the new order also spread in more public narratives, as "a story of egotism, jealousy, mistrust, fear, law-breaking and finally war."[15] Seen from this perspective, Byron's epic poem *Don Juan*, too, is one more example of the Concert of Europe as "a symbol of the very problem—autocratic leadership, bellicosity, an incomprehension of the value of freedom and the power of social change."[16] In the longer view of an evolving international order, the Congress of Vienna offers a material, equally controversial focus for reflection on the significance of the Concert's multilateralism. A century later, British historian Ramsay Muir marked the Congress of Vienna's *centennial* by celebrating the 1885 Congress of Berlin as the Concert of

Europe's most remarkable achievement, because the Berlin gathering allowed the "European powers" to peacefully and mutually cooperate in the "partition of Africa."[17] Muir's murky imperialist memory of the international past is indicative of the moral abyss into which imperial powers had thrown their conferencing ambitions, and the Vienna template, by the late nineteenth century. Muir does not mention, but we know from other memoirs and archival documents, bankers and lawyers featured at Berlin, notoriously redeploying the Vienna ideals of free trade (in a "Congo Free State") and free navigation (on the Congo and Niger rivers) in order to enable colonial exploitation.[18]

In 1899, the Concert of Europe became the sign under which Tsar Nicholas II summoned a peace congress at The Hague, this time deliberately evoking Alexander I's peacemaking aspirations. Nicholas II hoped to remind his fellow European sovereigns of this longer history of Russian leadership to the ends of peace and its relevance for deescalating the militarized imperial rivalry dominating the continent. The Hague peace congress too became an iconic historical moment in repertoires of "law and peace" as the instruments of internationalism. Importantly, the innovative centerpiece of modern diplomacy at this time was legal arbitration: international law would prevent conflict between states and mitigate the barbarity of war. The Hague congress's processes and outcomes were reported through a worldwide press with access to the almost immediate messaging of the telegraph. Non-state actors self-consciously organized as "international" did not hesitate to make their own political demands for abolition, or even decolonization, heard alongside their interest in humanizing war.[19] Delegations came from the United States, China, and Thailand as well as Italy and Germany—these relatively *new* European imperial states were products of continental wars fought between the European powers, even pitting Protestants against Catholics.

Over the last two hundred years, peacemaking viewed through the lens of the Concert of Europe and the Congress of Vienna has been deployed as a heuristic for extracting both positive and negative lessons. In 1907, the 2nd Hague Congress, organized through the efforts of a woman, the Austrian aristocrat and pacifist Bertha von Suttner, launched the ideal of a "solidarity that unites the members of a society of civilized nations," in contrast to Congress of Vienna–style diplomacy that worked against a peace based on "law principles."[20] When, a hundred years after the "theater of the world" gathered in Vienna, another European war erupted, triggered by a European system of alliances that split the continent, some historians took aim at the "reactionary and shortsighted" Concert of Europe and its imperializing tendencies.[21] For German historians, peacemaking at the end of the Napoleonic wars rewarded "avaricious mercantilism" by handing Britain a global network of trading colonies in Tobago, St. Lucia, Ceylon, South Africa, Malta, and Heligoland. British historians were no less inclined to equate the Concert of Europe with the Holy Alliance, and both as a rehearsal of the German dream of *Mitteleuropa* in full blush on the Western Front.[22] French historian Charles Seignobos was almost alone in arguing that the Congress of Vienna was the origin of a European state system that respected the sovereignty of public opinion and recognized "the moral authority of international rules."[23] He saw in the record of the Congress of Vienna an omen of the possibility of "a new [international] settlement" in the midst of the conflagration of Europe and suggested that a century on it is time for this political deference to public opinion to bear fruit as a necessary "revolution . . . in [the principles of] international life."[24] Other European public forces reimagined the multilateral dream of a "science of European government" on a radically expanded scale of representative international government, eventually known as the League of Nations.[25]

Reinventing

In the early twentieth century, in state policymaking contexts, selective memories of the principles of international order established at the end of the Napoleonic wars cut deep into the cloth of the purposes and methods of peacemaking. The Congress of Vienna, like the Concert of Europe, might represent a useless idealism, or a realism past its use-by date. In 1918, U.S. president Woodrow Wilson—the historian-cum-president and famous proponent of nationality and the League of Nations—makes his case for American participation in the European war by attacking the Congress of Vienna's legacy of a "shreds and patches" diplomacy. As Wilson rouses his country, he purposely singles out peacemaking at the end of the Napoleonic wars as the opposite of how to arrive at "permanent peace." He sees virtue in invoking its "arrangements between state and state" "discussed separately or in corners."[26] In its place, he conjures images of a future peace "based upon broad and universal principles of right and justice," conducted "in a spirit of unselfish and unbiased justice, with a view to the wishes, the natural connections, the racial aspirations, the security, and the peace of mind of the peoples involved." What is required a century later, according to Wilson, is "international action and . . . international counsel."[27]

Implicit in the president's attacks on the past is the idea that the generation of 1814 failed to foretell the intrinsically national shape of a modern international future. (This is dissimilar only in scope from Friedrich Meinecke's contemporaneous evaluation of Humboldt's shortcomings.) Wilson wields the word and meaning of "international" with a grandiloquent confidence because he can now attach it to the "principle of nationality" as a new unambiguous complementary objective of peacemaking. In practice, however, peacemaking in 1919 under Wilson's supervision is no more the antithesis of Vienna than the 1899 Hague peace congress.

At the end of World War I, the methods and terms, even ambitions, of multilateral peacemaking have not altered significantly, except to the extent that they reflect changes in political, social, economic, and cultural life. The peacemakers are men who gather around tables in discussion, often in closed-off, smoke-filled rooms—just as the earlier tableaus of peacemaking depicted. This time, much as President Wilson promised, nationality is confirmed as a principle of international order even before they meet. However, when commissions are tasked with researching specific territorial issues they turn to statistics or agree that whole populations should be moved on religious-*cum*-ethnic grounds to meet abstract ideas about borders, as happened before.

At the same time, Europe is now represented by an expanded number of empire-nations, invested in expansive economic-imperial connectivity and enabling enlarged public spheres filled with popular political demands, such as universal suffrage. Although few countries give women the vote, women of all political stripes, and from around the world, organize in international associations, in order to bring to the congressing men in Paris their requests for equal status and recognition of their "self-determination." Individual bankers are once again invited to intervene in political and economic crises in Europe and beyond; economic actors now have their own international organizations such as the International Chamber of Commerce to represent their interests. Imperial and national foreign ministries are staffed with men who can rise through public exam systems to meritocratic appointments; some women who train in new public educational institutions find themselves acting as *unofficial* advisors on geopolitical questions (Russia's Alexandra Kollontai and Hungary's Rosika Schwimmer stand out as women who are given formal plenipotentiary roles in the immediate postwar).[28]

The homosociality of diplomatic reunions is institutionalized in international and national settings alike, not least in the establishment of the League of Nations, with its conferencing methods, diplomatic bureaucracy, and world-scale membership. Women interrupt this setting too—as replacement delegates, on a few occasions as national delegates, mostly working in the bureaucracy behind the scenes and networking for representation in humanitarian and social justice questions. The League is depicted as an upscaled version of the allied administrative machinery that cooperated during the Great War. We can also connect its invention to the allied commissions of the Napoleonic wars and consequent peacemaking, melded with the influence of popular wartime League of Nations' associations made up of women and men supporting peace through law, international government, and "international thinking."[29]

That women are involved in this new international multilateral machinery is in part due to decisions taken at the peace to make sure they are excluded from national politics. The enlarged circle of peacemakers (and former alliance partners) are able to agree unanimously that women's demands for political "self-determination" within states presented to them in the conference setting are not akin to the demands of nations for statehood as self-determination; the status of women cannot be an international question, they argue, because determining women's status is the prerogative of nations.[30] At the same time, as Wilson fights off requests from his

FIGURE 39. Helen Johns Kirtland, *Dignitaries gathered in the Hall of Mirrors at Versailles to sign the peace treaty ending World War I, 28 June 1919*, 1919. Library of Congress, Prints and Photographs Division, Washington, D.C.

Japanese and Chinese allies for a racial equality convention in the League's founding charter, the peace process makes further refinements to the civilizational as well as gender ordering of a century earlier.

Even though the postwar peace is decided in Europe, "Europe" is no longer the dominant authority in this new international community. Nor is Russia party to the expanding institutional basis of the politics between states manifest in the League of Nations (even though Alexandra Kollontai attends as a Soviet delegate).[31] Russia has cut itself adrift after the 1917 Bolshevik Revolution, which entrenches the appeal of an alternative international imaginary based on the connections between the working classes of the world. The success of the Bolshevik Revolution is the provocation for an expanded view of the kind of politics relevant to the international domain. The peacemakers create a sister body to the League, the International Labor Organization (ILO), with constitutional obligations to "sentiments of justice and humanity" and "social justice."[32] For those attentive to the thinner strands of the memory of the Concert of Europe, the ILO's interest in the "conditions of labour . . . involving such injustice, hardship, and privation to large numbers of people" because of their threat to "the peace and harmony of the world," is traceable to the congress predictions of Robert Owen.[33] In all these direct and indirect ways, peacemaking in 1919 reinvents the processes of "ordering" and possibilities that shaped the international domain of politics a century earlier—even if there is little memory of the more complex history of that process or of the range of public and popular political ambitions it inspired.[34]

By the mid-twentieth century, another consuming, exhausting, devastating world war returns some minds to a memory of the Concert of Europe. One of its most curious appearances is in Karl Polanyi's classic study *The Great Transformation: The Political and Economic Origins of Our Time*, published in 1944.[35] Polanyi argues that after the original generation of statesmen died out, a "subgroup of financiers," specifically the House of Rothschild, carried the torch. On this view, the financiers who benefited from both the multilateral principle of peacemaking and the commercial benefits of peace became the communicative *and* cultural memory-makers of "abstract internationalism" and "pragmatic pacifism."[36] This emphasis on the symbiotic relationship between the invention of an international politics and international finance situates nationalism as the refuge of a "countermovement," against the negative social effects of free-range market capitalism without borders.[37] Polanyi invites reflection on the extent to which the point of a *liberal* international order has become more simply the principle of free trade alone.

In that same wartime moment, it is as evident that a free trade version of multilateralism is not the only focus. The vast United Nations Conference on International Organization is assembled by the allies in San Francisco in April 1945 to draft a charter for a new multilateral body. It conceives the new organization much like an international version of a national parliament: a UN overseen by an "upper house" in the guise of the Security Council, freezing in time an omniscient "Committee of Five," with Russia back in the fold, alongside Britain, France, China, and the United States. When the IMF and the World Bank are added to the UN system (the WTO would come later), the ties *between* international finance and politics are further entrenched. However, the contemporaneous establishment of UNESCO, with its mission to educate the world in peace and cooperation, substantiates a different strand of multilateral international thinking. Together with the ongoing functions of the ILO, it gives institutional form to Robert Owen's proposals to the Congress of Aix-la-Chapelle, without knowing it.

The connections between the new international order introduced at the end of World War II and the range of ambitions, or even breadth of politics, attached to the promise of peacemaking at the end of the Napoleonic wars are rarely remembered. We can plot their multilateral dimensions in the popularity of concepts such as the "solidarism" touted in the late nineteenth century by the French prime minister-cum-foreign minister Léon Bourgeois, or the late twentieth-century concept of "international society," defined by political scientist Hedley Bull as the "perception of common interests" at an international level and "cooperation in the working of common international institutions."[38] On occasion, governments have interpreted the remaking of Europe after Napoleon to national ends. In 2016 the Russian government commemorated Tsar Alexander as one of the founders of a system of *European* security, when "'conditions for the so-called balance were created, based not only on mutual respect for the interests of different countries, but also on moral values.'" Turkish discourses on the value of the European Union have referenced the 1856 Paris congress, with the intention of dispelling any doubts about Turkey's own European character.[39] But mostly, it is hard not to agree with historians of the wars of the French Revolution and Napoleonic Empire who argue that in the early twentieth century, the early nineteenth-century chapter of the past is closed and "has long since ceased to haunt the memory of European societies."[40]

More than two hundred years after the end of the Napoleonic wars, the cultural memory of the spectrum of ideas and innovations that comprise the international past is thin. In the West, popular and political discourse tends to locate the origins of the existing international order in 1945, while dwelling on the cultural, economic, political, and military leadership of the United States.[41] It is as if our age is characteristically the opposite of the early nineteenth-century *Sattelzeit*, with its unprecedented tendency to question decisions and events "depending on how the past was valued and how the future was anticipated."[42] It is worth returning to an older, more capacious history of peacemaking and the invention of international order—whether understood as revolution or evolution, as restoration or aberration—in order to understand and imagine the possibilities of multilateralism in the future. We might take from that history the lesson that there are no uninterrupted lines connecting the past and present, that the borders between forward- and backward-looking political imaginaries are blurred, and that the international order is a matter of perpetual reinvention. History is also a reminder that the possibilities of politics between states, like the question of who gets to do politics and how the past and future are imagined, have mattered for at least 200 years.

EPILOGUE

Paradoxes

All of the contradictions of Europe are gathered here, and preserve a balance somewhat.

—KARL VARNHAGEN TO MARCUS THEODOR, 20 JANUARY 1815

Reading for paradox requires a different kind of reading than historians are accustomed to.

—JOAN SCOTT, *ONLY PARADOXES TO OFFER*

AT THE end of the Napoleonic wars, no one set out to invent an international order. Even now, this abstract concept does not easily translate into a topic for policymaking. According to some analyses, the international order is "a collective design effort by world leaders coming together to reconcile their interests"; alternatively, it emerges "not from cooperation and deliberation but from a cruder calculus of power and material constraints."[1] Scholars of international relations at times define the source of international order as the political organization of authority, pressing us to think beyond individual motivations to the nature of politics itself. Who has authority? How do they get it? What ordering enables that authority, or is produced by it?

Once we consider the messiness of individual actions and ideas, caught up in the flow of time—to borrow from Metternich one last time, "floating between present and future"—such questions are riddled with paradox and contradiction. In early 1815, the Prussian diplomat Karl Varnhagen wrote to his banker brother-in-law in Berlin that the Congress of Vienna was "the strangest friction of old forms and notions, and the comprehension of brand-new conditions. The heads of great forces move without direction, the heads of single states are confused, and one cannot foresee what should come of it all."[2] Some of the paradoxes of this period were also the deliberate result of the choices the "heads" made, not least a version of European political modernity that came at a cost to women's authority and legitimacy as political actors.

For historians of gender in political history, there are no surprises in the conjunction of political modernity and the political marginalization of women. Historian Joan Scott has argued that, in the European context, "the discursive practices of democratic politics . . . have equated individuality with masculinity"; as a consequence, we should read with an eye to "the unsettledness that paradox, contradiction, and ambiguity imply."[3] In this epilogue, my aim is to review some of the unsettledness of the modern international order at a moment of invention: from its gender conundrum to its simultaneously imperial and international, international and national, political and capitalist, liberal and conservative characteristics. While Varnhagen thought "all of the contradictions of Europe" preserved "a balance somewhat," with hindsight, reading for paradox reveals the historical extent of seemingly contrary ambitions heaped onto the politics between states. Reading for paradox is also a reminder of the stakes of this international history: how the balance tipped in favor of some voices and views and not others; how the possibilities of international politics both opened up and closed off; how political authority and hierarchy were exercised and somehow ordered.

Masculine/Feminine

For most of the last two hundred years, international historians have designated diplomacy and the politics between states as the natural terrains of states*men* and (masculine) state actors—even when non-state actors, including women, have been visible and their voices on the record, ready to be heard. By contrast, historians of nation-states have been more attentive to gendered boundaries of the making of modern politics in the nineteenth century, including the public spheres that engendered national identification and agency, such as the all-male "dining societies" and coffeehouse communities interspersed across Europe's municipalities. These same national developments are mirrored in the international history of the professionalization and bureaucratization of diplomacy as a site of masculine authority and sociability, and the intersecting decline of the female-led salon as an authoritative site of mixed sociability and political negotiation. This coincided with a view of women as overly subject to their feelings and, as a result, illegitimate political agents—although a woman such as Germaine de Staël, for example, was as likely to consider a woman's capacity to be both rational and emotional as the basis of her superiority.[4]

Tested at the level of individual lives and ideas over the course of decades, noticeable gendered structural and ideological shifts were inconsistent and incomplete. When we probe the international contexts of this history, we find that the emotional authenticity of homosocial communities and the self-mastery of men are equally inscribed in national and international narratives. In the midst of emerging typologies of the masculine modern statesman, diplomat, and civil servant (and eventually the international lawyer), the aristocratic duel remained popular. In 1809 Castlereagh, then Britain's minister for war, challenged George Canning, foreign secretary at the time, to a duel for disrespecting him. In 1813, Staël's wayward son Albert, who traveled with the Coalition campaign as Bernadotte's assistant, was killed in a duel fought over reputation. The following year, Baron Wilhelm von Humboldt took a crucial role in defining the practices and purposes of modern conferencing, and dueled with the Prussian minister of war over a slight. In 1822, the philosopher Benjamin Constant (Staël's erstwhile collaborator) famously fought a duel against the French ultra-royalist deputy Forbin des Issarts as settlement of a political disagreement. Despite Constant's fifty-five years of age and his crippling ill health (to the extent he could barely stand), the philosopher opted for a method of conflict resolution that he had relied upon since his youth. Dueling's relevance as a method of resolving differences and salvaging "honor" persisted through the last decades of the nineteenth century. It became the masculine metaphor of choice for the purpose and functioning of international law and the invented international tradition of a "rules-based" order.[5]

In the nineteenth-century remaking of Europe after Napoleon, the gendering of separate public and private spheres became the default premise of diplomatic conferencing, in contradistinction to an older, more ambiguous congress sociability. Nevertheless, it was hard to change the habits of a generation, or those generations that followed. In 1817, the English diplomat Frederick Lamb wrote from Frankfurt where the German confederation was under discussion that the lack of women opening their homes had stymied negotiations.[6] In 1856, in the context of the Congress of Paris, after the Crimean War, the French government chose to recapture the ancien sociability of the Congress of Vienna, alongside its show of modern bureaucratic diplomacy. This was in the midst of an evolving emphasis on the training and meritocratic careers of diplomats and on the recasting of the role of *ambassadrice* as assistant to her husband's career.[7] Of course, individual women continued to utilize the ancien salon as a method of soft-power diplomacy through the nineteenth century. In the 1850s, Napoleon III's wife, Empress Eugenie, and mistress, the Countess Castiglione, both had strong views on French diplomacy and foreign policy and the Italian question, which they impressed on their man.[8]

In the mid-nineteenth century, ancien practices overlapped with new gendered humanitarian norms that we can trace back to the Napoleonic wars. The Crimean War legend of nurse Florence Nightingale echoed politics "of the bandaging kind" as an acceptable form of women's political engagement; that now became a female-focused humanitarianism on the battlefield, embedded in science and law. At the same time, the expanded international public sphere in which women's individual diplomacy was frowned upon also gave women a space to organize collectively on a transnational basis, to exert their moral or humanitarian influence on international issues such as abolition, peace, and war, and on behalf of their political rights within national and imperial states. However, it was only in the late twentieth century that women were likely to be appointed to political roles as diplomats and more likely to lead foreign affairs portfolios—unlike their absence in other ministerial or political offices and regardless of the liberal or conservative cast of government.[9] This development constitutes its own paradoxical logic, given the long European history of women's involvement in diplomacy and the politics between states, their simultaneous presence and absence, and their erasure.

Imperial/International

Through the first decade of peacemaking, innovations in diplomatic practice and political expectations, philanthropic and Christian moral purpose projected the authority of Europe in the world. It is significant that this Europe was the project of a handful of imperial powers often pitted against each other. Outside the reduced circle sat states and empires that had otherwise taken roles during the war or immediately after, whether Sweden, Spain, Portugal, the Netherlands, or Switzerland, as well as some smaller principalities. The imperial "Committee of Four" gave legitimacy to the cultural ideas of Poland and Germany in limited political forms, sometimes out of strategic concerns, at others in response to petitioning and publicity; these same empires/national states also supplemented and contradicted the promise of multilateral Europe by making unilateral and bilateral secret arrangements.

The Concert of Europe's simultaneously universal and Christian moral agenda also came with a long list of paradoxes, ambiguities, and exemptions that suited their imperial/state and overlapping religious interests: Jewish rights were canvassed in territories formerly occupied by the French but not in the victors' sovereign lands; by the 1820s, Britain, Russia, and Austria pivoted to demanding protection for the rights of Christians living in the Ottoman Empire but ignored religious discrimination in their own sovereign lands. Sometimes these European governments denied Jews and other non-Christians equality before the law in their empires, or burdened religious minorities with onerous taxes, or even targeted Christian minorities, whether Protestants in France or Catholics in Britain.[10] Serfdom in Orthodox Russia was not on the multilateral abolition agenda and did not affect Russia's liberal leadership.

The irregular deployment of ambassadorial conferences reflects the strange selectivity of those institutions and the Concert of Europe's remit: yes, when revolution threatened European internal political stability; no, when it concerned France annexing Algeria in 1830 at a cost of one million Algerian and 100,000 French lives.

In 1845, when the respective French foreign ministers Guizot and Aberdeen agreed to blockade the Argentinian confederation, neither the Monroe Doctrine nor the "Allied Machine" was a hindrance. Instead, their governments could rely on the cover of well-rehearsed rationales such as the universal relevance of free trade and the imperatives of humanity, patriotism, and international law. The Concert of Europe concerned itself with Ottoman imperial practices, but not Christians kidnapping Muslims, nor the long-established Russian practice of kidnapping native women and children in the Alaskan and Siberian territories as hostages in exchange for animal furs.[11] Advocacy of the abolition of the slave trade coincided with the expansion of the trade in some member European states, while Concert members did not touch on slavery as a practice. The Concert of Europe never registered the benchmark set by the "black republic" of Haiti, which had ended slavery before any European power, to the extent that it resisted Haiti's claims for diplomatic recognition, a status that would allow the young republic to participate in the system of free trade the Europeans now touted. Indeed, the Christian Haitians were forced to turn to the Vatican as a kin-Catholic power. The Vatican of course was itself excluded from the Concert of Europe club and forced to seek out its own diplomatic arrangements, despite the Coalition's consistent invocations of Christian brotherhood.[12]

This same history points to the extra-European legacies of the Concert of Europe's new machinery, as well as the selective internal limits of its universalism. When, in 1825, France ordered Haitians to pay former slave owners for revenues lost by its emancipation of slaves, in return for diplomatic recognition, there was no outcry from the European alliance, despite the valence of abolition as its cause célèbre. The Haitian reparations count as a forgotten point of continuity with the institutions of the new era of international politics. The French had taken a cynical history lesson from the reparations the victorious powers had forced on *them* in 1815. A decade later, France demanded from post-revolutionary Haiti compensation of 150 million francs, a rapacious overestimation that was to be paid in French currency rather than local *gourds*, through a sovereign debt loan package ten times Haiti's annual revenue. Having surrounded Haiti with its navy, the French forced the government to meet a payment schedule and take out the indemnity loans from especially nominated French bankers.[13] The terms of the second indemnity installment of 30 million francs alone earned the bankers thirty-five times the borrowed capital and filled the coffers of the French state and French banks well into the twentieth century.[14] Among the successful bidders for the rights to oversee that loan was a French syndicate led by the Rothschilds and Jacques Lafitte—the liberal Christian backer of Saint-Simon—who fought off competition from Delessert and André & Cottier, allied with Jean-Gabriel Eynard.[15]

The idea that the economic and political ambitions of a few European imperial governments were being foisted upon the world, for better or worse, was not uncommon in the early nineteenth century.[16] In 1823, U.S. president James Monroe famously declared that European rules drawn up at the Congress of Verona allowing French intervention on behalf of the Spanish Bourbon monarchy had no legitimacy in Spanish colonies south of a 54th parallel. Asserting the role of America as "the future of the world," he reminded the Europeans (as if they were one) that their voices existed in a larger society of interests. Similarly, even though a Russian ukase might unilaterally claim the Northwest Pacific area of Alaska as exclusively Russian territory for commercial purposes, America would not accept Russian rules as binding. The United States' public repudiation of European hegemony was driven by its government's own imperial ambitions and backed secretly by British strategists. There is also evidence that it was not consistently enforced—it was only two years after the Monroe Doctrine was announced that the French navy encircled slave-free Haiti in Caribbean waters without encountering opposition from the Concert of Europe, let alone a feisty United States. The civilizational repercussions of this new order had implications for Europe's borders as well. Before a new Russian tsar sought a path away from collective responsibility and security, the Russian polity found itself gradually and selectively marginalized from the European heart of the new international order. The Ottoman Empire too, long an entrenched member of Europe's commercial and even cultural networks, was eventually rendered a legal and economic pariah.

Politics/Capitalism

The emerging international order had a complex inner life that connected political and economic actors, and mimicked and supported the capitalist trends shaping national cultures. When Staël called "credit" the engine of liberal principles, she had politics in mind: credit was "the true modern discovery which binds a government to its people [because] it obliges the executive power to treat public opinion with consideration."[17] In the international context of peacemaking, "credit" bound investors to the fate of distant national communities, even when there was no national sentiment or identification at stake and the nations themselves were still more imagined than actual. As a result, the subscribers of French and Greek bonds might espouse religious, humanitarian, and patriotic motivations, or they were simply interested in interest rate returns.

As non-state actors in this new realm of politics otherwise dominated by states, economic actors represented a broader public, but they too might act according to their personal interests. Among the allegations that Staël faced from critics of her diplomacy was the possibility that she was acting in the interest of her investments in North America, for example, not political ideals. Ironically, diplomats were less likely to be criticized for financial conflict of interest; receiving payment or gifts was accepted as part of the job or deciding the timing of bond payouts within their remit. Wilhelm von Humboldt's conception of the public good was not in evidence in the politics practiced between states at this threshold moment.

Meanwhile, the importance of credit and commerce bolstered the significance of the public opinion and political agency of economic actors in international as well as national settings. Banking families such as the Rothschilds exploited their fiscal-political networks, and their influence extended to wives and daughters, allowing them to do politics as soft-power diplomacy. Saint-Simon's utopian political thinking was bankrolled by his capitalization of Church property confiscated during the French Revolution (he bought the property cheaply and resold at great profit); when those financial sources ran dry, he turned to like-minded bankers. Robert Owen was another of these rare utopian socialist figures of the "second class."

Ultimately, there was no inevitability to the influence of "capital." Owen is evidence of how a new money culture encouraged and enabled the entry of non-aristocrats into the formal sphere of national and international politics, to the ends of equality or radical restructuring of political institutions and social mores. By contrast, that ennobled Jews lacking civil rights joined liberal Catholics in the exploitation of the Haitian republic is evidence of the intersecting, and ultimately hierarchical, scales of political, economic, and "civilizational" inequality in the capitalist political framing of an international order. The death of Anna Eynard-Lullin's Protestant banker father in Haiti destitute, a failed speculator, is a reminder that *capitalistes* were also losers.

International/National

Historians have shown that the Napoleonic wars sparked nationalist movements, whether in industrial bourgeois Britain or at the other end of Europe. In feudal Russia, an "international Romantic civilization" breathed life into existing ideas about national differences alongside plans for perpetual peace.[18] Peacemaking as a site of cultural exchange reinforced the realism of national difference, whether in fashion trends or ways of organizing ministries. It was through the processes of peacemaking that the use of statistics and even the convenience of population transfers became legitimate methods for the disambiguation of national sovereign borders. The money for nation-building too was increasingly raised through the methods of international finance—specifically transnational sovereign debt loans. These became an integral dimension of the operation of Europe-based multilateral politics.

The invention of an Italian kingdom nation-state within a few years of the Congress of Paris underscores the rapidity with which the national landscape of international politics under the sign of Europe and humanity could change. Nevertheless, through the first half of the nineteenth century, diplomats and state actors representing empires or other kinds of polities were not expected to be "nationals," not as subjects of those sovereignties, nor as speakers of the local language. Such simple inconsistencies locate the infancy of the national state as a political idea in this period. They point to the relevant range of national emotions and practices concealed in histories of nineteenth-century state-building and conceptions of patriotism. Individuals supported national causes with which they had no personal cultural or religious identification: Dorothea Lieven was Lutheran Baltic-born, Jean-Gabriel Eynard was Protestant Swiss, yet both strategized the international political status of Greek autonomy on religious and cultural grounds. A Greek national state was not always the objective of such support; alternative versions of autonomy existed. Conversely, some *national* projects on the international agenda of the time have since disappeared from teleological view, including plans for a Septinsular Republic in the Ionian Sea and the unification of the Danubian principalities—neither of which corresponds to our contemporary view of European nation-states, so their existence has been forgotten.

Over this same period, the word "society" was of as much, if not more, interest to contemporaries as the setting in which politics took shape as Bentham's neologism "international"—although that too was growing in use. "Europe" could stand for the geopolitical unity of Napoleon's strategizing, and "une diaspora des esprits," or a tower of Babel.[19] From Staël's perspective, Europe liberated from French hegemony could be the cosmopolitan sum of national diversity. Cosmopolitanism was still likely be in vogue in ways that delighted the philosopher Benjamin Constant but dismayed Tadeusz Kościuszko, who felt that only if he were to cast aside his "Polish sentiments" in peacemaking society, "everybody would welcome me with delight and would be pleased."[20] By contrast, Caroline von Humboldt spoke for an exclusivist interpretation of national patriotism that foreshadowed the narrowing of national imaginaries and discourses in the latter nineteenth century.

Once we begin to layer our historical themes we find intriguing social intersections, some more familiar than others. The processes of international/national ordering involved individual agency, even enforced acquiescence. They were woven out of and into private relationships as well as public negotiations and legal documents, even as structural shifts entwined the popularity of cosmopolitan and nation-identified politics in international contexts.

Liberal/Conservative

The modern international order is often characterized as "liberal," even though its foundational practices—diplomacy through conferencing, consensus through law—owe their origins to a moment often defined as deeply conservative, when "order" won out "over equality, stability over justice."[21] Few of the statesmen identified with the passage from "balance of power" to multilateralism were or are thought of as liberals. Castlereagh's biographer John Bew advises that the problem lies as much with the hard borders placed around political classifications since then. Castlereagh—a member of the British Whig and Tory parties at various times—was like the literary heroes of the time, "trapped between two extremes, with 'fluctuating sympathies' for both sides."[22] The "decent and all-embracing" Castlereagh who had no sympathy for abolition read widely in the reformist literature of the Enlightenment (including Staël's novels and studies). As foreign secretary, Castlereagh believed that "both reactionary and revolutionary regimes were likely to disturb European peace and both, therefore, should be equally discouraged."[23] He was not a liberal in Staël's understanding, but he was a supporter of the "science" of European government.

"Fluctuating sympathies" and a disinclination for violent extremes also suits Metternich.[24] The Austrian foreign minister represented an absolutist empire and curried no favor with Staël, or her liberal ideas, let alone her support of the tsar. Metternich's reputation has been built on his role in the 1819 German Confederation congress held at Carlsbad, which shut down the idea of a free press and public opinion. In his later life, Metternich continued to claim "the shape of the conferences is my own invention" and blamed any relative shortcoming on liberalism (in France and England).[25] Yet, he also stood for the ideal of a "society of states," the characteristics of which, in the modern era, are conventionally described as a liberal, even romantic, interpretation of the foundation of international order. Metternich's policy choices were not motivated by the same temper of political opposition as Sagan's hatred of Bonaparte and liberalism. Rather, like Castlereagh—to whom Metternich drew close once Austria joined the Coalition—the point of cooperation was to end the tumult and violence, even bloodiness, of political revolution. Likewise, his embrace of the promise of science (both natural or social) and his arbitration of gender roles complemented the future-oriented modern foundations of bourgeois politics.

Staël's history of this period (published posthumously) captures the anomalies, inconsistencies, and contradictions in the liberal ambitions associated with peacemaking. It condemns Castlereagh for the weakness of the liberal political institutions put in place in France, the toll on French political morale of the allied occupation, the failure of the occupation government to bolster freedom of the press or to prevent the religious persecution and murder of Protestants in the French countryside, and their inability to more effectively stamp the postwar peace with the cause of abolition. England, the great model of a liberal political system, Staël writes, had failed to support the cause of liberty, not only in France but also in Ireland and Europe's colonies.[26] She blames not only English diplomats but her fair-weather friend Talleyrand, who made a small fortune out of the peace decisions. She attempts to salvage the importance of idealism from the encroachment of cynicism by defending the tsar's political views against attacks that they were too often attributed to personal calculations "as if in our days disinterested sentiments could no longer enter the human heart"—the sovereign she knew from St. Petersburg was unaffected, calm, penetrating, judicious, wise, and consistent in his commitment to "the progress of social order" and "those rights which human reason at present calls for in all directions."[27] By declaring that he was the person who stood for love of what was just and for posterity, *and* that he was ruled by his opinions more than by his passions, she reinforced a liberal agenda that saw no contradiction with religious objectives. From Staël's 1816 perspective, a long-anticipated opportunity to reshape European political institutions in the image of liberty had been lost.

At the end of the Napoleonic wars, diplomats and non-state actors alike juggled competing political visions of the future that we now discern more clearly as liberal and conservative, in the midst of intersecting secular and religious, political and economic expectations, all of which made the conferencing model—like the salon, or even public *esprit*—crucial for how the politics between states was imagined. Staël's own salon constituted "ce foyer imaginaire du libéralisme européen."[28] Its practices were intended as evidence of the importance of not only ideas, or a political program, but also a liberal impulse anchored in public *esprit*, "an animated sentiment of public life."[29] While constitutions were an important focus of this international history of liberal thinking, a more substantial conception of what constituted liberty was at stake.

In the period after Napoleon, the extent of public *esprit* can be discerned in the breadth of expectations, not only the pacifist promise of commerce but also the equitable distribution of wealth. The arc of failed political ideas—whether social contracts or ideal republics, freedom or democracy—marks out the horizon of public expectations, whether articulated from the modest podium of the salon or among a community of men, in pamphlet form or in personal correspondence. The expectations are valuable in themselves, pointing to the breadth of investment in the possibilities of politics between states.

Past/Future

At the beginning of a century in which the growing popularity of the term "international" was inextricable from the status of "national," the universalist language and authority of the Enlightenment gained traction in new contexts, connecting the past and the future. Staël's prediction in 1800 "that all major events lead towards the same goal of a world civilization" rehearsed Metternich's assertion in the 1830s that the difference between "the present world" and the "ancient" lay in "the tendency of nations to draw closer together and to set up a kind of corporate body resting on the same basis as the great human society which grew up at the heart of Christianity."[30] Eventually, variations on these ideas would echo through the vital debates of World War I around international government, during World War II around world government, and in the context of planetary politics, global governance, and even globalization from the Cold War détente of the 1970s and after.

As international orders have been reinvented, and as the world has changed around and through those reinventions, the capacity of and for politics, for imagining the point of the politics between states, is worth remembering. In the early nineteenth century, the invention of international order encouraged the engagement of a broader community of non-state actors than historians have tended to notice; these actors engaged new political possibilities in unprecedented ways, to diverse ends. The paradox lay in the fact that this same moment of modern possibility led to the official exclusion of women's political engagement in this international sphere and, eventually, a civilizational ordering that reinforced the interests of a few imperial powers and the conflation of Europe and international society. At our own moment of unmoored, uncertain transformation, on the cusp of losing the "international order," as we know it, can remembering the events of two hundred years ago help us revive engagement with the scope of international politics, its economic and political interests? At the least, seeing the unsettledness, unpredictability, and unevenness of the past should remind us of the relevance of continuing to ask questions of the contemporary international order: What and whom is it for? Just how wide can the horizon of our own expectations be?

NOTES

Introduction

1. Gaétan de Raxis de Flassan, *Histoire du Congrès de Vienne* (Paris: Treuttel et Wurtz, 1829).

2. Friedrich von Gentz, 18 April 1818, *Dépêches inédites du chevalier de Gentz aux hospodars de Valachie pour servir à l'histoire de la politique européenne (1813 à 1828)* (Paris: E. Plon, 1877), 388.

3. Robert Stewart, Viscount Castlereagh, to 1st Earl of Liverpool, 20 October 1818, Aix, Add MS 38566, fols. 67–68, Liverpool Papers, British Library, London (hereafter BL).

4. Viscount Castlereagh to the Earl of Liverpool, September and October 1814; letter to Charles-Maurice de Talleyrand, 30 September 1814; and "Protocole séparé de la conférence du 22 septembre," report compiled by Robert Stewart, Viscount Castlereagh, for the Earl of Liverpool, all in FO 92/7, vol. 7, Congress of Vienna, National Archives, London (hereafter TNA).

5. Cited in Guillaume de Bertier de Sauvigny, *Metternich and His Times* (London: Darton, Longman, and Todd, 1962), 30–32.

6. Paul W. Schroeder, *The Transformation of European Politics, 1763–1848*, Oxford History of Modern Europe (Oxford: Clarendon Press, 1994), 802–3.

7. Fabian Klose, ed., *The Emergence of Humanitarian Intervention: Ideas and Practice from the Nineteenth Century to the Present* (Cambridge: Cambridge University Press, 2015); Gary Bass, *Freedom's Battle: The Origins of Humanitarian Intervention* (New York: Vintage, 2009).

8. Woodrow Wilson, "Address to Congress, Analyzing German and Austrian Peace Utterances (February 11, 1918)," in *President Wilson's State Papers and Addresses*, ed. Albert Shaw (New York: George H. Doran, 1918), 475. See chapter 16 for a full survey of these views.

9. See the important and detailed work of Brian Vick in *The Congress of Vienna: Power and Politics after Napoleon* (Cambridge, MA: Harvard University Press, 2014).

10. Leo Tolstoy, epilogue in *War and Peace*, trans. Rosemary Edmunds (1869; London: Penguin, 1957), 1406–7.

11. Of course, for Tolstoy this historical approach did not go far enough because it ignored the social history of the masses, who, he argued, were the real engine of change.

12. In the twenty-first century, an Austrian bicentennial commemoration documentary opted for a bodice-ripper history. *Diplomatische Liebschaften: Die Mätressen des Wiener Kongresses*, directed by Monika Czernin and Melissa Müller (Makido,

2014), https://www.filmfonds-wien.at/filme/diplomatische-liebschaften---die-maetressen-des-wiener-kongresses.

13. Hilde Spiel, ed., *The Congress of Vienna: An Eyewitness Account*, trans. Richard H. Weber (Philadelphia: Chilton Book Co., 1968), 244.

14. Vick, *The Congress of Vienna*, chap. 3. See also Glenda Sluga, "On the Historical Significance of the Presence, and Absence, of Women at the Congress of Vienna, 1814–1815," *L'Homme* 25, no. 2 (2014): 49–62; Glenda Sluga, "Women, Diplomacy, and International Politics, Before and After the Congress of Vienna," in *Women, Diplomacy and International Politics since 1500*, ed. Glenda Sluga and Carolyn James (New York: Routledge, 2016), 120–32; and Agnes Husslein-Arco, Sabine Grabner, and Werner Telesko, eds., *Europe in Vienna: The Congress of Vienna, 1814/15* (Chicago: University of Chicago Press, 2015).

15. "From the Diary of Archduke John of Austria," 25 October 1814, in Friedrich Freksa, *A Peace Congress of Intrigue (Vienna, 1815); a Vivid, Intimate Account of the Congress of Vienna Composed of the Personal Memoirs of Its Important Participants* (New York: Century Co., 1919), 238.

16. For a useful summary, see Barbara Caine and Glenda Sluga, *Gendering European History, 1780–1920* (London: Continuum, 2000).

17. See Reinhart Koselleck, "Goethe's Untimely History," in *Sediments of Time: On Possible Histories*, ed. Reinhart Koselleck et al. (Stanford: Stanford University Press, 2018); and Mark Mazower, *Governing the World: The History of an Idea* (New York: Penguin, 2012).

Chapter 1

Note to epigraph: Adam Jerzy Czartoryski [under pseudonym Toulouzan, M.], *Essai sur la Diplomatie: Manuscrit d'un Philhellène* (Paris: Firmin Didot Frères, 1830), 342.

1. Cited in Eli F. Heckscher, *The Continental System: An Economic Interpretation*, ed. Harald Westergaard (Oxford: Clarendon Press, 1922), 74.

2. The heirless Swedish king Karl XIII appointed Bernadotte head of the Swedish state in 1810, and then adopted him.

3. Hamish Scott, "Diplomatic Culture in Old Regime Europe," in *Cultures of Power in Europe during the Long Eighteenth Century* (Cambridge: Cambridge University Press, 2007), 58–59.

4. Fred Anderson, "The Peace of Paris, 1763," in *The Making of Peace: Rulers, States, and the Aftermath of War*, ed. Williamson Murray and James Lacey (Cambridge: Cambridge University Press, 2009), 109.

5. François de Callières, *De la manière de négocier avec les souverains* [*The Practice of Diplomacy*] (Amsterdam: Pour La Companie, 1716).

6. Patricia Kennedy Grimsted, *The Foreign Ministers of Alexander I: Political Attitudes and the Conduct of Russian Diplomacy, 1801–1825* (Berkeley: University of California Press, 1969), 12.

7. Ibid., 15.

8. Ibid.

9. Ibid., 28.

10. Alexander Etkind, *Internal Colonisation: Russia's Imperial Experience* (Cambridge: Polity Press, 2011), 16.

11. See also Beatrice de Graaf, *Fighting Terror after Napoleon: How Europe Became Secure after 1815* (Cambridge: Cambridge University Press, 2020), 29.

12. Charles Webster, ed., *British Diplomacy, 1813–1815: Select Documents Dealing with the Reconstruction of Europe* (London: G. Bell & Sons, 1921), 222–23.

13. Earl of Liverpool to Viscount Castlereagh, 27 February 1814, Fife House, in Charles Webster, ed., *The Foreign Policy of Castlereagh, 1812–1815: Britain and the Reconstruction of Europe* (London: G. Bell & Sons, 1925–37), appendix B, clibrary-org-works.angelfire.com/castlereagh3.html.

14. See the Lord William Bentinck scandal, Castlereagh to Liverpool, 11 March 1814, Fife House, in Webster, *The Foreign Policy of Castlereagh*, appendix B; John Bew, *Castlereagh: A Life* (Oxford: Oxford University Press, 2002), 359.

15. Born as Klemens Wenzel Nepomuk Lothar Fürst von Metternich-Winneburg zu Beilstein.

16. Wolfram Siemann, *Metternich: Stratege und Visionär; Eine Biografie* (Munich: C. H. Beck, 2016), 736–63.

17. Ibid., 737–43.

18. Klemens von Metternich to Wilhelmine, Duchess of Sagan, 8 March 1814, 2:00 a.m., Chaumont, in *Clemens Metternich, Wilhelmine von Sagan: Ein Briefwechsel, 1813–1815*, ed. Maria Ullrichova (Graz-Koln: Verlag Hermann Bohlaus Nachf, 1966), 176, 227. Unless otherwise cited, all letters between Metternich and Sagan are from this volume, and translations are my own.

19. Jürgen Osterhammel, *Unfabling the East: The Enlightenment's Encounter with Asia*, trans. Robert Savage (Princeton: Princeton University Press, 2018), 250.

20. Etkind, *Internal Colonisation*, 54.

21. Frank Castiglione, "'Levantine' Dragomans in Nineteenth-Century Istanbul: The Pisanis, the British, and Issues of Subjecthood," *Osmanlı Araştırmaları/Journal of Ottoman Studies* 44 (2014): 169–95.

22. Cemil Aydin, *The Idea of the Muslim World: A Global Intellectual History* (Cambridge, MA: Harvard University Press, 2017), 40.

23. Miroslav Šedivý, *Metternich, the Great Powers and the Eastern Question* (Pilsen: University of West Bohemia, 2013), 182.

24. Roderic H. Davison, *Nineteenth Century Ottoman Diplomacy and Reforms* (Istanbul: Isis Press, 1999), 429.

25. See the essays in Sluga and James, *Women, Diplomacy and International Politics since 1500*.

26. Jennifer Mori, *The Culture of Diplomacy: Britain in Europe, c. 1750–1830* (Oxford: Manchester University Press, 2014), 214–15.

27. Susan Tenenbaum, "The Coppet Circle: Literary Criticism as Political Discourse," *History of Political Thought* 1, no. 3 (1980): 456.

28. Édouard Chapuisat, *Jean-Gabriel Eynard et son temps, 1775–1863* (Geneva: A. Julien, 1952), 61.

29. Callières, *De la manière de négocier avec les souverains*, cited in Benedetta Craveri, *The Age of Conversation* (New York: New York Review Books, 2005), 289.

30. Metternich to Sagan, 17 January 1814, 9:00 a.m., Basel, in Ullrichova, *Clemens Metternich*, 176.

31. Victor du Bled, "La société russe: Les salons de Petersbourg et de Moscou," *La revue hebdomadaire* 12 (November 1905): 89.

32. Germaine de Staël, *Considerations on the Principal Events of the French Revolution*, ed. Aurelian Craiutu (Indianapolis: Liberty Fund, 2008), 252.

33. Robert Escarpit, *L'Angleterre dans l'oeuvre de Madame de Staël* (Paris: J. Pechade, 1954), 49, 166.

34. Anne Jean Marie René Savary, 1st Duke of Rovigo, *Mémoires du duc de Rovigo, pour servir à l'histoire de l'empereur Napoléon* (Paris: A Bossange, 1828), 3:95.

35. Cited in Steven D. Kale, "Women, Salons, and the State in the Aftermath of the French Revolution," *Journal of Women's History* 13, no. 4 (2002): 64.

36. Staël, *Considerations on the Principal Events of the French Revolution*, 508.

37. Steven D. Kale, *French Salons: High Society and Political Sociability from the Old Regime to the Revolution of 1848* (Baltimore: Johns Hopkins University Press, 2004), 93.

38. Scott, "Diplomatic Culture," 83.

39. Grimsted, citing Joseph le Maistre, the Sardinian ambassador to Russia (born in France), requesting an assistant from the Sardinian ministry in 1803 (*Foreign Ministers*, 21). For more on this broader argument about the gendering of diplomacy, see Mori, *The Culture of Diplomacy*, 120, 213, who traces the effect of a shift to a new era of meetings on the old courtiership system.

40. Harold Nicolson, *Diplomacy* (London: Oxford University Press, 1963), 101; Markus Mosslang and Torsten Riotte, introduction to *The Diplomats' World: The Cultural History of Diplomacy, 1815–1914*, ed. Markus Mosslang and Torsten Riotte (Oxford: Oxford University Press, 2008); Robyn Adams and Rosanna Cox, introduction to *Diplomacy and Early Modern Culture*, ed. Robyn Adams and Rosanna Cox (Houndmills, Basingstoke: Palgrave Macmillan, 2011), 2.

Chapter 2

Note to epigraphs: Staël, *Considerations on the Principal Events of the French Revolution*, 553; Mme. de Chastenay, *Mémoires de Mme de Chastenay, 1777–1815*, ed. Alphonse Roserot (Paris: Plon, 1896), 2:445.

1. Eventually published as Germaine de Staël, *De l'Allemagne*, in *Oeuvres complètes de Madame la Baronne de Stäel-Holstein*, vol. 2 (1861; Geneva: Slatkine Reprints, 1967).

2. Karl Nesselrode, "A S.E.N. le Chancelier de l'Empire, Vienne 10/22 Septembre 1811," in *Lettres et papiers du chancelier Comte de Nesselrode, 1760–1850, extraits de ses archives*, ed. Anatol von Nesselrode (Paris: A. Lahure, 1811), 3:387–94.

3. James Mackintosh, "Review of Madame de Staël's *De l'Allemagne*," in *The Miscellaneous Works* (New York: D. Appleton & Co., 1871), 261–71.

4. Paul Gautier, *Madame de Staël et Napoléon* (Paris: Plon, 1903), 314.

5. Ibid.

6. "De L'Allemagne par Mme la Baronne de Stael," *Edinburgh Review: Or Critical Journal* 44 (October 1813): 204.

7. See Norman King, "Mme de Staël et la chute de Napoléon," in *Madame de Staël et l'Europe* (Paris: Klincksieck, 1970), 63–75.

8. Marquise de Dax d'Axat, *Souvenirs sur Mme de Stael* (Paris: Revie de Paris, 1933), cited in Georges Solovieff, "Madame de Stael vue par ses contemporains," *Revue d'histoire littéraire de la France* 1 (1966): 137.

9. See Craveri, *The Age of Conversation*, 372; and Simone Balayé, "De la persistence des clichés," *Europe* (January–February 1987): 107–12.

10. Eric Bollmann, "Memoirs of Varnhagen von Ense," *Foreign Quarterly Review* 26, no. 52 (1841): 147.

11. See Glenda Sluga, "Passions, Patriotism, and Nationalism, and Germaine de Staël," *Nations and Nationalism* 15, no. 2 (2009): 299–318; Glenda Sluga, "The Nation," in *The Palgrave Guide to Women Writing History*, ed. M. Spongberg (Basingstoke: Palgrave, 2005); Glenda Sluga, "Defining Liberty: Italy and England in Madame de Staël's *Corinne*," *Women's Writing* 1 (2003): 241–51.

12. For the transnational and international context of her activism in the 1790s, see Paul S. Spalding, "Germaine de Staël's Role in Rescuing Lafayette, 1792–1797," in *Germaine de Staël: Forging a Politics of Mediation*, ed. Karyna Szmurlo (Liverpool: Liverpool University Press, 2011), 56–68.

13. Helena Rosenblatt, *The Lost History of Liberalism* (Princeton: Princeton University Press, 2018), 51–52. Rosenblatt explains that the primary meaning of liberal "still referred to a cluster of moral and civic values, such as magnanimity and generosity, openness and toleration, values that had virtually disappeared during the revolution's radical phase."

14. See Sluga, "Defining Liberty."

15. Germaine de Staël to Alexandre de Lameth, 1794, Coppet, "given to me by Charles du Verac, J d'Estournel, 7 January 1843," do44-066 to do/44-068, Bibliothèque de Genève, Geneva, Switzerland (hereafter BGE). See also Germaine de Staël, *Réflexions sur le procès de la Reine par une femme* [August 1793], https://gallica.bnf.fr/ark:/12148/bpt6k42632j.texteImage.

16. See Kale, "Women, Salons, and the State," 64.

17. Staël, *Considerations on the Principal Events of the French Revolution*, 473. See also Chinatsu Takeda, "Deux origines du courant libéral en France," *Revue française d'histoire des idées politiques* 18, no. 2 (2003): 233–58.

18. Gérard Gengembre, "Fréquentation et sociabilité mutuelles," *Revue française d'histoire des idées politiques* 18, no. 2 (2003): 259–70.

19. Germaine de Staël, *Considérations sur les principaux événemens de la révolution françoise* (Paris: Libraires Delaunay, Bossange et Masson, 1818), 624.

20. "La comtese Charles de Nesselrode à son mari, Kamenni-Ostrof, 7 Octobre 1812," in Nesselrode, *Lettres et papiers*, 4:97.

21. Germaine de Staël to John Adams, 19 April 1813, St. Petersburg, and to John Adams, St. Petersburg, 22 March 1813, in John Quincy Adams, *Writings of John Quincy Adams*, ed. Worthington Chauncey Ford (New York: Macmillan, 1914), 4:473, 450.

22. Staël, *De l'Allemagne*, 1:28.

23. Hannah Alice Straus, *The Attitude of the Congress of Vienna toward Nationalism in Germany, Italy, and Poland* (New York: Columbia University Press, 1949), 47.

24. Moritz von Arndt, the future German hero of the crucial Battle of Nations in October 1813, was also listening. "Stein, 31 August 1812," in *Briefe und Samtliche Schriften*, ed. Von E. Botzenhart and W. Hubatech (Stuttgart: Neue Ausgabe, 1961–70), 3:719; Norman King, "A. W. Schlegel et la guerre de liberation: Le mémoire sur l'état de l'Allemagne," *Cahiers Staëliens* 16 (1973): 4.

25. "To John Adams, St. Petersburg," in *Writings of John Quincy Adams*, 4:451.

26. Ibid.

27. King, "Mme de Staël," 63.

28. Ibid., 65; Mme de Stael to Bernadotte, 25 May 1813, Letter 404, in *Madame de Staël, ses amis, ses correspondants: Choix de lettres (1778–1817)*, ed. Georges Solovieff (Paris: Éditions Klincksieck, 1970), 446.

29. Colonel Lowe to Colonel Bunbury, 17 February 1813, Stockholm, Correspondence and Papers of Col. Henry E. Bunbury, Add MS 37051, fol. 9, BL.

30. Pauline de Pange, *Auguste Wilhelm Schlegel et Madame de Staël d'après des documents inédit par la comtesse Jean de Pange* (Paris: Albert, 1938), 399.

31. Ibid., 393.

32. Comtesse de Remusat, *Memoirs of Mme de Remusat, 1802–1808* (Paris: Calmann-Levy, 1880), 2:155.

33. Sophie von Knorring, cited in Paul Tisseau, "Les Illusions de la Baronne Sophie con Knorring," *Cahiers Staëliens* 60 (2009): 102.

34. Gautier, *Madame de Staël et Napoleon*, 325; Sheilagh Margaret Riordan, "Sentiments of Travel: Madame de Staël, on Sweden," *Moderna Sprak* 90, no. 2 (1996): 190–99.

35. Cited in M. Trail, "Mme de Staël: Her Russian-Swedish Journey" (PhD diss., University of Southern California, 1946), 262.

36. Ibid., 282; Gautier, *Madame de Staël*, 365; Riordan, "Sentiments," 191.

37. Cabre reported to Talleyrand. Charlotte Blennerhasset, *Talleyrand* (London: Murray, 1894), 2:193; Michel Winock, *Madame de Staël* (Paris: Fayard, 2010), 2:329.

38. Letter, 5 May 1813, in Norman King, "Correspondances suédoises de Germaine de Staël (1812–1816)," *Cahiers Staëliens* 39 (1988): 75. See also J. Christopher Herold, *Mistress to an Age: A Life of Madame de Staël* (New York: Grove Press, 1958), 444; and Rovigo, *Mémoires*, 3:91–94.

39. See Trail, "Mme de Staël," 298.

40. Gautier, *Madame de Staël*, 335.

41. John Quincy Adams to John Adams, 19 April 1813, St. Petersburg, in *Writings of John Quincy Adams*, 4:469, 473.

42. Rovigo, *Mémoires*, 3:95.

43. Marie-Claire Hoock-Demarle, *L'Europe des lettres: Reseaux épistolaires et construction de l'espace européen* (Paris: Albin Michel, 2008), 143.

44. Herold concludes that "the most important negotiations between Sweden and Russia were conducted, not through the embassies, but through Madame de Staël and Galiffe" (*Mistress to an Age*, 431).

45. Sheilagh Margaret Riordan, "Politics and Romanticism: Germaine de Staël's Forgotten Influence on Nineteenth-Century Sweden," *Australian Journal of French Studies* 35, no. 3 (1998): 335.

46. Germaine de Staël to Dorothea Lieven, November 1813, Stockholm, Add MS 47374, fols. 59–63, Papers of Princess Lieven, BL.

47. King, "Correspondances suédoises de Germaine de Staël," 68.

48. Germaine de Staël to Jean Bernadotte, 2 July 1813, letter 408, in Solovieff, *Madame de Staël*, 450.

49. Germaine de Staël to Jean Bernadotte, 11 October 1813, letter 420, in Solovieff, *Madame de Staël*, 460.

50. Germaine de Staël to Jean Bernadotte, 8 July 1813, letter 410; end of October 1813, letter 421, both in Solovieff, *Madame de Staël*, 451.

51. Cited in Trail, "Mme de Staël," 263.

52. Bollmann, "Memoirs of Varnhagen von Ense," 148.

53. John Quincy Adams had no difficulty believing it to be Staël's work. "To John Adams," 19 April 1813, St. Petersburg, in *Writings of John Quincy Adams*, 4:473.

54. August Wilhelm von Schlegel and Germaine de Staël, *Sur le système continental* (Hamburg: Bibliotheek der Deutschen Literatur, 1813).

55. Schroeder, *The Transformation of European Politics*, 459.

56. Trail, "Mme de Staël," 265.

57. King, "Mme de Staël," 70; Riordan, "Politics and Romanticism," 337.

58. Staël to Lieven, May 1813, Add MS 47374, fol. 75, Lieven Papers, BL.

59. King, "Mme de Staël," 70.

60. Franklin D. Scott, *Bernadotte and the Fall of Napoleon* (Cambridge, MA: Harvard University Press, 1935), 101.

61. Carl Wilhelm Bergman von Schinkel, *Minnen ur Sveriges nyare historia* (Stockholm: P. A. Norstedt & Söner, 1853), 7:69; Riordan, "Sentiments," 190; Riordan, "Politics and Romanticism," 335.

Chapter 3

1. Isabel Hull, *Sexuality, State, and Civil Society in Germany, 1700–1815* (Ithaca: Cornell University Press, 1997), 410.

2. Joan Landes, *Women in the Public Sphere in the Age of the French Revolution* (Ithaca: Cornell University Press, 1988), 106.

3. See Gertrud Maria Roesch, "The Liberation from Napoleon as Self-Liberation: The Year 1813 in the Letters of Rahel Varnhagen," in *Women against Napoleon: Historical and Fictional Responses to His Rise and Legacy*, ed. Waltraud Maierhofer,

Gertrud Roesch, and Caroline Bland (Chicago: University of Chicago Press, 2008), 121, 133; and Wilhelm von Humboldt, "9. Über den Geschlechtsunterschied und dessen Einfluss auf die organische Natur," in *Gesammelte Schriften* (1785–1795) (Berlin: De Gruyter, 1903), https://doi.org/10.1515/9783110818284-009.

4. Staël, *Considerations on the Principal Events of the French Revolution*, 736.

5. Landes, *Women in the Public Sphere*, 23.

6. Chastenay, *Mémoires*, 2:445.

7. Jean Hanoteau, ed., *Lettres de Prince de Metternich à la Contesse de Lieven, 1818–1819* (Paris: Plon-Nourrit, 1909), 186, 196; Charles Zorgbibe, *Metternich: Le seducteur diplomate* (Paris: Fallois, 2009), 53.

8. Simone Balayé, *Madame de Staël: Lumières et liberté* (Paris: Éditions Klincksieck, 1979), 232.

9. Unknown (possibly Dorothea Lieven) to Lamb, 28 February 1816, Add MS 60482, fol. 16, Beauvale Papers, BL.

10. Georges Solovieff, *Rahel Varnhagen: Une revoltée féministe à l'époque romantique* (Paris: L'Harmattan, 2000), 9; see also Karen Hagemann, "Female Patriots: Women, War and the Nation in the Period of the Prussian-German Anti-Napoleonic Wars," *Gender and History* 16, no. 2 (2004): 406.

11. Dagmar von Gersdorff, *Caroline von Humboldt: Eine Biographie* (Leipzig: Insel Verlag GmbH, 2011), 153.

12. Stella Musulin, *Vienna in the Age of Metternich: From Napoleon to Revolution* (London: Faber and Faber, 1975), 57–58.

13. Catherine Pavlovna to Alexander I, 26 December 1813, in Irene de Vries de Gunzburg, *Catherine Pavlovna: Grande-Duchesse Russe, 1788–1819* (Amsterdam: J. M. Meulenboff, 1941), 54.

14. Gunzburg, *Catherine Pavlovna*, 59.

15. Catherine Pavlovna to Alexander I, 30 July 1813, in ibid., 193.

16. Catherine Pavlovna to Alexander I, Stuttgart, 4 January 1814, in Gunzburg, *Catherine Pavlovna*, 202–3.

17. Gunzburg, *Catherine Pavlovna*, 142.

18. See Linda Colley, *Britons: Forging the Nation, 1707–1837* (New Haven: Yale University Press, 1992).

19. Colley, *Britons*, 260; On total wars, see David A. Bell, *The First Total War: Napoleon's Europe and the Birth of Warfare as We Know It* (Boston: Houghton Mifflin, 2007).

20. Hagemann, "Female Patriots," 403.

21. Rahel Levin to Karl Varnhagen, 12 October 1813, in Rahel Varnhagen von Ense, *Rahel: Ein Buch des Andenkens für ihre Freunde*, Bd. 2, Berlin, 1834, S. 131–32, in Deutsches Textarchiv, http://www.deutschestextarchiv.de/varnhagen_rahel02_1834/140. The English translation is taken from Christopher Clark, *Iron Kingdom: The Rise and Downfall of Prussia, 1600–1947* (New York: Penguin, 2006).

22. Rahel Levin to Varnhagen, 16 April 1814, in Rahel Levin Varnhagen, *Familienbriefe*, ed. Renata B. M. Barovero (Munich: Verlag C. H. Beck, 2009), 128.

23. Gersdorff, *Caroline von Humboldt*, 157–58.

24. Ibid., 159.

25. Adela Pinch, *Strange Fits of Passion: Epistemologies of Emotion, Hume to Austen* (Stanford: Stanford University Press, 1996), 11, 16.

26. Ibid., 1.

27. See discussion in Sluga, "Passions, Patriotism and Nationalism."

28. Ibid.

29. Hannah Arendt, *Rahel Varnhagen: The Life of a Jewess*, ed. L. Weissberg, trans. Richard Winston and Clara Winston (Baltimore: Johns Hopkins University Press, 1997), 233.

30. See Hoock-Demarle, *L'Europe des lettres*, 305.

31. Cited in Arendt, *Rahel Varnhagen*, 234.

32. Levin to Varnhagen, 27 June 1815, in ibid., 358.

33. Solovieff, *Rahel Varnhagen*, 103; see also Hoock-Demarle, *L'Europe des lettres*, 109, 287.

34. Heidi Thomann Tewarson, *Rahel Levin Varnhagen: The Life and Work of a German Jewish Intellectual* (Lincoln: University of Nebraska Press, 1998), 217.

35. John Claiborne Isbell, *The Birth of European Romanticism: Truth and Propaganda in Staël's "De l'Allemagne," 1810–1813* (Cambridge: Cambridge University Press, 1994), 9.

36. Staël, *De l'Allemagne*, 1:28; see Sluga, "Defining Liberty."

37. George Mosse, *Nationalism and Sexuality: Respectability and Abnormal Sexuality* (New York: H. Fertig, 1985), 6.

38. Karen Hagemann, "Of 'Manly Valor' and 'German Honor': Nation, War, and Masculinity in the Age of the Prussian Uprising against Napoleon," *Central European History* 30, no. 2 (1997): 187–220; Karen Hagemann, "'Be Proud and Firm, Citizens of Austria!' Patriotism and Masculinity in Texts of the 'Political Romantics' Written during Austria's Anti-Napoleonic Wars," *German Studies Review* 29, no. 1 (2006): 53.

39. Bew, *Castlereagh*, 336.

40. Metternich to Sagan, 20 January 1814, Bale, and 21 January 1814, in Ullrichova, *Clemens Metternich*, 182–83.

41. Staël, *Considerations on the Principal Events of the French Revolution*, xiv, 560.

42. Niels Rosenkrantz, *Journal du Congrès de Vienne, 1814–1815* (Copenhagen: G.E.C. Gad, 1953), 72, 98, 105.

43. Gentz, cited in Dorothy Gies McGuigan, *Metternich and the Duchess* (Garden City, NY: Doubleday, 1975), 151.

44. Metternich to Sagan, 29 November 1813, in Ullrichova, *Clemens Metternich*, 147.

45. Clara Tuite, *Lord Byron and Scandalous Celebrity* (Cambridge: Cambridge University Press, 2015), 118, 120, 122.

46. Ibid., 123, 126.

47. On Humboldt's sexual expenses, see Gersdorff, *Caroline von Humboldt*, 32.

48. Ibid., 156.

49. Sagan to Metternich, 8 October 1813, Prague and Fribourg, 8 January 1814, in Ullrichova, *Clemens Metternich*, 16, 104.

Chapter 4

Note to epigraphs: Metternich to Sagan, 13 December 1813, Offenburg, in Ullrichova, *Clemens Metternich*, 135; Metternich to Sagan, 1 March 1814, 9:00 a.m., Chaumont, in Ullrichova, *Clemens Metternich*, 220.

1. "Autobiographie du Comte Charles-Robert de Nesselrode," in Nesselrode, *Lettres et papiers*, 2:99, 132.

2. Reichenbach today is better known as Dzierzoniow.

3. Cited in Paul R. Sweet, *Friedrich von Gentz: Defender of the Old Order* (Madison: University of Wisconsin Press, 1941), 187.

4. Metternich to Sagan, 6 June 1813, 9:00 a.m., Gitschin, in Ullrichova, *Clemens Metternich*, 21.

5. Metternich to Sagan, 12 June 1813, Prague, in Ullrichova, *Clemens Metternich*, 34.

6. Metternich to Sagan, 12 October 1813, 9:00 p.m., Chemnitz, in Ullrichova, *Clemens Metternich*, 80.

7. Metternich to Sagan, 1 March 1814, 9:00 a.m., n. 24, in Ullrichova, *Clemens Metternich*, 220.

8. Schroeder argues convincingly that Metternich's overall aim in this period isn't clear and possibly was directed toward creating an independent Central Europe and an Austria that relied on its relationship with France to fend off Russia, Prussia, and Britain as Austria's competitors. Schroeder, *The Transformation of European Politics*, 465.

9. Metternich to Sagan, 13 February 1814, 12:00 a.m., n. 20, Troyes, in Ullrichova, *Clemens Metternich*, 207.

10. Metternich to Sagan, 28 December 1813, in Ullrichova, *Clemens Metternich*, 148.

11. Sagan to Metternich, 31 August 1813, in Ullrichova, *Clemens Metternich*, 54.

12. Metternich to Sagan, 19 November 1813, Frankfurt, in Ullrichova, *Clemens Metternich*, 111.

13. Sagan to Metternich, 31 October 1813, Prague, in Ullrichova, *Clemens Metternich*, 92; Sagan to Metternich, 4 October 1813, Prague, in Ullrichova, *Clemens Metternich*, 96.

14. Sagan to Metternich, 15 January 1814, Vienna, in Ullrichova, *Clemens Metternich*, 171.

15. Rosalynd Pflaum, *By Influence and Desire* (New York: Evans and Co., 1984), 127.

16. Metternich to Sagan, 2 July 1813, Dresden, and 12 June 1813, Prague, in Ullrichova, *Clemens Metternich*, 28, 24.

17. Metternich to Sagan, 13 December 1813, Offenburg, in Ullrichova, *Clemens Metternich*, 135.

18. Helena Sobkova, *Katerina Zahanska* (Prague: Paseka, 2007), 100.

19. Dominic Lieven, *The Aristocracy in Europe, 1815–1914* (New York: Columbia University Press, 1992), 150.

20. Ibid.

21. Sagan had once been part of Bohemia and Saxony; Nachod is now in the Czech Republic.

22. Sagan to Metternich, 20 August 1813, in Ullrichova, *Clemens Metternich*, 44.

23. Pflaum, *By Influence and Desire*, 138.

24. Ibid., 117.

25. Sagan to Metternich, 14 April 1814, Vienna, in Ullrichova, *Clemens Metternich*, 245.

26. Sagan to Metternich, 20 August 1813, in Ullrichova, *Clemens Metternich*, 43, and 29 October 1813, Prague, in Ullrichova, *Clemens Metternich*, 69.

27. Sagan to Metternich, 11 June 1813, Ratiborz, in Ullrichova, *Clemens Metternich*, 23.

28. Metternich to Sagan, 12 June 1813, Prague, in Ullrichova, *Clemens Metternich*, 24.

29. Metternich to Sagan, 13 June 1813, evening, in Ullrichova, *Clemens Metternich*, 25; see also Pflaum, *By Influence and Desire*, 138.

30. Friedrich von Gentz, 14 June 1813, Koniggratz, *Dépêches inédites du chevalier de Gentz aux hospodars de Valachie: Pour servir à l'histoire politique européenne (1813–1828)* (Paris: Plon, 1876), 1:17.

31. See Wilhelm von Humboldt, *Wilhelm von Humboldts Gesammelte Schriften*, ed. Albert Leitzmann and Bruno Gebhardt (Berlin: Behr's, 1903), 11:73.

32. Paul R. Sweet, *Wilhelm von Humboldt: A Biography* (Columbus: Ohio State University Press, 1980), 2:128.

33. See Graaf, *Fighting Terror after Napoleon*, 41.

34. Ibid.

35. Sagan to Metternich, 22 February 1814, Vienna, in Ullrichova, *Clemens Metternich*, 218.

36. Metternich to Sagan, 27 December 1813, Fribourg, in Ullrichova, *Clemens Metternich*, 147.

37. Metternich to Sagan, 17 September 1813, 8:00 a.m., Teplitz, in Ullrichova, *Clemens Metternich*, 65.

38. Metternich to Sagan, 8 November 1813, 12:00 a.m., Frankfurt, in Ullrichova, *Clemens Metternich*, 105.

39. Metternich to Sagan, 7 November 1813, in Ullrichova, *Clemens Metternich*, 128.

40. Metternich to Sagan, 8 March 1814, 2:00 a.m., Chaumont, in Ullrichova, *Clemens Metternich*, 227; Sagan to Metternich, 8 March 1814, Vienna, in Ullrichova, *Clemens Metternich*, 229.

41. Sagan to Metternich, 2 October 1813, Prague, in Ullrichova, *Clemens Metternich*, 96.

42. Metternich to Sagan, 21 August 1813, 6:00 p.m., Teplitz, in Ullrichova, *Clemens Metternich*, 42.

43. Metternich to Sagan, 28 December 1813, in Ullrichova, *Clemens Metternich*, 148.

44. Metternich to Sagan, 5 November 1813, Frankfurt, in Ullrichova, *Clemens Metternich*, 99.

45. Metternich to Sagan, 13 January 1814, 12:00 a.m., Basel, in Ullrichova, *Clemens Metternich*, 196.

46. Metternich to Sagan, 8 March 1814, 2:00 a.m., Chaumont, in Ullrichova, *Clemens Metternich*, 227.

47. Metternich to Sagan, 25 February 1814, Chaumont, in Ullrichova, *Clemens Metternich*, 217.

48. Metternich to Sagan, 25 October 1813, Weimar, in Ullrichova, *Clemens Metternich*, 99.

49. Metternich to Sagan, 7 November 1813, 12:00 a.m., in Ullrichova, *Clemens Metternich*, 101.

50. Metternich to Sagan, 14 January 1814, 12:00 a.m., in Ullrichova, *Clemens Metternich*, 169.

51. Metternich to Sagan, 21 October 1813, 11:00 p.m., Leipzig, in Ullrichova, *Clemens Metternich*, 83.

52. Metternich to Sagan, 25 February 1814, Chaumont, in Ullrichova, *Clemens Metternich*, 217.

53. Sagan to Metternich, 12 October 1813, Prague, in Ullrichova, *Clemens Metternich*, 61.

54. Metternich to Sagan, 13 October 1813, Teplitz, in Ullrichova, *Clemens Metternich*, 62.

55. Sagan to Metternich, 8 October 1813, Prague, in Ullrichova, *Clemens Metternich*, 105.

56. Metternich to Sagan, 11 October 1813, Commothau, in Ullrichova, *Clemens Metternich*, 75.

57. "Mais je te permets bien de faire de la politique comme de la charpier." Metternich to Sagan, 8 November 1813, 12:00 a.m., Frankfurt, in Ullrichova, *Clemens Metternich*, 105.

58. Metternich to Sagan, 6 April 1814, 1:00 a.m., Dijon, in Ullrichova, *Clemens Metternich*, 240.

59. Metternich to Sagan, 6 January 1814, in Ullrichova, *Clemens Metternich*, 159.

60. Metternich to Sagan, 16 March 1814, Troyes, in Ullrichova, *Clemens Metternich*, 233.

61. Metternich to Sagan, 8 January 1814, Fribourg, in Ullrichova, *Clemens Metternich*, 161.

62. Metternich to Sagan, 13 January 1814, Basel, in Ullrichova, *Clemens Metternich*, 167.

63. Sagan to Metternich, 23 October 1813, Prague, in Ullrichova, *Clemens Metternich*, 123.

64. Metternich to Sagan, 16 January 1814, Basel, in Ullrichova, *Clemens Metternich*, 175.

65. Gentz to Metternich, "Privatissime," 24 April 1814, cited in Siemann, *Metternich*, 570.

66. Gentz to Metternich, "Privatissime," 5 April 1814, cited in Ullrichova, *Clemens Metternich*, 571.

67. Golo Mann, *Secretary of Europe: The Life of Friedrich Gentz, Enemy of Napoleon*, trans. William H. Woglom (New Haven: Yale University Press, 1946), 57.

68. Wilhelmina von Sagan to Frederick Lamb, 20 April 1815, Vienna, Add MS 60480, fol. 86, Beauvale Papers, BL.

69. Metternich to Sagan, 12 February 1814, 2:00 a.m., Troyes, in Ullrichova, *Clemens Metternich*, 205.

Chapter 5

Note to epigraphs: Metternich to Sagan, 12 June 1813, Prague, in Ullrichova, *Clemens Metternich*, 24; Edward Thornton to Sir Hudson Lowe, 25 July 1813, Schwerin, Add MS 20111, fol. 62, copies of correspondence and papers, principally of an official character, of Sir Hudson Lowe, from the year 1794 to the year 1822, BL.

1. See Glenda Sluga, "Turning International: Foundations of Modern International Thought and New Paradigms for Intellectual History," *History of European Ideas* 41, no. 1 (2015): 103–15. Specific abstract nouns had not yet been invented as necessary for defining competing political ideologies. Staël is credited with the invention of *liberalisme*, *nationalité*, and even *culture*.

2. Friedrich Meinecke, *Cosmopolitanism and the National State*, trans. Robert B. Kimber (Princeton: Princeton University Press, 1970), 118.

3. Ibid., 126.

4. Glenda Sluga, *Internationalism in the Age of Nationalism* (Philadelphia: University of Pennsylvania Press, 2013), 11–44.

5. Marian Dziewanowski, "Czartoryski and His *Essai Sur La Diplomatie*," *Slavic Review* 30, no. 3 (1971): 603.

6. William Pitt and Lord Castlereagh, "Memorandum on the Deliverance and Security of Europe, 19 January 1805," FO 65/60, TNA; Webster, *British Diplomacy*, appendix 1, 389–94.

7. Emmanuel-Auguste-Dieudonné Las Cases, *Memoirs of the Life, Exile, and Conversations of the Emperor Napoleon* (London: Published for Henry Colburn, 1896), 4:104; Janet Hartley, "Is Russia Part of Europe? Russian Perceptions of Europe in the Reign of Alexander I," *Cahiers du monde russe et soviétique* 33, no. 4 (1992): 369–85.

8. David Laven and Lucy Riall, eds., *Napoleon's Legacy: Problems of Government in Restoration Europe* (Oxford: Berg, 2000), 21, 88, 90–92.

9. Biancamaria Fontana, "The Napoleonic Empire and the Europe of Nations," in *The Idea of Europe: From Antiquity to the European Union*, ed. Anthony Pagden (Cambridge: Cambridge University Press, 2002), 123.

10. Bew, *Castlereagh*, 326. See also "Memorandum on the Deliverance and Security of Europe, 19 January 1805," in *British Diplomacy*, appendix 1, 389–94.

11. Bew, *Castlereagh*, 350.

12. Metternich to Sagan, 21 January 1814, midday, in Ullrichova, *Clemens Metternich*, 183.

13. Immanuel Kant, *Idee zu einer allgemeinen Geschichte in weltbürgerlicher Absicht* (Göttingen: Vollstandige Neuausgabe, 2019 [in English in 1798]); see James Sofka, "Metternich's Theory of European Order: A Political Agenda for 'Perpetual Peace,'" *Review of Politics* 60, no. 1 (1998): 119, doi:10.1017/S0034670500043953.

14. See Immanuel. *Idee zu einer allgemeinen Geschichte in weltbürgerlicher Absicht.* (Gottingen: Vollstandige Neuausgabe), 2019; and Julia Horne and Glenda Sluga, "Cosmopolitanism: Its Past and Practices," *Journal of World History* 21, no. 3 (2010): 369–73.

15. Jennifer Pitts, "Empire and Legal Universalisms in the Eighteenth Century," *American Historical Review* 117, no. 1 (February 2012): 95.

16. Sofka, "Metternich's Theory of European Order," 129.

17. Jennifer Pitts, *Boundaries of the International: Law and Empire* (Cambridge, MA: Harvard University Press, 2018), 24.

18. Clemens Metternich, *Mémoires, documents et écrits divers*, ed. M. A. de Klinkowstroem (Paris: E. Plon, 1880–84), 1:31.

19. Šedivý, *Metternich*, 378.

20. Germaine de Staël, "Du principe de la morale dans la nouvelle philosophie allemande," in *Oeuvres complètes de madame la baronne de Staël-Holstein: Oeuvres posthumes de madame la baronne de Staël-Holstein, précédées d'une notice sur son caractère et ses écrits* (Paris: Chez Firmin Didot Freres, 1871), 2:210–12.

21. Staël, *De la littérature*, in *Oeuvres complètes*, 1:75.

22. Sluga, "Passions, Patriotism and Nationalism"; Joan Dejean, *Ancients against Moderns: Culture Wars and the Making of a Fin de Siècle* (Chicago: University of Chicago Press, 1997); Mosse, *Nationalism and Sexuality*, 6.

23. Sluga, "Passions, Patriotism and Nationalism, 304.

24. Germaine de Staël, "De la littérature: Considéré dans ses rapports avec les institutions sociales, "in *Oeuvres complètes de Madame la baronne de Staël-Holstein* (Paris: Firmin Didot, 1836), 236.

25. See Staël, *De la littérature*, in *Oeuvres complètes*, 2:44–46.

26. Sofka, "Metternich's Theory of European Order," 121.

27. Šedivý, *Metternich*, 40.

28. Ibid. The Ottoman Dynasty (or the Imperial House of Osman) ruled the Ottoman Empire from 1299 to 1922.

29. Cited in Anthony Pagden, ed., *The Idea of Europe: From Antiquity to the European Union* (New York: Cambridge University Press, 2002), 16.

30. Germaine de Staël, "An Appeal to the Sovereigns," in *Translating Slavery*, ed. Kadish and Massardier-Kenney, 159.

31. See Aydin, *The Idea of the Muslim World.*

32. Robert Wilson to Emperor Alexander I, 12 September 1812, St. Petersburg, in Robert Wilson, *Narrative of Events during the Invasion of Russia by Napoleon Bonaparte: And the Retreat of the French Army, 1812* (Cambridge: Cambridge University Press, 2013), 388.

33. Albert Sorel, *L'Europe et la révolution française*, vol. 3 (Paris: Plon, 1904).

34. Meinecke, *Cosmopolitanism and the National State*, 118.

35. Ibid.

Chapter 6

Note to epigraphs: Metternich, *Mémoires, documents et écrits divers*, 1:31; Meinecke, *Cosmopolitanism and the National State*, 119.

1. Metternich to Sagan, 8 March 1814, 2:00 a.m., Chaumont, in Ullrichova, *Clemens-Metternich*, 227; Schroeder, *The Transformation of European Politics*, 802.

2. Schroeder, *The Transformation of European Politics*, 802.

3. Randall Lesaffer, *The Peace of Aachen (1748) and the Rise of Multilateral Treaties* (Oxford: Oxford University Press, 2017), http://opil.ouplaw.com/page/Peace-Aachen.

4. Randall Lesaffer, "Perpetual Peace," in *Oxford Historical Treaties* (Oxford: Oxford University Press, 2017), http://opil.ouplaw.com/home/OHT. See also Randall Lesaffer, "The 18th-Century Antecedents of the Concert of Europe II: The Quadruple Alliance of 1718," *Oxford Historical Treaties* (Oxford: Oxford University Press, 2017), http://opil.ouplaw.com/page/quadruple-alliance; and Randall Lesaffer, "The 18th-Century Antecedents of the Concert of Europe I: The Triple Alliance of 1717," in *Oxford Historical Treaties* (Oxford: Oxford University Press, 2017), https://opil.ouplaw.com/page/The%2018th-century%20Antecedents%20of%20the%20Concert%20of%20Europe%20I:%20The%20Triple%20Alliance%20of%201717.

5. Metternich to Sagan, 21 January 1814, midday, in Ullrichova, *Clemens Metternich*, 183.

6. Bew, *Castlereagh*, 350.

7. Ibid., 322.

8. Graaf, *Fighting Terror after Napoleon*, 105.

9. Wolf Gruner, "The German Confederation: Cornerstone of the New European Security System," in *Securing Europe after Napoleon: 1815 and the New European Security Culture*, ed. Beatrice de Graaf, Ido de Haan, and Brian Vick (Cambridge: Cambridge University Press, 2019), 151.

10. *Continuation du Protocole des conferences de Chatillon sur seine, séance 7 Fevrier 1814*; *Protocole of the conference held with the French Plenipotentiary, Châtillon 7 Feb 1814*; *Enclosure in Lord Aberdeen's Dispatch no.5 Feb 17th 1814*; *Protocole des conferences de Châtillon sur seine*, all in FO 139/3, TNA.

11. *Protocole des conferences de Châtillon sur seine*; *Protocole of the Conference held with the French Plenip. Châtillon 5 Feb 1814, enclosure in Lord Aberdeen's despatch no. 2 Feb 7 1814*, FO 139/3, TNA.

12. *Protocole des conferences de Châtillon sur seine*; *Continuation du Protocole des conferences de Chatillon sur Seine, séance du 18–19 mars 1814*, FO 139/3, TNA.

13. Treaty of Chaumont, *Art, VI, Art. VII. Art. VIII*, in Jules de Clerq, *Recueil des traités de la France publ. sous les auspices du ministère des affaires étrangères* (Paris: A. Durand et Pedone-Lauriel, 1880–1917), 2:395–99.

14. See discussion in Glenda Sluga, "'Who Hold the Balance of the World?' Bankers at the Congress of Vienna and in International History," *American Historical Review* (December 2017): 1403–30.

15. Documents relatifs à un projet de papier-monnaie federatif, 1813, fol. 46 and Papiers François d'Ivernois et papiers Delor-d'Ivernois: 1728–1889, MS suppl. 976–1010, MS fr. 1299, BGE.

16. Bew, *Castlereagh*, 346.

17. Beatrice de Graaf, "The Allied Machine: The Conference of Ministers in Paris and the Management of Security, 1815–18," in *Securing Europe after Napoleon*, ed. Graaf, Haan, and Vick, 134.

18. Graaf, *Fighting Terror after Napoleon*, 49.

19. "Cette paix ne sera plus jamais que celle de l'Europe," published on 25 March 1814 in Vitry, *Protocole des conferences de Châtillon sur Seine*, FO 139/3, TNA.

20. *Continuation du Protocole des conferences de Chatillon sur Seine, séance du 10 mai 1814*, FO 139/3, TNA.

21. Bew, *Castlereagh*, 336.

22. Charles Stewart, "Narrative of the War in Germany and France," cited in ibid., 337.

23. Claude-Henri de Saint-Simon and Augustin Thierry, *De la réorganisation de la société européenne, ou De la nécessité et des moyens de rassembler les peuples de l'Europe en un seul corps politique, en conservant à chacun son indépendance nationale* (Paris: Delauney, 1814).

24. Ibid., 23.

25. Ibid., 51.

26. Maxime Leroy, *La vie véritable du comte Henri de Saint-Simon (1760–1825)* (Paris: B. Grasset, 1925), 259.

27. "Discours préliminaire," in Staël, *De la littérature*, in *Oeuvres complètes*, 1:17.

28. Cited in Frank Edward Manuel, *The New World of Henri Saint-Simon* (Ann Arbor: University of Michigan Press, 1963), 56.

29. See chapter 13.

30. Saint-Simon, *De la réorganisation*, 60.

31. Fontana, "The Napoleonic Empire," 126.

32. Joep Schenk, "The Central Commission for the Navigation of the Rhine: A First Step towards European Economic Security?" in *Securing Europe after Napoleon*, ed. Graaf, Haan, and Vick, 81.

33. See Brian Vick, "Power, Humanitarianism and the Global Liberal Order: Abolition and the Barbary Corsairs in the Vienna Congress System," *International History Review* 40, no. 4 (2018): 939–60.

34. Jean-Charles-Leonard Simonde de Sismondi, *De l'intérêt de la France à l'égard de la traite des nègres* (Geneva: J. J. Paschoud, 1814).

35. Aberdeen, 4 December 1813, Add MS 43259, fol. 66, Aberdeen Papers, BL; Sagan to Metternich, 4 and 5 January 1814, Vienna, in Ullrichova, *Clemens Metternich*, 171.

36. Castlereagh to Emily, Langres, 30 January 1814, in Webster, *The Foreign Policy of Castlereagh*.

37. Priscilla Anne Fane Westmorland, *The Letters of Lady Burghersh: (afterwards Countess of Westmorland) from Germany and France during the Campaign of 1813–14* (London: J. Murray, 1893).

38. Bew, *Castlereagh*, 341.

39. Staël, *Considerations on the Principal Events of the French Revolution*, 558; Blennerhasset, *Talleyrand*, 2:193; Winock, *Madame de Staël*, 2:193.

40. Bew, *Castlereagh*, 336.

41. Graaf, *Fighting Terror after Napoleon*, 12; Graaf, "The Allied Machine."

42. Robert Gordon to Alex, Freiburg, 29 December 1813, Add MS 43217, fol. 59, Aberdeen Papers, BL.

43. Lord Aberdeen to Lord Abercorn, 9 May 1814, Paris, Add MS 43217, Aberdeen Papers, BL.

44. *Protocole de la Commision des limites du 21 May 1814*, Overseen by Humboldt for Prussia, Wessenberg for Austria, Munster of Hanover for Britain, the Duke of Palmela (Don Pedro de Sousa Holstein) for Portugal, M. le Comte de Casa Flores for Spain, and M. le Marquis d'Osmond for France, FO 92/4, TNA.

45. For more on territorial questions of the commissions, see Straus, *The Attitude of the Congress of Vienna*.

46. Graaf, *Fighting Terror after Napoleon*, 70.

47. *Definitive treaty of Peace and Amity between his Britannic Majesty and his most Christian Majesty, signed at Paris, the 30th day of May 1814* (London: Printed by R. G. Clarke, 1814), 25, https://www.torontopubliclibrary.ca/detail.jsp?Entt=RDMDC-37131052110558D&R=DC-37131052110558D.

48. Egon Caesar Corti, *The Rise of the House of Rothschild*, trans. Brian Lunn and Beatrix Lunn (New York: Cosmopolitan Book Corporation, 1928), 160.

49. 7 May 1814, in Bew, *Castlereagh*, 359.

50. Metternich to Sagan, 25 February 1814, n. 22, Chaumont, in Ullrichova, *Clemens Metternich*, 217.

51. Biancamaria Fontana has summed up this new vision: "European stability could no longer be left to the operation of spontaneous forces or to opportunistic dynastic alliances; it had to be constructed and closely monitored at a continental level" ("The Napoleonic Empire," 127).

Chapter 7

1. Roger Boutet de Monvel, *Eminent English Men and Women in Paris* (New York: C. Scribner's Sons, 1913), 85.

2. Diary entries, Paris, 8 April–7 May 1814, *John Cam Hobhouse's Diary*, https://petercochran.files.wordpress.com/2009/12/30-18221.pdf; http://petercochran.files.wordpress.com/2009/12/00-introduction.pdf.

3. Colonel Lowe to Colonel Bunbury, 31 March 1814, Paris, Correspondence and Papers of Col. Henry E. Bunbury, Add MS 37051, fol. 187, BL.

4. Bew, *Castlereagh*, 335.

5. Metternich to Sagan, 13 April 1814, Paris, n. 37, in Ullrichova, *Clemens Metternich*, 243.

6. See Kelly L. Grotke and Markus J. Prutsch, eds., *Constitutionalism, Legitimacy, and Power: Nineteenth-Century Experiences* (Oxford: Oxford University Press, 2014).

7. Geneviève Tabouis and Albert Mousset, *Quand Paris résiste: L'occupation Romaine, Paris sous les anglais, l'occupation espagnole, l'occupation des "alliés," les prussiens en 1871* (Paris: Seimrha, 1951), 33.

8. Bulletins de l'état des esprit en France, 26 June 1814, Direction Générale de la Police de France, MC PO 3176/Vol. 337/7, France Affaires Intérieurs, 1814–1815, Archives of Ministères des Affaires Étrangères, Paris, France (hereafter MAE).

9. Staël was an early enthusiast of Bentham as a "jurisconsulte et un penseur très profonde" but became disenchanted with utilitarianism for its emphasis on the majority at the cost of liberal principles of pluralism. Germaine de Staël, *Considerations sur la révolution française*, vol. 3, *Ouevres complètes de Madame de Stael* (Brussels: Auguste Wahlen & Company, 1820), 321.

10. See Markus Prutsch, *Fundamentalismus: Das "Projekt der Moderne" und die Politisierung des Religiösen* (Vienna: Passagen-Verlag, 2007); and Markus Prutsch, *Making Sense of Constitutional Monarchism in Post-Napoleonic France and Germany* (Basingstoke: Palgrave Macmillan, 2013).

11. Jeremy Bentham to Alexander I, January 1814, n. 2266, in Jeremy Bentham, *The Correspondence of Jeremy Bentham* (London: Athlone, 1968), 8.

12. Nikolay Mikhailovich, *Imperator Alexander I. Opyt istoricheskogo issledovaniya* (St. Petersburg: Eksp. Zagot. Gosud. Bumag, 1912), 219–220.

13. Tsar Alexander to Louis XVIII, 5 April 1814, in A. Polovtsoff, ed., *Correspondance diplomatiques des ambassadeurs et ministers de Russie en France et de France en Russie, 1814–1816* (St. Petersburg: Édition de la société impérial d'histoire de Russie, 1902).

14. Prutsch, *Making Sense of Constitutional Monarchism*, 217.

15. Norman King, "Libéralisme et legitimité," *Europe* (1987): 65.

16. Likewise, Joseph de Maistre, the Sardinian ambassador to Russia and renowned Catholic philosopher, criticized Louis for having "jumped on Napoleon's throne and continued the Revolution by other means." Markus J. Prutsch, "'Monarchical Constitutionalism' in Post-Napoleonic Europe: Concept and Practice," in *Constitutionalism, Legitimacy, and Power*, ed. Grotke and Prutsch.

17. "Sur un trône solidement établi avec de véritables fondements monarchiques et constitutionnels qui devaient le rendre non seulement inébranlable, mais même inattaquable." Charles-Maurice Talleyrand-Périgord, *Mémoires du prince de Talleyrand, publiés avec une préface et des notes par Le duc de Broglie* (Paris: Calmann-Levy, 1891), 2:164–65.

18. Éléonore-Adèle Boigne, *Récits d'une tante: Mémoires de la comtesse de Boigne, née d'Osmond. publiés intégralement, d'après le manuscrit original, 1921–1923* (Paris: Emile-Paul Frere, 1921), 1:350–62; Count Nostitz, cited in Musulin, *Vienna in the Age of Metternich*, 150.

19. Emma Cust, *Slight Reminiscences of a Septuagenarian* (London: J. Murray, 1867), 94.

20. Micheline Dupuy, *La duchesse de Dino, princesse de Courlande, égérie de Talleyrand, 1793–1862* (Paris: Perrin, 2002).

21. Cust, *Slight Reminiscences of a Septuagenarian*, 93–94.

22. Sagan to Lamb, 1 July 1814, Vienna, Add MS 60480, Beauvale Papers, BL; Metternich to Sagan, 20 April 1814, n. 34, in Ullrichova, *Clemens Metternich*, 248.

23. Sagan to Metternich, Vienna, 26 April 1814, n. 38, in Ullrichova, *Clemens Metternich.*

24. Metternich to Sagan, 20 April 1814, n. 34, in Ullrichova, *Clemens Metternich*, 248.

25. Metternich to Sagan, 23 April 1814, Paris, n. 39, in Ullrichova, *Clemens Metternich*, 252.

26. Comte A. de la Garde-Chambonas, *Souvenirs du Congrès de Vienne, 1814–1815* (Paris: Emile Paul, 1901), 178.

27. Rose Sophia Weigall, *The Letters of Lady Burghersh afterwards Countess of Westmorland—from Germany and France during the Campaign of 1813–14* (London: John Murray, 1893), 231; Cust, *Slight Reminiscences of a Septuagenarian*, 91–93, 171.

28. Cust, *Slight Reminiscences of a Septuagenarian*, 97. According to Cust, only one other French house is included in their evening itineraries, that of Minister of War General Dupont, "where we met a number of marshals and their wives."

29. Cust, *Slight Reminiscences of a Septuagenarian*, 96.

30. Colonel Lowe to Colonel Bunbury, 5 May 1814, Paris, Correspondence and Papers of Col. Henry E. Bunbury, Add MS 37051, fol. 202, BL.

31. Cust, *Slight Reminiscences of a Septuagenarian*, 83.

32. Ibid., 92.

33. Corti, *The Rise of the House of Rothschild*, 168.

34. Ibid.

35. The authoritative account of Stäel is Simone Balayé's *Madame de Stäel: Lumières et liberté*. Paris: Éditions Klincksieck, 1979.

36. Journal entry, 13 May 1814, Benjamin Constant, *Journaux intimes, Journaux intimes, publiée, avec un index et des notes par Alfred Roulin et Charles Roth* (Paris: NRF, Librairie Gallimard, 1952), 403; Arthur Chuquet, *L'Année 1814: Lettres et memoirs* (Paris: Albert Fontemoing, 1914), 239.

37. Journal entry, 13 May 1814, Constant, *Journaux intimes*, 403.

38. Earl of Aberdeen, 14 May 1814, Paris, Add MS 4325, fol. 284, Aberdeen Papers, BL.

39. Germaine de Staël to Benjamin Constant, 22 March 1814, in Germaine de Staël, *Madame de Staël, Charles de Villers, Benjamin Constant: Correspondance*, ed. Kurt Kloocke (New York: P. Lang, 1993), 221–22.

40. Pierre Rain, *L'Europe et la restauration des Bourbons, 1814–1818* (Paris: Perrin, 1908), 50.

41. Blennerhasset, *Talleyrand*, 2:239.

42. Ibid., 2:430, 238.

43. See Hilde Spiel, *Fanny von Arnstein: A Daughter of the Enlightenment, 1758–1818*, trans. Christine Shuttleworth (New York: Berg, 1991), 279–80; Blennerhasset, *Talleyrand*, 2:232.

44. Pictet was an old flame of Staël's who was only ambivalently comfortable with the extent of her influence. Edmond Pictet, *Biographie, travaux et correspondance*

diplomatique de C. Pictet de Rochemont 1755–1824, député de Genève auprès du Congrès de Vienne, 1814, envoyé extraordinaire et ministre plénipotentiaire de la Suisse à Paris et à Turin, 1815 et 1816 (Genève: H. Georg, 1892), https://www.archivesfamillepictet.ch.

45. Comtesse de Rémusat, *Mémoires of Mme de Remusat* (London: Sampson Low, 1880), 2:155.

46. John Quincy Adams, *Memoirs of John Quincy Adams* (Philadelphia: J. B. Lippincott, 1874), 1:278–79, 371.

47. Gengembre, "Fréquentation et sociabilité mutuelles," 266, 268.

48. For more on Staël's politics in this period, see Aurelian Craiutu, *A Virtue for Courageous Minds: Moderation in French Political Thought, 1748–1830* (Princeton: Princeton University Press, 2012).

49. Viscount Castlereagh to the Earl of Liverpool, 17 May 1814, Paris, FO 92/1, TNA.

50. For a thorough account of the context for Staël's abolitionism, and all its recorded manifestations, see John Claiborne Isbell, "Voices Lost? Staël and Slavery, 1786–1830," in *Slavery in the Caribbean Francophone World*, ed. Doris Kadish (Atlanta: University of Georgia Press, 2000); Françoise Massardier-Kenney, "Staël, Translation, and Race," in *Translating Slavery: Gender and Race in French Women's Writing, 1783–1823*, ed. Doris Kadish and Françoise Massardier-Kenney (Kent, OH: Kent State University Press, 1994), 140; and A. T. Gardiner, "Representing Slavery: Germaine de Staël and the French Abolition Debate at the Revolutionary Turn of the 19th Century" (paper presented at Conference on Humanitarian Responses to Narratives of Inflicted Suffering, University of Connecticut Human Rights Institute, 13–15 October 2006), 10.

51. Staël, "An Appeal to the Sovereigns," 159.

52. On the Norwegian constitution, see Ruth Hemstad, *"Like a Herd of Cattle": Parliamentary and Public Debates Regarding the Cession of Norway, 1813–1814* (Oslo: Akademisk Publisering, 2014).

53. Kale, "Women, Salons, and the State."

54. Sagan to Frederick Lamb, 31 May 1815, Add MS 60480, Beauvale Papers, BL.

55. Straus, *The Attitude of the Congress of Vienna*, 51.

56. It was not until 1848 that slavery was "finally and definitively banned" by the intermediary revolutionary government. Gardiner, "Representing Slavery," 15.

57. Foreign Office, ed., *British and Foreign State Papers, 1812–1816* (London: Ridgway, 1838–42), 1:170. This is a secret article agreed at the same time as Treaty of Paris, among eight powers: Austria, France, Great Britain, Portugal, Prussia, Russia, Spain, and Sweden.

58. "Minutes of a conference of 2 June 1814," FO 92/1, TNA.

59. "Points de deliberation," *Protocole de conference*, 16 June 1814, FO 139/3, fol. 71, TNA.

60. Ibid.

61. Georg Herbert Münster-Ledenburg, Ernst Friedrich Herbert Münster, and Harriet Elizabeth St. Clair, *Political Sketches of the State of Europe, from 1814–1867,*

Containing Count Ernst Münster's Despatches to the Prince Regent, from the Congress of Vienna (Edinburgh: Edmonston & Douglas, 1868), 163.

62. Diary entry, 7 June 1814, Mary Berry, *Extracts of the Journals and Correspondence of Miss Berry: From the Year 1783 to 1852*, ed. Lady Theresa Lewis (London: Longmans, Green, 1865), 3:26.

63. Catherine Pavlovna to Alexander I, 14 April 1814, in Alexander I, *Scenes of Russian Court Life: Being the Correspondence of Alexander I. With His Sister Catherine*, trans. Henry Havelock (London: Jarrolds, 1915), 220.

64. Graaf, *Fighting Terror after Napoleon*, 66.

65. Lieven, in Alexander I, *Scenes of Russian Court Life*, 266.

66. See Albert Gallatin, *The Life of Albert Gallatin*, ed. Henry Adams (Philadelphia: J. B. Lippincott, 1879), 563. In October, Gallatin finally replies that he cannot tell her about the peace negotiations between America and Britain, adding, "I fully appreciate everything you have done to be of help to America." Germaine de Staël, *Madame de Staël on Politics, Literature, and National Character*, ed. Morroe Berger (London: Sidgwick and Jackson, 1964), 27.

67. Staël to Bernadotte, 20 August 1814, n. 451, Coppet, in Solovieff, *Madame de Staël*, 487.

68. Jean-Gabriel Eynard, *Au Congrès de Vienne* (Paris: Librairie Plon, 1914), 82. My translation.

69. Garde-Chambonas, *Souvenirs du Congrès de Vienne*, 125. Staël had organized for a selection of Ligne's letters to be published and had written a preface to help sell them.

70. Lady Romilly to Bentham, 9 October 1814, in Bentham, *The Correspondence*, 8:435.

71. Lady Melbourne to Lord Byron, Whitehall, 31 January 1815, in Jonathan David Gross, *Byron's "Corbeau Blanc": The Life and Letters of Lady Melbourne* (College Station: Texas A&M University Press, 1998), 281.

72. Jaucourt to Talleyrand at Vienna, Paris, 1 October 1814, in Arnail François Jaucourt, *Correspondance du Comte de Jaucourt, ministre interim: Des affaires étrangères avec le prince de Talleyrand* (Paris: Plon, 1905), 15.

73. Bulletins de l'état des esprit en France, 1 July 1814, Direction Générale de la Police de France, MC PO 3176/Vol. 337/7, France Affaires Intérieurs, 1814–1815, MAE.

74. Talleyrand to Staël, 21 October 1814, Vienne, n. 456, in Solovieff, *Madame de Staël*.

75. Staël, *Considérations*, 719.

76. Staël to Bernadotte, 20 August 1814, in Solovieff, *Madame de Staël*, 487.

Chapter 8

Note to epigraphs: "Baron Humboldt's Project for the Regulation of the Congress, Vienna, September 1814," in Great Britain Foreign Office, *Peace Handbooks*, no. 153, appendix IV (December 1945) (London: H. M. Stationery Office, 1920), 532–54;

Unknown (possibly Dorothea Lieven) to Lamb, 28 February 1816, Add MS 60482, fol. 16, Beauvale Papers, BL.

1. Viscount Castlereagh to the Earl of Liverpool, 30 September 1814, Vienna, FO 92/7, Congress Vienna, TNA.

2. Unknown (possibly Dorothea Lieven) to Lamb, 28 February 1816.

3. Humboldt, *Projet*, September 1814, in C. K. Webster, ed., *The Congress of Vienna* (London: H. Milford, 1919), appendix IV, pp. 175–83, "Proposal to Publish a Declaration," appendix V, pp. 183–85 and appendix VI, p. 185. See also Karl Griewank, *Der Wiener Kongress und die europäische Restauration 1814/15* (Leipzig: Koehler und Amelang, 1942), 104–8; Wilhelm Humboldt, "Mémoire [préparatoire] sur le travail de la Commission de la navigation, presenté par M. le Baron de Humboldt, 3 février 1815," Annexe no. 1, "Procès-verbale de la deuxième conférence de la commission pour la libre navigation des rivières—Vienne, Séance du 8 février 1815," in Comte d'Angeberg, *Le Congrès de Vienne et les traités de 1815* (Paris: Amyot, Éditeur des Archives Diplomatiques, 1863), 728–33.

4. "Points de deliberation," Protocole de conference, 16 June 1814, FO 139/3, TNA.

5. Viscount Castlereagh to the Earl of Liverpool, 24 September 1814, Vienna, "Secret and Confidential," FO 92/7, Congress Vienna, fols. 42–43, TNA.

6. Ozan Ozavci, *Dangerous Gifts: Imperialism, Security, and Civil Wars in the Levant, 1798–1864* (forthcoming), cited in Erik de Lange, "Menacing Tides: Security, Piracy and Empire in the Nineteenth-Century Mediterranean" (PhD diss., Utrecht University, 2020), 61.

7. Mavrogheni's note of a conversation with Lord Castlereagh, 16 February 1815, Vienna, FO 139/26, Continent conferences, Miscellaneous, Turkey, Vienna, TNA.

8. Ozavci, *Dangerous Gifts*, cited in Lange, "Menacing Tides."

9. Castlereagh to Liverpool, 24 September 1814.

10. Schroeder, *The Transformation of European Politics*, vii.

11. Copies of protocols, Viscount Castlereagh to the Earl of Liverpool, 22 September 1814, contained in Castlereagh to Liverpool, 24 September 1814.

12. Protocol of the Conference held with the French Plenipotentiary, Châtillon, 5 February 1814, enclosure in Lord Aberdeen's dispatch no. 2, 7 February 1814; Continuation du Protocole des conferences de Châtillon sur Seine, 7 February 1814; Protocol of the conference held with the French Plenipotentiary, Châtillon, 7 February 1814; enclosure in Lord Aberdeen's Dispatch no. 5, 17 February 1814; Continuation du Protocole des conferences de Châtillon sur Seine, 18–19 March 1814, all in FO 139/3, TNA.

13. "Rapport de la Commission des huit Plenipotentiaries pour régler le rang entre les Courronnes," FO 139/11, fols. 16, 24, 27, 30, TNA.

14. Ibid.

15. Harold Nicolson, *The Congress of Vienna: A Study in Allied Unity, 1812–1822* (London: Constable and Co., 1946), 14.

16. Norman Hill, *The Public International Conference: Its Function, Organization and Procedure* (Palo Alto: Stanford University Press, 1926), 38.

17. Straus, *The Attitude of the Congress of Vienna*, 124, 125, 135; Comte d'Angeberg, *Recueil des traités, conventions et actes diplomatiques concernant la Pologne, 1762–1862* (Paris: Amyot, 1862), 619.

18. Jürgen Wilke, "From Parish Register to the 'Historical Table': The Prussian Population Statistics in the 17th and 18th Centuries," *History of the Family* 9, no. 1 (2004): 63–79.

19. "Proces verbaux et Rapports de la commission statistique avec les pieces annexes, 24 December 1814," in Leonard Chodźko, *Le Congrès de Vienne et les traités de 1815* (Paris: Amyot, Éditeur des Archives Diplomatiques, 1864), 2:562–66.

20. Genevieve Peterson, "II. Political Inequality at the Congress of Vienna," *Political Science Quarterly* 60, no. 4 (1945): 532–54.

21. Straus, *The Attitude of the Congress of Vienna*, 131.

22. Ibid., 132.

23. Straus argues that "economic measures . . . were to remain a dead letter" (*The Attitude of the Congress of Vienna*, 132). See also Mark Jarrett, *The Congress of Vienna and Its Legacy: War and Great Power Diplomacy after Napoleon* (London: I. B. Tauris, 2013), 102–4.

24. Humboldt, "Mémoire [préparatoire]."

25. Graaf, *Fighting Terror after Napoleon*, 44.

26. See also Schenk, "The Central Commission for the Navigation of the Rhine," 84.

27. Jennifer Siegel, *For Peace and Money: French and British Finance in the Service of Tsars and Commissars* (New York: Oxford University Press, 2014), 115.

28. "Projet d'articles pour le règlement de ce qui concerne la navigation des grands fleuves traversant plusieurs territoires, présenté par M. le duc de Dalberg, plénipotentiare de France," in "Procès-verbale de la première conférence de la Commission relative à la libre navigation des rivières, Vienne, 2 février 1815," in Comte d'Angeberg, *Le Congrès de Vienne et les traités de 1815* (Paris: Amyot, Éditeur des Archives Diplomatiques, 1863), 694–97.

29. "Procès-verbale de la Commission relative à la libre navigation des rivières," 778, 799–800, 828–63.

30. Humboldt, "Mémoire [préparatoire]."

31. Joseph P. Chamberlain, *The Regime of the International Rivers: Danube and Rhine* (New York: Columbia University Press, 1923), 29.

32. Viscount Castlereagh to the Earl of Liverpool, 9 October 1814, FO 92/7, Congress of Vienna, TNA.

33. Viscount Castlereagh to the Earl of Liverpool, 25 October 1814, Vienna, FO92/7, Congress of Vienna, TNA; Comte d'Angeberg. *Le Congrès de Vienne et les traités de 1815* (Paris: Amyot, Éditeur des Archives Diplomatiques, 1863), 2:504, 613–14, 726.

34. Viscount Castlereagh to Lord Liverpool, 6 September 1814, Geneva, FO 92/7, Congress of Vienna, TNA.

35. Castlereagh to Liverpool, 25 October 1814; second conference, 28 January 1815, Kongress Akten 5, Österreichisches Staatsarchiv, Haus-, Hof- und Staatsarchiv, Vienna, Austria.

36. Stefan Krause, *Die Aechtung des Sklavenhandels auf dem Wiener Kongress: Ein Sieg der Humanitaet oder der Machtpolitik?* (Norderstedt, GRIN Verlag, 2009), 9.

37. Second conference, 28 January 1815.

38. Randall Lesaffer, "Vienna and the Abolition of the Slave Trade," *Oxford Public International Law* (2015), https://opil.ouplaw.com/page/498. Vick has described the abolitionist declaration as "the first truly humanitarian measure cast in universalist terms to emerge from a diplomatic gathering" (*The Congress of Vienna*, 204). Matthias Schulz has argued that the Final Acts were the "first general peace concluded as a multilateral treaty" and therefore they were considered "a kind of 'constitutional' order of Europe." Matthias Schulz, *Normen und Praxis: Das Europäische Konzert der Großmächte als Sicherheitsrat, 1815–1860*, Studien zur Internationalen Geschichte B.21 (Munich: R. Oldenbourg Verlag, 2009).

39. Vick, "Power, Humanitarianism and the Global Liberal Order."

40. Lesaffer, "Vienna and the Abolition of the Slave Trade."

41. The resolution gave the duchy to a prince from the female line and engineered Bouillon's allocation to the Duchy of Luxembourg and, by default, to the Kingdom of the Netherlands. Beatrice de Graaf, "Second-Tier Diplomacy: Hans Von Gagern and William I in Their Quest for an Alternative European Order, 1813–1818," *Journal of Modern European History/Zeitschrift Für Moderne Europäische Geschichte/Revue d'histoire Européenne Contemporaine* 12, no. 4 (2014): 546–66.

42. Catherine to Marie de Saxe-Weimar, Rotterdam, 19/7 March 1814, in Gunzburg, *Catherine Pavlovna*, 101.

Chapter 9

Note to epigraphs: "N à Madame de Staël," 27 November 1814, Vienna, in Solovieff, *Madame de Staël*, 463; Goethe, cited in Musulin, *Vienna in the Age of Metternich*, 139.

1. Hager à 00 (Confidentielle), Instructions adressées à l'agent 00, Vienne, 24 septembre 1814, in *Les Dessous du Congrès de Vienne d'après les documents originaux des Archives du Ministère Impèrial et royal de l'Intèrieur*. Vienne. Vol. 1. (Paris: Librairie Payot), 1917.

2. Jean Gaggiám, *Guide des étrangers à Vienne pendant le congrès, contenant les noms des souverains présents dans cette capitale ainsi que ceux des ministres et chargés d'affaires des differentes cours auprès de celle de Vienne au mois de Janvier 1815* (Vienna: Se trouve chez le Suisse de S.A.R. le Duc Albert de Saxe Teschen, 1815).

3. Von Hegardt, Swedish chargé d'affaires to Foreign Minister Engestrom, cited in Musulin, *Vienna in the Age of Metternich*, 163.

4. William Sidney Smith, *Mémoire sur la nécessité et les moyens de faire cesser les pirateries des états barbaresques*, January 1814, https://play.google.com/books/reader?id=1FBNAAAAcAAJ&hl=en_GB&pg=GBS.PA1.

5. Jean-Gabriel Eynard, "Notes prises au Congrès de Vienne du 30 Octobre 1814 au 10 Fevrier 1815," MS suppl. 1854, 17–19, BGE.

6. Queen Maria Luigia, *Memoir of the Queen of Etruria Written by Herself* (London: John Murray, 1814); Protesta dell/Imperatrice Maria Luigia, 15 February 1815,

Documenti Staccati, 91/20, Manoscritte venuti da S. Clena da mano incognito, Biblioteca Nazionale Centrale Vittorio Emanuele, Rome, Italy.

7. Review of "Memoirs of the Baron de Kolli," *Edinburgh Review* 39, no. 77 (1824): 245.

8. See Vick, *The Congress of Vienna*, 7, on women at the Congress of Vienna, particularly his conceptualization of their "influence politics."

9. Maurice Henri Weil, *Les Dessous du Congrès de Vienne d'après les documents originaux des Archives du Ministère Impérial et royal de l'Intérieur à Vienne* (Paris: Librairie Payot, 1917), 1:827.

10. Gräfin Hürheim, *Mein Leben: Erinnerungen Aus Österreicsh Grosse Welt, 1819–1852* (Munich: Müller, 1913), 258; Charles Robert de Nesselrode, "Le comte Charles de Nesselrode à son père, Viènne, 27 mai 1807," in Nesselrode, *Lettres et papiers*, 3:180.

11. "Le comte Charles de Nesselrode à son père, Viènne, 23 avril 1807," in Nesselrode, *Lettres et papiers*, 3:175. Bled, "La société russe," 80, 86.

12. Germaine de Staël's *On Germany* boosts a linguistic map of German-speaking lands extending from Austria through Prussia and the former lands of the Holy Roman Empire into Switzerland.

13. Stein cited in Meinecke, *Cosmopolitanism*, 121.

14. Ibid., 126.

15. Straus, *The Attitude of the Congress of Vienna*, 36.

16. Ibid., 51.

17. See Franziska Schedewie, "The Tsar's Sister as State Diplomat: Maria Pavlovna between Weimar and St. Petersburg on the Eve of the Congress of Vienna," in *Women, Diplomacy and International Politics since 1500*, ed. Glenda Sluga and Carolyn James (London: Routledge, 2015), 137–50.

18. Princess Dowager of Fürstenberg to the King, 31 October 1814, Vienna, "Les Mediatisés," FO 139/16, TNA.

19. Cited in Straus, *The Attitude of the Congress of Vienna*, 37.

20. Caroline von Humboldt to Wilhelm von Humboldt, 12 December 1814, Berlin, in Freksa, *Peace Congress*, 177.

21. Gersdorff, *Caroline von Humboldt*, 145.

22. Caroline to Wilhelm, 28 November 1814, Berlin, in Freksa, *Peace Congress*, 174.

23. Wilhelm to Caroline, 9 November 1814, Vienna, in Freksa, *Peace Congress*, 169.

24. Gersdorff, *Caroline von Humboldt*, 9.

25. Caroline to Wilhelm, 26 November 1814, Berlin, in Freksa, *Peace Congress*, 171.

26. Wilhelm to Caroline, 1 August 1814, Zurich, in Freksa, *Peace Congress*, 156.

27. Caroline to Wilhelm, 17 November 1814, Berlin, in Freksa, *Peace Congress*, 170.

28. Caroline to Wilhelm, 28 November 1814, Berlin, in Freksa, *Peace Congress*, 171.

29. Caroline to Wilhelm, 7 November 1814, Berlin, in Freksa, *Peace Congress*, 166.

30. Caroline to Wilhelm, 17 November 1814, Berlin, in Freksa, *Peace Congress*, 170.

31. Caroline to Wilhelm, 7 November 1814, Berlin, in Freksa, *Peace Congress*, 167.

32. Wilhelm to Caroline, 1 August 1814, Zurich, in Freksa, *Peace Congress*, 156.

33. See Gunzburg, *Catherine Pavlovna*.

34. Cited (in English) in S. Askenazy, "Polska a Europa, 1813–1815," *Biblioteka Warszawska* (1909): 1–30, 209–37.

35. Princess Jablonowska, Letter from Paris, 14 October 1814, in Maria Pia Casalena, *"Cher Sis": Scritture femminili nella corrispondenza di Sismondi* (Firenze: Edizioni Polistampa, 2008).

36. Maurice Henri Weil, *Autour du Congrès de Vienne: La princesse Bagration, la duchesse de Sagan, et la police secrète de l'Autriche* (Paris: Librairie Payot, 1913), 626, 841.

37. Caroline to Wilhelm, 17 November 1814, Berlin, in Freksa, *Peace Congress*, 170.

38. Letter dated 21 July 1814, cited in Niall Ferguson, *The House of Rothschild: Money's Prophets, 1798–1848* (New York: Viking, 1998), 173–74.

39. Max J. Kohler, *Jewish Rights at the Congresses of Vienna (1814–1815) and Aix-La-Chapelle (1818)* (New York: American Jewish Committee, 1918).

40. Ibid., 6.

41. Salo W. Baron, "Unveröffentliche Aktenstücke zur Judenfrage auf dem Wiener Kongress (1814–15)," *Monatsschrift für Geschichte und Wissenschaft des Judentums* 6 (1926): 457–75.

42. Ferguson, *The House of Rothschild*, 173; Kohler, *Jewish Rights*, 15.

43. *M. Rothschild to Lord Liverpool, London, Nov 1 1814, in favour of the Jews of Germany. Inclosed in a private letter from Lord Liverpool to Lord Castlereagh and the subject strongly recommended to his attention*, in Liverpool to Castlereagh, Fife House, 12 December 1814, Letter xxxvi, in Webster, *The Foreign Policy of Castlereagh*, 603. Charles Stewart, Castlereagh's half brother, was probably the Rothschilds' English "friend." See Ferguson's useful discussion in *The House of Rothschild*, 173–76.

44. Original in French, "[xx] à Hager," 18 December 1814, Vienna, in Weil, *Les Dessous*, 695. Spiel, *Fanny von Arnstein*, 300. Kohler (*Jewish Rights*) mentions the roles of other women in this question, including Rahel Levin and Mesdames Herz, Ephraim, Pereira, and Dorothea Mendelssohn von Schlegel, but with no evidence.

45. Cited in, Spiel, *Fanny von Arnstein*, 298.

46. Nathan Michael Gelber, *Aktenstücke zur Judenfrage am Wiener Kongress, 1814/1815* (Vienna: Verlag des "Esra," 1920) for the text of the memorials; Corti, *The Rise of the House of Rothschild*, 172; Spiel, *Fanny von Arnstein*, 70.

47. Alix de Watteville, *Anna Eynard-Lullin et l'époque des congrès et des révolutions* (Lausanne: Paul Feissly, 1955), 148.

48. Anna Eynard, *Journal* Congrès de Vienne, 1814–1815, 13 October 1815, MS suppl. 1959, fol. 21, BGE.

49. Both Anna and Jean-Gabriel kept diaries of the Congress.

50. Two copies of the letter from Anna Eynard-Lullin to Ms. Delessert, Annexes, MS suppl. 1915, BGE.

51. For more on these networks, see Vick, *The Congress of Vienna*, 115.

52. Anna Eynard, *Journal* Congrès de Vienne, 1814–1815, MS suppl. 1959, fol. 231, BGE.

53. Ibid., fol. 204.

54. Ibid., fol. 228.

55. Ibid., fol. 194. When Prince Eugene Beauharnais (Napoleon's nephew) visited the Eynards at Kuglerstrasse on numerous afternoons, the company would sing, and he would tell her things that she wished she could report as a military person.

56. Ibid., fol. 239.

57. For more on Geneva, see Jarrett, *The Congress of Vienna*, 137–38.

58. Vick, *The Congress of Vienna*, 168.

59. Sweet, *Humboldt*, 2:207–8; Vick, *The Congress of Vienna*, 175.

60. The former territory of the confederation today includes Austria, Belgium, Croatia, the Czech Republic, Germany, Italy, Liechtenstein, Luxembourg, the Netherlands, Poland, and Slovenia.

61. Staël to Prosper de Barante, 28 October 1814, Geneva, Lettres de divers ouvertes et copiées à la poste de Paris, vol. 675, fol. 395, France et Divers États de l'Europe, 1814, MAE.

62. My translation, intercepted letter, in Weil, *Autour du Congrès de Vienne*, 828.

63. Sagan to Lamb, 31 March 1815, Vienna, Add MS 60480, fol. 69, Beauvale Papers, BL.

64. Sagan to Lamb, 20 April 1815, Vienna, Add MS 60480, fol. 86, Beauvale Papers, BL.

65. Anna Eynard, *Journal* Congrès de Vienne, 1814–1815, 28 December 1814, Wednesday, MS suppl. 1959, BGE.

66. Ibid.

67. "N" à Madame de Staël, 27 November 1814, Vienna, in Solovieff, *Madame de Staël*, 463.

Chapter 10

Note to epigraphs: Germaine de Staël, "Necker's Plans of Finance," in *Considerations on the Principal Events of the French Revolution* (Indianapolis: Liberty Fund, 2008), 59; Benjamin Constant, *Commentaire sur l'ouvrage de Filangieri, Science de la Législation*, ed. Alain Laurent (Paris: Belles Lettres, 2004).

1. Friedrich von Gentz, *On the State of Europe Before and After the French Revolution*, trans. John Charles Herries (London: J. Hatchard, 1804), 38–39.

2. Leroy, *La vie véritable du comte Henri de Saint-Simon*, 262, 264–65.

3. Varnhagen, *Familienbriefe*, passim. See also David S. Landes, "Vieille Banque et Banque Nouvelle: La révolution financière du dix-neuvième siècle," *Revue d'histoire moderne et contemporaine* 3, no. 3 (July–September 1956): 204–22. "Capitalist" also reemerged as a catch-all noun for the scope of individuals representing "monied interests" in the early nineteenth century; see editor's note, Staël, *Considerations on the Principal Events of the French Revolution*, 42.

4. Jerrold Seigel, *Modernity and Bourgeois Life: Society, Politics, and Culture in England, France and Germany since 1750* (Cambridge: Cambridge University Press, 2012), 352.

5. Corti, *The Rise of the House of Rothschild*, 168.

6. Local Austrian Jews, too, were subject to discrimination, as the subjects of regular state surveillance and/or laws that forbid them to intermarry, to own land in the imperial dominions, to assume positions in the imperial administration or political office or higher posts in the army, or to become lawyers or teachers., They were also required to pay a special tax.

7. Varnhagen, *Familienbriefe*, 371, 527–31.

8. Fritz Redlich, "Eric Bollmann, Adventurer, Businessman, and Economic Writer," in *Essays in American Economic History: Eric Bollmann and Studies in Banking*, ed. Fritz Redlich (New York: G. E. Stechert & Co., 1944), 50. See also Corti, *The Rise of the House of Rothschild*, 168, 172; Ferguson, *The House of Rothschild*, 173; Rahel Levin and Moritz Robert-Tornow to Marcus Theodor, 20 November 1814, Berlin, in Varnhagen, *Familienbriefe*, 456–57.

9. Daniel Moran, *Toward the Century of Words: Johann Cotta and the Politics of the Public Realm in Germany, 1795–1832* (Berkeley: University of California Press, 1992), 125; "French Papers," *The Times*, 14 October 1814, 2.

10. Watteville, *Anna Eynard-Lullin*, 151.

11. Gunzburg, *Catherine Pavlovna*, 42.

12. Seigel, *Modernity and Bourgeois Life*, 87–91.

13. See Eynard, *Au Congrès de Vienne*.

14. See "Siber à Hager," 10 February 1815, in Weil, *Les Dessous*, 2:178.

15. Spiel, Fanny von Arnstein, 238; for more on bankers, see Sluga, "'Who Hold the Balance of the World?'."

16. Spiel, *Fanny von Arnstein*, 284, 300. Original in French, "XX à Hager," 18 December 1814, Vienna, in Weil, *Les Dessous*, 1:695.

17. Herman Freudenberger, *Lost Momentum: Austrian Economic Development, 1750s–1830s* (Cologne: Böhlau Verlag, 2003), 170.

18. Léon Poliakov, *Histoire de l'antisémitisme*, vol. 3, *De Voltaire à Wagner* (Paris: Calmann-Lévy, 1968), 3:202.

19. Cited in Spiel, *Fanny von Arnstein*, 283.

20. Ibid., 269.

21. Ibid., 287.

22. Ibid., 284.

23. Ibid., 269.

24. Garde-Chambonas, *Souvenirs du Congrès de Vienne*, 270–71.

25. Vienna became excessively expensive as a result of the congress's demand for housing and supplies. See Freudenberger, *Lost Momentum*, 174; see also Watteville, *Anna Eynard-Lullin*, 404–5.

26. Lämel had a long history of helping the Austrians fight Napoleon by personally financing the purchase of ammunition, acting as commissary for the army,

and eventually lending the state his entire fortune; his efforts were rewarded with ennoblement. His daughter was married to Herz. Spiel, *Fanny von Arnstein*, 302.

27. Wilhelm von Humboldt to Caroline von Humboldt, 30 April 1815, Vienna, in Freksa, *Peace Congress*, 204.

28. The total cook's bill, 21 April to 31 May, was £1596, 2s., "From Clancarty, April 19, 1814," FO 95 (Misc.), fol. 506.

29. *The Times*, 8 October 1818.

30. Musulin, *Vienna in the Age of Metternich*, 163.

31. Ibid., 158–59.

32. "From the Reminiscences of the Countess Bernstorff"; see Freksa, *A Peace Congress of Intrigue*, 15.

33. Garde-Chambonas, *Souvenirs du Congrès de Vienne*, 183.

34. Carlile Aylmer Macartney, "The Austrian Monarchy, 1792–1847," in *War and Peace in an Age of Upheaval*, ed. Charles William Crawley, vol. 9 of *New Cambridge Modern History* (Cambridge: Cambridge University Press, 1965), 401–2. See Eric Hobsbawm, *The Age of Revolution: 1789–1848* (London: Weidenfeld and Nicolson , 1996), 94–95; for more on the diversity of paper money, see Seigel, *Modernity and Bourgeois Life*, 273, 287–88, and Lynn Hunt, "The Global Financial Origins of 1789," in *The French Revolution in Global Perspective*, ed. Suzanne Desan, Lynn Hunt, and William Max Nelson (Ithaca: Cornell University Press, 2013).

35. A Russian issue of paper money collapsed to 20 percent of its original value under similar circumstances. For more on the diversity of paper money, see Seigel, *Modernity and Bourgeois Life*, 273. Hilde Spiel has linked the "fear of suffering once more under a financial debacle such as the one that attended Austria's national bankruptcy of 1811" to the "business instinct" that she argues drove women from far and wide to take up prostitution at the congress. Spiel, *Fanny von Arnstein*, 276.

36. Küster quoted in Spiel, *Fanny von Arnstein*, 24.

37. Karl Varnhagen to Marcus Theodor, 20 January 1815, in Varnhagen, *Familienbriefe*, 483–85.

38. Spiel, *Fanny von Arnstein*, 24.

39. "Carrissimo Marito," Premio dicembre 1814, Foscolo Speciale, Bentivoglio, Biblioteca Archigiannesi, Bologna, Italy.

40. Watteville, *Anna Eynard-Lullin*, 130, 152.

41. Tewarson, *Rahel Levin Varnhagen*, 140.

42. Levin to Marcus Theodor, 20 March 1815, Berlin, in Varnhagen, *Familienbriefe*, 532–34. See all of Rahel's letters to Moritz, January–February 1815, in Varnhagen, *Familienbriefe*, 495–500. Levin's letters reference bankers in Vienna (Arnstein, Eskeles, Geymüller), Prague (Lämel, Zdeckauer, Lesser, Ballanbene, Dessauer), Berlin (Mendelsson, Getschow, Schidkler, Lehmann, Speyer, Goldschmidt), Hamburg (Gontard), Frankfurt (Rothschildt [*sic*], Kongliche), Leipzig (Levy Salomon), and Paris (Rougemont). On her banking connections, see Hoock-Demarle, *L'Europe des lettres*, 275; on currency exchange, see David S. Landes, *Bankers and Pashas: International Finance and Economic Imperialism in Egypt* (London: Heinemann, 1958), 4.

43. By the time Levin was in Frankfurt, her brothers used the Frankfurt Rothschilds for sending credit. See Marcus Theodor to Rahel in Frankfurt am Main, 12 October 1816, 19–20 December 1814; Marcus asked if she liked her new apartment better. Varnhagen, *Familienbriefe*, 468–69.

44. Landes, *Bankers and Pashas*, 4.

45. Rahel to Moritz in Berlin, 30 January 1815, in Varnhagen, *Familienbriefe*, 495–97.

46. Rahel to Moritz in Berlin, 6 February 1815, in Varnhagen, *Familienbriefe*, 499–500.

47. Marcus Theodor to Rahel, 16 March 1815, in Varnhagen, *Familienbriefe*, 370, 525.

48. Rahel to Marcus Theodor in Berlin, 30–31 March 1815, in Varnhagen, *Familienbriefe*, 554–55.

49. Rahel and Moritz to Marcus Theodor, 20 November 1814, Berlin, in Varnhagen, *Familienbriefe*, 456–57; Redlich, "Eric Bollmann," 50. See also Arendt, *Rahel Varnhagen*; on Bollmann, see Redlich, "Eric Bollmann."

50. Rahel to Moritz and Ernestine, 15–16 January 1815, in Varnhagen, *Familienbriefe*, 481.

51. Rahel and Moritz to Ernestine in Berlin, 15–16 January 1815, Varnhagen, *Familienbriefe*, 481–483; Barings is involved as guarantor of the trade between South America and Austria.

52. Ibid.

53. Rahel to Moritz, 8 February 1815, in Varnhagen, *Familienbriefe*, 501–2.

54. Redlich, "Eric Bollmann," 51. For more on entrepreneurial interest in the congress, see Vick, *The Congress of Vienna*, 66–111.

55. Rahel to Moritz and Ernestine, 15–16 January 1815, in Varnhagen, *Familienbriefe*, 676–78.

56. Spiel, *Fanny von Arnstein*, 25.

57. Tewarson, *Rahel Levin Varnhagen*, 149.

58. Spiel, *Fanny von Arnstein*, 238.

59. Ibid., 271–73; Musulin, *Vienna in the Age of Metternich*, 155.

60. In 1813, Danish currency went into dramatic decline against Swedish currency, thanks in part to its dependence on "courant bank notes." See Håkan Lobell, "Foreign Exchange Rates, 1804–1914," in *Exchange Rates, Prices and Wages, 1277–2008*, ed. Rodney Edvinsson, Tor Jacobson, and Daniel Waldenström (Stockholm: Sveriges Riksbank, 2010), 295–96.

61. Spiel, *The Congress of Vienna*, 272.

62. See "Siber à Hager," 10 February 1815, in Weil, *Les Dessous*, 2:178.

63. For more on the threat posed by women at the congress, see Glenda Sluga, "Madame de Staël and the Transformation of European Politics, 1812–17," *International History Review* 37, no. 1 (2015): 142–66; Sluga, "On the Historical Significance"; Sluga, "Women, Diplomacy, and International Politics."

64. Maurice-Henri Weil, "Autour du congrès de Vienne: La princesse Bagration, la duchesse de Sagan et la police secrète de l'Autriche," *La Revue de Paris*, 1 and 15 June 1913.

65. "Nota à Hager," 2 October 1814, Vienna, in Weil, *Les Dessous*, 1:831; Rosenkrantz, *Journal du Congrès de Vienne*, 72, 98, 105.

66. Weil, "Autour du congrès de Vienne"; Spiel, *The Congress of Vienna*, 260.

67. "Nota à Hager," 2 October 1814, Vienna, in Weil, *Les Dessous*, 1:831.

68. Mme. la Comtesse de Bassanville, *Les salons d'autrefois: Souvenirs intimes* (Paris: Victorion, 1862), 2:122.

69. "XX to Hager," 9 February 1815, in Weil, *Les Dessous*, 2:168.

70. "Nota à Hager," 2 October 1814, Vienna, in Weil, *Les Dessous*, 1:831.

Chapter 11

1. Charles William Crawley, "International Relations, 1815–1830," in *War and Peace in an Age of Upheaval, 1793–1830*, vol. 9 of *New Cambridge Modern History* (Cambridge: Cambridge University Press, 1906), 665.

2. See Walter Alison Phillips, *The Confederation of Europe: A Study of the European Alliance, 1813–1823, as an Experiment in the International Organization of Peace* (New York: Howard Fertig, 1966), 305–6.

3. Ernest John Knapton, *The Lady of the Holy Alliance: The Life of Julie de Krüdener* (New York: Columbia University Press, 1939), 160.

4. The most thorough histories include Andrei Zorin, "'Star of the East': The Holy Alliance and European Mysticism." *Kritika: Explorations in Russian and Eurasian History* 4, no. 2 (Spring 2003): 313–42; and Stella Ghervas, *Réinventer la tradition: Alexandre Stourdza et l'Europe de la Sainte-Alliance* (Paris: Honoré Champion, 2008).

5. Ghervas, *Réinventer la tradition*, 196.

6. Ibid., 243.

7. Ibid., 248–47.

8. Ibid., 237.

9. Comte d'Haussonville, "Mme de Staël et Mme de Krüdener," correspondance inédite, *Le Figaro*, supplément littéraire Samedi 16 September 1911, 13.

10. Solovieff, *Rahel Varnhagen*, 25.

11. Kari Lokke, "Frederike Brun's *Briefe aus Rom* (1816): Cosmopolitanism, Nationalism, and the Politics of *Geistlichkeit*," in *Women against Napoleon*, ed. Maierhofer, Roesch, and Bland, 140.

12. Francis Ley, "Alexandre Ier, Chateaubriand, Lamartine et Madame de Krüdener, en 1815," *Cahiers du monde russe et soviétique* 9, no. 1 (January–March 1968): 59.

13. Solovieff, *Madame de Staël*, 513–14.

14. Staël to Mme de Gérando (née Annette de Rathsamhausen), Martigny, 27 September 1815, in ibid., 513.

15. Chateaubriand, 1802, cited in Matthijs Lok, "The Congress of Vienna as a Missed Opportunity: Conservative Visions of a New European Order after Napoleon," in *Securing Europe after Napoleon*, ed. Graaf, Haan, and Vick, 61–62.

16. Ghervas, *Réinventer la tradition*, 99.

17. Ibid., 23; see also Roksandra Skarlatovna Edling, "Zapiski," in *Derzhavnyi sfinks*, ed. Alexander Liberman (Moscow: Fond Sergeia Dubova, 1999), 223; Edward Vose Gulick, "The Final Coalition and the Congress of Vienna, 1813–1815," in *War and Peace in an Age of Upheaval, 1793–1830*, ed. Charles William Crawley, vol. 9 of *New Cambridge Modern History* (Cambridge: Cambridge University Press, 1965), 663.

18. Ghervas, *Réinventer la tradition*, 78; Zorin, "'Star of the East,'" 332.

19. Castlereagh to Liverpool, 28 September 1815, Paris, in Webster, *British Diplomacy*, 382.

20. Ibid.

21. Ibid., 383; Ghervas, *Réinventer la tradition*, 74, 76.

22. Crawley, "International Relations, 1815–1830," 9:671.

23. Bew, *Castlereagh*, 580.

24. Zorin, "'Star of the East,'" 325.

25. Ghervas, *Réinventer la tradition*, 47.

26. Ibid., 262.

27. Sauvigny, *Metternich and His Times*, 129–54.

28. Ghervas, *Réinventer la tradition*, 48–50.

29. Zorin, "'Star of the East,'" 313.

30. Lange, "Menacing Tides," 38.

31. Ibid., 32.

32. Aydin, *The Idea of the Muslim World*, 50.

33. Matija Nenadovic, *The Memoirs of Prota Matija Nenadovic*, trans. Lovett F. Edwards (Oxford: Clarendon Press, 1969), 195–96.

34. Ibid., 205.

35. Ibid., 212.

36. Lord Aberdeen to Castlereagh, undated letter [probably December 1821], Add MS 43260, fol. 165, Aberdeen Papers, BL.

37. Wednesday, 28 December 1814, Anna Eynard, *Journal* Congrès de Vienne, 1814–1815, BGE.

38. Ghervas, *Réinventer la tradition*, 69; see also William St. Clair, *That Greece Might Still Be Free: The Philhellenes in the War of Independence* (London: Oxford University Press, 1972), 222; Charles William Crawley, *The Question of Greek Independence* (Cambridge: Cambridge University Press, 1930); William Cobbett, "Greek Cause!" *Cobbett's Weekly Register* 60, nos. 5–7 (28 October, 4 and 11 November 1826).

39. Elisavet Papalexopoulou, "Tracing the 'Political' in Women's Work: Women of Letters in the Greek Cultural Space, 1800–1832," *Journal of Modern Greek Studies* 39 (May 2021).

40. Foreign Office, *1815–1816*, in *British and Foreign State Papers* (London: James Ridgway and Sons, 1838), 281.

41. Gulick says this was "the legal basis for the diplomacy by conference of the postwar era" ("The Final Coalition and the Congress of Vienna," 663).

42. Stella Ghervas is indispensable for understanding Stourdza through this period; see *Réinventer la tradition*, and *Conquering Peace: From the Enlightenment to the European Union* (Cambridge, MA: Harvard University Press, 2021).

43. Solovieff, *Madame de Staël*, 513–14.

44. Foreign Office, *British and Foreign State Papers*, 279.

Chapter 12

Note to epigraphs: Countess Roxandra Edling to Count Ioannis Antonios Kapodistrias, 27 January 1817, Weimar, in "Pismo Grafini Edling Grafu Kapodistrii," *Russky Arkhiv*, no. 11 (1891): 421; François-René vicomte de Chateaubriand, Maurice Levaillant, *Deux livres des Mémoires d'outre-tombe* (Venice: Delagrave, 1936), 2:206.

1. For a discussion of the gender implications of this Orientalism, see Sluga and Caine, "Sex and Race, Nations and Empires," in *Gendering European History*, 87–117.

2. Castlereagh to Liverpool, 28 September 1815, Paris, Add MS 38566, Liverpool Papers, BL; Marquise de Montcalm, diary entry from 1 November 1815, in Marquise de Montcalm, "Journal Inédit: Extraits," *Revue de Paris* (October 1934): 25–26; Stephanie M. Hilger, *Women Write Back: Strategies of Response and the Dynamics of European Literary Culture, 1790–1805* (New York: Rodopi, 2009), 274.

3. Gunzburg, *Catherine Pavlovna*, 73.

4. Alexander Martin, *Romantics, Reformers, Reactionaries: Russian Conservative Thought and Politics in the Reign of Alexander I* (DeKalb: Northern Illinois University Press, 1997), 169.

5. Charles Eynard, *Vie de Madame de Krüdener* (Paris: Cherbuliez, 1849), 2:9, 15.

6. Krüdener to Roxandra Stourdza, 27 October 1814, in Francis Ley, *Madame de Krüdener et son temps: 1764–1824* (Paris: Plon, 1962), 424–28.

7. Emperor Alexander I to Roxandra Sturdza, "Aleksandr I," in *Russkiy biograficheskiy slovar*, ed. Alexandre Polovtsoff (St. Petersburg: Imp. Istorich.Obshestvo, 1896), 1:337.

8. Zorin, "'Star of the East,'" 319, 339.

9. Knapton, *The Lady of the Holy Alliance*, 14.

10. Ibid., 152.

11. Zorin, "'Star of the East,'" 318.

12. Chateaubriand, cited in Knapton, *Lady of the Holy Alliance*, 54.

13. Julie Kavanagh, *French Women of Letters: Biographical Sketches* (London: Hurst and Blackett, 1862), 2:125.

14. John V. Fleming, *The Dark Side of the Enlightenment: Wizards, Alchemists, and Spiritual Seekers in the Age of Reason* (London: Norton, 2013), 304.

15. Kavanagh, *French Women of Letters*, 2:127.

16. See Sluga, "Women, Diplomacy, and International Politics."

17. Knapton, *Lady of the Holy Alliance*, 49.

18. Ibid., 53.

19. Fleming, *Dark Side of the Enlightenment*, 334.

20. Hilger, *Women Write Back*, 147.

21. There are chords of similarity in the Romantic view of religion. Knapton cites the opening lines of Novalis's *Christenheit oder Europas* in *Lady of the Holy Alliance*, 127.

22. Ibid., 143.

23. Gruner, "The German Confederation," 162.

24. Knapton, *Lady of the Holy Alliance*, 134.

25. Ibid., 136.

26. Ibid., 135.

27. Emmanuel Beau de Loménie, ed., *Lettres de Madame de Staël à Madame Récamier: Présentées et annotées par Emmanuel Beau de Loménie* (Paris: Editions Domat, 1952), 262;Haussonville, "Mme de Staël et Mme de Krüdener," 1.

28. For Stourdza, Krüdener was a sympathetic soul to whom she could pour out her heart about all her "grands chagrins." Ley, *Madame de Krüdener et son temps*, 406–7.

29. Knapton, *Lady of the Holy Alliance*, 138–39.

30. Cited in Martin, *Romantics, Reformers, Reactionaries*, 243.

31. Ghervas, *Réinventer la tradition*, 254.

32. Ley, *Madame de Krüdener et son temps*, 444–45.

33. Knapton, *Lady of the Holy Alliance*, 153; Ley, "Alexandre Ier," 59.

34. Haussonville, "Mme de Staël et Mme de Krüdener."

35. Montcalm, diary entry from 1 November 1815, in "Journal Inédit: Extraits," 25–26.

36. Haussonville, "Mme de Staël et Mme de Krüdener," 1.

37. Benjamin Constant, Lettre XLIII, *Lettres de Benjamin Constant a Mme. Récamier* (Paris: E. Dentu, 1864), 112.

38. Knapton, *Lady of the Holy Alliance*, 155.

39. Montcalm, "Journal Inédit: Extraits," 26.

40. Boigne, *Récits d'une tante*, vol. 2, chap. 7.

41. Montcalm, "Journal Inédit: Extraits," 26.

42. Webster, *British Diplomacy*, 382.

43. Kavanagh, *French Women of Letters*, 2:150; Knapton, *Lady of the Holy Alliance*, 158.

44. Knapton, *Lady of the Holy Alliance*, 157.

45. Following Golitsyn, as cited in Zorin, "'Star of the East,'" 326–27.

46. Dupuy, *La duchesse de Dino*, 204.

47. Jean-Gabriel Eynard, *Journal de Jean-Gabriel Eynard*, ed. Édouard Chapuisat (Paris: Plon, 1924), 2:70.

48. Zorin, "'Star of the East,'" 339.

49. Montcalm, diary entry, 1 November 1815, in Montcalm, "Journal Inédit: Extraits," 25.

50. Ley, "Alexandre Ier," 60.

51. Zorin, "'Star of the East,'" 314.

52. Ibid., 330.

53. Victor du Bled, "La société russe: La Cour de Russie," *La revue hebdomadaire* 24 (16 June 1906): 291.

54. Ghervas, *Réinventer la tradition*, 182; Knapton, *Lady of the Holy Alliance*, 163.

55. Graaf, *Fighting Terror after Napoleon*, 268, 275, 279–80.

56. Knapton, *Lady of the Holy Alliance*, 4.

57. Krüdener to Alexander I (1817–1821), fol. 967, op. 1, d. 50, ll. 15–26, Institute of Russian Literature (Pushkinsky Dom), St. Petersburg.

58. Kavanagh, *French Women of Letters*, 2:151.

59. See Ido De Haan and Jeroen Van Zanten, "Constructing an International Conspiracy: Revolutionary Concertation and Police Networks in the European Restoration," in *Securing Europe after Napoleon*, ed. Graaf, Haan, and Vick, 171–92.

60. Sagan to Lamb, 25 May 1814, Vienna, Add MS 60480, fol. 10, Beauvale Papers, BL.

61. Rosenkrantz, *Journal du Congrès de Vienne*, 159.

62. Klemens von Metternich to Wilhelmine, Duchess of Sagan, 16 January 1814, Basel, in Ullrichova, *Clemens-Metternich*, 175.

63. Kavanagh, *French Women of Letters*, 2:153.

64. Ibid., 2:151.

65. Hilger, *Women Write Back*, 147.

Chapter 13

1. *The Times*, 12 October 1818.

2. *The Times*, 9 October 1818, 3.

3. Ernest Daudet, *Une vie d'ambassadrice au siecle dernier, La Princesse de Lieven* (Paris: Plon, 1903), 79.

4. Report from Aix-la-Chapelle, 5 and 12 October 1818, *The Times*.

5. Jean-Gabriel Eynard, "Voyage à Aix-la-Chapelle pendant le Congrès en octobre 1818 et retour par Paris en décembre 1818.- Lausanne, Aix-la-Chapelle et Paris," MS suppl. 1862, fol. 20, BGE.

6. Jean-Gabriel Eynard, 24 October 1818, samedi matin, fol. 15; 31 October 1818, fol. 21; 9 October 1818, 10 heures, fol. 22, all in BGE.

7. See Graaf, *Fighting Terror after Napoleon*, 440, 442; Jarrett, *The Congress of Vienna*, 182.

8. The history of the indemnity is covered in detail in Eugene N. White, "Making the French Pay: The Costs and Consequences of the Napoleonic Reparations," *European Review of Economic History* 5, no. 3 (2001): 337–65, especially 350–51; and Peter Austin, *Baring Brothers and the Birth of Modern Finance* (London: Routledge, 2007), 11; see also D.C.M. Platt, *Foreign Finance in Continental Europe and the United States, 1815–1870: Quantities, Origins, Functions, and Distribution* (London: Routledge, 1984), 8–9. On the background to credit questions in peacemaking, see H. Neufeld, *The International Protection of Private Creditors from the Treaties of Westphalia to the Congress of Vienna (1648–1815): A Contribution to the History of the Law of Nations* (Leiden: Sijthoff, 1971); Richard Bithell, *A Counting-House Dictionary* (London: Routledge, 1881), 265; for the later nineteenth century, see Siegel, *For Peace and Money*.

9. White, "Making the French Pay," 341, 346–47; Philip Ziegler, *The Sixth Great Power: A History of One of the Greatest of All Banking Families, the House of Barings, 1762–1929* (New York: Alfred A. Knopf, 1988), 82, 85; Austin, *Baring Brothers*, 10–13.

10. White, "Making the French Pay," 341, 346–47; see Ziegler, *The Sixth Great Power*, 82, 85.

11. Austin, *Baring Brothers*, 13–14: "it was the management of the loans for the rebuilding of Europe that gave Barings its greatest triumph . . . it expanded their role in a specifically international realm of operations."

12. Paul Emden, *Money Powers of Europe in the Nineteenth and Twentieth Centuries* (New York: D. Appleton-Century Company, 1938), 10–12. See also *The Times*, 12 and 14 October 1818.

13. Charles Stewart to James de Rothschild, 18 October 1817, Paris, XI/109/8/1/65, Rothschild Archive, London.

14. Ferguson, *The House of Rothschild*, 153, 161.

15. See Marc Flandreau and Juan H. Flores, "Bonds and Brands: Foundations of Sovereign Debt Markets, 1820–1830," *Journal of Economic History* 69, no. 3 (2009): 646.

16. Sweet, *Humboldt*, 2:289. In 1818, Humboldt is at Aix-la-Chapelle, although no longer at the center of congress diplomacy—he has missed out on the top job, as Hardenberg is replaced by the Danish ambassador to Berlin, Count von Bernstorff.

17. The French *rentes* were paid out only in francs.

18. Fritz Redlich, "Jacques Lafitte and the Beginnings of Investment Banking in France," *Bulletin of the Business Historical Society* 22, no. 4/6 (December 1948): 151.

19. Florian Kerschbaumer and Korinna Schönhärl, "Der Wiener Kongress als 'Kinderstube' des Philhellenismus: Das Beispiel des Bankers Jean-Gabriel Eynard," in *Vormärz und Philhellenismus, Forum Vormärz Forschung 18, Jahrbuch 2012*, ed. Anne-Rose Meyer (Bielefeld: Aisthesis Verlag, 2013), 103.

20. My translation, Jean-Gabriel Eynard to Marc-Auguste Pictet, 5 February 1825 and 23 March 1825, Paris, Diverses copies du précédent [Notes journalières.- 1821–1830], MS suppl. 1871, fols. 17, 157–58, BGE; Chapuisat, *Jean-Gabriel Eynard et son temps*, 115, 118.

21. Chapuisat, *Jean-Gabriel Eynard et son temps*, 115; Emmanuel Waresquiel, *Talleyrand Immobile* (Paris: Fayard, 2003), 578.

22. Denys Barau, "La mobilisation des philhellènes en faveur de la Grèce, 1821–1829," *Populations réfugiées: De l'exil au retour*, ed. L. Cambrézy and V. Lassailly-Jacob (Montpellier: IRD Editions, 2001), 60; Catherine Duprat, *"Pour l'amour de l'humanité": Le temps des philanthropes: La philanthropie parisienne des lumières à la monarchie de Juillet*, 2 vols. (Paris: Editions du C.T.H.S, 1995), 1:54–55.

23. Chatziioannou claims these loans "essentially constitute the first international recognition of the Greek state," although she focuses on the London Greek Committee, not Eynard: Maria Christina Chatziioannou, "War, Crisis and Sovereign Loans: The Greek War of Independence and British Economic Expansion in the 1820s," *Historical Review/La Revue Historique* 10 (2013): 33, 45–47; see also Christopher Montague Woodhouse, *Capodistria: The Founder of Greek Independence* (Oxford: Oxford University Press, 1973), 346, 392; Foreign Office, 5 July 1836, Années 1836–1837, Supplément de la correspondance relative à la Grèce.- 1831–1873, MS suppl. 1887, fol. 93, BGE. These sales promised 8.5% and 8.8%, respectively; "Ricardo was an avowed

seller of junk bonds" (Flandreau and Flores, "Bonds and Brands," 673; St. Clair, *That Greece Might Still Be Free*, 222).

24. Staël, *Considerations on the Principal Events of the French Revolution*, 58; see Sluga, "Madame de Staël and the Transformation of European Politics."

25. Robert Owen, "Memorial of Robert Owen of New Lanark, in Scotland," in *Manifesto of Robert Owen: The Discoverer and Founder of the Rational System of Society, and of the Rational Religion* (London: Social Institution, 1840), 31–34. Between 1818 and 1858, the memoranda were printed five times in five different forms in London alone. They were also published by *The Times*: "Private Correspondent," 26 October 1818. See also Albert Tangeman Volwiler, "Robert Owen and the Congress of Aix-la-Chapelle, 1818," *Scottish Historical Review* 19, no. 74 (1922): 96–105.

26. "Memorandum, Aix-la-Chapelle, 21 October 1818," in Owen, *Manifesto of Robert Owen*, 35.

27. Robert Owen, "Memorandum, Aix-la-Chapelle October 22," cited in "Private Correspondent," *The Times*, 26 October 1818.

28. Robert Owen, "Memorandum, Frankfurt, 20 September 1818," in Owen, *Manifesto of Robert Owen*, 29–30.

29. "Private Correspondence, Aix-La-Chapelle, 23 October 1818," *The Times*.

30. Ibid.

31. "Private Correspondence, Aix-La-Chapelle, 26 October 1818," *The Times*.

32. Mme. Eynard to unknown recipient, 17 August 1827, "Copie des Letters de Mme Eynard pendant son sejour en Angleterre, 1827," MS suppl. 1961, fol. 82, Bibliothèque de Genève, Geneva, Switzerland.

33. Seigel, *Modernity and Bourgeois Life*, 393; Deborah Sadie Hertz, *Jewish High Society in Old Regime Berlin* (Syracuse: Syracuse University Press, 2005), 84.

34. Kohler, *Jewish Rights*, 59–60.

35. Egon Caesar Corti, *The Rise of the House of Rothschild*, trans. Brian Lunn and Beatrix Lunn (New York: Cosmopolitan Book Corporation, 1928), 203.

36. Kohler, *Jewish Rights*, 11–12, 30.

37. Ibid., 46, 59–60.

38. Corti, *The Rise of the House of Rothschild*, 191–92, 216.

39. Amschel Rothschild to James Rothschild, 6 March 1817, Frankfurt, XI/109/6/2/11, Rothschild Archive.

40. Irby C. Nichols, *The European Pentarchy and the Congress of Verona, 1822* (The Hague: Nijhoff, 1971), 129–30; Ferguson, *The House of Rothschild*, 158–59; Corti, *The Rise of the House of Rothschild*, 228.

41. Corti, *The Rise of the House of Rothschild*, 228. Although Gentz is close to Rahel Levin, he is ambivalent about her Jewishness.

42. Austin, *Baring Brothers*, 11; Corti, *The Rise of the House of Rothschild*, 224.

43. Corti, *The Rise of the House of Rothschild*, 308.

44. See Ferguson, *The House of Rothschild*, 130, 234–35, 158–59; Corti, *The Rise of the House of Rothschild*, 308; Nichols, *European Pentarchy*, 129–30.

45. Cited in Chapuisat, *Jean-Gabriel Eynard et son temps*, 208.

46. See Eric Strand, "Byron's 'Don Juan' as a Global Allegory," *Studies in Romanticism* 43, no. 4 (Winter 2004): 503–36; on Saint-Simon, see Le Roy, *La vie véritable du comte Henri de Saint-Simon.*

Chapter 14

1. See Etkind, *Internal Colonisation*, 150–51.

2. See Lesaffer, "Vienna and the Abolition of the Slave Trade."

3. Graaf, "The Allied Machine," 132, 136.

4. Mostafa Minawi, "International Law and the Precarity of Ottoman Sovereignty in Africa at the End of the Nineteenth Century," *International History Review* (May 2020): 1–24.

5. For a detailed discussion of the governance of piracy, see Vick, "Power, Humanitarianism and the Global Liberal Order," 952.

6. Lange, "Menacing Tides." Between the sixteenth and eighteenth centuries, "North African rulers had largely turned corsair captures from an uncertain source of income, dependent on chance takings at sea, into a latent threat that generated regular payments" (32).

7. Betty Anderson, *A History of the Modern Middle East: Rulers, Rebels and Rogues* (Stanford: Stanford University Press, 2016), 43–44, 46.

8. Lange, "Menacing Tides," 39.

9. Smith, *Mémoire sur la nécessité*, 1, cited in Lange, "Menacing Tides," 47.

10. Castlereagh to William Cathcart, 26 May 1816, St. Petersburg, in Graaf, *Fighting Terror after Napoleon*, 120–23.

11. Vick, "Power, Humanitarianism and the Global Liberal Order," 942.

12. Erik de Lange, "From Augarten to Algiers: Security and 'Piracy' around the Congress of Vienna," in *Securing Europe after Napoleon*, ed. Graaf, Haan, and Vick, 232.

13. Ibid., 234.

14. Taken from a draft on the problem delivered to the ambassadorial conference held in London prior to the congress by the well-positioned. See Vick, *The Congress of Vienna*, 279.

15. Lange, "Menacing Tides," 16.

16. Diary entry, 9 November 1822, *John Cam Hobhouse's Diary*, 160, https://petercochran.files.wordpress.com/2009/12/30-18221.pdf.

17. Dorothea Lieven to Neumann, 18 November 1822, Verona, Dorothea Lieven Papers, BL.

18. Juan Luis Simal and Juan Pan-Montojo, "Exil, finances internationales et construction de l'État: Les libéraux et 'joséphins' espagnols (1813–1851)," *Revue d'histoire du XIXe siècle* 53 (2016): 59–77.

19. François-René vicomte de Chateaubriand, *The Congress of Verona: Comprising a Portion of Memoirs of His Own Times*, Volume 1 of 2 (London: Richard Bentley, 1834), 174, 194.

20. Aberdeen to Castlereagh, undated [probably December 1821], Add MS 43260, fol. 165, Aberdeen Papers, BL.

21. Šedivý, *Metternich*, 62.

22. Chateaubriand had experience as ambassador to Prussia (1821) and Britain (1822), and took Montmorency's position as foreign minister (28 December 1822–4 August 1824).

23. Aberdeen to Castlereagh, undated [probably December 1821]. Aberdeen—who would be foreign secretary from 1828 to 1830, and again from 1841 to 1846, and prime minister from 1851 to 1855, crucial years of the Greek question—offered his opinion, based on "no peculiar means of knowledge or information" and unbiased by "the associations of ancient history, or under the effects of early enthusiasm."

24. "Copie des lettres de Madame Eynard-Lullin pendant son séjour en Angleterre.- 1827," MS suppl. 1961 and notes from 2 June 1822, 10 October 1822, Florence, in "Notes prise en 1822 & 1823 à Turin, à Florence, et à Geneve, à Paris," MS suppl. 1868, BGE.

25. Madame Eynard-Lullin, 17 August 1827, MS suppl. 1961, fol. 82, BGE. The view of Greek independence as a major episode in the history of philanthropy is still repeated; see the work of Gary J. Bass (*Freedom's Battle*, 48), who calls it the "distant but unmistakable ancestor of Amnesty International and Human Rights Watch."

26. On Kapodistrias's congress visions, see Graaf, *Fighting Terror after Napoleon*, 211.

27. Chapuisat, *Jean-Gabriel Eynard et son temps*, 199.

28. Nichols, *European Pentarchy*, 130.

29. These men included the bankers Lafitte, Delessert, Cottier, and Louriottis. "Notes écrits à Paris," 13 April 1824, 3 February 1825, fol. 7; see also "Notes écrits à Paris du 15 avril 1822 à 12 juin 1822," all in MS suppl. 1871, BGE.

30. Eynard quotes from his own letter to the Phanariot, Mavrocordato, 31 March 1821, MS suppl. 1871, fol. 152; 3 February 1825, Paris, MS suppl. 1871, fol. 154, n. 2; February, March, April, 1825, MS suppl. 1871, fol. 7, all in BGE; Barau, "La mobilisation des philhellènes," 47; all my translation. Lafitte has a curious place in this history as speculator, establishment figure, and financial backer of utopian socialism.

31. In the original French they were: "un comité pour l'organisation d'une souscription en faveur des réfugiés grecs" and "Société de la moral chrétienne." See St. Clair, *That Greece Might Still Be Free*, 266; Barau, "La mobilisation des philhellènes," 43.

32. Chapuisat, *Jean-Gabriel Eynard et son temps*, 208.

33. Ibid., 115–16, 118–19.

34. Barau, "La mobilisation des philhellènes," 44. Barau notes other committees were formed in Marseilles, Lyons, Nimes, Mulhouse, Toulouse, Brussels, The Hague, Copenhagen, Stockholm, Berlin, Munich, New York, Boston, Philadelphia, and Baltimore.

35. Chapuisat credits Eynard with inspiring London developments, but it is difficult to prove this chronologically. Chapuisat, *Jean-Gabriel Eynard et son temps*, 105.

36. Woodhouse, *Capodistria*, 392.

37. "Notes prises à Paris au mois d 8bre 1829," Manuscrits de Jean-Gabriel Eynard, BGE.

38. British Foreign Office, 5 July 1836, MS suppl. 1887, fol. 93, BGE.

39. Bew, *Castlereagh*, 137.

40. Aberdeen to Castlereagh, undated letter [probably December 1821], Add MS 43260, fols. 36, 165, BL.

41. Vick, "Power, Humanitarianism and the Global Liberal Order," 940.

Chapter 15

Note to epigraphs: Cited in Hanoteau, *Lettres du Prince de Metternich à la Comtesse de Lieven*, 333; Earl of Aberdeen and the Princesse de Lieven from 13 October 1838 to 11 November 1841, Add MS 43272, Aberdeen Papers, BL.

1. The phrasing reflects Kant's argument in his *Idea for a Universal History with a Cosmopolitan Intent*: expecting the world to run "to a certain rational goal" is the stuff of "*romance*"; history reveals a less predictable world ruled by individual and state self-interest, in which a cosmopolitan society of states is even more crucial.

2. Harold Temperley, "Princess Lieven and the Protocol of 4 April 1826," *English Historical Review* 39, no. 153 (1924): 55.

3. Harold Temperley, ed., *The Unpublished Diary and Political Sketches of Princess Lieven Together with Some of Her Letters* (London: Jonathan Cape, 1925), 46, 98. Looking back on her life she will also takc credit for saving the tsar's reputation from the damage of his sister Catherine's maladroit diplomacy in 1814, during the London postwar celebrations.

4. See for example, *Distaff Diplomacy: The Empress Eugenie and the Foreign Policy of the Second Empire* (Austin: University of Texas Press, 1967), Nancy Nichols Barker has explored the kinds of influence that Napoleon III's wife had on his diplomatic practices and foreign policy, including a rapprochement with Spain (her native land) and the Italian question of the 1860s. Barker argues that Eugenie's influence is negative and destructive.

5. See Sluga, "Women, Diplomacy, and International Politics.", p. 131.

6. Daudet, *Une vie d'ambassadrice*, 9, 12.

7. Temperley, *The Unpublished Diary*, 76.

8. Crawley, *The Question of Greek Independence*, 4.

9. Mori, *The Culture of Diplomacy*, 76. See also D. H. Thomas, "Princess Lieven's Last Diplomatic Confrontation," *International History Review* 5, no. 4 (1983): 550–56.

10. Cited in Hanoteau, *Lettres du Prince de Metternich à la Comtesse de Lieven*, 47.

11. Dorothea Lieven, *The Private Letters of Princess Lieven to Prince Metternich, 1820–1836*, ed. Peter Quennell (New York: E. P. Dutton, 1938). See also Siemann, *Metternich*, 573.

12. Metternich to Dorothea Lieven, 21 February 1819, in Siemann, *Metternich*, 580.

13. Metternich to Lieven, 9 May 1821, in Siemann, *Metternich*, 581.

14. Daudet, *Une vie d'ambassadrice*, 97.

15. Her letters are going to Chandos House, Cavendish Square, London, 1 December 1822, Verona, Add MS 47366, Lieven Papers, BL.

16. Daudet, *Une vie d'ambassadrice*, 98.

17. Šedivý, *Metternich*, 89–90, 93.

18. Sofka, "Metternich's Theory of European Order," 138.

19. Šedivý, *Metternich*, 161, 165.

20. Dorothea Lieven to Metternich, 16 May 1826, in Peter Quennell, ed., *Vertrauliche Briefe der Fürstin Lieven* (Berlin: Steuben-Verlag, 1939), 348, 584.

21. Siemann, *Metternich*, 596.

22. Temperley, *The Unpublished Diary*, 107.

23. Ibid., 233.

24. Temperley describes her role as having Britain and Russia agree on establishing "in the East an order of things conformable to the interests of Europe and to the laws of religion and humanity" (*The Unpublished Diary*, 97).

25. Protocol of Conference between Great Britain and Russia, signed at St. Petersburg, 23 March (4 April) 1826, https://opil.ouplaw.com/view/10.1093/law:oht/law-oht-76-CTS-175.regGroup.1/law-oht-76-CTS-175.

26. The "former proprietors" are to be indemnified, "either by an annual sum to be added to the tribute . . . or by some other arrangement." Cited in Thomas Erskine Holland, *The European Concert in the Eastern Question* (Oxford: Clarendon Press, 1885), 4–69, https://en.wikisource.org/wiki/The_European_Concert_in_the_Eastern_Question/Chapter_2.

27. Kale, *French Salons*, 189.

28. Henry John Temple, 3rd Viscount Palmerston, Prime Minister to Princess Dorothea Lieven, 17 August 1827, Add MS 47366, Lieven Papers, BL.

29. Duchesse de Dino, *Chronique de 1831–1862*, 4 vols., ed. Princesse Castellane née Radziwill (Paris: Plon-Nourrit, 1909–10).

30. George Weill, *La France sous la monarchie constitutionnelle* (Paris: Alcan, 1912).

31. Kale, *French Salons*, 147.

32. Ibid., 149.

33. Ibid. In practice, the diverse circle is of limited social capital, representative of the court society in which Lieven has been trained. It organizes farewell gifts when someone leaves or gleans snippets of private and sometimes public relevant information.

34. Lord Aberdeen to Princess Lieven, London, 8 September 1853, Letter 473, in George Hamilton Gordon Earl of Aberdeen, *The Correspondence of Lord Aberdeen and Princess Lieven, 1832–1854* (London: Royal Historical Society, 1938), 647.

35. Zorgbibe, *Metternich*, 478.

36. See, for example, "Enclosure. Copy. Peter Meyendorff to Princess Lieven, Warsaw, 3 October 1853"; Princess Lieven to Lord Aberdeen Paris, 10 October 1853, both in *Correspondence of Lord Aberdeen and Princess Lieven*, 476, 650.

37. Winfred Baumgart, *The Peace of Paris, 1856: Studies in War, Diplomacy, and Peacemaking* (Oxford: Clio Press, 1981), 59.

38. Princess Lieven to Lord Aberdeen, 3 October 1853, Letter 475, and Lord Aberdeen to Princess Lieven, 23 May 1853, London, Letter 470, both in *Correspondence of Lord Aberdeen and Princess Lieven*, 649, 644.

39. Lord Aberdeen to Princess Lieven, 8 September 1853, London, Letter 473, in *Correspondence of Lord Aberdeen and Princess Lieven*, 647.

40. Aberdeen ordered the British fleet into the Black Sea despite the 1841 Straits Convention.

41. Bell, *First Total War*, 309.

42. Yves Bruley, "L'organisation et le déroulement du congrès," in *Le Congrès de Paris de 1856, un acte fondateur*, ed. Gilbert Ameil, Isabelle Nathan, and Georges-Henri Soutou (Brussels: Peter Lang, 2009), 33–44.

43. Jean-Claude Yon, "En marge des négociations: Mondanités et spectacles pendant le congrès de Paris," in *Le Congrès de Paris de 1856, un acte fondateur*, ed. Ameil, Nathan, and Soutou, 171, 178.

44. Ibid., 174.

45. Baumgart, *The Peace of Paris*, 171.

46. Ibid., 169.

47. Candan Badem, *The Ottoman Crimean War, 1853–1856* (Leiden: Brill, 2010), 40.

48. See Jacob Coleman Hurewitz, "Ottoman Diplomacy and the European State System," *Middle East Journal* 15, no. 2 (1961): 151.

49. Minawi, "International Law," 7.

50. Baumgart, *The Peace of Paris*, 60.

51. Badem, *The Ottoman Crimean War*, 69.

52. Baumgart, *The Peace of Paris*, 165.

53. Cedomir Antic, *Neutrality as Independence: Great Britain, Serbia and the Crimean War* (Belgrade: Institute for Balkan Studies, 2007), 169.

54. Badem, *The Ottoman Crimean War*, 15.

55. Baumgart, *The Peace of Paris*, 161.

56. Ibid., 159.

57. Minawi, "International Law"; see Emre Öktem, "Le traité de Paris de 1856 revisité à son 150e anniversaire: Quelques aspects juridiques internationaux," in *Le Congrès de Paris*, ed. Ameil, Nathan, and Soutou, 151, 169.

58. Baumgart, *The Peace of Paris*, 164–65.

59. According to that treaty, a population exchange of Greeks defined as Christians and Turks defined as Muslims allows proper national borders to be drawn between Greece and a reduced Turkish republic.

60. Beatrice de Graaf, "Bringing Sense and Sensibility to the Continent: Vienna 1815 Revisited," *Journal of Modern European History* 13, no. 4 (2015): 447–57; Sluga, "Passions, Patriotism and Nationalism."

61. Sauvigny, *Metternich and His Times*, 30–32.

62. Badem, *The Ottoman Crimean War*, 403.

Chapter 16

Note to epigraph: Hedley Bull, *The Anarchical Society*, 2nd ed. (Basingstoke: Macmillan, 1997), 13.

1. See the discussion in Jasper Heinzen, "Transnational Affinities and Invented Traditions: The Napoleonic Wars in British and Hanoverian Memory, 1815–1915," *English Historical Review* 127, no. 529 (December 2012): 1407.

2. A. Necker de Saussure, *Notice sur le caractère et les écrits de Madame de Staël* (Paris: Treuttel and Wiirtz, 1820), viii.

3. Helen P. Jenkins, "Madame de Staël," in *The Congress of Women*, ed. Mary Kevenaugh Oldham Eagle (Chicago: Monarch Book Company, 1894), 2:690. Some in the scientific world claimed a place for Staël alongside Adam Smith, Linnaeus, and Lavoisier because of her identification of social institutions as the determinant of a people or nation's education, its character, and even its "interior destiny." *Blackwood's Edinburgh Magazine* (December 1818): 278; John Isbell, introduction to Madame de Staël, *Corinne, or, Italy*, trans. S. Raphael (Oxford: Oxford University Press, 1998), x.

4. See chapter 2.

5. Duvergier de Hauranne, *Histoire du gouvernement parlementaire en France, 1814–1848* (Paris: Michel Levy Freres, 1860), 4:97.

6. Lord Acton to George Eliot, May 1887, *Selections from the Correspondence of the First Lord Acton*, ed. John Neville Figgis (London: Longmans, 1917), 1:277.

7. For more discussion of these points, see Sluga, "Madame de Staël and the Transformation of European Politics."

8. Jarrett, *The Congress of Vienna*, 420 n179.

9. Étienne François, "The Revolutionary and Napoleonic Wars as a Shared and Entangled European Lieu de Mémoire," in *War Memories: The Revolutionary and Napoleonic Wars in Modern European Culture*, ed. Alan Forrest, Étienne François, and Karen Hagemann (London: Palgrave, 2012). See also Richard Hart Sinnreich, "In Search of Military Repose: The Congress of Vienna and the Making of Peace," in *The Making of Peace: Rulers, States, and the Aftermath of War*, ed. Williamson Murray and Jim Lacey (Cambridge: Cambridge University Press, 2009), 132.

10. Defendente Sacchi, *Lavori all'Arco della Pace in Milano*, in *Biblioteca Italiana ossia Giornale di letteratura scienze ed arti* (Milan: A. F. Stella, 1832), 57:3–12.

11. Viscount Castlereagh to the Earl of Liverpool, 30 September 1814, FO 92/7, TNA.

12. William Butler, "Congress of Nations: A Nineteenth Century View," *World Affairs* 128, no. 2 (1965): 102–6, http://www.jstor.org/stable/20670645.

13. See chapter 15.

14. Cemil Aydin, "The Emergence of Transnational Muslim Thought, 1774–1914," in *Arabic Thought beyond the Liberal Age: Towards an Intellectual History of the Nahda*, ed. Jens Hanssen and Max Weiss (Cambridge: Cambridge University Press, 2016), 121–41.

15. Šedivý, *Metternich*, 1.

16. Mazower, *Governing the World*, 12.

17. Ramsay Muir, *Nationalism and Internationalism* (London: Constable Limited, 1917), 35, 179.

18. See Andrew Fitzmaurice, *King Leopold's Ghostwriter* (Princeton: Princeton University Press, 2021).

19. See Maartje Abbenhuis, *The Hague Conferences and International Politics, 1898–1915* (London: Bloomsbury, 2018).

20. Caroline Tixier, "The Legacy of Léon Bourgeois: From the Solidarist Doctrine to the Emergence of International Arbitration," in *Reconsidering Peace and Patriotism during the First World War*, ed. Justin Olmstead (Cham: Palgrave Macmillan, 2017), 37.

21. Sinnreich, "In Search of Military Repose," 132.

22. Wilhelm Hausenstein, "Das Zeitalter von Waterloo: Zur Widerkehr des Tags der Schlacht vom 18. Juni 1815," in *Eine Wochenschrift-Zweiter Band-April-Juni 1915* (Berlin: Marz Verlag, 1915), 222.

23. Charles Seignobos, *1815–1915: From the Congress of Vienna to the War of 1914* (Paris: Librairie Armand Colin, 1915), 35.

24. Ibid., 36.

25. See Glenda Sluga, "From F. Melian Stawell to E. Greene Balch: International Thinking at the Gender Margins, 1919–1947," in *Women's International Thought: A New History*, ed. Katharina Rietzler and Patricia Owens (Cambridge: Cambridge University Press, 2021), 223–44.

26. "11 February 1918: President Wilson's Address to Congress, Analyzing German and Austrian Peace Utterances," in *The World War I Document Archive*, ed. Richard Hacken, http://wwi.lib.byu.edu.

27. Ibid.

28. See essays in Sluga, Glenda, and Patricia Clavin, eds. *Internationalisms: A Twentieth-Century History*. Cambridge: Cambridge University Press, 2017.

29. See Sluga, *Internationalism in the Age of Nationalism*, chaps. 1 and 2.

30. Glenda Sluga, *Nation, Psychology and International Politics* (London: Palgrave, 2006).

31. Madeleine Herren, "Gender and International Relations through the Lens of the League of Nations," in *Women, Diplomacy and International Politics*, ed. James and Sluga, 182–201.

32. Covenant of the International Labor Organization, https://www.loc.gov/law/help/us-treaties/bevans/m-ust000002-0241.pdf.

33. Ibid.

34. For a newer reading of the end of World War I as a new international order, see Natasha Wheatley, "Central Europe as Ground Zero of the New International Order," *Slavic Review* 78, no. 4 (2019): 900–911.

35. For more on Polanyi's connection to international thinking, see Glenda Sluga, "Habsburg Histories of Internationalism," in *Remaking Central Europe: The League of Nations and the Former Habsburg Lands*, ed. Peter Becker and Natasha Wheatley (Oxford: Oxford University Press, 2021).

36. Marc Flandreau and Juan Flores, "The Peaceful Conspiracy: Bond Markets and International Relations during the Pax Britannica," *International Organization* 66, no. 2 (2012): 211–41.

37. Gareth Dale, "In Search of Karl Polanyi's International Relations Theory," *Review of International Studies* 42, no. 3 (2016): 401–24.

38. Bull, *The Anarchical Society*, 67.

39. See Glenda Sluga, "Anfänge und Ende(n) der Weltordnung," *Merkur* 816 (2017): 72–81 (also published in English as "The Beginnings and Ends of International

Orders," *E-IR* [May 2017], http://www.e-ir.info/2017/05/22/the-beginnings-and-ends-of-the-international-order/); and Öktem, "Le traité de Paris de 1856 revisité à son 150e anniversaire," 151, 169. Angela Merkel's critique of Putin's own disregard for a European system "restrained by consensus and bounded by law" that relied on a global vision of international politics found no resonance in the *longue durée* European past.

40. François, "The Revolutionary and Napoleonic Wars as a Shared and Entangled European Lieu de Mémoire."

41. See Glenda Sluga, "Inventing an International Order," *After Disruption: Historical Perspectives on the Future of International Order*, CSIS, September 2020, https://csis-website-prod.s3.amazonaws.com/s3fs-public/publication/200901_Bates_History_FullReport_v1.pdf.

42. Koselleck, "Goethe's Untimely History," 63.

Epilogue

Note to epigraphs: Karl and Rahel Varnhagen to Marcus Theodor, 20 January 1815, Vienna, Letter 348, in *Briefwechsel zwischen Carl August Varnhagen von Ense und Oelsner nebst Briefen von Rahel*, ed. Ludmilla Assing (Stuttgart: Kroner, 1865), 483–85; Joan Scott, *Only Paradoxes to Offer: French Feminists and the Rights of Man* (Cambridge, MA: Harvard University Press, 1996), 16.

1. Adam Tooze, "Everything You Know about Global Order Is Wrong," *Foreign Policy*, 30 January 2019, https://foreignpolicy.com/2019/01/30/everything-you-know-about-global-order-is-wrong/.

2. Karl and Rahel Varnhagen to Marcus Theodor, 20 January 1815.

3. Scott, *Only Paradoxes to Offer*, 4–5.

4. See Susan Tenenbaum, "Liberal Heroines: Mme de Stäel on the Woman Question and the Modern State," *Annales Benjamin Constant* 5 (1985): 37–52.

5. See Robert A. Nye, "Mobilization for War: Gendered Military Cultures in Nineteenth-Century Western Societies," in *The Oxford Handbook of Gender, War, and the Western World since 1600*, ed. Karen Hagemann, Stefan Dudink, and Sonya O. Rose (Oxford: Oxford University Press, 2020).

6. Frederick Lamb to his mother, 19 January 1817, Frankfurt, Add MS 45546, fol. 174, Beauvale Papers, BL.

7. See Vick, *The Congress of Vienna*, 305.

8. Barker, *Distaff Diplomacy*.

9. See Sluga and James, introduction to *Women, Diplomacy and International Politics since 1500*, 1.

10. Baumgart, *The Peace of Paris, 1856*, 158.

11. Etkind, *Internal Colonisation*, 76, 105.

12. Julia Gaffield, "The Racialization of International Law in the Aftermath of the Haitian Revolution: The Holy See and National Sovereignty," *American Historical Review* 125, no. 3 (June 2020): 841–68; Mary Lewis, "Repairing Damage: The

Slave Ship *Marcelin* and the Haiti Trade," *American Historical Review* 125, no. 3 (June 2020): 869–98.

13. Jean-Baptiste Honoré Raymond, *Emprunts, bourses, crédit public, grands capitalistes de l'Europe, 1814–1852* (Paris: Amyot, 1858), 3:144–46.

14. The first loan was contracted to Ternaux Grandolphe et Cie, 30 million francs principal, of which the bankers took 6 million francs in fees. Gusti-Klara Gaillard, *L'experience Haitiènne de la dette exterieur, 18–19* (Port-au-Prince: Impr. H. Deschamps, 1990); Thomas Madiou, *Histoire d'Haiti* (Port-au-Prince: Impr. H. Deschamps, 1988), vol. 4. The loans were renegotiated through the nineteenth century; see Victor Bulmer-Thomas, *The Economic History of the Caribbean since the Napoleonic Wars* (Cambridge: Cambridge University Press, 2013).

15. Redlich, "Jacques Laffitte and the Beginnings of Investment Banking in France," 146.

16. See for example, Sismondi, *De l'intérêt de la France à l'égard de la traite des nègres*.

17. Staël, *Considerations on the Principal Events of the French Revolution*, 59.

18. Etkind, *Internal Colonisation*, 25, 54.

19. Hoock-Demarle, *L'Europe des lettres*, 132–33.

20. Cited in Askenazy, "Polska a Europa," 289.

21. Mazower, *Governing the World*, 15.

22. Bew, *Castlereagh*, 160.

23. Ibid., 359.

24. See the discussion of Metternich in Pitts, "Empire and Legal Universalisms in the Eighteenth Century."

25. Metternich to Count Rudolf Apponyi, 1852, cited in Sauvigny, *Metternich and His Times*, 121.

26. Staël, *Considerations on the Principal Events of the French Revolution*, 598, 709–11; Victor de Pange, *Madame de Staël et le duc de Wellington, correspondance inédite, 1815–1817* (Paris: Gallimard, 1962).

27. Staël, *Considerations on the Principal Events of the French Revolution*, v, iv, 553–55.

28. Gengembre, "Fréquentation et sociabilité mutuelles," 266–68.

29. Norman King, "'The Airy Form of Things Forgotten': Madame de Staël, l'utilitarisme et l'impulsion libérale," *Cahiers Staëliens* 11 (1970): 5–26, quote on 24.

30. Cited in Sauvigny, *Metternich and His Times*, 30–32.

BIBLIOGRAPHY

Archives

Archives Nationales de France, Paris
Archives of Ministères des Affaires Étrangères, Paris, France
Biblioteca Archigiannesi, Bologna, Italy
Biblioteca Nazionale Centrale Vittorio Emanuele, Rome, Italy
Bibliothèque de Genève, Geneva, Switzerland
British Library, London, United Kingdom
Fondation des Archives de la Famille Pictet, Geneva, Switzerland
Institute of Russian Literature (Pushkinsky Dom), St. Petersburg
National Archives, London, and Norwich, United Kingdom
Österreichisches Staatsarchiv, Haus-, Hof- und Staatsarchiv, Vienna, Austria
Rothschild Archive, London, United Kingdom

Sources

Abbenhuis, Maartje. *The Hague Conferences and International Politics, 1898–1915*. London: Bloomsbury, 2018.

Aberdeen, George Hamilton Gordon, Earl of. *The Correspondence of Lord Aberdeen and Princess Lieven, 1832–1854*. London: Royal Historical Society, 1938.

Adamovsky, Ezequiel. "Euro-Orientalism and the Making of the Concept of Eastern Europe in France, 1810–1880." *Journal of Modern History* 77, no. 3 (September 2005): 591–628.

Adams, Henry. *The Life of Albert Gallatin*. Philadelphia: J. B. Lippincott, 1879.

Adams, John Quincy. *Memoirs of John Quincy Adams*. Vol. 1. Philadelphia: J. B. Lippincott, 1874.

———. *Writings of John Quincy Adams*. Ed. Worthington Chauncey Ford. 7 vols. New York: Macmillan, 1913–17.

Adams, Robyn, and Rosanna Cox. Introduction to *Diplomacy and Early Modern Culture*, ed. Robyn Adams and Rosanna Cox. Houndmills, Basingstoke: Palgrave Macmillan, 2011.

Aldridge, Alfred Owen. "Madame de Staël and Hannah More on Society." *Romanic Review* 38, no. 4 (December 1947): 330–39.

Alexander I. *Scenes of Russian Court Life: Being the Correspondence of Alexander I. With His Sister Catherine*. Trans. Henry Havelock. London: Jarrolds, 1915.

Allgor, Catherine. *Parlor Politics: In Which the Ladies of Washington Help Build a City and a Government*. Charlottesville: University of Virginia Press, 2002.

Amrith, Sunil, and Glenda Sluga. "New Histories of the United Nations." *Journal of World History* 19, no. 3 (2008): 251–74. DOI: 10.1353/jwh.0.0021.

Anderson, Betty. *A History of the Modern Middle East: Rulers, Rebels and Rogues*. Stanford: Stanford University Press, 2016.

Anderson, Fred. "The Peace of Paris, 1763." In *The Making of Peace: Rulers, States, and the Aftermath of War*, ed. Williamson Murray and James Lacey, 100–129. Cambridge: Cambridge University Press, 2009.

Anderson, M. S. "The Continental System and Russo-British Relations during the Napoleonic Wars." In *Studies in International History*, ed. K. Bourne and D. C. Watts, 68–80. London: Longmans, Green, 1967.

André, Roger. *L'Occupation de la France par les alliés en 1815 (juillet–novembre)*. Paris: E. de Boccard, Éditeur, 1924.

Angeberg, Comte d'. *Le Congrès de Vienne et les traités de 1815*. Paris: Amyot, Éditeur des Archives Diplomatiques, 1863.

——. *Recueil des traités, conventions et actes diplomatiques concernant la Pologne, 1762–1862*. Paris: Amyot, 1862.

Antic, Cedomir. *Neutrality as Independence: Great Britain, Serbia and the Crimean War*. Belgrade: Institute for Balkan Studies, 2007.

Appleby, Joyce Oldham. *The Relentless Revolution: A History of Capitalism*. New York: W. W. Norton, 2010.

Arendt, Hannah. *Rahel Varnhagen: The Life of a Jewess*. Ed. L. Weissberg. Trans. Richard Winston and Clara Winston. Baltimore: Johns Hopkins University Press, 1997.

Askenazy, Szymon. "Polska a Europa, 1813–1815." *Biblioteka Warszawska* (1909): 1–30, 209–37.

Assing, Ludmilla, ed. *Briefwechsel zwischen Carl August Varnhagen von Ense und Oelsner nebst Briefen von Rahel*. Stuttgart: Kroner, 1865.

Aubret-Ehnert, Françoise. "Les femmes au congrès de Vienne." In *Communication faite au colloque de février 2004 sur "Talleyrand, prince des diplomates."* 2008. http://www.dames-de-courlande.fr/fr/.

Austin, Peter. *Baring Brothers and the Birth of Modern Finance*. London: Routledge, 2007.

Axat, Marquise de Dax d'. *Souvenirs sur Mme de Stäel*. Paris: Revie de Paris, 1933.

Aydin, Cemil. "The Emergence of Transnational Muslim Thought, 1774–1914." In *Arabic Thought beyond the Liberal Age: Towards an Intellectual History of the Nahda*, ed. Jens Hanssen and Max Weiss, 121–41. Cambridge: Cambridge University Press, 2016.

——. *The Idea of the Muslim World: A Global Intellectual History*. Cambridge, MA: Harvard University Press, 2017.

Badem, Candan. *The Ottoman Crimean War, 1853–1856*. Leiden: Brill, 2010.

Balayé, Simone. *Les carnets de voyage de Madame de Staël: Contribution à la genèse de ses oeuvres*. Geneva: Librairie Droz, 1971.

——. "De la persistence des clichés." *Europe* (January–February 1987): 107–12.

——. *Madame de Staël: Lumières et liberté*. Paris: Éditions Klincksieck, 1979.

Baldensperger, Fernand. "Paul de Krüdener en Lorraine et en Alsace (1812–1813)." *Bulletin de la Société Philomatique Vosgienne, 1905–1906*, 4–28. Saint-Dié: C. Cuny, 1906.

Barau, Denys. "La mobilisation des philhellènes en faveur de la Grèce, 1821–1829." In *Populations réfugiées: De l'exil au retour*, ed. Luc Cambrézy and V. Lassailly-Jacob, 37–75. Paris: IRD Editions, 2001.

Barker, Nancy Nichols. *Distaff Diplomacy: The Empress Eugenie and the Foreign Policy of the Second Empire*. Austin: University of Texas Press, 1967.

Baron, Salo W. "Unveröffentliche Aktenstücke zur Judenfrage auf dem Wiener Kongress (1814–15)." *Monatsschrift für Geschichte und Wissenschaft des Judentums* 70, no. 11/12 (1926): 457–75.

Bass, Gary. *Freedom's Battle: The Origins of Humanitarian Intervention*. New York: Vintage, 2009.

Bassanville, Mme. la Comtesse de. *Les salons d'autrefois: Souvenirs intimes*. Vol. 2. Paris: Victorion, 1862.

Baumgart, Winfred. *The Peace of Paris, 1856: Studies in War, Diplomacy, and Peacemaking*. Oxford: Clio Press, 1981.

Bayard, James. *Papers of James A. Bayard, 1796–1815*. Ed. Elizabeth Donnan. New York: Da Capo Press, 1971.

Belgioso, La Princesse Christine Trivulce de. *Histoire de la Maison de Savoie*. Paris: Michel Lévy Frères, 1860.

Bell, David A. *First Total War: Napoleon's Europe and the Birth of Warfare as We Know It*. Boston: Houghton Mifflin, 2007.

Bentham, Jeremy. *The Correspondence of Jeremy Bentham*. Vol. 8. London: Athlone, 1968.

Berry, Mary. *Extracts of the Journals and Correspondence of Miss Berry: From the Year 1783 to 1852*. Vol. 3. Ed. Lady Theresa Lewis. London: Longmans, Green, 1865.

Bew, John. *Castlereagh: A Life*. Oxford: Oxford University Press, 2002.

Birnie, Arthur. *An Economic History of Europe, 1760–1930*. New York: Dial Press, 1931.

Bishara, Fahad Ahmad. *A Sea of Debt: Law and Economic Life in the Western Indian Ocean, 1780–1950*. Cambridge: Cambridge University Press, 2017.

Bithell, Richard. *A Counting-House Dictionary*. London: Routledge, 1881.

Bled, Victor du. "La société russe: Les salons de Petersbourg et de Moscou." 2 pts. *La revue hebdomadaire* 12 (November 1905): 72–91; 13 (December 1905): 76–89.

Blennerhasset, Charlotte. *Talleyrand*. 2 vols. London: Murray, 1894.

Boigne, Éléonore-Adèle. *Récits d'une tante: Mémoires de la comtesse de Boigne, née d'Osmond, publiés intégralement, d'après le manuscrit original, 1921–1923*. 5 vols. Paris: Emile-Paul Frere, 1921.

Bollmann, Eric. "Memoirs of Varnhagen von Ense." *Foreign Quarterly Review* 26, no. 52 (1841): 135–48.

———. *Paragraphs on Banks*. Philadelphia: C. & A. Conrad & Co., 1811.

Bordo, Michael, and Eugene White. "British and French Finance during the Napoleonic Wars." NBER working papers series, No. 3517. Cambridge, MA: NBER, 1990.

Bourne, Kenneth. *Palmerston: The Early Years, 1784–1841*. London: Allen Lane, 1982.

Boutet de Monvel, Roger. *Eminent English Men and Women in Paris*. New York: C. Scribner's Sons, 1913.

Braudel, Fernand. *Civilisation matérielle, économie et capitalisme, XVe–XVIIIe siècle*. Paris: Armand Colin, 1979.

Bresson, Jacques. *Histoire financière de la France, depuis l'origine de la monarchie jusqu'à l'année 1828*. Paris: Au Bureau de la Gazette des Chemins de Fer, 1857.

Bruley, Yves. "L'organisation et le déroulement du congrès." In *Le Congrès de Paris de 1856, un acte fondateur*, ed. Gilbert Ameil, Isabelle Nathan, and Georges-Henri Soutou. Brussels: Peter Lang, 2009.

Bull, Hedley. *The Anarchical Society*. 2nd ed. Basingstoke: Macmillan, 1997.

Bulmer-Thomas, Victor. *The Economic History of the Caribbean since the Napoleonic Wars*. Cambridge: Cambridge University Press, 2013.

Butler, William. "Congress of Nations: A Nineteenth Century View." *World Affairs* 128, no. 2 (1965): 102–6. http://www.jstor.org/stable/20670645.

Byron, George Gordon. *Don Juan*. Ed. T. G. Steffan, E. Steffan, and W. W. Pratt. Harmondsworth: Penguin, 1982.

Caine, Barbara, and Glenda Sluga. *Gendering European History, 1780–1920*. London: Continuum, 2000.

Callières, François de. *De la manière de négocier avec les souverains* [*The Practice of Diplomacy*]. Amsterdam: Pour La Companie, 1716.

Camaviano, Nestor. *Alexandre Mavrocordato, le grand dragoman: Son activité diplomatique (1673–1709)*. Thessaloniki: Institute for Balkan Studies, 1970.

Capefigue, M. *Les cent jours*. Brussels: Société Belge de Librairie, Hauman, 1841.

———. *Les diplomates européens*. Paris: Librairie D'Amyot, 1845–47.

———. *The Diplomatists of Europe*. Ed. Major-General Monteith. London: G. W. Nickisson, 1845.

———. *Histoire des Grandes Opérations Financières—Banques, Bourses, Emprunts, Compagnies industrielles*. Paris: Librairie D'Amyot, Paris, 1855–60.

Casalena, Maria Pia. *"Cher Sis": Scritture femminili nella corrispondenza di Sismondi*. Firenze: Edizioni Polistampa, 2008.

Cases, Emmanuel-Auguste-Dieudonné Las. *Memoirs of the Life, Exile, and Conversations of the Emperor Napoleon*. Vol. 4. London: Published for Henry Colburn, 1896.

Cassis, Youssef, and Philip Cottrell. *Private Banking in Europe: Rise, Retreat, and Resurgence*. Oxford: Oxford University Press, 2015.

———, eds. *The World of Private Banking*. Burlington, VT: Ashgate, 2009.

Castiglione, Frank. "'Levantine' Dragomans in Nineteenth-Century Istanbul: The Pisanis, the British, and Issues of Subjecthood." *Osmanlı Araştırmaları/Journal of Ottoman Studies* 44 (2014): 169–95.

Chaldecott, John. "Justus Erich Bollmann and Francisco Antonio Zea: Efforts to Meet the Demand for Columbian Platinum in England over the Years 1816 to 1822." *Platinum Metals Review* 23, no. 2 (1983): 81–90.

Chamberlain, Joseph P. *The Regime of the International Rivers: Danube and Rhine*. New York: Columbia University Press, 1923.

Chapuisat, Édouard. "Les cent-jours et l'invasion de 1815 vus de Genève." *Revue de Paris* (15 January 1917): 384–93.

———. "Empereurs, rois, ministres au congrès de Vienne." *Revue de Paris*, 15 July 1914.

———. *Jean-Gabriel Eynard et son temps, 1775–1863*. Geneva: A. Julien, 1952.

Chastenay, Mme de. *Mémoires de Mme de Chastenay, 1777–1815*. 2 vols. Ed. Alphonse Roserot. Paris: Plon, 1896.

Chateaubriand, François-René, Maurice Levaillant. *Deux livres des Mémoires d'outre-tombe*. Vol. 2. Venice: Delagrave, 1936.

Chateaubriand, François-René de. *The Congress of Verona: Comprising a Portion of Memoirs of His Own Times*, Volume 1 of 2. London: Richard Bentley, 1834.

Chatziioannou, Maria Christina. "War, Crisis and Sovereign Loans: The Greek War of Independence and British Economic Expansion in the 1820s." *Historical Review/La Revue Historique* 10 (2013): 33–55.

Chodźko, Leonard. *Le Congrès de Vienne et les traités de 1815*. Paris: Amyot, Éditeur des Archives Diplomatiques, 1864.

Chuquet, Arthur. *L'Année 1814: Lettres et memoirs*. Paris: Albert Fontemoing, 1914.

Clark, Christopher. *Iron Kingdom: The Rise and Downfall of Prussia, 1600–1947*. New York: Penguin, 2006.

Clavin, Patricia. "Men and Markets: Global Capital and the International Economy." In *Internationalisms: A Twentieth Century History*, ed. Glenda Sluga and Patricia Clavin. Cambridge: Cambridge University Press, 2017.

Clerq, Jules de. *Recueil des traités de la France publ. sous les auspices du Ministère des affaires étrangères*. Vol. 2. Paris: A. Durand et Pedone-Lauriel, 1880–1917.

Cobbett, William. "Greek Cause!" (nos. 5–6) and "Greek Pie" (nos. 7, 8, 10). *Cobbett's Weekly Register*. London: W. Cobbett, 1826, 291–312, 363–79, 385–443, 448–92, 581–615.

Cohen, Lucy. *Lady de Rothschild and Her Daughters, 1821–1931*. London: J. Murray, 1935.

Colley, Linda. *Britons: Forging the Nation, 1707–1837*. New Haven: Yale University Press, 1992.

"Commission des porteurs d'annuités d'Haïti." *Emprunt d'Haïti* [mémoires adressées aux Ministres du Roi], Paris, 15 December 1830, 29 January 1831. Paris: L'Imprimerie d'Adrien, 1830–31.

Constant, Benjamin. *Commentaire sur l'ouvrage de Filangieri, Science de la Législation*. Ed. Alain Laurent. Paris: Belles Lettres, 2004.

———. *Journaux intimes, Journaux intimes, publiée, avec un index et des notes par Alfred Roulin et Charles Roth*. Paris: NRF, Librairie Gallimard, 1952.

———. *Lettres de Benjamin Constant a Mme. Récamier*. Paris: E. Dentu, 1864.

———. *The Spirit of Conquest and Usurpation and Their Relation to European Civilization*. In *The Political Writings of Benjamin Constant*. Trans. and ed. Biancamaria Fontana. Cambridge: Cambridge University Press, 1988.

Cope, S. R. *Walter Boyd: A Merchant Banker in the Age of Napoleon*. Gloucester: Alan Sutton Publishing, London School of Economics and Political Science, 1983.

Corti, Egon Caesar. *The Rise of the House of Rothschild*. Trans. Brian Lunn and Beatrix Lunn. New York: Cosmopolitan Book Corporation, 1928.

Covenant of the International Labor Organisation. https://www.loc.gov/law/help/us-treaties/bevans/m-ust000002-0241.pdf.

Craig, Gordon. "Problems of Coalition Warfare: The Military Alliance against Napoleon, 1813–1814." *Harmon Memorial Lectures in Military History*, no. 7. United States Air Force Academy, 1965.

———. "Wilhelm von Humboldt as Diplomat." In *Studies in International History*, ed. K. Bourne and D. C. Watts, 81–102. London: Longmans, Green, 1967.

Craiutu, Aurelian. *A Virtue for Courageous Minds: Moderation in French Political Thought, 1748–1830*. Princeton: Princeton University Press, 2012.

Craveri, Benedetta. *The Age of Conversation*. New York: New York Review Books, 2005.

Crawley, Charles William. "John Capodistrias and the Greeks before 1821." *Cambridge Historical Journal* 13, no. 2 (1957): 162–82.

———. *The Question of Greek Independence*. Cambridge: Cambridge University Press, 1930.

———, ed. *War and Peace in an Age of Upheaval, 1793–1830*. Vol. 9 of *New Cambridge Modern History*. Cambridge: Cambridge University Press, 1906.

Crétineau-Joly, J. *Histoire des Traités de 1815 et de leur exécution, publiée sur les documents officiels et inédits*. Paris: Colomb des Batines, 1842.

Croker, Walter. "A Letter to a Member of Parliament, on the Slavery of the Christians at Algiers." *Edinburgh Review* 26, no. 52 (June 1816): 449–57.

Cust, Emma. *Slight Reminiscences of a Septuagenarian*. London: J. Murray, 1868.

Czartoryski, Adam Jerzy. "An Appeal to the Allies, and the English Nation, in Behalf of Poland." *Edinburgh Review* 22, no. 44 (1 January 1814): 294–331.

———. [under pseudonym Toulouzan, M.]. *Essai sur la Diplomatie: Manuscrit d'un Philhellène*. Paris: Firmin Didot Frères, 1830.

Dale, Gareth. "In Search of Karl Polanyi's International Relations Theory." *Review of International Studies* 42, no. 3 (2016): 401–24.

Daudet, Ernest. "Autour du Congrès d'Aix-la-Chapelle (1818), d'après des documents inédits." *Le Correspondant* 228 (10 July 1907).

———. "La politique extérieure." *La revue hebdomadaire* 9 (7 September 1918): 12–30.

———. "Un roman du Prince de Metternich 1819." *Revue hebdomadaire* (July–August 1899): 648–69.

———. *Une vie d'ambassadrice au siecle dernier: La Princesse de Lieven*. Paris: Plon, 1903.

Daunton, Martin. "'Gentlemanly Capitalism' and British Industry, 1820–1914." *Past & Present* 122 (February 1989): 119–58.

Davison, Roderic H. *Nineteenth Century Ottoman Diplomacy and Reforms*. Istanbul: Isis Press, 1999.

Dejean, Joan. *Ancients against Moderns: Culture Wars and the Making of a Fin de Siecle*. Chicago: University of Chicago Press, 1997.

"De L'Allemagne par Mme la Baronne de Stäel." *Edinburgh Review: Or The Critical Journal* 44 (October 1813): 198–238.

Dickson, P.G.M. *Finance and Government under Maria Theresia, 1740–1780*. Oxford: Clarendon Press, 1987.

Dino, Duchesse de. *Chronique de 1831–1862*. 4 vols. Paris: Plon-Nourrit, 1909–10.

Duprat, Catherine. *"Pour l'amour de l'humanité": Le temps des philanthropes: La philanthropie parisienne des lumières à la monarchie de Juillet*. Vol. 1. Paris: Editions du C.T.H.S., 1995.

Dziewanowski, Marian. "Czartoryski and His *Essai Sur La Diplomatie*." *Slavic Review* 30, no. 3 (1971): 589–605.

"11 February 1918: President Wilson's Address to Congress, Analyzing German and Austrian Peace Utterances." In *The World War I Document Archive*, ed. Richard Hacken. http://wwi.lib.byu.edu.

Emden, Paul. *Money Powers of Europe in the Nineteenth and Twentieth Centuries*. New York: D. Appleton-Century Company, 1938.

Escarpit, Robert. *L'Angleterre dans l'oeuvre de Madame de Staël*. Paris: J. Pechade, 1954.

Etkind, Alexander. *Internal Colonisation: Russia's Imperial Experience*. Cambridge: Polity Press, 2011.

Eynard, Charles. *Vie de Madame de Krüdener*. Geneva: Libraire G. Bridel, 1849.

Eynard, Jean-Gabriel. *Au Congrès de Vienne*. Paris: Librairie Plon, 1914.

———. *Journal de Jean-Gabriel Eynard*. Ed. Édouard Chapuisat. 2 vols. Paris: Plon-Nourrit, 1914, 1924.

Ferguson, Niall. *The House of Rothschild: Money's Prophets, 1798–1848*. New York: Viking, 1998.

Figgis, John Neville, ed. *Selections from the Correspondence of the First Lord Acton*. Vol. 1. London: Longmans, 1917.

Fitzmaurice, Andrew. *King Leopold's Ghostwriter*. Princeton: Princeton University Press, 2021.

Flandreau, Marc, and Juan H. Flores. "Bonds and Brands: Foundations of Sovereign Debt Markets, 1820–1830." *Journal of Economic History* 69, no. 3 (2009): 646–84.

———. "The Peaceful Conspiracy: Bond Markets and International Relations during the Pax Britannica." *International Organization* 66, no. 2 (2012): 211–41.

Flandreau, Marc, and Nathan Sussman. "Old Sins: Exchange Rate Clauses and European Foreign Lending in the 19th Century." CEPR Discussion Paper no. 4248, CEPR [Centre for Economic Policy Research], London, February 2004. http://ssrn.com/abstract=511303.

Flassan, Gaétan de Raxis. *Histoire du Congrès de Vienne*. Paris: Treuttel et Wurtz, 1829.

Fleming, John. *The Dark Side of the Enlightenment: Wizards, Alchemists, and Spiritual Seekers in the Age of Reason*. London: Norton, 2013.

Fleming, K. E. *The Muslim Bonaparte: Diplomacy and Orientalism in Ali Pasha's Greece*. Princeton: Princeton University Press, 1999.

Fontana, Biancamaria. "The Napoleonic Empire and the Europe of Nations." In *The Idea of Europe: From Antiquity to the European Union*, ed. Anthony Pagden, 116–28. Cambridge: Cambridge University Press, 2002.

Ford, Clarence. *The Life and Letters of Madame de Krüdener*. London: Adam and Charles Black, 1893.

Foreign Office, ed. *British and Foreign State Papers, 1812–1816*. Vol. 1. London: Ridgway, 1838–42.

Fournier, August. *Die Geheimpolizei auf dem Wiener Kongress: Eine Auswahl aus ihren Papieren*. Vienna: F. Tempsky & G. Freytag, 1913.

———. *Der Kongress von Châtillon: Die Politik in Kriege von 1814: Ein historische Studie*. Vienna: Verlag von F. Tempsky, 1900.

François, Étienne. "The Revolutionary and Napoleonic Wars as a Shared and Entangled European Lieu de Mémoire." In *War Memories: The Revolutionary and Napoleonic Wars in Modern European Culture*, ed. Alan Forrest, Étienne François, and Karen Hagemann. London: Palgrave, 2012.

Freksa, Frederick. *A Peace Congress of Intrigue (Vienna, 1815); a Vivid, Intimate Account of the Congress of Vienna Composed of the Personal Memoirs of Its Important Participants*. New York: Century Co., 1919.

Freudenberger, Herman. *Lost Momentum: Austrian Economic Development, 1750s–1830s*. Cologne: Böhlau Verlag, 2003.

Gaggiam, Jean, Coureur de S.A.R. le Duc Albert de Saxe-Teschen. *Guide des étrangers à Vienne pendant le congrès, contenant les noms des souverains présents dans cette capitale ainsi que ceux des ministres et chargés d'affaires des différentes cours auprès de celle de Vienne au mois d'Octobre 1814*. Vienna: Imprimerie des P. P. Méchitaristes, 1814.

———. *Supplément du guide des étrangers, auquel on a joint la liste générale des cavaliers employés par sa majesté l'empereur et roi en qualité de grands maîtres, aides de camp généraux, adjudants, chambellans et pages auprès des augustes étrangers à Vienne 1814*. Vienne: Imprimerie des P. P. Arméniens Méchitaristes, chez le Suisse de S.A.R. le Duc Albert de Saxe Teschen, 1814.

Gaffield, Julia. "The Racialization of International Law in the Aftermath of the Haitian Revolution: The Holy See and National Sovereignty." *American Historical Review* 125, no. 3 (June 2020): 841–68.

Gaillard, Gusti-Klara. *L'experience Haitiènne de la dette exterieur, 18–19*. Port-au-Prince: Impr. H. Deschamps, 1990.

Gallatin, Albert, ed. *A Great Peace Maker: The Diary of James Gallatin, Secretary to Albert Gallatin*. London: William Heinemann, 1914.

———. *The Writings of Albert Gallatin*. Ed. Henry Adams. Philadelphia: J. B. Lippincott, 1879.

Gandara, Marquis de la. "Quelques influences féminines dans la vie du prince de Metternich." *La revue hebdomadaire* (5 December 1936): 32–50.

Garde-Chambonas, Comte A. de la. *Souvenirs du Congrès de Vienne, 1814–1815*. Paris: Emile Paul, 1901.

Gardiner, T. "Representing Slavery: Germaine de Staël and the French Abolition Debate at the Revolutionary Turn of the 19th Century." Paper presented at Conference on Humanitarian Responses to Narratives of Inflicted Suffering, University of Connecticut Human Rights Institute, 13–15 October 2006.

Gariup, Monica. *European Security Culture: Language, Theory, Policy*. Aldershot: Ashgate, 2009.

Gautier, Paul. *Madame de Staël et Napoléon*. Paris: Plon, 1903.

Gay, Sophie. *Salons célèbres*. Paris: Michel Lévy, 1864.

Gelber, Nathan Michael. *Aktenstücke zur Judenfrage am Wiener Kongress, 1814/1815*. Vienna: Verlag des "Esra," 1920.

Gengembre, Gérard. "Fréquentation et sociabilité mutuelles." *Revue française d'histoire des idées politiques* 18, no. 2 (2003): 259–70.

Gentz, Friedrich von. *Dépêches inédites du chevalier de Gentz aux hospodars de Valachie: Pour servir à l'histoire politique européenne (1813–1828)*. 3 vols. Paris: Plon, 1876.

———. *On the State of Europe Before and After the French Revolution*. Trans. John Charles Herries. London: J. Hatchard, 1804.

———. *Tagebücher von Friedrich von Gentz*. Ed. Ludmilla Assing. Leipzig: F. A. Brockhaus, 1874.

Gersdorff, Dagmar von. *Caroline von Humboldt: Eine Biographie*. Leipzig: Insel Verlag GmbH, 2011.

Ghervas, Stella. *Conquering Peace: From the Enlightenment to the European Union*. Cambridge, MA: Harvard University Press, 2021.

———. *Réinventer la tradition: Alexandre Stourdza et l'Europe de la Sainte-Alliance*. Paris: Honoré Champion, 2008.

———. "Voyage au pays des mystiques: Une aristocrate russe dans les cours allemandes de la Restauration." In *Voyager en Europe de Humboldt à Stendhal (1790–1840)*, ed. Nicholas Bourguinat and Sylvain Venayre, 385–412. Paris: Nouveau Monde éditions, 2007.

Gille, Bertrand. *Histoire de la Maison Rothschild*. Geneva: Librairie Droz, 1967.

Goethe, J. W. von. *Faust, Part Two*. Trans. David Luke. Oxford: Oxford University Press, 1994.

Graaf, Beatrice de. "The Allied Machine: The Conference of Ministers in Paris and the Management of Security, 1815–18." In *Securing Europe after Napoleon: 1815 and the New European Security Culture*, ed. Beatrice de Graaf, Ido de Haan, and Brian Vick, 130–49. Cambridge: Cambridge University Press, 2019.

———. "Bringing Sense and Sensibility to the Continent: Vienna 1815 Revisited." *Journal of Modern European History* 13, no. 4 (2015): 447–57.

———. *Fighting Terror after Napoleon: How Europe Became Secure after 1815*. Cambridge: Cambridge University Press, 2020.

———. "Second-Tier Diplomacy: Hans Von Gagern and William I in Their Quest for an Alternative European Order, 1813–1818." *Journal of Modern European History/Zeitschrift Für Moderne Europäische Geschichte/Revue d'histoire Européenne Contemporaine* 12, no. 4 (2014): 546–66.

Graaf, Beatrice de, Ido de Haan, and Brian Vick, eds. *Securing Europe after Napoleon: 1815 and the New European Security Culture*. Cambridge: Cambridge University Press, 2019.

Graaf, Beatrice de, and Cornel Zwierlein. "Historicizing Security—Entering the Conspiracy Dispositive." *Historical Social Research/Historiche Sozialforschung* 38, no. 1 (2013): 46–64.

Gray, Richard. *Money Matters: Economics and the German Cultural Imagination, 1770–1850*. Seattle: University of Washington Press, 2008.

Great Britain Foreign Office. *1815–1816*. In *British and Foreign State Papers*. London: James Ridgway and Sons, 1838.

——. *Peace Handbooks*. No. 153. Appendix IV. London: H. M. Stationery Office, 1920.

Green, Abigail. *Moses Montefiore: Jewish Liberator, Imperial Hero*. Cambridge, MA: Belknap Press of Harvard University Press, 2010.

Greenfield, Jerome. "Financing a New Order: The Payment of Reparations by Restoration France, 1817–18." *French History* 30, no. 3 (2016): 1–26.

Grimsted, Patricia Kennedy. *The Foreign Ministers of Alexander I: Political Attitudes and the Conduct of Russian Diplomacy, 1801–1825*. Berkeley: University of California Press, 1969.

Gronow, Rees Howell. *The Reminiscences and Recollections of Captain Gronow: Anecdotes of the Camp, Court, Clubs and Society, 1810–1860*. London: John C. Nimmo, 1900.

Gross, Jonathan David. *Byron's "Corbeau Blanc": The Life and Letters of Lady Melbourne*. College Station: Texas A&M University Press, 1998.

Grotke, Kelly L., and Markus J. Prutsch, eds. *Constitutionalism, Legitimacy, and Power: Nineteenth-Century Experiences*. Oxford: Oxford University Press, 2014.

Gruner, Wolf. "The German Confederation: Cornerstone of the New European Security System." In *Securing Europe after Napoleon: 1815 and the New European Security Culture*, ed. Beatrice de Graaf, Ido de Haan, and Brian Vick. Cambridge: Cambridge University Press, 2019.

Grunwald, Constantin de. *Trois siècles de diplomatie russe*. Paris: Calmann-Lévy, Éditeurs, 1945.

Guizot, François. "Nécrologie [de Mme de Staël]." In *Archives philosophiques politiques et littéraires*, 237–45. Paris: Chez Fournier, Libraire, 1817.

Gulick, Edward Vose. "The Final Coalition and the Congress of Vienna, 1813–1815." In *War and Peace in an Age of Upheaval, 1793–1830*, ed. W. Crawley, 639–67. Vol. 9 of *New Cambridge Modern History*. Cambridge: Cambridge University Press, 1965.

Gunzburg, Irene de Vries de. *Catherine Pavlovna: Grande-Duchesse Russe, 1788–1819*. Amsterdam: J. M. Meulenboff, 1941.

Hagemann, Karen. "'Be Proud and Firm, Citizens of Austria!' Patriotism and Masculinity in Texts of the 'Political Romantics' Written during Austria's Anti-Napoleonic Wars." *German Studies Review* 29, no. 1 (2006): 41–62.

——. "Female Patriots: Women, War and the Nation in the Period of the Prussian-German Anti-Napoleonic Wars." *Gender and History* 16, no. 2 (2004): 397–424.

——. "Of 'Manly Valor' and 'German Honor': Nation, War, and Masculinity in the Age of the Prussian Uprising against Napoleon." *Central European History* 30, no. 2 (1997): 187–220.

Hanoteau, Jean, ed. *Lettres de Prince de Metternich à la Contesse de Lieven, 1818–1819*. Paris: Plon-Nourrit, 1909.

Hartley, Janet. "Is Russia Part of Europe? Russian Perceptions of Europe in the Reign of Alexander I." *Cahiers du monde russe et soviétique* 33, no. 4 (1992): 369–85.

Hauranne, Duvergier de. *Histoire du gouvernment parlementaire en France, 1814–1848*. Vol. 4. Paris: Michel Levy Freres, 1860.

Hausenstein, Wilhelm. "Das Zeitalter von Waterloo: Zur Widerkehr des Tags der Schlacht vom 18. Juni 1815." In *Eine Wochenschrift-Zweiter Band-April-Juni 1915*. Berlin: Marz Verlag, 1915.

Haussonville, Comte d'. "Mme de Staël et Mme de Krüdener—Correspondance inédite." *Le Figaro Supplément littéraire* 31 (16 September 1911).

Heckscher, Eli F. *The Continental System: An Economic Interpretation*. Ed. Harald Westergaard. Oxford: Clarendon Press, 1922.

Heinzen, Jasper. "Transnational Affinities and Invented Traditions: The Napoleonic Wars in British and Hanoverian Memory, 1815–1915." *English Historical Review* 127, no. 529 (December 2012): 1404–34.

Hemstad, Ruth. *"Like a Herd of Cattle": Parliamentary and Public Debates Regarding the Cession of Norway, 1813–1814*. Oslo: Akademisk Publisering, 2014.

Henning, Ian Allan. *L'Allemagne de Mme de Staël et la polémique romantique: Première fortune de l'ouvrage en France et en Allemagne (1814–1830)*. Paris: Librairie Ancienne Honoré Champion, 1929.

Hermant, Abel. "Madame de Krüdener." *Revue de Paris* 1933–34 (3 pts.): 1. "La danse du schall" (1 and 15 December 1933: 481–96, 783–808); 2. "Litterarum intemperantia" (1 January 1934): 125–46; 3. "Le commerce des anges" (15 January, 1 February 1934): 366–85, 607–35.

Herold, J. Christopher. *Mistress to an Age: A Life of Madame de Staël*. New York: Grove Press, 1958.

Herren, Madeleine. "Gender and International Relations through the Lens of the League of Nations." In *Women, Diplomacy and International Politics*, ed. Carolyn James and Glenda Sluga, 182–201. London: Routledge: 2015.

Hertz, Deborah Sadie. *Jewish High Society in Old Regime Berlin*. Syracuse: Syracuse University Press, 2005.

Hetherington, Philippa, and Glenda Sluga. "Liberal and Illiberal Internationalisms." *Journal of World History* 31, no. 1 (March 2020): 1–9.

Hilger, Stephanie. *Women Write Back: Strategies of Response and the Dynamics of European Literary Culture, 1790–1805*. New York: Rodopi, 2009.

Hill, Norman. *The Public International Conference: Its Function, Organization and Procedure*. Palo Alto: Stanford University Press, 1926.

Hobsbawm, Eric. *The Age of Revolution: 1789–1848*. 1962. London: Weidenfeld and Nicolson, 1996.

Holland, Thomas Erskine. *The European Concert in the Eastern Question*. Oxford: Clarendon Press, 1885.

Holmes, Stephen. *Benjamin Constant and the Making of Modern Liberalism*. New Haven: Yale University Press, 1984.

Hoock-Demarle, Marie-Claire. *L'Europe des lettres: Réseaux epistolaires et construction de l'espace européen*. Paris: Albin Michel, 2008.

Horne, Julia, and Glenda Sluga. "Cosmopolitanism: Its Past and Practices." *Journal of World History* 21, no. 3 (2010): 369–73.

Houssaye, Henry. "France en 1814." *Revue des Deux Mondes* 83 (15 October 1887): 788–820.

Hull, Isabel. *Sexuality, State, and Civil Society in Germany, 1700–1815*. Ithaca: Cornell University Press, 1997.

Humboldt, Wilhelm. "Mémoire [préparatoire] sur le travail de la Commission de la navigation, presenté par M. le Baron de Humboldt, 3 février 1815," Annexe no. 1, "Procès-verbale de la deuxième conférence de la commission pour la libre navigation des rivières—Vienne, Séance du 8 février 1815." In Comte d'Angeberg, *Le Congrès de Vienne et les traités de 1815*, pt. 1, pp. 728–33. Paris: Amyot, Éditeur des Archives Diplomatiques, 1863.

———. *Wilhelm von Humboldts Gesammelte Schriften*. Vol. 11. Ed. Albert Leitzmann and Bruno Gebhardt. Berlin: Behr's, 1903–36.

Hunt, Lynn. "The Global Financial Origins of 1789." In *The French Revolution in Global Perspective*, ed. Suzanne Desan, Lynn Hunt, and William Max Nelson. Ithaca: Cornell University Press, 2013.

Hurewitz, Jacob Coleman. "Ottoman Diplomacy and the European State System." *Middle East Journal* 15 (1961): 141–52.

Hürheim, Gräfin. *Mein Leben: Erinnerungen Aus Österreicsh Grosse Welt, 1819–1852*. Munich: Müller, 1913.

Husslein-Arco, Agnes, Sabine Grabner, and Werner Telesko, eds. *Europe in Vienna: The Congress of Vienna, 1814/15*. Chicago: University of Chicago Press, 2015.

"Interchange: The History of Capitalism." *Journal of American History* 101, no. 2 (2014): 503–36. https://doi.org/10.1093/jahist/jau357.

Isbell, John Claiborne. *The Birth of European Romanticism: Truth and Propaganda in Staël's "De l'Allemagne," 1810–1813*. Cambridge: Cambridge University Press, 1994.

———. Introduction to Madame de Staël, *Corinne, or, Italy*. Trans. S. Raphael. Oxford: Oxford University Press, 1998.

———. "Voices Lost? Staël and Slavery, 1786–1830." In *Slavery in the Caribbean Francophone World*, ed. Doris Kadish. Atlanta: University of Georgia Press, 2000.

James, Harold. "Finance Capitalism." In *Capitalism: The Reemergence of a Historical Concept*, ed. Jürgen Kocka and Marcel van der Linden. London: Bloomsbury Academic, 2016.

Jarrett, Mark. *The Congress of Vienna and Its Legacy: War and Great Power Diplomacy after Napoleon*. New York: I. B. Tauris, 2013.

Jaucourt, Arnail Francois. *Correspondance du Comte de Jaucourt, ministre interim: Des affaires étrangères avec le prince de Talleyrand*. Paris: Plon, 1905.

Jeffery, Francis. "De la littérature considérée dans ses rapports avec les institutions sociales." *Edinburgh Review* 21 (1813): 1–50.

Jenkins, Helen. "Madame de Staël." In *The Congress of Women*, ed. Mary Kavanaugh Oldham Eagle. Vol. 2. Chicago: Monarch Book Company, 1894.

Jennings, Mrs. Vaughan. *Rahel: Her Life and Letters*. London: Henry S. King & Co., 1876.

Kale, Steven. *French Salons: High Society and Political Sociability from the Old Regime to the Revolution of 1848*. Baltimore: Johns Hopkins University Press, 2004.

———. "Women, Salons, and the State in the Aftermath of the French Revolution." *Journal of Women's History* 13, no. 4 (2002): 54–80.

Kalman, Julie. "Rothschildian Greed: 'This New Variety of Despotism.'" In *French History and Civilization: Papers from the George Rudé Seminar* (2004), ed. Ian Coller, Helen Davies, and Julie Kalman. Vol. 1. George Rudé Society, University of Melbourne, 2005. www.h-france.net/rude/2005conference/Kalman2.pdf.

Kant, Immanuel. *Idee zu einer allgemeinen Geschichte in weltbürgerlicher Absicht*. Göttingen: Vollstandige Neuausgabe, 2019.

Kapp, Friedrich. *Justus Erich Bollmann, Ein Lebensbild aus zwei Welttheilen*. Berlin: Julius Springer, 1880.

Karmin, Otto. *Sir Francis D'Ivernois, 1757–1842: Sa vie, son oeuvre et son temps*. Geneva: Librairie Ancienne Bader et Mongenet/Revue historique de la Révolution Française et de l'empire, 1920.

Kavanagh, Julie. *French Women of Letters: Biographical Sketches*. Vol. 2. London: Hurst and Blackett, 1862.

Kerschbaumer, Florian, and Korinna Schönhärl. "Der Wiener Kongress als 'Kinderstube' des Philhellenismus: Das Beispiel des Bankers Jean-Gabriel Eynard." In *Vormärz und Philhellenismus, Forum Vormärz Forschung 18, Jahrbuch 2012*, ed. Anne-Rose Meyer. Bielefeld: Aisthesis Verlag, 2013.

Kindleberger, Charles. *A Financial History of Western Europe*. New York: Oxford University Press, 1993.

King, Norman. "A. W. Schlegel et la guerre de liberation: Le mémoire sur l'état de l'Allemagne." *Cahiers Staëliens* 16 (1973): 1–31.

———. "Correspondances suédoises de Germaine de Staël (1812–1816)." *Cahiers Staëliens* 39 (1988): 11–137.

———. "Libéralisme et legitimité." *Europe* (1987): 64–80.

———. "Mme de Staël et la chute de Napoléon." In *Madame de Staël et l'Europe*, 63–75. Paris: Klincksieck, 1970.

Kirshner, Jonathan. *Appeasing Bankers: Financial Caution on the Road to War*. Princeton: Princeton University Press, 2007.

Klose, Fabian, ed. *The Emergence of Humanitarian Intervention: Ideas and Practice from the Nineteenth Century to the Present*. Cambridge: Cambridge University Press, 2015.

Knapton, Ernest John. *The Lady of the Holy Alliance: The Life of Julie de Krüdener*. New York: Columbia University Press, 1939.

———. "An Unpublished Letter of Mme de Krüdener." *Journal of Modern History* 9, no. 4 (December 1937): 483–92.

Kohler, Max. *Jewish Rights at the Congresses of Vienna (1814–1815) and Aix-La-Chapelle (1818)*. New York: American Jewish Committee, 1918.

Koselleck, Reinhart. "Goethe's Untimely History." In *Sediments of Time: On Possible Histories*, ed. Reinhart Koselleck et al., 60–79. Stanford: Stanford University Press, 2018.

Krause, Stefan. *Die Aechtung des Sklavenhandels auf dem Wiener Kongress: Ein Sieg der Humanität oder der Machtpolitik?* Norderstedt: GRIN Verlag, 2009.

Krüdener, Barbara Juliane von. *Le Camp de Vertus, ou, La Grande revue de l'armée russe, dans la plaine de ce nom, par l'empereur Alexandre*. Lyon: Guyot Frères, 1815.

——. *Valérie*. 1804. Paris: Charpentier, Libraire-Éditeur, 1840.

La Garde-Chambonas, Comte A. de. *Souvenirs du Congrès de Vienne, 1814–1815*. Paris: Librairie Historique et Militaire, Henri Vivien, 1901.

Landes, David. *Bankers and Pashas: International Finance and Economic Imperialism in Egypt*. London: Heinemann, 1958.

——. "A Chapter in the Financial Revolution of the Nineteenth Century: The Rise of French Deposit Banking." *Journal of Economic History* 23, no. 2 (June 1963): 224–31.

——. *Dynasties: Fortunes and Misfortunes of the World's Great Family Businesses*. New York: Viking Penguin, 2006.

——. "Vieille Banque et Banque Nouvelle: La révolution financière du dix-neuvième siècle." *Revue d'histoire moderne et contemporaine* 3, no. 3 (July–September 1956): 204–22.

Landes, Joan. *Women in the Public Sphere in the Age of the French Revolution*. Ithaca: Cornell University Press, 1988.

Lange, Erik de. "Menacing Tides: Security, Piracy and Empire in the Nineteenth-Century Mediterranean." PhD diss., Utrecht University, 2020.

Lanier, Amelie. "The Budapest Chain Bridge." *Rothschild Archive Review of the Year* (April 2003–March 2004): 34–39.

Laurence, Anne, Josephine Maltby, and Janette Rutterford, eds. *Women and Their Money, 1700–1950: Essays on Women and Finance*. London: Routledge, 2009.

Laven, David, and Lucy Riall, eds. *Napoleon's Legacy: Problems of Government in Restoration Europe*. Oxford: Berg, 2000.

Lenormand, Mlle. M. A. *La Sibylle au Congrès d'Aix-la-Chapelle suivi d'un coup-d'oeil sur celui de Carlsbad*. Paris: chez l'Auteur, 1819.

Leroy, Maxime. *La vie véritable du comte Henri de Saint-Simon (1760–1825)*. Paris: B. Grasset, 1925.

Lesaffer, Randall. "The 18th-Century Antecedents of the Concert of Europe I: The Triple Alliance of 1717." In *Oxford Historical Treaties*. Oxford: Oxford University Press, 2017. https://opil.ouplaw.com/page/The%2018th-century%20Antecedents%20of%20the%20Concert%20of%20Europe%20I:%20The%20Triple%20Alliance%20of%201717.

——. "The 18th-Century Antecedents of the Concert of Europe II: The Quadruple Alliance of 1718." In *Oxford Historical Treaties*. Oxford: Oxford University Press, 2017. http://opil.ouplaw.com/page/quadruple-alliance.

——. *The Peace of Aachen (1748) and the Rise of Multilateral Treaties*. Oxford: Oxford University Press, 2017. http://opil.ouplaw.com/page/Peace-Aachen.

——. "Perpetual Peace." In *Oxford Historical Treaties*. Oxford: Oxford University Press, 2017. http://opil.ouplaw.com/home/OHT.

——. "Vienna and the Abolition of the Slave Trade." *Oxford Public International Law* (2015). https://opil.ouplaw.com/page/498.

Lewis, Mary. "Repairing Damage: The Slave Ship *Marcelin* and the Haiti Trade." *American Historical Review* 125, no. 3 (June 2020): 869–98.

Ley, Francis. "Alexandre Ier, Chateaubriand, Lamartine et Madame de Krüdener, en 1815." *Cahiers du monde russe et soviétique* 9, no. 1 (January–March 1968): 58–64.

——. *Bernardin de Saint-Pierre, Madame de Stäel, Chateaubriand, Benjamin Constant et Madame de Krüdener*. Paris: Aubier, Éditions Montaigne, 1967.

——. "Madame de Krüdener à Paris (1802–1804)." *Revue d'histoire littéraire de la France* 99, no. 1 (January–February 1999): 99–108.

——. *Madame de Krüdener et son temps: 1764–1824*. Paris: Plon, 1962.

Lieven, Dominic. *The Aristocracy in Europe, 1815–1914*. New York: Columbia University Press, 1992.

Lieven, Dorothea. *The Private Letters of Princess Lieven to Prince Metternich, 1820–1826*. Ed. Peter Quennell. New York: E. P. Dutton, 1938.

Lobell, Håkan. "Foreign Exchange Rates, 1804–1914." In *Exchange Rates, Prices and Wages, 1277–2008*, ed. Rodney Edvinsson, Tor Jacobson, and Daniel Waldenström. Stockholm: Sveriges Riksbank, 2010.

Loménie, Emmanuel Beau de, ed. *Lettres de Madame de Staël à Madame Récamier: Présentées et annotées par Emmanuel Beau de Loménie*. Paris: Editions Domat, 1952.

Lowenstein, Steven. *The Berlin Jewish Community: Enlightenment, Family and Crisis, 1770–1830*. New York: Oxford University Press, 1994.

——. "Jewish Upper Crust and Berlin Jewish Enlightenment: The Family of Daniel Itzig." In *Profiles in Diversity: Jews in a Changing Europe, 1750–1870*, ed. Frances Malino and David Sorkin. Detroit: Wayne State University Press, 1998.

Luigia, Queen Maria. *Memoir of the Queen of Etruria Written by Herself*. London: John Murray, 1814.

Macartney, Carlile Aylmer. "The Austrian Monarchy, 1792–1847." In *War and Peace in an Age of Upheaval*, ed. C. W. Crawley, 401–2. Vol. 9 of *New Cambridge Modern History*. Cambridge: Cambridge University Press, 1965.

Mackintosh, James. "Review of Madame de Staël's *De l'Allemagne*." In *The Miscellaneous Works*. New York: D. Appleton & Co., 1871.

Madiou, Thomas. *Histoire d'Haiti*. Vol. 4. Port-au-Prince: Impr. H. Deschamps, 1988.

Mann, Golo. *Secretary of Europe: The Life of Friedrich Gentz, Enemy of Napoleon*. Trans. William H. Woglom. New Haven: Yale University Press, 1946.

Manuel, Frank Edward. *The New World of Henri Saint-Simon*. Ann Arbor: University of Michigan Press, 1963.

Martin, Alexander. *Romantics, Reformers, Reactionaries: Russian Conservative Thought and Politics in the Reign of Alexander I.* DeKalb: Northern Illinois University Press, 1997.

Massardier-Kenney, Françoise. "Staël, Translation, and Race." In *Translating Slavery: Gender and Race in French Women's Writing, 1783–1823*, ed. Doris Kadish and Françoise Massardier-Kenney. Kent, OH: Kent State University Press, 1994.

Mazower, Mark. *Governing the World: The History of an Idea.* New York: Penguin, 2012.

McGuigan, Dorothy Gies. *Metternich and the Duchess.* Garden City, NY: Doubleday, 1975.

Meinecke, Friedrich. *Cosmopolitanism and the National State.* Trans. Robert B. Kimber. Princeton: Princeton University Press, 1970.

Metternich, Clemens. *Clemens Metternich-Wilhelmine von Sagan: Ein Briefwechsel, 1813–1815.* Köln: Bohlau, 1966.

———. *Lettres à la Comtesse de Lieven, 1818–1819.* Paris: Plon-Nourrit, 1909.

———. *Mémoires, documents et écrits divers.* Ed. M. A. de Klinkowstroem. Paris: E. Plon, 1880–84.

Minawi, Mostafa. "International Law and the Precarity of Ottoman Sovereignty in Africa at the End of the Nineteenth Century." *International History Review* (May 2020): 1–24.

Mistler, Jean. *Madame de Staël et Maurice O'Donnell 1805–1817 d'après des lettres inédites.* Paris: Calmann-Lévy, Éditeurs, 1926.

Mitchell, Harvey. *The Underground War against Revolutionary France: The Missions of William Wickham, 1794–1800.* Oxford: Clarendon Press, 1965.

Montcalm, Marquise de. "Journal Inédit: Extraits." *Revue de Paris* (October 1934): 9–28.

Montet, Alexandrine Baronne du. *Souvenirs de la baronne du Montet, 1785–1866.* Paris: Librairie Plon, Plon-Nourrit, 1904.

Moran, Daniel. *Toward the Century of Words: Johann Cotta and the Politics of the Public Realm in Germany, 1795–1832.* Berkeley: University of California Press, 1992.

Mori, Jennifer. *The Culture of Diplomacy: Britain in Europe, c. 1750–1830.* Oxford: Manchester University Press, 2014.

Morton, Frederic. *The Rothschilds: A Family Portrait.* London: Secker & Warburg, 1962.

Mosse, George. *Nationalism and Sexuality: Respectability and Abnormal Sexuality.* New York: H. Fertig, 1985.

Mösslang, Markus, and Torsten Riotte. Introduction to *The Diplomats' World: The Cultural History of Diplomacy, 1815–1914*, ed. Markus Mösslang and Torsten Riotte. Oxford: Oxford University Press, 2008.

Mueller-Vollmer, Kurt. "Wilhelm von Humboldt." In *Stanford Encyclopedia of Philosophy*, ed. Edward N. Zalta (Winter 2014). http://plato.stanford.edu/archives/win2014/entries/wilhelm-humboldt/.

Müller, Klaus. *Quellen zur Geschichte des Wiener Kongresses 1814/1815, Ausgewählte Quellen zur deutschen Geschichte der Neuzeit*. Darmstadt: Wissenschaftliche Buchgesellschaft, 1986.

Münster-Ledenburg, Georg Herbert, Ernst Friedrich Herbert Münster, and Harriet Elizabeth St. Clair. *Political Sketches of the State of Europe, from 1814–1867, Containing Count Ernst Münster's Despatches to the Prince Regent, from the Congress of Vienna*. Edinburgh: Edmonston & Douglas, 1868.

Muir, Ramsay. *Nationalism and Internationalism*. London: Constable Limited, 1917.

Muir, Rory. *Wellington*. New Haven: Yale University Press, 2013, 2015.

Musulin, Stella. *Vienna in the Age of Metternich: From Napoleon to Revolution*. London: Faber and Faber, 1975.

Nesselrode, Anatol von. *Lettres et papiers du chancelier Comte de Nesselrode, 1760–1850, extraits de ses archives*. 11 vols. Paris: A. Lahure, 1904–11.

Neufeld, H. *The International Protection of Private Creditors from the Treaties of Westphalia to the Congress of Vienna (1648–1815): A Contribution to the History of the Law of Nations*. Leiden: Sijthoff, 1971.

Nichols, Irby C. *The European Pentarchy and the Congress of Verona, 1822*. The Hague: Nijhoff, 1971.

Nicoll, André. *Comment la France a payé après Waterloo*. Paris: E. de Boccard, Éditeur, 1929.

Nicolson, Harold. *The Congress of Vienna: A Study in Allied Unity, 1812–1822*. London: Constable and Co., 1946.

———. *Diplomacy*. London: Oxford University Press, 1963.

Nigohosian, V.-A. *La libération du territoire français après Waterloo (1815–1818)*. Paris: E. de Boccard, Éditeur, 1929.

———. *L'observateur au congrès d'Aix-la-Chapelle*. Paris: Chez Eymery, 1818.

Nye, Robert A. "Mobilization for War: Gendered Military Cultures in Nineteenth-Century Western Societies." In *The Oxford Handbook of Gender, War, and the Western World since 1600*, ed. Karen Hagemann, Stefan Dudink, and Sonya O. Rose. Oxford: Oxford University Press, 2020.

Oldfield, J. R. *Popular Politics and British Anti-slavery: The Mobilization of Public Opinion against the Slave Trade, 1787–1807*. London: Frank Cass, 1998.

O'Neill, Eileen. "Disappearing Ink: Early Modern Women Philosophers and Their Fate in History." In *Philosophy in a Feminist Voice: Critiques and Reconstructions*, ed. J. A. Kourany, 17–62. Princeton: Princeton University Press, 1998.

Orbell, John. "Baring, Alexander, First Baron Ashburton (1773–1848)." In *Oxford Dictionary of National Biography*. Oxford: Oxford University Press, 2004.

Osterhammel, Jürgen. *The Transformation of the World: A Global History of the Nineteenth Century*. Trans. Patrick Camiller. Princeton: Princeton University Press, 2014.

———. *Unfabling the East: The Enlightenment's Encounter with Asia*. Trans. Robert Savage. Princeton: Princeton University Press, 2018.

Osterhammel, Jürgen, and Niels P. Petersson. *Globalization: A Short History*. Trans. Dona Geyer. Princeton: Princeton University Press, 2005.

Ouvrard, Gabriel Julian. *Mémoires de G.-J. Ouvrard, sur sa vie et ses diverses opérations financières*. Paris: Moutardier, Libraire, 1826–27.

Owen, Robert. *Manifesto of Robert Owen: The Discoverer, Founder, and Promulgator, of the Rational System of Society, and of the Rational Religion*. London: Social Institution, 1840.

Pagden, Anthony, ed. *The Idea of Europe: From Antiquity to the European Union*. New York: Cambridge University Press, 2002.

Pange, Pauline de. *Auguste Wilhelm Schlegel et Madame de Staël d'après des documents inédit par la comtesse Jean de Pange*. Paris: Albert, 1938.

Pange, Victor de. *Madame de Staël et le duc de Wellington, correspondance inédite, 1815–1817*. Paris: Gallimard, 1962.

Papalexopoulou, Elisavet. "Tracing the 'Political' in Women's Work: Women of Letters in the Greek Cultural Space, 1800–1832." *Journal of Modern Greek Studies* 39 (May 2021).

Pearce, Adrian. "The Hope-Barings Contract: Finance and Trade between Europe and the Americas, 1805–1808." *English Historical Review* 124, no. 511 (December 2009): 1324–52.

Penn, Virginia. "Philhellenism in Europe, 1821–1828." *Slavonic and East European Review* 16, no. 48 (April 1938): 638–53.

Peterson, Genevieve. "II. Political Inequality at the Congress of Vienna." *Political Science Quarterly* 60, no. 4 (1945): 532–54.

Pflaum, Rosalynd. *By Influence and Desire*. New York: Evans and Co., 1984.

Phillips, Walter Alison. *The Confederation of Europe: A Study of the European Alliance, 1813–1823, as an Experiment in the International Organization of Peace*. New York: Howard Fertig, 1966.

Pictet, Edmond. *Biographie, travaux et correspondance diplomatique de C. Pictet de Rochemont 1755–1824, député de Genève auprès du Congrès de Vienne, 1814, envoyé extraordinaire et ministre plénipotentiaire de la Suisse à Paris et à Turin, 1815 et 1816*. Genève: H. Georg, 1892.

Pinch, Adela. *Strange Fits of Passion: Epistemologies of Emotion, Hume to Austen*. Stanford: Stanford University Press, 1996.

"Pismo Grafini Edling Grafu Kapodistrii." *Russky Arkhiv*, no. 11 (1891): 420–24.

Pitts, Jennifer. *Boundaries of the International: Law and Empire*. Cambridge, MA: Harvard University Press, 2018.

———. "Empire and Legal Universalisms in the Eighteenth Century." *American Historical Review* 117, no. 1 (February 2012): 92–121.

Platt, D.C.M. *Foreign Finance in Continental Europe and the United States, 1815–1870: Quantities, Origins, Functions, and Distribution*. London: Routledge, 1984.

Polanyi, Karl. *The Great Transformation: The Political and Economic Origins of Our Time*. New York: Farrar & Rinehart, 1944.

Poliakov, Léon. *Histoire de l'antisémitisme*. Vol. 3, *De Voltaire à Wagner*. Paris: Calmann-Lévy, 1968.

Polovtsoff, Alexandre, ed. *Correspondance diplomatiques des ambassadeurs et ministres de Russie en France et de France en Russie, 1814–1816*. St. Petersburg: Édition de la société impérial d'histoire de Russie, 1902.

——. *Russkiy biograficheskiy slovar*. Vol. 1. St. Petersburg: Imp. Istorich.Obshestvo, 1896.

"Proces verbaux et Rapports de la commission statistique avec les pieces annexes, 24 December 1814." In Leonard Chodźko, *Le Congrès de Vienne et les traités de 1815*, 2:562–66. Paris: Amyot, Éditeur des Archives Diplomatiques, 1864.

"Projet d'articles pour le règlement de ce qui concerne la navigation des grands fleuves traversant plusieurs territoires, présenté par M. le duc de Dalberg, plénipotentiare de France," Annexe no. 1, in "Procès-verbale de la première conférence de la Commission relative à la libre navigation des rivières, Vienne, 2 février 1815." In Comte d'Angeberg, *Le Congrès de Vienne et les traités de 1815*, pt. 1, pp. 693–97. Paris: Amyot, Éditeur des Archives Diplomatiques, 1863.

Protocol of Conference between Great Britain and Russia, signed at St. Petersburg, 23 March (4 April) 1826. https://opil.ouplaw.com/view/10.1093/law:oht/law-oht-76-CTS-175.regGroup.1/law-oht-76-CTS-175.

Prutsch, Markus. *Fundamentalismus: Das "Projekt der Moderne" und die Politisierung des Religiösen*. Vienna: Passagen-Verlag, 2007.

——. *Making Sense of Constitutional Monarchism in Post-Napoleonic France and Germany*. Basingstoke: Palgrave Macmillan, 2013.

——. "'Monarchical Constitutionalism' in Post-Napoleonic Europe: Concept and Practice." In *Constitutionalism, Legitimacy, and Power: Nineteenth-Century Experiences*, ed. Kelly L. Grotke and Markus J. Rutsch. Oxford: Oxford University Press, 2014.

Quennell, Peter, ed. *Vertrauliche Briefe der Fürstin Lieven*. Berlin: Steuben-Verlag, 1939.

Rain, Pierre. *L'Europe et la restauration des Bourbons, 1814–1818*. Paris: Perrin, 1908.

Raymond, Jean-Baptiste Honoré. *Emprunts, bourses, crédit public, grands capitalistes de l'Europe, 1814–1852*. Vol. 3. Paris: Amyot, 1858.

Reddy, W. H. *The Navigation of Feeling: A Framework for the History of Emotions*. Cambridge: Cambridge University Press, 2001.

Redlich, Fritz. "The Business Activities of Erich Bollmann: An International Business Promoter, 1797–1821." *Bulletin of the Business Historical Society* 17, nos. 5 and 6 (November and December 1943): 81–91, 103–12.

——. "Eric Bollmann: Adventurer, Businessman, and Economic Writer." In *Essays in American Economic History: Eric Bollmann and Studies in Banking*, ed. Fritz Redlich, 1–106. New York: G. E. Stechert & Co., 1944.

——. "Jacques Laffitte and the Beginnings of Investment Banking in France." *Bulletin of the Business Historical Society* 22, no. 4/6 (December 1948): 137–61.

——. *The Molding of American Banking: Men and Ideas*. New York: Hafner, 1947–51.

——. "Payments between Nations in the Eighteenth and Early Nineteenth Centuries." *Quarterly Journal of Economics* 50, no. 4 (August 1936): 694–705.

Reinerman, Alan. "Metternich, Italy and the Congress of Verona, 1821–1822." *Historical Journal* 14, no. 2 (June 1971): 263–87.

Reinert, Sophus. "Lessons on the Rise and Fall of Great Powers: Conquest, Commerce, and Decline in Enlightenment Italy." *American Historical Review* 115, no. 5 (December 2010): 1395–1425.

Remusat, Comtesse de. *Mémoires of Mme de Remusat*. Vol. 2. London: Sampson Low, 1880.

———. *Memoirs of Madame de Rémusat, 1802–1808*. 3 vols. Paris: Calmann-Levy, 1880.

Review of "Memoirs of the Baron de Kolli." *Edinburgh Review* 39, no. 77 (1824): 234–46.

Rietzler, Katharina, and Patricia Owens, eds. *Women's International Thought: A New History*. Cambridge: Cambridge University Press, 2021.

Riley, James. *International Government Finance and the Amsterdam Capital Market, 1740–1815*. Cambridge: Cambridge University Press, 1980.

Riordan, Sheilagh Margaret. "Politics and Romanticism: Germaine de Staël's Forgotten Influence on Nineteenth-Century Sweden." *Australian Journal of French Studies* 35, no. 3 (1998): 333–45.

———. "Sentiments of Travel: Madame de Staël on Sweden." *Moderna Sprak* 90, no. 2 (1996): 190–99.

Rochechouart, Count de. *Memoirs of the Count de Rochechouart, in France, in southern Russia, The Napoleonic wars, 1812–1815, and as commandant of Paris 1788–1816*. Trans. Frances Jackson. New York: E. P. Dutton & Co., 1920.

Roesch, Gertrud Maria. "The Liberation from Napoleon as Self-Liberation: The Year 1813 in the Letters of Rahel Varnhagen." In *Women against Napoleon: Historical and Fictional Responses to His Rise and Legacy*, ed. Waltraud Maierhofer, Gertrud Roesch, and Caroline Bland. Chicago: University of Chicago Press, 2008.

Romanov, Nikolay Mikhailovich, *Imperator Alexander I. Opyt istoricheskogo issledovaniya*. St. Petersburg: Eksp. Zagot. Gosud. Bumag, 1912.

Rorty, Amelie Oksenberg, and James Schmidt, eds. *Kant's Idea for a Universal History with a Cosmopolitan Aim: A Critical Guide*. Cambridge: Cambridge University Press, 2009.

Rosenberg, Emily. "Revisiting Dollar Diplomacy: Narratives of Money and Manliness." *Diplomatic History* 22, no. 2 (Spring 1998): 154–76.

Rosenblatt, Helena. *The Lost History of Liberalism*. Princeton: Princeton University Press, 2018.

Rosenhaft, Eve. "Women Investors and Financial Knowledge in Eighteenth-Century Germany." In *Women and Their Money, 1700–1950: Essays on Women and Finance*, ed. Anne Laurence, Josephine Maltby, and Janette Rutterford. London: Routledge, 2009.

Rosenkrantz, Niels. *Journal du Congrès de Vienne, 1814–1815*. Copenhagen: G.E.C. Gad, 1953.

Rothschild, Emma. *Economic Sentiments: Adam Smith, Condorcet, and the Enlightenment*. Cambridge, MA: Harvard University Press, 2001.

———. "Isolation and Economic Life in Eighteenth-Century France." *American Historical Review* 119, no. 4 (2014): 1055–82.

———. "What Is Security?" *Daedalus* 124, no. 3 (Summer 1995): 53–98.

Rowlands, Guy. *Dangerous and Dishonest Men: The International Bankers of Louis XIV's France*. Basingstoke: Palgrave Macmillan, 2014.

Sacchi, Defendente. *Lavori all'Arco della Pace in Milano*. In *Biblioteca Italiana ossia Giornale di letteratura scienze ed arti*. Vol. 57. Milan: A. F. Stella, 1832.

Sainte-Beuve, C.-A. "Madame de Krüdner." *Revue des Deux Mondes* 11 (July 1837): 33–53.

Saint-Simon, Claude-Henri de, and Augustin Thierry. *De la réorganisation de la société européenne, ou, De la nécessité et des moyens de rassembler les peuples de l'Europe en un seul corps politique, en conservant à chacun son indépendance nationale*. Paris: Delauney, 1814.

Sarkowicz, Hans. *Die grossen Frankfurter*. Frankfurt am Main: Insel, 1994.

Saussure, A. Necker de. *Notice sur le caractère et les écrits de Madame de Staël*. Paris: Treuttel and Wiirtz, 1820.

Sauvigny, Guillaume de Bertier de. *Metternich and His Times*. London: Darton, Longman, and Todd, 1962.

Savary, Anne Jean Marie René, 1st Duke of Rovigo. *Mémoires du duc de Rovigo, pour servir à l'histoire de l'empereur Napoléon*. 4 vols. Paris: A. Bossange, 1828.

Schenk, Hans Georg. *The Aftermath of the Napoleonic Wars: The Concert of Europe, An Experiment*. London: Kegan Paul, Trench, Trubner & Co., 1947.

Schenk, Joep. "The Central Commission for the Navigation of the Rhine: A First Step towards European Economic Security?" In *Securing Europe after Napoleon: 1815 and the New European Security Culture*, ed. Beatrice de Graaf, Ido de Haan, and Brian Vick, 75–94. Cambridge: Cambridge University Press, 2019.

Schinkel, Carl Wilhelm Bergman von. *Minnen ur Sveriges nyare historia*. 10 vols. Stockholm: P. A. Norstedt & Söner, 1853.

Schlegel, August Wilhelm von, and Germaine de Staël. *Sur le système continental*. Hamburg: Bibliotheek der Deutschen Literatur, 1813.

Schnee, Heinrich. *Die Hoffinanz und der moderne Staat*. Berlin: Duncker & Humblot, 1953.

Schnurmann, Claudia. "His Father's Favored Son: David Parish (1778–1826)." In *From the Colonial Economy to Early Industrialization, 1720–1840*, ed. Marianne S. Wokeck. Vol. 1 of *Immigrant Entrepreneurship: German-American Business Biographies: 1720 to the Present*. https://www.immigrantentrepreneurship.org/entry.php?rec=12.

Schroeder, Paul W. "Did the Vienna Settlement Rest on a Balance of Power?" *American Historical Review* 97, no. 3 (June 1992): 683–706.

———. *The Transformation of European Politics, 1763–1848*. Oxford History of Modern Europe. Oxford: Clarendon Press, 1994.

Schulz, Matthias. "The Construction of a Culture of Peace in Post-Napoleonic Europe: Peace through Equilibrium, Law and New Forms of Communicative Interaction." *Journal of Modern European History* 13 (2015): 464–74.

———. *Normen und Praxis: Das Europäische Konzert der Großmächte als Sicherheitsrat, 1815–1860*. Studien zur Internationalen Geschichte B.21. Munich: R. Oldenbourg Verlag, 2009.

Scott, Franklin D. *Bernadotte and the Fall of Napoleon*. Cambridge, MA: Harvard University Press, 1935.

Scott, Hamish. "Diplomatic Culture in Old Regime Europe." In *Cultures of Power in Europe during the Long Eighteenth Century*. Cambridge: Cambridge University Press, 2007.

Scott, Joan. *Only Paradoxes to Offer: French Feminists and the Rights of Man*. Cambridge, MA: Harvard University Press, 1996.

Šedivý, Miroslav. *Metternich, the Great Powers and the Eastern Question*. Pilsen: University of West Bohemia, 2013.

Seigel, Jerrold. *Modernity and Bourgeois Life: Society, Politics, and Culture in England, France and Germany since 1750*. Cambridge: Cambridge University Press, 2012.

Seignobos, Charles. *1815–1915: From the Congress of Vienna to the War of 1914*. Paris: Librairie Armand Colin, 1915.

Sewell, William. "A Strange Career: The Historical Study of Economic Life." *History and Theory* 49, no. 4 (December 2010): 146–66.

Shankland, Peter. *Beware of Heroes: Admiral Sir Sydney Smith's War against Napoleon*. London: William Kimber, 1975.

Sherwood, Marika. *After Abolition: Britain and the Slave Trade since 1807*. London: I. B. Tauris, 2007.

Shilder, Nikolay. *Imperator Aleksandr Pervyi*. St. Petersburg: Isdanie A. S. Suvorina, 1897–98.

Siegel, Jennifer. *For Peace and Money: French and British Finance in the Service of Tsars and Commissars*. New York: Oxford University Press, 2014.

Siemann, Wolfram. *Metternich: Stratege und Visionär; Eine Biografie*. Munich: C. H. Beck, 2016.

Silberling, Norman. "Financial and Monetary Policy of Great Britain during the Napoleonic Wars." 2 pts. *Quarterly Journal of Economics* 38, nos. 2–3 (1924): "I. Financial Policy," no. 2 (February 1924): 214–33; "II. Ricardo and the Bullion Report," no. 3 (May 1924): 397–439.

Simal, Juan Luis, and Juan Pan-Montojo. "Exil, finances internationals et construction de l'État: Les libéraux et 'joséphins' espagnols (1813–1851)." *Revue d'histoire du XIXe siècle* 53 (2016): 59–77.

Singer, Isidore, ed. *The Jewish Encyclopedia: A Descriptive Record of the History, Religion, Literature, and Customs of the Jewish People from the Earliest Times to the Present Day*. New York: Funk and Wagnalls, 1901.

Sinnreich, Richard Hart. "In Search of Military Repose: The Congress of Vienna and the Making of Peace." In *The Making of Peace: Rulers, States, and the Aftermath of War*, ed. Williamson Murray and Jim Lacey, 131–59. Cambridge: Cambridge University Press, 2009.

Sismondi, Jean-Charles-Leonard Simonde de. *De l'intérêt de la France à l'égard de la traite des nègres*. Geneva: J. J. Paschoud, 1814.

Skaerved, Peter Sheppard [violinist]. Blog, on Fries, http://www.peter-sheppard-skaerved.com/author/peter/.

Skolnik, Fred, and Michael Berenbaum, eds. *Encyclopaedia Judaica*. Detroit: Macmillan, 2007.

Sluga, Glenda. "Anfänge und Ende[n] der Weltordnung." *Merkur* 816 (2017): 72–81.

——. "Defining Liberty: Italy and England in Madame de Staël's Corinne." *Women's Writing* 1 (2003): 241–51.

——. "Economic Insecurity, 'Securities' and a European Security Culture after the Napoleonic Wars." In *Securing Europe after Napoleon: 1815 and the New European Security Culture*, ed. Beatrice de Graaf, Ido de Haan, and Brian Vick. Cambridge: Cambridge University Press, 2019.

——. "From F. Melian Stawell to E. Greene Balch: International Thinking at the Gender Margins, 1919–1947." In *Women's International Thought: A New History*, ed. Katharina Rietzler and Patricia Owens. Cambridge: Cambridge University Press, 2021.

——. "Habsburg Histories of Internationalism." In *Remaking Central Europe: The League of Nations and the Former Habsburg Lands*, ed. Peter Becker and Natasha Wheatley. Oxford: Oxford University Press, 2021.

——. *Internationalism in the Age of Nationalism*. Philadelphia: University of Pennsylvania Press, 2013.

——. "Inventing an International Order." In *After Disruption: Historical Perspectives on the Future of International Order*, CSIS, September 2020. https://csis-website-prod.s3.amazonaws.com/s3fs-public/publication/200901_Bates_History_FullReport_v1.pdf.

——. "Madame de Staël and the Transformation of European Politics, 1812–17." *International History Review* 37, no. 1 (2013): 142–66.

——. "The *Nation*." In *The Palgrave Guide to Women Writing History*, ed. M. Spongberg. Basingstoke: Palgrave, 2005.

——. *Nation, Psychology and International Politics*. London: Palgrave, 2006.

——. "On the Historical Significance of the Presence, and Absence, of Women at the Congress of Vienna, 1814–1815." *L'Homme* 25, no. 2 (2014): 49–62.

——. "Passions, Patriotism and Nationalism, and Germaine de Staël." *Nations and Nationalism* 15, no. 2 (2009): 299–318.

——. "Sexual Congress." *History Today* 64, no. 9 (September 2014): 33–39.

——. "Turning International: Foundations of Modern International Thought and New Paradigms for Intellectual History." *History of European Ideas* 41, no. 1 (2015): 103–15.

——. "Was the Twentieth Century the Great Age of Internationalism?" In *Taking Stock: The Humanities in Australia*, ed. Mark Finnane and Ian Donaldson. Perth: UWA Publishing, 2012.

——. "'Who Hold the Balance of the World?' Bankers at the Congress of Vienna and in International History." *American Historical Review* (December 2017): 1403–30.

——. "Women at the Congress of Vienna." *Eurozine*, 28 January 2015. https://www.eurozine.com/women-at-the-congress-of-vienna/.

——. "Women, Diplomacy, and International Politics, Before and After the Congress of Vienna." In *Women, Diplomacy and International Politics since 1500*, ed. Glenda Sluga and Carolyn James, 120–36. New York: Routledge, 2016.

Sluga, Glenda, and Patricia Clavin, eds. *Internationalisms: A Twentieth-Century History*. Cambridge: Cambridge University Press, 2017.

Sluga, Glenda, and Carolyn James, eds. *Women, Diplomacy and International Politics since 1500*. New York: Routledge, 2016.

Smith, Michael. *The Emergence of Modern Business Enterprise in France, 1800–1930*. Cambridge, MA: Harvard University Press, 2005.

Smith, William Sidney. *Mémoire sur la nécessité et les moyens de faire cesser les pirateries des états barbaresques*. January 1814. https://play.google.com/books/reader?id=1FBNAAAAcAAJ&hl=en_GB&pg=GBS.PA1.

Sobkova, Helena. *Katerina Zahanska*. Prague: Paseka, 2007.

Sofka, James. "Metternich's Theory of European Order: A Political Agenda for 'Perpetual Peace.'" *Review of Politics* 60, no. 1 (1998): 115–49. doi:10.1017/S0034670500043953.

Soll, Jacob. "From Virtue to Surplus: Jacques Necker's *Compte rendu* (1781) and the Origins of Modern Political Rhetoric." *Representations* 134, no. 1 (Spring 2016): 29–63.

Solovieff, Georges. *Madame de Staël, ses amis, ses correspondants: Choix de lettres (1778–1817)*. Paris: Editions Klincksieck, 1970.

——. "Madame de Stäel vue par ses contemporains." *Revue d'histoire littéraire de la France* 1 (1966): 130–39.

——. *Rahel Varnhagen: Une revoltée féministe à l'époque romantique*. Paris: L'Harmattan, 2000.

Sorel, Albert. *L'Europe et la révolution française*. Vol. 3. Paris: Plon, 1904.

Spalding, Paul. "Germaine de Staël's Role in Rescuing Lafayette, 1792–1797." In *Germaine de Staël: Forging a Politics of Mediation*, ed. Karyna Szmurlo, 56–68. Liverpool: Liverpool University Press, 2011.

Spang, Rebecca. *Stuff and Money in the Time of the French Revolution*. Cambridge, MA: Harvard University Press, 2015.

Sparrow, Elizabeth. *Secret Service: British Agents in France, 1792–1815*. Suffolk: Woodbridge, 1999.

Spiel, Hilde, ed. *The Congress of Vienna: An Eyewitness Account*. Trans. Richard H. Weber. Philadelphia: Chilton Book Co., 1968.

——. *Fanny von Arnstein: A Daughter of the Enlightenment, 1758–1818*. Trans. Christine Shuttleworth. New York: Berg, 1991.

——. "Jewish Women in Austrian Culture." In *The Jews of Austria: Essays on Their Life, History and Destruction*, ed. Josef Frankel. London: Vallentine, Mitchell, 1970.

Squire, P. S. "Metternich and Benckendorff, 1807–1834." *Slavonic and Eastern Review* 45, no. 104 (January 1967): 35–62.

St. Clair, William. *That Greece Might Still Be Free: The Philhellenes in the War of Independence*. London: Oxford University Press, 1972.

Staël, Germaine de. "An Appeal to the Sovereigns." In *Translating Slavery*, ed. Doris Kadish and Françoise Massardier-Kenney, 157–59. Kent, OH: Kent State University Press, 2010.

———. "The Author of 'Souvenirs of Madame Récamier.'" In *Madame de Staël and the Grand-Duchess Louise*. London: Saunders, Otley & Co., 1862.

———. *Considerations on the Principal Events of the French Revolution*. Ed. Aurelian Craiutu. Indianapolis: Liberty Fund, 2008.

———. *Considérations sur la révolution française*. Ed. Jacques Godechot. Paris: Tallandier, 1983.

———. *Considérations sur la révolution française*. Vol. 3 of *Ouevres complètes de Madame de Stäel*. Brussels: Auguste Wahlen & Company, 1820.

———. *Considérations sur les principaux événemens de la révolution françoise*. Paris: Libraires Delaunay, Bossange et Masson, 1818.

———. *Corinne, or, Italy*. 1807. New Brunswick, NJ: Rutgers University Press, 1987.

———. *De la littérature*. Ed. Paul Can Tieghem. Genève: Droz, 1959.

———. *De la littérature considérée dans ses rapports avec les institutions sociales*. In *Oeuvres complètes de Madame la Baronne de Stäel-Holstein*. 1800. Geneva: Slatkine Reprints, 1967.

———. *De l'Allemagne*. In *Oeuvres complètes de Madame la Baronne de Stäel-Holstein*. Vol. 2. 1861. Geneva: Slatkine Reprints, 1967.

———. *De l'Esprit des Traductions*. In *Oeuvres complètes de Madame la Baronne de Stäel-Holstein*, 294–97. Geneva: Slatkine Reprints, 1967.

———. *Dix années d'exil: Fragmens d'un ouvrage inédit*. In *Oeuvres inédites de Mme La Baronne de Staël*. Paris: Treuttel et Würtz, Libraires, 1821.

———. "Du principe de la morale dans la nouvelle philosophie allemande." In *Oeuvres complètes de madame la baronne de Staël-Holstein: Oeuvres posthumes de madame la baronne de Staël-Holstein, précédées d'une notice sur son caractère et ses écrits*. Paris: Chez Firmin Didot Freres, 1871.

———. *Germany by the Baroness Staël Holstein, Translated from the French in Three Volumes*. London: John Murray, 1813.

———. *The Influence of Literature upon Society Translated from the French of Madame de Staël-Holstein the Second Edition, to which is prefixed a Memoir of the life and writings of the author in two volumes*. London: Henry Colburn, 1812.

———. *Madame de Staël, Charles de Villers, Benjamin Constant: Correspondance*. Ed. Kurt Kloocke. New York: P. Lang, 1993.

———. *Madame de Staël on Politics, Literature, and National Character*. Ed. Morroe Berger. London: Sidgwick and Jackson, 1964.

———. *Réflexions sur le procès de la Reine par une femme* [August 1793]. https://gallica.bnf.fr/ark:/12148/bpt6k42632j.texteImage.

———. *Ten Years of Exile*. Trans. Doris Beik. 1821. Toronto: Doubleday, 1972.

———. *A treatise on the influence of the passions, upon the happiness of individuals and of nations: illustrated by striking references to . . . the French Revolution from the French of the Baroness Stäel de Holstein; to which is prefixed a sketch of her life, by the translator*. London: G. Cawthorn, 1798.

Steinmetz, Greg. *The Richest Man Who Ever Lived: The Life and Times of Jacob Fugger*. New York: Simon and Schuster, 2016.

Stern, Fritz. *Gold and Iron: Bismarck, Bleichröder, and the Building of the German Empire*. New York: Knopf, 1979.

Strand, Eric. "Byron's 'Don Juan' as a Global Allegory." *Studies in Romanticism* 43, no. 4 (Winter 2004): 503–36.

Straus, Hannah Alice. *The Attitude of the Congress of Vienna toward Nationalism in Germany, Italy, and Poland*. New York: Columbia University Press, 1949.

Sturdza, Mikhail-Dimitri. *Dictionnaire historique et généalogique des grandes familles de Grèce, d'Albanie et de Constantinople*. Paris: M-D Sturdza, 1983.

Süslü, Dr. Azmi. "Un aperçu sur les ambassadeurs ottomanes et leurs sefaratname." *Tarih Araştırmaları Dergisi* (1981). https://doi.org/10.1501/Tarar_0000000365.

Sweet, Paul R. "Erich Bollmann at Vienna in 1815." *American Historical Review* 46, no. 3 (April 1941): 580–87.

———. *Friedrich von Gentz: Defender of the Old Order*. Madison: University of Wisconsin Press, 1941.

———. *Wilhelm von Humboldt: A Biography*. Vol. 2. Columbus: Ohio State University Press, 1980.

Takeda, Chinatsu. "Deux origines du courant libéral en France." *Revue française d'histoire des idées politiques* 18, no. 2 (2003): 233–58.

Talleyrand-Périgord, Charles-Maurice, duc de. *Mémoires du prince de Talleyrand, publiés avec une préface et des notes par Le duc de Broglie*. Vol. 2. Paris: Calmann-Levy, 1891.

Taylor, Barbara. *Eve and the New Jerusalem: Socialism and Feminism in the Nineteenth Century*. London: Virago Press, 1983.

Temperley, Harold. "Princess Lieven and the Protocol of 4 April 1826." *English Historical Review* 39, no. 153 (1924): 55–78.

———, ed. *The Unpublished Diary and Political Sketches of Princess Lieven Together with Some of Her Letters*. London: Jonathan Cape, 1925.

Temperley, Harold, and Lillian M. Penson. *A Century of Diplomatic Blue Books, 1814–1914*. London: Cambridge University Press, 1938.

Tenenbaum, Susan. "The Coppet Circle: Literary Criticism as Political Discourse." *History of Political Thought* 1, no. 3 (1980): 453–73.

———. "Liberal Heroines: Mme de Stäel on the Woman Question and the Modern State." *Annales Benjamin Constant* 5 (1985): 37–52.

Tewarson, Heidi Thomann. *Rahel Levin Varnhagen: The Life and Work of a German Jewish Intellectual*. Lincoln: University of Nebraska Press, 1998.

Thomas, D. H. "Princess Lieven's Last Diplomatic Confrontation." *International History Review* 5, no. 4 (1983): 550–56.

Tilly, Charles. *Coercion, Capital, and European States, AD 990–1990*. Cambridge, MA: Blackwell, 1990.

Tisseau, Paul. "Les Illusions de la Baronne Sophie con Knorring." *Cahiers Staëliens* 60 (2009): 93–104.

Tixier, Caroline. "The Legacy of Léon Bourgeois: From the Solidarist Doctrine to the Emergence of International Arbitration." In *Reconsidering Peace and Patriotism during the First World War*, ed. Justin Olmstead. Cham: Palgrave Macmillan, 2017.

Tolstoy, Leo. *War and Peace*. 1869. Trans. Rosemary Edmunds. London: Penguin, 1957.

Tooze, Adam. "Everything You Know about Global Order Is Wrong." *Foreign Policy*, 30 January 2019. https://foreignpolicy.com/2019/01/30/everything-you-know-about-global-order-is-wrong/.

Trail, M. "Mme de Staël: Her Russian-Swedish Journey." PhD diss., University of Southern California, 1946.

Tuite, Clara. *Lord Byron and Scandalous Celebrity*. Cambridge: Cambridge University Press, 2015.

Turquan, Joseph. *Une illuminée au XIXe siècle (La baronne de Krüdener), 1766–1824*. Paris: Emile-Paul, 1906.

Ullrichova, Maria, ed. *Clemens Metternich, Wilhelmine von Sagan: Ein Briefwechsel, 1813–1815*. Graz-Koln: Verlag Hermann Bohlaus Nachf, 1966.

Varnhagen, Rahel Levin. *Familienbriefe*. Ed. Renata B. M. Barovero. Munich: Verlag C. H. Beck, 2009.

Vick, Brian. *The Congress of Vienna: Power and Politics after Napoleon*. Cambridge, MA: Harvard University Press, 2014.

———. "Power, Humanitarianism and the Global Liberal Order: Abolition and the Barbary Corsairs in the Vienna Congress System." *International History Review* 40, no. 4 (2018): 939–60.

Vincent, Patrick. *Romantic Poetess: European Culture, Politics and Gender, 1820–1840*. Durham: University of New Hampshire Press, 2004.

Volwiler, Albert Tangeman. "Robert Owen and the Congress of Aix-la-Chapelle, 1818." *Scottish Historical Review* 19, no. 74 (1922): 96–105.

Vovsi, Eman. "Service of Antoine-Henri Baron de Jomini in 1812–13: A New Retrospective View." PhD diss., Florida State University, 2006.

Ward, Adolphus William. *The Period of Congresses*. London: Society for Promoting Christian Knowledge, 1919.

Ward, Adolphus William, G. W. Prothero, and Stanley Leathes, eds. Preface to *The Restoration, Cambridge Modern History*. Cambridge: Cambridge University Press, 1907.

Waresquiel, Emmanuel de. *Talleyrand: Dernières nouvelles du Diable*. Paris: CNRS Edition, 2011.

———. *Talleyrand Immobile*. Paris: Fayard, 2003.

Watteville, Alix de. *Anna Eynard-Lullin et l'époque des congrès et des révolutions*. Lausanne: Paul Feissly, 1955.

Webster, Charles, ed. *British Diplomacy, 1813–1815: Select Documents Dealing with the Reconstruction of Europe*. London: G. Bell & Sons, 1921.

———. *The Congress of Vienna*. London: H. Milford, 1919.

———. "England and the Polish-Saxon Problem at the Congress of Vienna." *Transactions of the Royal Historical Society* 7 (1913): 49–101.

———. *The Foreign Policy of Castlereagh, 1812–1815: Britain and the Reconstruction of Europe*. London: G. Bell & Sons, 1931.

———. *The Foreign Policy of Castlereagh, 1815–1822: Britain and the European Alliance*. London: G. Bell & Sons, 1963.

Weigall, Rose Sophia, ed.. *The Letters of Lady Burghersh afterwards Countess of Westmorland—from Germany and France during the Campaign of 1813–14*. London: John Murray, 1893.

Weil, Maurice-Henri. "Autour du congrès de Vienne." *La Revue de Paris*, 3:599–628, 825–57. Paris: Bureaux de la Revue de Paris, 1913.

———. *Autour du congrès de Vienne: La princesse Bagration, la duchesse de Sagan, et la police secrète de l'Autriche*. Paris: Librairie Payot, 1913.

———. *Les Dessous du Congrès de Vienne d'après les documents originaux des Archives du Ministère Impérial et royal de l'Intérieur à Vienne*. Vol. 1. Paris: Librairie Payot, 1917.

———. "Talleyrand et la frontière ouverte." *Revue Militaire Générale*, July 1923.

———. "Le vol de l'Aigle." In *La Revue de Paris*, 1:128–53, 408–36. Paris: Bureaux de la Revue de Paris, 1915.

Weill, George. "Le financier Ouvrard." *Revue Historique* 127, fasc. 1 (1918): 31–61.

———. *La France sous la monarchie constitutionnelle*. Paris: Alcan, 1912.

Wellington, Field Marshal Arthur, Duke of. *Supplementary Despatches, Correspondence and Memoranda*. Ed. Duke of Wellington, K. G. London: John Murray, 1862.

Wheatley, Natasha. "Central Europe as Ground Zero of the New International Order." *Slavic Review* 78, no. 4 (2019): 900–911.

White, Eugene N. "Making the French Pay: The Costs and Consequences of the Napoleonic Reparations." *European Review of Economic History* 5, no. 3 (2001): 337–65.

Wilhelmy-Dollinger, Petra. "Berlin Salons: Late Eighteenth to Early Twentieth Century." *Jewish Women: A Comprehensive Historical Encyclopedia*, 1 March 2009, *Jewish Women's Archive*. http://jwa.org/encyclopedia/article/berlin-salons-late-eighteenth-to-early-twentieth-century.

———. "Fanny Baronin Von Arnstein." *Jewish Women: A Comprehensive Historical Encyclopedia*, 1 March 2009, *Jewish Women's Archive*. http://jwa.org/encyclopedia/article/arnstein-fanny-baronin-von.

Wilke, Jürgen. "From Parish Register to the 'Historical Table': The Prussian Population Statistics in the 17th and 18th Centuries." *History of the Family* 9, no. 1 (2004): 63–79.

Wilson, Robert. *Narrative of Events during the Invasion of Russia by Napoleon Bonaparte: And the Retreat of the French Army, 1812*. Cambridge: Cambridge University Press, 2013.

Wilson, Woodrow. "Address to Congress, Analyzing German and Austrian Peace Utterances (February 11, 1918)." In *President Wilson's State Papers and Addresses*. Ed. Albert Shaw. New York: George H. Doran, 1918.

Winock, Michel. *Madame de Staël*. Vol. 2. Paris: Fayard, 2010.

Wolff, Otto. *Ouvrard, Speculator of Genius, 1770–1846*. Trans. Stewart Thomson. London: Barrie and Rockcliff, 1962.

Woodhouse, Christopher Montague. *Capodistria: The Founder of Greek Independence*. Oxford: Oxford University Press, 1973.

Zamoyski, Adam. *Rites of Peace: The Fall of Napoleon & the Congress of Vienna*. London: HarperPress, 2007.

Ziegler, Philip. *The Sixth Great Power: A History of One of the Greatest of All Banking Families, the House of Barings, 1762–1929*. New York: Alfred A. Knopf, 1988.

Zorin, Andrei. "'Star of the East': The Holy Alliance and European Mysticism." *Kritika: Explorations in Russian and Eurasian History* 4, no. 2 (Spring 2003): 313–42.

Zwierlein, Cornel, and Beatrice de Graaf. "Security and Conspiracy in Modern History." *Historical Social Research/Historiche Sozialforschung* 38, no. 1 (2013): 7–45.

Zorgbibe, Charles. *Metternich: Le seducteur diplomate*. Paris: Fallois, 2009.

INDEX

A NOTE ON THE TYPE

THIS BOOK has been composed in Miller, a Scotch Roman typeface designed by Matthew Carter and first released by Font Bureau in 1997. It resembles Monticello, the typeface developed for The Papers of Thomas Jefferson in the 1940s by C. H. Griffith and P. J. Conkwright and reinterpreted in digital form by Carter in 2003.

Pleasant Jefferson ("P. J.") Conkwright (1905–1986) was Typographer at Princeton University Press from 1939 to 1970. He was an acclaimed book designer and AIGA Medalist.

The ornament used throughout this book was designed by Pierre Simon Fournier (1712–1768) and was a favorite of Conkwright's, used in his design of the *Princeton University Library Chronicle.*

www.ingramcontent.com/pod-product-compliance
Ingram Content Group UK Ltd.
Pitfield, Milton Keynes, MK11 3LW, UK
UKHW041813221224
452558UK00001B/1